MW01283597

English Prepositions

English Prepositions

Their Meanings and Uses

R. M. W. DIXON

Central Queensland University

OXFORD

UNIVERSITY PRESS

OXFORD

UNIVERSITY PRESS

Great Clarendon Street, Oxford, OX2 6DP,
United Kingdom

Oxford University Press is a department of the University of Oxford.
It furthers the University's objective of excellence in research, scholarship,
and education by publishing worldwide. Oxford is a registered trade mark of
Oxford University Press in the UK and in certain other countries

© R. M. W. Dixon 2021

The moral rights of the author have been asserted

First Edition published in 2021

Impression: 1

All rights reserved. No part of this publication may be reproduced, stored in
a retrieval system, or transmitted, in any form or by any means, without the
prior permission in writing of Oxford University Press, or as expressly permitted
by law, by licence or under terms agreed with the appropriate reprographics
rights organization. Enquiries concerning reproduction outside the scope of the
above should be sent to the Rights Department, Oxford University Press, at the
address above

You must not circulate this work in any other form
and you must impose this same condition on any acquirer

Published in the United States of America by Oxford University Press
198 Madison Avenue, New York, NY 10016, United States of America

British Library Cataloguing in Publication Data
Data available

Library of Congress Control Number: 2021932405

ISBN 978-0-19-886868-2 (hbk.)
ISBN 978-0-19-886871-2 (pbk.)

DOI: 10.1093/oso/9780198868682.001.0001

Printed and bound by
CPI Group (UK) Ltd, Croydon, CR0 4YY

Links to third party websites are provided by Oxford in good faith and
for information only. Oxford disclaims any responsibility for the materials
contained in any third party website referenced in this work.

Contents

Preliminaries

Prepositions include the shortest words in English, yet they play a vital role in the language. They serve to indicate how and where, when and why, purpose and association, inclusion, connection, and many other things.

Every clause must have core elements: a subject slot, filled by a noun phrase (NP)—such as *The tall woman*—and a predicate slot, filled by a verb phrase (VP)—such as *has apologised*. This suffices for an intransitive clause:

[The tall woman]_{NP:SUBJECT} [has apologised]_{VP:PREDICATE}

A transitive clause also includes an object slot, filled by another NP; for example:

[The fat man]_{NP:SUBJECT} [told]_{VP:PREDICATE} [a story]_{NP:OBJECT}

It is convenient to have abbreviatory labels for these core functions in clause structure —'S' for intransitive subject, 'A' for transitive subject, and 'O' for transitive object. Some verbs (such as *apologise* and *arrive*) only go into an intransitive predicate slot, others (such as *tell* and *recognise*) only go into a transitive predicate slot, while some (such as *cook* and *break*) may go into either slot. (There is a third clause type, copula clauses; see sections 2.4b and 2.5.)

One could just speak using core clauses, but this would produce a rather barren discourse. We need to add trimmings, and this is achieved through peripheral constituents (PERI), each of which is an NP or a clause introduced by a preposition; for example, *inside the bedroom, on Tuesday, for the queen, after we have eaten*.

Do we really need prepositions? After all, one NP is recognised as being in subject function since it precedes the VP and another as being in object function since it immediately follows the VP. Why couldn't a peripheral NP just be placed after the object NP? For example:

[The tall woman]_{NP:S} apologised [her husband]_{NP:PERI}

This is unclear. There are several ways in which the apologising could relate to the tall woman's husband. These are shown by inserting an appropriate preposition to introduce the peripheral NP:

[The tall woman]$_{NP:S}$ apologised [to her husband]$_{NP:PERI}$

> (she said to her husband that she was sorry for something she had done which affected him; this is the 'beneficiary' sense of *to*; see section 7.2c)

[The tall woman]$_{NP:S}$ apologised [for her husband]$_{NP:PERI}$

> (she offered an apology, on his behalf, concerning something which he had done; this is the 'benefit' sense of *for*; see section 5.3a)

[The tall woman]$_{NP:S}$ apologised [about her husband]$_{NP:PERI}$

> (she expressed regret that, for instance, he was always so rude to all her relatives; see section 12.3c)

[The tall woman]$_{NP:S}$ apologised [before/after her husband]$_{NP:PERI}$

> (the tall woman and her husband spoke in temporal sequence, one and then the other; these are the temporal senses of *before* and *after*; see section 14.4a)

Every core clause may take a variety of peripheral additions, each introduced by its own preposition. As another example, we can add *the bridge* as a peripheral NP after the transitive core *The fat man told a story*:

[The fat man]$_{NP:A}$ told [a story]$_{NP:O}$ [the bridge]$_{NP:PERI}$

There are again a number of ways in which the bridge may relate to the storytelling, and these are shown by the inclusion of an appropriate preposition. First, *the bridge* may be the topic of the story and then preposition *about* or *concerning* (section 12.3c) should be used:

[The fat man]$_{NP:A}$ told [a story]$_{NP:O}$ [about/concerning the bridge]$_{NP:PERI}$

Alternatively, *the bridge* could refer to the location of the storytelling. The fat man could place himself above or below or adjacent to the bridge:

[The fat man]$_{NP:A}$ told [a story]$_{NP:O}$ [on the bridge]$_{NP:PERI}$

[The fat man]$_{NP:A}$ told [a story]$_{NP:O}$ [under/underneath/beneath the bridge]$_{NP:PERI}$

[The fat man]$_{NP:A}$ told [a story]$_{NP:O}$ [by/beside the bridge]$_{NP:PERI}$

Prepositions *under*, *beneath*, and *underneath* have slightly different senses and possibilities for usage; these are explained in section 11.1. *By* is a very common preposition with one of its senses 'near to, not quite reaching' (section 6.1a), having similar meaning to *beside* (section 9.4c).

There are a handful of verbs which have three semantic roles. For instance, *give* requires Donor, Gift, and Recipient. Two of these can relate to subject and object functions, but for the third a peripheral NP, marked by preposition *to* is generally needed:

[The student]$_{\text{DONOR:A}}$ gave [an apple]$_{\text{GIFT:O}}$ to the teacher]$_{\text{RECIPIENT:PERI}}$

There is an alternative construction:

[The student]$_{\text{DONOR:A}}$ gave [the teacher]$_{\text{RECIPIENT:O}}$ [an apple]$_{\text{GIFT}}$

Here the Recipient NP, *the teacher*, moves next to the verb, taking on O function. The Gift NP, *an apple*, follows it without a preposition. Grammarians differ as to what the function of *an apple* is in this sentence. Is it a 'second object', or a peripheral NP with zero marking?

* * *

This book aims to provide an integrated account of the main prepositions of English, together with associated adverbs. The prepositions are grouped together in terms of similar meanings and functions. For instance, *beneath* and *underneath* are linked to *over* and *under*, and *above* and *below*, as varying expressions of 'vertical position'; *among(st)*, *amid(st)*, *between*, and *in-between* are exemplars of 'distribution', while *along*, *alongside*, *across*, and *through* describe kinds of 'passage'.

For each preposition there is an account of its genetic origin and shifts of form and meaning over the centuries. An instructive way to appreciate the meanings of prepositions is by studying instances where two prepositions may be used in the same frame with meanings which show some similarity but also a significant difference. For instance, what is the difference between *These elm trees have died out* and *These elm trees have died off* (see section 9.2d-2), and between *Shut the door behind you!* and *Shut the door after you!* (section 14.4e-3)? This technique of comparison is employed throughout the book.

Nomenclature

There are a number of varieties of prepositions and it is useful to employ the following labels:

- **Simple prepositions**, such as *in*, *of*, *since*, *under*, and *through*. Note that some derive from two elements historically but function as a single unit in the present-day language; for example, *across*, *behind*, and *within*.
- **Complex prepositions**, each being composed of two simple prepositions. These include *into*, *out-of*, *upon*, and *in-between*. Note that some of them are conventionally written as one word, others as two; the latter are here provided with a hyphen, to show that they do each constitute a single preposition.
- **Phrasal prepositions,** each made up of adverb, noun, adjective, or conjunction, sometimes preceded by a simple preposition and always followed by one. By far the most common final element is *of*; others are *for*, *to*, *from*, and *with*. Phrasal prepositions include, among many others (hyphens are again inserted to show that each functions as single unit): *ahead-of*, *in-spite-of*, *by-means-of*, *but-for*, *close-to*, *far-from*, and *together-with*.

The organisation of this book

Language can be likened to a theatre (the theatre of life) and explaining how it works is like recounting a tale. Indeed, the introductory chapter is entitled 'A story to tell'. It introduces the reader to the roles of prepositions in English, outlining their various forms and illustrating contrastive senses.

Three chapters make up Part I 'The Stage is Set'. These delineate grammatical contexts of occurrence, and special uses. Chapter 2, 'Grammatical roles', distinguishes between 'inner' and 'outer' prepositional phrases, examines syntactic functions, and investigates the effects of inserting or omitting a preposition. Chapter 3 provides a detailed account of 'phrasal verbs'; these are complex verbs each consisting of a simple verb (which can occur alone) plus one or two prepositions or adverbs. The meaning of a phrasal verb cannot be obviously inferred from the basic meanings of its components. Thus, it must be accorded an entry all of its own in the dictionary; for example, *The rain has set in*, *He is going to lay off booze*, *She made a story up*. Chapter 4 is concerned with 'prepositional verbs'; these are verbs which cannot be used on their own but must be accompanied by a preposition. For example, *dispose of, long for, deal with*. The noun phrase following the preposition functions in many ways like the object of a transitive verb.

The stage having been set in Part I, the chapters of Part II describe the prepositions which strut upon the stage. Each chapter deals with a set of related prepositions, providing an integrated account of the meanings for each, and how these are linked to their grammatical properties. There are two chapters on relational prepositions—principally *of, for, by*, and *with*—which have only minor reference to space or time. These are followed by seven chapters on prepositions whose basic meaning is spatial, with many extensions to abstract senses. Chapter 14 ties together the varied ways through which prepositions deal with time.

Each chapter unites a group of prepositions which have similar meanings. They are often a mixture with respect to their status—simple prepositions, complex prepositions, and phrasal prepositions. Some adverbs are also included in the discussion when they are part of the pattern; for example, *forth* and *back* (section 11.2). Every simple preposition and complex preposition is dealt with quite thoroughly, but only those phrasal prepositions which feature as members of the various semantic sets are included in the analysis.

The final chapter tells how some people have attempted to prescribe how language should be used; it also mentions dialect variation, foreign learners' errors, and prospects for the future.

Care has been taken to make the book accessible to a broad spectrum of readers by avoiding esoteric technical terms. Although a wide range of data sources has been used, the judgements are basically mine, on the basis of my native speaker competence in Standard British English. There are a number of references throughout to differences in Standard American English, and a summary of some of these in section 15.3a.

For each preposition, a set of basic senses and uses have been outlined. These summarise what my researches have shown to be its canonical character. Around this there will be variation of many kinds—social, regional, individual. The way in which each person uses language always bears a measure of creativity. But variation is always with respect to a norm, and this is what I have tried to delineate.

Check list of prepositions discussed

Note: * indicates that this form also functions as an adverb; ** indicates that *up* and *down* are primarily adverbs, secondarily prepositions.

(1) **Simple prepositions**

  (a) Realised as clitics unless stressed (see section 1.6):
  at, for, from, of, to; plus *by, with* which are sometimes realised as clitics

  (b) Other monosyllabics:
  *down**, in*, off*, on*, out*, past, since, till, up***

  (c) Polysyllabics:
  about, above, across*, after, against, along*, amid(st), among(st), (a)round*, before, behind, below, beneath, beside(s)*, between, beyond, concerning, despite, during, over*, through*, toward(s), under, underneath, until, within*, without**

(2) **Complex prepositions**, each being a combination of two simple prepositions

  (a) Realised as a clitic unless stressed:
  into, off-of, onto, out-of, upon, up-to

  (b) Others:
  in-between, throughout, up-until, alongside* (treated as basically *along* plus *besides*; see section 11.4a-1)

(3) **Having two forms**:

  (a) As **simple preposition**, and (b) Adding one *of* or *for* or *to*, creating a **complex preposition**—realised as a clitic (by virtue of their final component) unless stressed:
  except(-for), inside(-of), near(-to), outside(-of)**

(4) **Phrasal preposition**. Adverb, noun, adjective, or conjunction plus one or more simple prepositions—realised as a clitic (by virtue of their final component) unless stressed. Note that only some of the several dozen phrasal prepositions are dealt with in this book; basically, those which fit into the semantic sets featuring simple and complex prepositions.

  (a) Based on an adverb:
  ahead-of, apart-from, aside-from, away-from, instead-of, together-with

(b) Based on a noun or adjective:
close-to, far-from, in-exchange-for, in-front-of, in-return-for, in-spite-of

(c) Based on a conjunction:
because-of, but-for

A number of adverbs are mentioned in connection with the discussion of prepositions: *afterwards, back, beforehand, forth, forward(s), backward(s), upward(s), downward(s), inward(s), outward(s),* and *onward(s).*

There are a number of other items which have marginal status as prepositions and/or have been listed as prepositions by some grammarians. They are not included here since there had to be a limit, or else the book would have expanded on and on. They include: *as* (which has very minor use as a preposition), *abroad, astride, following, including, like, notwithstanding, plus, opposite, qua, re, regarding, sans, than,* and *via.*

Abbreviations and conventions

Abbreviations

Syntactic functions

A	transitive subject core function
S	intransitive subject core function
O	transitive object core function
CS	copula subject core function
CC	copula complement core function
PERI	peripheral function

Constituents

NP	noun phase
VP	verb phrase
pNP	peripheral noun phrase (noun phrase introduced by preposition, showing its meaning and function)
CoCl	complement clause (clause filling a core argument slot in a main clause, as an alternative to an NP in that slot; see section 2.5c)

Languages

OE	Old English (also known as Anglo-Saxon), spoken from the fifth to the twelfth century
ME	Middle English, spoken from the twelfth to the end of the fifteenth century

In chapter 15

BrE	standard British English
AmE	standard American English
L1	person who learns a language as their first language; native speaker
L2	person who learns a language as their second language; foreign learner

Conventions

=	clitic boundary; see section 1.6
/.../	encloses phonological representation
[...]	encloses constituent
	typically used with a subscript indicating syntactic function; for example: [the truth]$_O$, or constituent type; for example: [that he is fat]$_{CoCl}$; or both: [the truth]$_{NP:O}$, [that he is fat]$_{CoCl:CS}$
(...)	adds an additional, explanatory portion to the sentence
	for example: John was jealous of Jill (since she had got the job he wanted)
*	unacceptable sentence

If a complex preposition or a phrasal preposition is conventionally written as a sequence of separate words, they are here joined by hyphens to show that they constitute one prepositional unit; for example: *out-of, near-to, in-spite-of.*

When a phrasal verb is quoted within a sentence, it is underlined; for example: *The manager <u>put down</u> Tom's loss <u>to</u> inexperience.*

Slots in phrasal verb structures are in bold type: **a, p**; see section 3.2.

1

A story to tell

The function of a preposition in English is to mark a noun phrase (NP) which is neither subject nor object, but ancillary to the core elements of a clause.

The role of language is to express meanings, and typically for a meaning to be communicated from speaker (or writer) to addressee(s). Each preposition carries a meaning, as does each verb, noun, and adjective. Which preposition is used in a particular circumstance, and which sense of it is appropriate, is determined by the meanings of the words it is combined with. This can be shown by examples.

English Prepositions: Their Meanings and Uses. R. M. W. Dixon. Oxford University Press (2021). © R. M. W. Dixon.
DOI: 10.1093/oso/9780198868682.003.0001

Every preposition has a range of senses, and the most common prepositions have the widest ranges. Which sense is appropriate in a given instance of use may depend on the verb it follows. Consider:

(1)   Sam baked a cake for Christmas   <reason for the activity>
(2)   Sam visited her parents for Christmas   <duration of the activity>

The 'reason' sense in (1) is also shown in *Sheila is saving for a rainy day* and *Frederick thanked Matilda for the flowers* (see section 5.3b), while the 'duration' sense in (2) is further illustrated by *Jason slept for an hour* and *Robin has been angry for quite a while* (see section 5.3f). Which sense is appropriate is determined by the meaning of verb-plus-object— *baked a cake* or *visited her parents*.

In both (1) and (2), *for* is followed by *Christmas*. An alternative is for the core of the clause to be the same, but for the NP following *for* to differ, with this entailing different senses of the preposition, as in:

(3)   Mary bought the book for Tom   <benefit>
(4)   Mary bought the book for ten dollars   <exchange>

Other examples of the 'benefit' sense in (3) include *Uncle Fred coached me for the exam* and *Maria was a witness for the defence* (see section 5.3a). The 'exchange' sense, of (4), also occurs in: *Chris exchanged his gun for a bicycle*, and *Simon has to pay compensation for the damage caused* (see section 5.3e).

The nature of the NP following *for* determines which sense of the preposition is appropriate—'benefit' when the NP refers to a person, and 'exchange' when it indicates a sum of money. In this instance, both *for* phrases can be included:

(5)   Mary bought the book for Tom for ten dollars

This is the most felicitous ordering of the *for phrases*, with 'benefit' before 'exchange' (see section 5.3i). If the reverse order were employed we would expect juxtapositonal intonation (shown in writing by a comma) before *for Tom*, indicating that this is something of an afterthought: *Mary bought the book for ten dollars, for Tom*.

There are occasions when a preposition may be used with two different senses in the same sentence. For instance:

(6)   The lowlanders fought with the highlanders

This sentence is ambiguous. It can carry the meaning of 'association' (see section 6.2b-4)—the lowlands were allied with the highlanders in fighting the invaders. Further examples of this sense are *Stella talked with Cressida* and *Maisie played with the dog*. *With* in (6) can be extended to *together-with*, making the sentence unambiguous:

(7)　The lowlanders fought together-with the
　　　highlanders　　　　　　　　　　　　　　　　　　　　　　<association>

The other meaning of (6) is 'directed activity' (see section 6.2e). Under this interpretation, the lowlanders were opposed to the highlanders. A further example of the confrontation sense is: *James struggled with incipient dementia* and *She is quite up to competing with the best in the world*. In this sense, *with* can be replaced by *against*, and the sentence is unambiguous:

(8)　The lowlanders fought against the
　　　highlanders　　　　　　　　　　　　　　　　　　　　　　<directed activity>

We saw in (5) that a sentence may include two *for* phrases, one in the 'benefit' and one in the 'exchange' sense. This is not possible for *with*. One can say:

(9)　The lowlanders fought (together-) with the
　　　highlanders　　　　　　　　　　　　　　　　　　　　　　<association>
(10)　The lowlanders fought with/against the
　　　invaders　　　　　　　　　　　　　　　　　　　　　　<directed activity>

But not

(11)　*The lowlanders fought (together-) with the highlanders with
　　　the invaders

This has to be stated as:

(12)　The lowlanders fought (together-) with the highlanders against
　　　the invaders

What is fascinating is instances where two prepositions may be used in the same frame, with meanings which show some similarity but also a significant difference. This is an instructive way to appreciate the meanings of prepositions—by well-chosen comparisons—and will be employed throughout the book. Here are three preliminary examples.

1.1 Selected contrasts

1.1a To and at

One can say either of:

(13) Mike threw the ball to Ian (implied: for Ian
      to catch it)   <beneficiary>
(14) Mike threw the ball at Ian (implied: for it to
      hit Ian)   <target>

The use of *to* in (13) indicates a link of 'receiving' between the participants in the activity; Ian is the 'destination' of the throw, and he now has
the benefit of holding the ball. Other instances of this sense of the preposition include *Susan gave the ball to Tom* and *Robin explained the
nature of the problem to Martin* (see section 7.2c). When *to* is replaced
by *at*, as in (14), the NP following the preposition becomes the target of
the activity. This sense of *at* is also shown in *The actress smiled at me* and
The judge wanted to get at the truth (see section 7.1c).

Throw has a wide range of meaning, enabling it to be used in both a
'beneficiary' and a 'target' context. Specialised verbs of throwing are
more restricted. *Hurl* refers to throwing with force and is likely only to
be used in a 'target' construction, *Mike hurled the ball at Ian*. In contrast,
the verb *toss* is used for gentle throwing and is most at home in a 'beneficiary' sentence such as *Mike tossed the ball to Ian*.

There are other contexts within which *to* and *at* contrast in similar
fashion. For instance, *talk* generally implies a joint activity. On hearing:

(15) Peter talked to Jean   <beneficiary>

one infers that this was a conversation, with Jean responding. However,
suppose that Peter just bombarded Jean with his opinions, not inviting
her to respond. *At* could then be used to indicate a 'target' meaning:

(16) Peter talked at Jean   <target>

Other verbs of communication have more limited meaning and, consequently, restricted grammatical possibilities. *Bawl* indicates aggressive
vocal activity; one hears *Peter bawled at Jean* but never **Peter bawled to
Jean*. And with the verb *pray*, one could say *The proselyte prayed to his
god* (as a way of engaging with the deity) but not **The proselyte prayed
at his god*.

1.1b Of *and* about

There are many contexts in which either *of* or *about* may be used. There is always a contrast between them—sometimes obvious, other times more subtle. We can commence with a clear example:

(17)   A book of poetry   \<expansion>
(18)   A book about poetry   \<general topic>

Noun phrase (17), with *of*, refers to a book including a number of poems. The *of poetry* expands on the referent of *book*, indicating what sort of book it is. This construction, *X of Y*, states that X consists of Y. Similar examples of this sense of preposition *of* include *a bottle of wine, a tour of the factory*, and *the theory of relativity* (see section 5.2b).

In contrast, in (18) the book just concerns poetry, perhaps a critical discussion of the genre. The NP following *about* refers to some general topic. Other examples are: *a dispute about property rights* and *He's glad about the good results* (see section 12.3c). Another contrast is:

(19)   Kate thought of a solution to the problem   \<knowledge>
(20)   Mark thought about a solution to the
           problem   \<general topic>

Kate had been searching her brain to come up with a solution (see section 5.2g) but Mark was doing something quite different. He was ruminating over a possible solution—its difficulty, its ramifications, how nice it would be to receive the prize offered for the correct solution.

Granpa has for some time been *complaining about his poor health* (a general topic). But today he *complained of a new pain in his back* (something specific). Ted is *hopeful of a good result* (a specific outcome) whereas Fred is simply *hopeful about the outcome* (something more general).

Language is not a cut-and-dried matter, like the properties of rocks or neutrons. The use of language is fuzzy so that it is often not possible to come to yes-or-no conclusions (or not sensible to try to do so). We deal instead with tendencies and proclivities. In (17) and (18) the contrastive use of *about* and *of* is quite definite. For other examples, the interpretations given are the predominant ones. However there are some instances of people employing *of* where I have preferred *about*, and vice versa. Some would criticise such deviations as sloppy usage; others would hail them as tokens of the elasticity of present-day English.

1.1c In *and* out-of

Quite a few prepositions group into pairs of 'opposites'; for example: *to* and *from*, *on* and *off*, *up* and *down*, *over* and *under* (see section 1.5). Also *in* and *out-of*, as in:

(21)   Jane is standing in the sun
(22)   Kate is standing out-of the sun
(23)   Joseph is still in hiding
(24)   Matthew is now out-of hiding

In and *out-of* plainly have opposite meanings here.

How then do we explain the fact that the following two sentences have the same pragmatic effect:

(25)   Bill hit Fred in anger   <in a state of>
(26)   Bill hit Fred out-of anger   <arising from>

Both sentences describe Bill hitting Fred, with the reason being anger. But the circumstances differ. For (25), Bill experienced a flair-up of anger (a fit of anger) in the course of an encounter with Fred and hit him impetuously, without having planned to do so (he may regret it later and perhaps apologise). Further examples of this 'in a state of' sense of preposition *in* include: *The victim cried out in pain*, and *Mavis sat in silence* (section 8.1c).

In contrast, (26) is likely to refer to a premeditated act of hitting, which Bill had planned because he had been angered by something Fred had done earlier on (in this instance, he is unlikely to feel any need to apologise later). Other examples of the 'arising from' sense of *out-of* include: *Jane voted for Hannah out-of loyalty*, and *Charlie forgave Sam out-of love* (section 8.2b).

1.2 Meanings

Each preposition has a basic meaning and a number of extensions from this, mostly of a more abstract nature. Language is founded on the concrete world; as a consequence most prepositions have a basic meaning relating to space or to time.

I. **Basic meanings spatial.** There are here two subtypes.
    Ia. With a secondary sense relating to time. These include: *at, to, from, in, on, behind, between,* and about twenty more.
    Ib. With no temporal sense. These include: *upon, onto, beside(s), among, beneath, despite, above,* and just a few more.
II. **Basic meaning temporal.** We again find two subtypes:
    IIa. With a secondary sense relating to space: *before, after, past.*
    IIb. With no spatial sense: *since, until/till, during.*
III. **Basic meaning purely relational.** These are frequent and wide-ranging prepositions—*of, for, by,* and *with.* Both *for* and *by* also show secondary temporal senses (for example, *The meeting is planned for late June* and *Be home by five o'clock!*) and *by* can refer to space (as in *Sally stood by the tree*).

The sense which a preposition assumes in each instance of use is determined in large part by the verb (and other words and grammatical elements) it is used with. This can be briefly illustrated with *against*.

The meaning of **against** is 'opposed to'. Basic spatial uses are: *Tony swam against the tide* and *Martha pushed against the door.* The latter sentence implies that the door was not easy to open, being perhaps stiff or stuck. Note the comparison with *Martha pushed on the door* which just implies making contact with the door to open it easily, with no impedance involved. Extensions of meaning for *against* include reference to mental attitude (for example, *have a prejudice against*) and contrast (*The red roof stood out against the blue sky*). A full account is in section 9.3.

We saw that in the context *push — the door, on* and *against* imply different degrees of force. However, in some frames the two prepositions appear synonymous; for example, *wage war on the invaders* and *wage war against the invaders.*

Now consider use of the two prepositions for the placement of a picture with respect to a wall:

(27) Igor hung the picture on the wall
(28) Elena turned the picture against the wall

Sentence (27) describes a normal activity—the picture is placed on the wall (so that it does not fall down). It will be put front-out since being able to see the front is the whole point of the exercise. Then (28) describes something entirely different. Elena takes a dislike to what is portrayed on the picture and reverses it. The front of the picture is now towards the wall; the use of *against* indicates that it is opposite to the way it should be.

On (and *onto*) are common prepositions with a wide range of uses and meanings. We can here just provide a sample, which is a smallish fraction of the whole. Note that *on* and *onto* are sometimes interchangeable, other times not. There is a full account in section 9.1.

On(to) indicates 'connection', and generally carries positive overtones. Its pairing, *off*, shows 'disconnection' which is typically (but by no means always) negative.

(i)   The basic sense is 'connection'. This can be supported by gravity, as in: *Put the cup on the table!* or by some physical means, as in *Sew the button on the shirt!* or *They fixed the undercarriage on the plane.*

(ii) *On(to)* is used for the prolongation of connection, as in *Hang onto the other end of the rope, so that we don't get separated in the dark!*

(iii) This basic sense can be extended to where there is just oversight. For example: *Hang onto your late father's desk!* is an injunction not to let anyone take it away. This does not necessarily imply holding on to it physically (although this may well be appropriate if someone attempts to remove it).

(iv) The verb *live* has a range of meanings—just for existence (*Is he still living?*) or for where the existence takes place, or the dependency by which it is maintained. *On* can be used, in rather different senses, for these two kinds of statement—*He lives on the coast*, and *He lives on beans and rice.*

(v)   The focus of an activity may be marked by *on*, as in *The detective tapped on the wall with his mallet until he heard a hollow sound, indicating the secret hiding place.* Then he knew: *He had hit on the hollow.*

(vi) One can say: *Our new house is built on the existing foundations.* An abstract extension of this is: *Our new project is built on Aaron's insight.*

1.3 Phrasal verbs

Present-day English has hundreds of what are called 'phrasal verbs'. These are complex verbs each consisting of a simple verb (which can occur alone) plus one or two prepositions or adverbs. The meaning of a phrasal verb cannot be obviously inferred from the basic meanings of its components—verb, preposition, adverb. Thus, it must be accorded an entry all of its own in the dictionary. Sentential examples (with the phrasal verbs underlined) are: *The rain set in*, *The boy turned against his father*, and *Derek made the company over to his brother*.

It is true that the meaning of a phrasal verb cannot be easily inferred from the basic meanings of its components. However, its meaning is not simply idiosyncratic. In very many instances it relates not to basic meanings but to extended meanings of the words making it up.

A preliminary illustration can be provided for three phrasal verbs which each involve *on(to)* and one with *against*. (Many further analyses are provided in chapter 3 and throughout the chapters of part II).

(a) ***Hang onto***, as in:

(29) Make sure you hang onto this job Uncle Peter has organised for you; if you misbehave and get fired, you'll find it difficult to get another job

Senses (ii) and (iii) just given for *on(to)* relate to concrete objects: *Hang onto the end of the rope!* and *Hang onto your father's desk!*, the latter indicating oversight rather than necessary physical contact. These naturally extend to *hang onto* this job, describing something that is more abstract. The message is, once again, 'prolong it, don't let it get away!'.

(b) ***Live on***, as in

(30) He can barely live on the small monthly allowance from his mother

This is an extension from the dependency of *on*—given under (iv)—as in *He lives on beans and rice*. A monthly allowance has a more general reference; it is not something that can be directly eaten, like beans and rice, but it provides the wherewithal for purchasing food which will assist in maintaining life.

(c) *Hit on,* as in

(31)   Aaron thought about it a lot and has just <u>hit on</u> an interesting idea

Under sense (v) for *on* we had *The detective had hit on the hollow.* Substituting 'brain' for 'mallet', and 'an interesting idea' for 'the hollow', the sense of discovery conveyed by the phrasal verb of (31) is seen to be an extension from the basic sense of *on.*

(d) *Turn against*, as in:

(32)   The wicked stepmother <u>turned</u> the boy <u>against</u> his father

This is plainly an extension from the basic sense of against, as illustrated in (28), *Elena turned the picture against the wall*, meaning that it was opposite to the way it should be. The normal situation is for a picture to be face-out and for a boy to have positive feelings towards his father. The replacement of these by hostility is shown by using *against* (this is similar to the hostility of *have a prejudice against*).

There need not be any causer involved. One may hear, simply, *The boy <u>turned against</u> his father.* (There is no similar intransitive sentence with 'picture', since pictures do not turn all by themselves.)

There is a syntactic criterion which helps to recognise what is a phrasal verb. When a question involves a regular peripheral NP, the preposition may either be fronted with the question word or else left behind. For example, a question based on *The cat sat on the mat* could be either *On what did the cat sit?* or *What did the cat sit on?* In contrast, with a phrasal verb, it is often the case that the preposition may not be fronted. Based on *The boss <u>laid off</u> the workers* we can have *Who did the boss <u>lay off</u>?*, but not **<u>Off</u> who did the boss <u>lay</u>?* That is, in a phrasal verb, simple verb and preposition should remain together.

Chapter 3 has a full discussion of the semantics and syntax of phrasal verbs.

1.4 Prepositional verbs

There are a number of verbs which cannot be used on their own but must be accompanied by a preposition. For example *dispose of, long for, deal with, refer to, depend on.* The NP following the preposition functions in many ways like a transitive object; for example, from *They disposed of the body* is derived the passive sentence *The body was disposed of.* The verb plus preposition makes up a complex lexical unit, the whole functioning like a transitive verb. (During the detailed discussion of prepositional verbs, in chapter 4, it will be seen that the NP following the preposition differs in minor respects from a straightforward transitive object; the reason for this is explained in section 4.3.)

Note that these 'prepositional verbs' are quite different from phrasal verbs, where the verbal component may occur on its own. *Turn* can be used outside phrasal verbs such as *turn against, turn down (the offer),* and *turn to (the vicar for help),* whereas *dispose* requires its 'inherent preposition' *of.*

The meaning of a prepositional verb can be related to extended senses of its components, in a similar way to that just exemplified for phrasal verbs. Consider, for instance, prepositional verb *depend on,* exemplified in:

(33)   The success of our new project depends on Aaron's insight

This plainly relates to sense (vi) of *on,* with *Our new project is built on Aaron's insight.*

Similarly to phrasal verbs, the components of a prepositional verb should be kept together; one can ask *What did he deal with?* but scarcely **With what did he deal?*

There is a full discussion of prepositional verbs in chapter 4.

1.5 Pairings—major and minor members

There are natural **pairings** for some of the most important prepositions whose basic meanings relate to space or time. For each pair one member can be considered **major** and the other **minor**, with the following properties:

(i)   The major member is far more common than the minor one.

(ii)   The major member has a wider range of meanings and grammatical possibilities; it is likely to feature in more phrasal verbs and prepositional verbs than the minor member. Some of the senses of the major member also apply for the minor member, mutatis mutandis. Other major member senses have no correspondents. The minor member has some independent senses, but rather few (in comparison with those of the major member).

(iii) In most instances, the basic meaning of the major member is provided with a positive specification, with that of the minor member being, in a rather rough sense, the opposite of this.

The pairings are:

MAJOR MEMBER		MINOR MEMBER		
to	approaching	from	departing	chapter 7
in	enclosed	out	unenclosed	chapter 8
on	connected	off	disconnected	chapter 9
up	high, superior	down	low, inferior	chapter 10
over	relatively higher area	under	relatively lower area	section 11.1a
above	relatively higher vertically	below	relatively lower vertically	section 11.1b
after	later time	before	earlier time	section 14.4

The major and minor members of each pairing can be conjoined, all but one in that order: *to and from, in and out, on and off, up and down, over and under, above and below.* (Conjunctions in the reverse order do occur but are rare; for example there are almost ninety times as many *up and down* as there are *down and up* in the COCA corpus.) The exception, where the minor member comes first is *before and after* (this is the order which shows temporal sequence).

There are also the idiomatic combinations *ins and outs* 'all the details of a situation' and *ups and downs* 'mixture of good and bad happenings'.

Discussion of the meanings and functions of individual prepositions, in part II, is conducted in terms of these pairings.

1.6 Realisation as clitics

A number of short grammatical elements (almost all monosyllabic) although written as if they were distinct words are typically pronounced as clitics. That is, their vowel is reduced, they lose primary stress, and they attach to a following full word (proclitic) or a preceding full word (enclitic). A clitic boundary is shown by '='. For example:

WRITTEN | SPOKEN

He set her to work   /hi=ˈset=ə tə=ˈwəːk/

Whereas the sentence is written as five orthographic works, when spoken it consists of just two phonological words, each centred on a lexical root which bears primary stress (shown by ˈ). To /ˈset/ 'set' is attached the proclitic subject pronoun /hi=/ 'he' and the enclitic object pronoun /=ə/ 'her'. And to /ˈwəːk/ 'work' is attached the proclitic preposition /tə=/ 'to'.

Proclitics include articles, possessive pronouns, subject pronouns, some verbal auxiliaries, and a number of conjunctions. Plus a small selection of prepositions. These are:

| | FULL FORM | REDUCES TO A PROCLITIC FORM | |
	(STRESSED)	BEFORE A CONSONANT	BEFORE A VOWEL
of	/ˈɔv/	/ə(v)=/	/(ə)v=/
for	/ˈfɔː(r)/	/fə=/ or /f=/	/fər=/ or /fr=/
at	/ˈat/	/ət=/ or /ə/=/	/ət=/
to	/ˈtuː/	/tə=/ or /t=/	/tu=/ or /tə=/
from	/ˈfrɔm/	/frəm=/ or /frm=/	
upon	/əˈpɔn/	/əpən=/	
with	/ˈwið/	/wið=/ or /wi=/	/wið=/
by	/ˈbai/	/bi=/ or /bə=/	/bai=/

We can see that the proclitic prepositions consist of the four whose basic meaning is relational (*of, for, by, with*) and the three central spatial forms (*at, to, from*) plus *upon* (see section 2.3).

By and *with* are only sometimes pronounced as proclitics whereas the other six prepositions invariably are, except in a context of contrast. For example, suppose someone says, with normal proclitic reduction:

(34)   Mary moved from France   /ˈmeri ˈmuːvd frəm=ˈfraːns
       to Spain   tə=ˈspein/

However, you may know that this is not true. In correcting it you employ the full stressed forms of *to* and *from* to emphasise places of destination and departure:

(35)   No, Mary moved *to* France   /'nou 'meri 'muvd 'tu: 'fraːns
       from Spain   'frɔm 'spein/

The possibilities for omitting the NP which follows a preposition (in certain circumstances) are discussed in the next chapter; for example, *She put the shoes on her feet* may be shortened to *She put the shoes on*. It is noteworthy that the six prepositions which are always typically pronounced as clitics belong to the set of prepositions which may not omit a following NP; if this were to be omitted, there would be no following word for the proclitic preposition to attach to. In addition, they do not function as adverbs. The same applies for *with*, which is only sometimes reduced to a proclitic (there is here a non-cognate adverb, *together*). *By* has a minor spatial sense, and this does also function as an adverb.

When a peripheral NP is replaced by a question word, this generally moves to the beginning of the clause. It may take its preposition with it—for example, *At what did John aim?*—or leave it behind—*What did John aim at?* Such a 'stranded' preposition no longer has anything following to which it can cliticise, and it is thus stressed.

Complex prepositions which end in *to* or *of* are also proclitic: *into*, *onto*, *up-to*, *out-of*, *off-of*, as is *upon* (reasons are given in section 2.3 for treating each of these as a single preposition rather than as a sequence of two prepositions). Phrasal prepositions—for example, *in-front-of*, *in-return-for*, *close-to*, *away-from*, and *together-with*—end in a simple preposition which is prototypically a clitic and thus themselves cliticise onto a following NP.

There are many prepositions, both monosyllabic and disyllabic, which do not reduce—*in*, *out*, *on*, *off*, *up*, *down*, *over*, *under*, *about*, among others. All of these may omit a following NP if it could be understood from context. And there are prepositions which may not omit a following NP and which do not have a reduced clitic form; they include *among* and *until/till*.

There is one other kind of clitic which is relevant for the study of prepositions. This is object pronouns which are generally enclitic to the preceding verb. For example *you* may be pronounced as /'yu/, with a full vowel and primary stress, in a contrastive context such as: *I didn't say* 'who' I said 'you' /'ai 'didnt 'sei 'hu: 'ai 'sed 'yu/. But it is generally an enclitic /=yə/ attached to the preceding word, as in *Sam likes you* /'sam 'laiks=yə/.

There are certain circumstances in which a preposition may move to the left over a preceding NP (see section 2.1c). For example *Meg let the cat into the house* may be reduced to *Meg let the cat in*, and then this rejigged to *Meg let in the cat*. However, this left movement is not possible if the NP is a pronoun. One can say *Meg let it in* but not **Meg let in it*. The reason is that an object pronoun is enclitic to its verb:—/'let=it 'in/ 'let it in'—and neither a preposition nor anything else can intervene between verb and enclitic object pronoun.

1.7 Prepositions and adverbs

An adverb is a word which functions on its own (without any following NP) to add meaning to a sentence. Many manner adverbs are derived from adjectives by adding *-ly*; for example, *carefully*, *quickly*, *cleverly*. There are a number of general quantifying adverbs, including *almost*, *possibly*, *really*. The adverbs which concern us here are those relating to space—*away* in *John ran away*—which have properties similar to those of prepositions.

It is often possible to omit an NP following a preposition if its identity is clear from the context. Consider:

(36)   Mark took his hat off the peg
(37)   Mark took his hat off his head

Sentence (37) could be reduced to just *Mark took his hat off* if one were describing what Mark did as he entered church, since it is an expected act in this situation. (In contrast (36) could be reduced to *Mark took his hat off* only in very special circumstances.)

The question now to ask is: since *off* is no longer followed by an NP in *Mark took his hat off*, should it now be considered an adverb (rather than as a preposition)? My answer would be 'no', since a following NP is clearly understood from the situation. This is just a situation-engendered reduction of a prepositional NP.

However, *off* does clearly function as an adverb in:

(38)   Larry ran off

Around behaves in a similar way. *Pete just sat around the house yesterday* can, in an appropriate context, be reduced to *Pete just sat around yesterday*. *Around* is still functioning as a preposition; the following NP is not stated but is understood from the context. But *around* does also function as an adverb, as in *The wind veered around*.

With respect to adverb possibilities, prepositions may be classified as follows:

(1) **Function as preposition only, not as adverb**. There is no context-determined omission of a following NP and no adverbial function. These include: *of, for, except, despite, at, to, from, toward(s), among(st), since, until/till*.

(2) **Function as preposition, not really as adverb, but there can be occasional context-determined omission of a following NP**. They have no true adverbial function. These include: *under, above, below, against, beside(s), between*.

(3) **Function equally as preposition and as adverb**. These include: *in, on, off, over, about, around, along*.

(4) **Function primarily as adverb** (with a wide range of senses) **and secondarily as preposition** (with limited spatial reference): *out, up, down*.

(5) **There are a number of other preposition/adverb correspondences**. For example, adverb *together* relates to prepositions *with* and *together with*. And there are compound prepositions based on adverbs, such as:

ADVERB	PREPOSITION
ahead	ahead-of
apart	apart-from
away	away-from
forward(s)	forward(s)-of

The relationship of prepositions *on, onto,* and *upon* with adverb *on*, prepositions *into* and *in* with adverb *in*, and suchlike, are discussed in the first few pages of chapters 8 and 9.

1.8 Further functions

There are various, rather limited, possibilities for prepositions undertaking 'double duty'; that is, having a secondary function in some other word class.

(i) Just a few prepositions also function as **adjectives**; for example: *the outside toilet, the down track, the above statement, (he died in) near poverty.*

(ii) A noun following such an adjectival-use of preposition may, in appropriate circumstances, be omitted, leaving the preposition-adjective appearing to be head of its NP, superficially behaving like a **noun**. For instance, *Varnish the underneath part of the boat!* can be reduced to *Varnish the underneath of the boat!*

(iii) A handful of prepositions may also function as **verbs**. Alongside *He drank the beer down* one can say *He downed the beer.* And a re-statement of *We were near the finishing point* is *We neared the finishing point.*

(iv) Just a few prepositions can be used as predicate of an imperative sentence, in each case followed by a *with* phrase:
- *Out,* as in *Out with it!* (meaning 'Don't keep the news to yourself!')
- *Off,* as in *Off with you!* (meaning 'Go away!') and *Off with his head!*
- *Down,* as in *Down with the monarchy!*
- *Up,* as in *Up with the Rangers!* (when cheering on a sports team)

Perhaps the most notable example of a preposition being used as a verb is when Lady Macbeth attempts to remove the blood from her hand: *Out, damned spot, out, I say* (*Macbeth*, Act 5, scene 1).

(v) A preposition may be related to a **conjunction,** notably *because-of* and *because, but-for* and *but. Since* functions as a temporal preposition and as a conjunction indicating 'consequence'; see section 14.1.

(vi) Two of the relational prepositions (*for* and *by*) and also *to,* whose basic meaning is spatial, **mark grammatical constructions**. In

17

a passive derivation, the erstwhile agent is marked with *by*, as in *I was bitten by a dog*. The 'potential' variety of complement clauses uses *for* and *to*; for example, *We had hoped for Isaac to be elected* (see sections 2.5c, 5.3d, 6.1c, and 7.2d).

1.9 Related prefixes

There are eleven grammatical elements, each of which could function as preposition or as derivational prefix in early stages of English, and they maintain these uses today. In some instances, the verbal derivation can be paraphrased using the corresponding preposition. For example:

PREFIX	PREPOSITION
There was an <u>out</u>-burst of laughter	Laughter burst <u>out</u>
An <u>in</u>-house magazine	A magazine only circulated <u>in</u> the house (i.e. company)
Phoebe was just an <u>on</u>-looker	Phoebe was just looking <u>on</u>
Her <u>off</u>-screen personality was quite different	Her personality was quite different <u>off</u> the screen
They live <u>up</u>-river	They live <u>up</u> the river
There was a <u>down</u>-pour of rain	The rain poured <u>down</u>
She felt mud <u>under</u>-foot	She felt mud <u>under</u> her feet
He wore an <u>over</u>-coat	He wore a coat <u>over</u> his clothes
There was a <u>through</u>-draught in the room	There was a draught right <u>through</u> the room (between two open windows)
I don't believe in an <u>after</u>-life	I don't believe in life <u>after</u> death
They are building a <u>by</u>-pass at Slough	They are building a road which passes <u>by</u> Slough (not going through it)

However, a goodly number of words involving these prefixes have a meaning some way removed from that of the corresponding preposition. Among many others can be mentioned *out-number*, *on-set*, *off-season*, *up-beat*, *down-home*, *under-go*, and *over-shadow*.

An interesting contrast is that between derived verb *over-take* and phrasal verb *take over*:

(39) Dr Lewis <u>over</u>-took the blue van
        (she drove her car past the van so that she was in front of it)

(40) Dr Lewis <u>took over</u> the company
        (she bought the company and had control over it)

There is a similar contrast between *over-look* and *look over*.

1.10 Endings -s and -st

In ME there was a suffix *-s* (homonymous with the genitive) which could be added to a noun or adjective to form an adverb or preposition. In some instances a final *-t* was also added, giving *-st*. There are a variety of ways in which this has come through into the modern language:

(1) Preposition *among* has an alternative form *amongst* /əˈmʌŋst/ (see section 12.1).
(2) Preposition/adverb *along* had an alternative form *alongst* /əˈlɔŋst/, which has now pretty well dropped out of use (see section 11.4a).
(3) Preposition *against*, /əˈgenst/ or /əˈgeinst/, included *-st* to distinguish it from adverb *again*, which has the same source (section 9.3).
(4) Preposition *beside* has an alternative form *besides* /bəˈsaidz/ (section 9.4).
(5) Preposition *toward* has an alternative form *towards* /təˈwɔːdz/ (section 7.3).

There is a phonological principle involved. Where the basic form ends in a nasal, as in (1–3) then *-t* is added after the *-s* on grounds of euphony. However, when the basic form ends in *d*, there is no addition of *-t* (to avoid a sequence *-dst*).

While came down to us from OE. In the fourteenth century, it was augmented to become *whiles* (which is now scarcely used), and *whilst* /wailst/, which is a present-day alternative for *while*. The *-st* was here acceptable after the lateral, *l*.

There is one further example. In the seventeenth century, *-st* was added to another form which ends in a nasal, giving *unbeknownst*; this gained general acceptance and is today far commoner than *unbeknown*. (*Unknownst* also made an entry, but the plain *unknown* is preferred here.)

However, there appears to be an exception—preposition *amid* ends in *d* but has an alternative form *amidst* (see section 12.1). The factor here may be the quality of the vowel. The final syllable of *amid* /əˈmid/ has a short stressed vowel /i/ and this may accept a final coda /dst/; the form /əˈmidst/ sounds quite harmonious. In contrast, the stressed final syllables of the words in (4–5) have stronger vowels—a diphthong, in *beside* /bəˈsaid/, and a long vowel, in *toward* /təˈwɔːd/. For these, adding *-st* would produce a word which sounds discordant.

* * *

The next three chapters, in Part I, outline the grammatical possibilities for prepositions. This sets the stage for the ten chapters of Part II, which feature characterisation of each preposition, these being arranged in semantic sets.

Part I
The Stage is Set

2

Grammatical roles

2.1 Inner and outer peripheral noun phrases

The core components of a clause—subject, predicate, object if the clause is transitive—are obligatory. To these may be added a peripheral NP (pNP)—an NP introduced by a preposition—which is in most cases

English Prepositions: Their Meanings and Uses. R. M. W. Dixon. Oxford University Press (2021). © R. M. W. Dixon.
DOI: 10.1093/oso/9780198868682.003.0002

optional. The role of the preposition is to indicate the semantic role of its NP; for instance, whether it refers to an instrument, a purpose, an ability, a location, or any of many other possibilities.

Dealing with prepositions in their basic spatial or temporal meanings, there are two kinds of pNP:

- An **inner pNP**, which provides spatial modification of a verb—the meaning of the preposition correlates with the meaning of the verb. The pNP almost always follows the core components of the clause and may, in specific circumstances, omit its NP.
- An **outer pNP**, which provides spatial or temporal modification of a complete sentence. There is no necessary connection between the preposition and the verb of the clause. An outer pNP generally comes at the end of the sentence but can be placed at the beginning. The NP part of the pNP can never be omitted.

2.1a Inner peripheral noun phrases

There are two varieties of inner pNPs:

- **Motion.** One or more pNPs indicating motion may be used with a verb of motion. This is the primary use of prepositions *to, toward(s),* and *from,* as in:

  The boy went from the haystack to the sundial

  Many other prepositions may have a motion sense. For example *She came through the tunnel, He jumped over the wall, They ran along the path.*

- **Location.** One or more pNPs indicating location may be used with a verb of rest. Besides *at,* quite a number of other prepositions may have a location sense. For example:

  The girl stayed in the kitchen at home

  Also: *He lives behind the school, She sat below the window, He replaced the top on the canister.*

Some prepositions may indicate either motion or location, depending on the verb they are used with. For instance *under* refers to motion in *The mouse ran under the table* ('to under') and location in *The mouse hid under the table* ('at under').

2.1b Omission of the noun phrase from an inner peripheral noun phrase

A feature of inner pNPs is that the NP can sometimes be omitted from the pNP. The conditions for this are:

(i) **The preposition may not be a clitic.** *To, from,* and *at* are proclitic to the following NP; this NP may not be omitted or there would then be nothing for the preposition to attach to.

(ii) **The full combination**—core components plus pNP—**must refer to a familiar circumstance**, such that when the NP is omitted its identity will be understood from the context.

If several people are in a dining room, one could say to another: *Please put the cloth on the table!* and then, a couple of hours later: *Please take the cloth off the table!* These are likely to be reduced to: *Please put the cloth on!* and *Please take the cloth off!*, since in this context the normal object which a cloth is put onto, and then taken off from, is understood to be a table.

Suppose a courier comes delivering a parcel, enquires where it should be put and is instructed: *Put the package on the bed!* There is no way in which *the bed* could be omitted here (giving: *Put the package on!*) since putting a package on a bed is not a familiar activity, in the way that putting a cloth on a table is.

A customer entered a bank, went up to a cashier standing on the other side of a counter and wished to withdraw some money. What happened is described by:

> The cashier passed the money over the counter

A cashier passing money over a counter in a bank is a familiar activity, and consequently the NP *the counter* could be omitted here, giving *The cashier passed the money over*. What the money was passed over is understood from the context. In contrast, the final NP is rather unlikely to be omitted from *The cook passed the cake through the window*, since this is not so recurrent an activity as passing money over a counter.

Omission of an NP in a familiar circumstance is found most often with the more common non-proclitic spatial prepositions: *in, out, on, off, through, over, across,* and *around*. It is unlikely with, for example, *behind* and *against*.

2.1c Left movement of preposition or adverb over a preceding noun phrase

If there is an inner pNP following a transitive verb, and the NP is omitted from the pNP under circumstances just described, the preposition may optionally move to the left of the object NP of the transitive verb. (As mentioned in section 1.6 this is not possible if the object NP is a pronoun, since an object pronoun is enclitic to the preceding verb and cannot be detached from it.) Thus:

He put the cloth on (the table)	→	He put on the cloth
He took the cloth off (the table)	→	He took off the cloth
He put the hat on (his head)	→	He put on the hat
She passed the money over (the counter)	→	She passed over the money

Some grammarians would maintain that once its following NP is omitted, the preposition becomes an adverb and the rule is then that an adverb can be moved over a preceding object NP. (This is essentially a matter of terminology and does not alter the facts.) My view is that, since the reference of the omitted NP is understood, the preposition maintains this function.

Spatial adverbs have a similar role to inner pNPs and do also undergo left movement. For example:

He threw the rubbish away	→	He threw away the rubbish
She couldn't tell the twins apart	→	She couldn't tell apart the twins

Movement of a spatial preposition or adverb over a preceding object NP is rather unexpected, in the context of the overall grammatical organisation of the language. Generally, a manner adverb—something like *quickly* or *carefully* or *cleverly*—can be placed at the end or at the beginning of a sentence, or before the verb (or after the first word of a multi-verb VP), but not between verb and object. One may say *He put his hat on his head quickly* or *Quickly he put his hat on his head* or *He quickly put his hat on his head* but not **He put quickly his hat on his head.* It is thus somewhat surprising that *on* can move to precede *his hat,* giving: *He put on his hat.*

The explanation is that an inner pNP is determined by the meaning of the verb. When the NP of the pNP has been omitted (under circumstances where its reference is clear) and the preposition is left unencumbered, it may naturally be moved to the left—over the object NP—so that it is adjacent to the verb with which it is associated.

There is one point of difference between a preposition when following and when preceding an object NP. As discussed in section 2.6, there are limited possibilities for modification of a preposition; a common modifier is *right,* as in:

He took the cloth right off (the table)

When the preposition is moved to the left, it cannot take its modifier with it. That is, one can say *He took off the cloth,* but not **He took right off the cloth.* The close association between verb and preposition which is established by left movement may not be interrupted by a modifier.

We have been discussing inner NPs involving prepositions used in their basic spatial senses. More abstract meanings are an extension from these, as are the uses of prepositions in phrasal verbs. Left movement of a preposition also happens here. There is discussion in section 3.5 of factors influencing its application.

2.1d Outer peripheral noun phrases

Most types of activity are located in some place and at some time. This can be specified by a selection of outer pNPs. The difference from inner pNPs is that there is no association between the verb of the sentence and the outer pNPs. Whereas an inner pNP augments the reference of the verb, an outer pNP relates to the complete sentence, locating the activity it describes in space and time.

For example, we can describe a few happenings, chosen pretty well at random:

Jack broke the plate	Jill ate the mango
Robin proved the theorem	Fred admitted his guilt
Jane likes to exercise	Jason complained about his liver

To each of these core clauses (and to an indefinite number more) can be added one or more spatial and/or temporal pNPs, such as:

> in the garden at the vicarage at ten o'clock on Monday

or   before breakfast under the oak tree beyond the shed

The complete sentence must be plausible but—unlike for inner pNPs—there is no particular association between the preposition and the meaning of the verb.

There are significant differences between the two varieties of pNP:

(i) **Prepositions involved**
- An inner pNP only relates to space (motion or location) and can be marked by any preposition which has a spatial sense.
- An outer pNP specifies space or time and can be marked by any preposition which has a location (not motion) or a temporal sense. Thus, the main motion prepositions—*to*, *from*, and also *toward(s)*—only occur in inner, never in outer, pNPs. Note though that *at* is used in both varieties.
- The relational prepositions—*of*, *for*, and *with*—have grammatical functions and do not feature in outer pNPs. *By* does have a minor spatial sense so that it can occur in both inner and outer pNPs.

(ii) **Possibility of reduction.** Unlike an inner pNP, an outer pNP cannot omit its NP; there is thus no possibility of left movement of the preposition over a preceding transitive object NP.

(iii) **Placement.** An inner pNP is generally placed after the verb (plus the object NP if it has one). With just a few prepositions, the pNP may come at the beginning of the clause but only in a contrived poetic-like style. For example: *Over the counter, the cashier passed the money* and *Across the lawn, the rabbit ran*.

An outer pNP most often follows the core components of a clause but it can, fairly freely, precede them. Or there can be one or more pNPs before and other(s) after. Consider:

Jack broke the plate [in the garden] [at the pub] [at noon] [on Monday]
                    1   2   3

The two spatial outer pNPs are linked—the garden is at the pub—as are the two temporal outer pNPs—noon is on Monday—and cannot be separated. Nor should spatial and temporal pNPs be interspersed.

The two spatial pNPs, 2, could either precede or follow the temporal pNPs, 3. Either or both of 2 and 3 could precede the clausal core, 1, in either order. That is, we could have 123, or 132, or 231, or 321, or 213, or 312.

2.2 Preposition stranding

There are several grammatical operations which affect the position or the integrity of a pNP. One of the most frequent consists in questioning the NP component of a pNP. The question word is generally moved to the beginning of the clause and either (a) it may leave its preposition behind, or (b) it may take it with it.

We can start with a straightforward statement:

Sylvia is living with friends

It would be possible to just substitute *who* for *friends*, creating an 'echo question': *Sylvia is living with who?* But the more normal practice is to move the question word (here *who*) to the beginning of the sentence. There are the two possibilities.

(a)   Fronting who and leaving the preposition in its original position (it is then said to be 'stranded'):

Who is Sylvia living with?

(b)   Fronting the entire pNP; that is, the preposition plus *who*:

With whom is Sylvia living?

The same two possibilities apply for relative clause formation:

(a)   The friends [who Sylvia is living with] come from Birmingham
(b)   The friends [with whom Sylvia is living] come from Birmingham

Note that the same alternatives apply for questioning, for relative clause constructions and for other techniques for fronting all or part of a pNP.

In some circumstances—as in the examples just quoted—(a) and (b) are equally acceptable. In others, one possibility is good and the other either unacceptable or marginal. This can be roughly summarised in a table:

(a) front NP and leave preposition stranded	(b) front preposition plus NP	
yes	no	Phrasal verbs—verb and prepositions/ adverbs must stay together. See section 3.6.
yes	few	Prepositional verbs— verb and preposition generally stay together. See section 4.1a.
no	yes	Temporal prepositions *since, until/till, after,* and *before*—whole pNP must stay together. See chapter 14.
yes	sometimes (varies)	Most other prepositions

Sometimes neither (a) nor (b) are fully acceptable. This applies for several of the least common prepositions, such as *within, beside(s), beyond,* and *despite.*

Whether alternative (b) is possible for a preposition—in the bottom row of the diagram—depends in part on the meaning of the verb and NPs involved. Consider preposition *for*. Both (a) and (b) are acceptable for the following:

I'm waiting for the postman

(a)   Who are you waiting for?

(b)   For whom are you waiting?

However, when we change verb and NPs, (a) is fine but (b) sounds rather less good:

The dealer bid for the picture

(a)   What did the dealer bid for?

(b)   *For what did the dealer bid?

As we find throughout the grammar, judgements concerning the acceptability of a particular sentence are essentially subjective and personal. Nevertheless there usually is general agreement; for instance most speakers would consider that with the *dealer bid* pair, (b) is less felicitous than (a). (One factor may be the fact that for *wait* the NP following *for* has animate reference, whereas the corresponding NP for *bid* refers to something inanimate.)

2.3 Complex prepositions

There can be a sequence of two prepositions, as in the following phrasal verbs:

Marcia <u>took</u> her anger <u>out on</u> Henry

Martha <u>tied</u> the reunion <u>in with</u> her wedding

His uncle <u>set</u> John <u>up in</u> business

The fact that the two prepositions are quite separate is shown by the fact that the first may move to the left over a preceding object NP:

Marcia <u>took out</u> her anger <u>on</u> Henry

Martha <u>tied in</u> the reunion <u>with</u> her wedding

His uncle <u>set up</u> John in business

In contrast, there are instances of what might appear on the surface to be a sequence of prepositions but actually each constitutes a single complex preposition. There are *into, out-of, up-to, onto, upon,* and *off-of.* (English orthography is inconsistent, writing three of these as single words and the others as two words. I add a hyphen to indicate that each is a single preposition.)

Consider the following examples:

The wizard turned Dan into a frog

We talked Sally out-of applying for that job

You can change your preference up-to three times

She put Martin onto the possibilities

He dropped his jacket upon the chair

She took the book off-of the shelf

If each of these had a sequence of two prepositions, we would expect the first to be able to be moved to the left over the preceding object NP. This is not possible. That is, the following are absolutely unacceptable:

*The wizard turned in Dan to a frog
*We talked out Sally of applying for that job
*You can change up your preference to three times
*She put on Martin to the possibilities
*He dropped up his jacket on the chair
*She took off the book of the shelf

Five of the complex prepositions end in *of* or *to* which are proclitics; as a consequence, the complex prepositions are proclitics (at least before a word commencing with a consonant). *Upon* is the only one of these complex prepositions not to end in *of* or *to* but it patterns with them in also having proclitic form (even though its components, *up* and *on*, are non-proclitic). The forms are:

into	/intə=/	out-of	/autəv=/	up-to	/ʌptə=/
onto	/ɔntə=/	upon	/əpən=/	off-of	/ɔfəv=/

These are thus solely prepositions. They must be followed by an NP to which they attach, and they cannot function as adverbs.

Note though that, quite apart from the complex prepositions, we do sometimes find the 'components' as a sequence of two prepositions. For example:

Fred hung the picture up on the wall
Billy worked the crowd up to a fever pitch of excitement
Tony handed the baton on to the next runner in the relay

Here, the first preposition can be moved to the left over the object NP, showing that it is separate from the second preposition:

Fred hung up the picture on the wall
Billy worked up the crowd to a fever pitch of excitement
Tony handed on the baton to the next runner in the relay

In fact, the last part of each of these two sentences is optional. We can have just *Fred hung the picture up*, *Fred hung up the picture*, *Billy worked the crowd up*, *Billy worked up the crowd*, and *Tony handed the baton on*, *Tony handed on the baton*.

In some instances either a simple or a complex preposition may be used, with little difference in meaning. For example, *in* and *into* in:

She brought the cat into the   *or*   She brought the cat in the
house   house

When the NP, *the house*, of the pNP can be understood from the context, this may be omitted, However, only the non-proclitic pronoun is then possible: *She brought the cat in*, not **She brought the cat into*. This preposition can then undergo left movement, giving: *She brought in the cat*.

For Standard British English, *out-of* is generally used, rather than just *out*, for the basic spatial sense. For example:

The pastrycook took the cake out-of the oven

When its identity would be understood, the NP may be omitted from the pNP and then the proclitic *out-of* must be reduced to the non-proclitic form *out*. Thus, *The pastrycook took the cake out* and, with left movement, *The pastrycook took out the cake*.

Chapter 8 has detailed discussion of prepositions *in*, *into*, *out*, and *out-of*, and chapter 10 of *up* and *up-to*. The rather more intricate relations between *on*, *onto*, *upon*, *off*, and *off-of* are dealt with in chapter 9.

There are just a few complex prepositions (each made up of two simple prepositions) that do not end in a clitic—*in-between*, *throughout*, and *up-until*.

2.4 Other roles for a peripheral noun phrase

2.4a With a noun

The inclusion of a pNP with a verb naturally extends to inclusion with a cognate noun. For example:

They stayed at the inn   →   [Their stay at the inn] was enjoyable
We walked to the station   →   [Our walk to the station] was pleasant

Our walk to the station refers to the activity of our walking. *The walk to the station* could have this meaning, or it could describe the path for the walk (how pretty it was).

A motion pNP can be used with any noun which may relate to motion, such as *the train into town*, *the tunnel through the mountain*,

and *the road to the river*. There could, alternatively, be location specification, such as *the road at the end of the valley*.

In essence, any noun with concrete reference can have its place specified through a spatial location pNP; for instance: *the shop on the corner*,
the struggle in the corridor, the bridge over the freeway, and *the meeting
at headquarters*. This extends to temporal location as in *the meeting on
Monday*. If the referent of the noun is extended in time, this can also be
described through a temporal pNP; for example *the rain during the
night*, and *his unhappiness since the divorce*.

When a verb (plus object if transitive) is followed by two pNPs, there
can be ambiguity as to whether (a) both pNPs directly modify the verb,
or (b) only the first pNP does, with the second pNP modifying the head
noun of the first pNP. Compare:

(a)   The rabbit ran [to the shed] [across the lawn]

which relates both *to the shed* and *across the lawn* to the rabbit's running, and:

(b)   The rabbit ran [to the shed [across the lawn]]

This states that the rabbit ran to the shed which was situated across the
lawn.

Note that there is no such ambiguity with *The rabbit ran [across the
lawn][to the shed]*. The noun *lawn* can be modified by a location pNP
(as in: *the lawn on the north side*) but not by a motion pNP such as *to the
shed*.

2.4b As copula complement

A copula clause will have a copula subject (CS), which is an NP, a copula
verb (*be*, or *become* in some instances), and a copula complement (CC).
There is a wide range of possibilities for copula complement. It can be
an NP (as in, *My daughter is a lawyer*) or an adjective (*This apple is ripe*)
or a possessive phrase (*The red car is the tall doctor's*) or a pNP.

However, only a pNP showing spatial or temporal location may function as copula complement. For example, *The road is at the end of the
valley, The struggle was in the corridor*, and *The meeting will be on Monday*.

A pNP referring to spatial motion or to temporal duration may not
felicitously make up a copula complement; these require a non-copula
verb. Rather than *The road is to the river*, one should say something like

The road goes to the river. And *The rain fell during the night* is preferable to **The rain was during the night.*

2.4c With an adjective

Adjectives from the HUMAN PROPENSITY semantic type are typically followed by a pNP. Which preposition is used in the pNP depends on the adjective. *Busy* prefers a pNP marked by *with* and *clever* one introduced by *at*—*Jo is busy (with the visa requirements)* and *Anna is clever (at kite-making)*. Some adjectives may occur with several prepositions, each relating to one segment of its range of meaning. For instance *Sara was angry with Tom, Robin was angry about the decision, Mary was angry at the man who stole her camera.*

An adjective describes a general property and a following pNP specifies what the property relates to in a particular instance. *Anna is clever* is a general statement but vague; she is unlikely to be clever in all possible ways. *Anna is clever at kite-making* is fully informative. In almost every case, a pNP is optional after an adjective. It may be sufficient to say just *Robin is angry*, with the context making clear the reason for his emotion in this instance. Or the reason could be explicitly stated through a following pNP. (An exception to this optionality is *fond*, which requires a pNP marked by *of*; for example, *Richard is fond of dogs.*)

Discussion so far in this chapter has centred on the basic senses of spatial and temporal prepositions as they mark pNPs which are ancillary to the core elements of a clause. For each preposition, the basic sense is extended, in various ways, to more abstract meanings with verbs, and thence—for some prepositions—to use after adjectives. This can be exemplified with *at*:

At relates to a purely spatial target in:	Anna threw the dart at the bullseye
This is extended to an abstract target, still with a verb referring to physical activity over a length of time in:	Anna works at kite-making
Then further extended to use with a verb of positive judgement in:	Anna excels at kite-making
And naturally extended to an adjective describing prowess in:	Anna is clever at kite-making
Or just an adjective describing competence in:	Anna is good at kite-making

35

About marks pNPs which can follow several kinds of adjectives. Once more, these develop to form the basic spatial sense of *about* with verbs, extended to more abstract senses with verbs, and thence to use with adjectives.

About relates to the spatial focus of a verb of motion in:	Robin walked about the garden
This can be extended to the focus of a general verb of speaking in:	Robin talked about the decision
The verb can be more specific, where the focus relates to something considered unsatisfactory:	Robin complained about the decision
Alternatively, a very similar sentiment may be conveyed through an adjective:	Robin was angry about the decision
Another extension from the basic meaning of *about* is to the focus of a general verb of cognition in:	Sam was thinking about Peg's wealth
The verb can be more specific, enquiring for information concerning what is focussed on:	Sam was wondering about Peg's wealth
This enquiring attitude may also be expressed with an adjective:	Sam was curious about Peg's wealth
For is a relational preposition one of whose senses is 'purpose', which can relate to mental aspiration, as in:	John yearns for recognition
A similar sense is shown by the adjective *eager* in:	John is eager for recognition
With, another relational preposition, can indicate 'activity directed towards', as in:	Jo is experimenting with a new approach
The verb describing the activity may be less specific:	Jo is dealing with the visa requirements
Using the adjective *busy* conveys a similar meaning:	Jo is busy with the visa requirements

These examples have illustrated how the choice of a pNP which optimally follows an adjective is often motivated by similar extensions from the basic meaning of the preposition when it is used with verbs. Not all adjectival pNPs may be linked to verbal extensions in this way, but many can be.

2.5 Manipulating prepositions

There are three types of main clause:

- **Intransitive clause**, with a single core argument in intransitive subject (S) function.
- **Transitive clause**, with two core arguments in transitive subject (A) and transitive object (O) functions. (A variant of this, involving a prepositional verb, was mentioned in section 1.4 and is the topic of chapter 4.)
- **Copula clause**, with two core arguments in copula subject (CS) and copula complement (CC) functions.

S, A, O, and CS functional slots must be filled by an NP or a complement clause (CoCl); for example $Sam_{NP:A}$ knows [that Alice is clever]$_{CoCl:O}$ and [That Alice is clever]$_{CoCl:CS}$ is [a well-known fact]$_{NP:CC}$. The CC functional slot may be filled by an NP, a complement clause, an adjective, a possessive phrase, or a pNP.

To the core of an intransitive or transitive clause—verbal predicate plus core argument(s)—may be added one or more pNPs. With respect to copula clauses, the CC may be a pNP and, in addition, a pNP may be added to the core (copula verb predicate plus core arguments). For example [That apple]$_{CS}$ will be ripe$_{CC}$ [in a few days], Tony$_{CS}$ was [in the bathroom]$_{CC}$ [during the vote], and [Winter nights]$_{CS}$ are [of long duration]$_{CC}$ [in the north].

The referent of S, the sole core argument in an intransitive clause, will in some instances exercise volitional control over the activity—for example, Dick jumped off the bridge—but other times there is no control—as in Dick fell from the balcony.

For a transitive clause, that core argument whose referent could initiate or control the activity (if anything could) is in A function, the other core argument being in O function. In many cases the referent of the O argument will be affected by the activity, but this does not always hold (for instance in *John*$_A$ *saw [a flash of lightning]*$_O$ there is no way in which the flash of lightning is affected). For every transitive clause, both the referent of the A argument and the referent of the O argument are integral features of the activity. This is in contrast to the referent of the NP within a pNP, which is a peripheral element.

We can now describe how a preposition may be inserted into, or deleted from, a prototypical clause scheme to indicate some deviation from the norm.

2.5a Inserting a preposition

Verb *pull* indicates that the referent of the O argument is moved; for example, *Bill pulled the rope.* The rope, referent of the O argument, has its position affected. Now, suppose that Bill exerts a pulling force on the rope but it does not move; the fact that in this instance the rope was not affected in the expected way is shown by inserting preposition *on* before the O NP: *Bill pulled on the rope.*

When *bite* is used with a non-animate object, it generally refers to separating off a portion with one's teeth, as in *Enid bit the apple, and ate the portion she had bitten off.* But someone can also bite to relieve tension. For instance, if being operated on without anaesthetic, the patient may sink their teeth into a leather strap. One would not say *Enid bit the leather strap* (which would imply removing a piece from it) but rather *Enid bit on the leather strap.* Inserting preposition *on* before the O NP indicates that the referent of this argument is not affected in the expected way.

Verb *hold* refers to grasping something and keeping control over it. For example, *Archie held the baby, Mavis held the lantern*; the referent of the O argument is affected by the control exerted over it by the referent of the A argument. *Hold* could also be used if there were a fierce wind, and Tom grasped a pole to stop being blown away; but in this instance one would say *Tom held onto the pole.* The fact that here it is the pole which is securing Tom (and not the other way round) is shown by inserting preposition *onto* before the O NP.

In each of these examples, the fact that the referent of the O argument is not affected in the way expected for that verb is shown by specially marking it with a preposition (here *on* or *onto*). A further example involves preposition *at*. If Steve moves his foot to come into forceful contact with a ball so that this propels the ball away, one would say *Steve kicked the ball.* However, if Steve aimed his foot towards the ball but missed it entirely, one could only say *Steve kicked at the ball.* The insertion of *at* before the O NP indicates that its referent is not affected in the way one would expect the object of *kick* to be. (Using *at* indicates that the ball was here a target.)

Inserting a preposition does not always relate to how the referent of the O argument is (or is not) affected. It may also be used to draw attention to the emotional state of the referent of the A argument. In the plain transitive clause *Mary kicked the door*, it is implied that she directed a foot at the door to move it (to make it open). Suppose that Mary gets a temper up with the physical manifestation of this being wild gestures of arms and legs. We then might say *Mary kicked at the door* to describe where her irate kicks landed. In this instance, inserting preposition *at* before the O NP *the door* indicates that what happens to the door is of secondary importance. The focus here is on Mary, the referent of the A argument, how she is behaving—just kicking out in fury, and it was perhaps chance that it was the door (and not something else) which received the kicks.

In summary, inserting a preposition (typically *on, onto,* or *at*) before an O NP indicates that the referent of this NP is not affected in the expected manner by the activity described by the verb.

2.5b Omitting a preposition

Jump is an intransitive verb describing a type of motion. One can just say *Stella jumped.* Or the jump can be to get over something, and a pNP with *over* may be added: *Stella jumped over a stone.* We are here talking about jumping and the stone is a peripheral element in the activity. But suppose that Stella is an athlete and she jumped over something really significant (which few other people could achieve). This could be described by *Stella jumped over the perimeter fence.* The fact that the perimeter fence is a notable thing to jump over could be indicated by grammatical adjustment—*the perimeter fence* sheds its preposition and moves from being an NP in the pNP, *over the perimeter fence*, to be the O argument of the verb, which now becomes transitive. Thus:

Stella$_A$ jumped [the perimeter fence]$_O$

We are now not talking just about jumping (as in *Stella jumped over a stone*) but about a definite achievement, getting to the other side of this high fence by jumping. (Note that it would not be felicitous to say *Stella jumped a stone.*)

Similar remarks apply for jumping across. The preposition *across* should be included in *Charlie jumped across a tiny stream*. But it could be omitted for a jump showing unusual prowess—*Charlie jumped [the wide chasm]$_O$*. Again, the verb becomes transitive and the NP from the pNP, *across the wide chasm*, sheds its preposition and moves into the O argument slot for *jump*, which is now functioning transitively.

Climb is also an intransitive verb, which may be augmented by a pNP; for example, *Ted climbed up the high tower* or *Ted climbed down the deep mineshaft*. An *up* pNP with *climb* may refer to something inconsequential, as in *Ted climbed up the grassy bank*; preposition *up* would be unlikely to be omitted here. But if the object climbed up were significant such that few people had achieved the feat, then the same grammatical scenario could be enacted. Starting with *Ted$_S$ climbed [up Mt Everest]*, the NP *Mt Everest* could cast off its preposition, *up*, and become O argument for *climb*, which is now transitive:

Ted$_A$ climbed [Mt Everest]$_O$

Note that *Mt Everest* has all the properties of an O argument. For instance, it can enter into a passive derivation such as *[Mt Everest]$_S$ has been climbed [by many people] [this year]*. Similarly, *[The perimeter fence]$_S$ hadn't been jumped [by anyone] before*.

A manner adverb may come at the end or beginning of a sentence, or before the verb, or immediately before an inner or outer pNP; for example, *Ted climbed slowly up Mt Everest*. An adverb may not intrude between verb and direct object; the fact that one cannot say *Ted climbed slowly Mt Everest* confirms that status of *Mt Everest* as O argument here.

In section 1.5 it was mentioned that some prepositions are paired—the major member is more common and has a wider range of meanings and grammatical possibilities than the minor member. What is interesting is that the 'preposition omission' just described only applies for a major member, not for a minor one. Suppose that Ted descends a mineshaft of incredible depth; *down* could not be omitted from *Ted$_S$ climbed [down the very deep mineshaft]* in the way that *up* can be omitted if the object climbed up is significant. Similarly with the *over/under* pairing—*over* may be omitted but never *under*. Stella may have been greatly admired for the feat described by *Stella$_S$ crawled [under a thousand metre overhang]*, but the preposition *under* could not be omitted.

What we have seen is that if an NP is regarded as an integral part of an activity, then in certain circumstances it may be moved out of a pNP, which is an ancillary component of the clause, to be a core constituent (in O function). A somewhat similar example involves the verb *speak*. This can be intransitive—we can say just *[The President]$_S$ spoke*—or transitive—*[The President]$_A$ spoke [some harsh words]$_O$*. This sentence may be augmented by a pNP specifying the language being used and/or a pNP indicating who the harsh words were addressed to:

> [The President]$_A$ spoke [some harsh words]$_O$ [in French] [to his
> secretary]

In this sentence it is the harsh words which are in focus and this NP is thus placed in the core grammatical function O. But suppose that what the President actually said is considered immaterial with the focus being on the language used. This can be shown by stripping *French* of its preposition and moving it into O slot, replacing *some harsh words*, which is now discarded, yielding:

> [The President]$_A$ spoke [French]$_O$ [to his secretary]

The core constituents are together crucial for the particular message to be conveyed, and prepositions may be manipulated to ensure that appropriate elements are placed in core slots.

All of the pNPs just mentioned—which may, in special circumstances, omit their preposition—have been inner pNPs. There is another type of preposition omission, from an outer pNP, which shows semantic similarities to what has just been described but is grammatically rather different. It involves a pNP referring to a measure of temporal or spatial duration.

Specification of how long an activity lasts may be provided by an outer pNP introduced with *for*, followed by a number word and then a noun referring to a unit of time, as in:

> Baby Emma only cried [for about three minutes]
> Your assistant didn't work [for more than about ten minutes
> yesterday]

Preposition *for* would be unlikely to be omitted from these sentences. However, if the period of time were significant with respect to the kind of activity described, this could be marked by the omission of *for*, as in:

Baby Emma cried [three hours non-stop]

Your assistant worked [seven hours yesterday]

Statements of spatial duration behave in a similar way. For instance, *for* could be omitted from *My sister always runs [(for) three miles before breakfast]* in order to draw attention to the fact that is an unusual amount of exercise to undertake before the first meal of the day. Another example is: *[From the top of that mountain] one can see [(for) thirty miles on a clear day]*.

After this omission of *for*, the outer pNP remains an outer pNP—a special variety of outer pNP not marked by a preposition. That is, its NP does not become O argument to the verb; one cannot passivise and say **Seven hours was worked by your assistant yesterday*.

A measure phrase may be used without a preposition when that particular measure carries implications about the completion of the activity. *She followed the thief seven miles into the forest* might be used when he travelled seven miles to his hide-out and she followed him all the way, whereas *She followed the thief for seven miles into the forest* could be appropriate when he travelled further, but she only followed him for the first seven miles.

It will be seen that, although the grammatical status of preposition omission is quite different for inner and for outer pNPs, the semantic implications are similar—the referent of the NP within the pNP is significant with respect to the kind of activity being described.

2.5c Preposition dropping before a complementiser

For some verbs each core argument slot must be filled by an NP. Other verbs may—for one or more argument slots—allow either an NP or a complement clause (CoCl).

This can be illustrated for the O argument of verb *remember*, commencing with an NP as O in (1a).

(1a)   Father$_{NP:A}$ remembered [the inoculations]$_{NP:O}$

(1b)   Father$_{NP:A}$ remembered [(that) the children had been inoculated]$_{CoCl:O}$

(1c)   Father$_{NP:A}$ remembered [the children('s) having been inoculated]$_{CoCl:O}$

(1c′)   Father$_{NP:A}$ remembered [having been inoculated]$_{CoCl:O}$

(1d) Father$_{\text{NP:A}}$ remembered [for the children to be inoculated]$_{\text{CoCl:O}}$

(1d') Father$_{\text{NP:A}}$ remembered [to be inoculated]$_{\text{CoCl:O}}$

There are three main varieties of CoCl in English:

I. **A THAT clause**, as in (1b). The CoCl has the structure of a main clause, simply preceded by complementiser *that* (which may often be omitted). It refers to **the fact** that something took place.

II. **An -ING clause**, as in (1c). The verb phrase (VP) is not marked for tense, instead the first word of the VP takes suffix *-ing*. The subject (A or S) NP of an -ING CoCl may take suffix -'*s*, although it is quite often omitted. This type of CoCl refers to something **extended in time.** If the main clause and CoCl have the same subject, this can be omitted from the CoCl, as in (1c').

III. **A (FOR) TO clause**, as in (1d). The VP is again not marked for tense; complementiser *for* comes at the beginning of the CoCl (it may sometimes be omitted) and *to* is placed before the VP. This type of CoCl describes the **potentiality or intention** of the referent of the subject (S or A) in the CoCl becoming involved in the activity described. If the main clause and CoCl have the same subject, this can be omitted from the CoCl, together with the *for*, as in (1d').

What varieties of complement clause each verb may take depends on the meaning of the verb and the meanings of the complement clause, and how these match together.

Prepositional verbs were briefly introduced in section 1.4—these are verbs which cannot be used on their own but must be accompanied by a preposition. The preposition may be followed by either an NP or a CoCl, just as in the O slot for a straightforward transitive verb. However there is here a dropping rule:

A preposition drops before complementiser *that, for*, or *to*

This can be illustrated for the prepositional verb *decide on*, using sentences similar to (1a–d) for the transitive verb *remember* (adjusting time specification a little, in accord with the meanings of the two verbs):

(2a) Father$_{\text{NP:A}}$ decided on [the inoculations]$_{\text{NP:O}}$

(2b) Father$_{\text{NP:A}}$ decided — [(that) the children should be inoculated]$_{\text{CoCl:O}}$

(2c)   Father$_{NP:A}$ decided on [the children('s) being inoculated]$_{CoCl:O}$

(2c')   Father$_{NP:A}$ decided on [being inoculated]$_{CoCl:O}$

(2d)   Father$_{NP:A}$ decided — [for the children to be inoculated]$_{CoCl:O}$

(2d')   Father$_{NP:A}$ decided — [to be inoculated]$_{CoCl:O}$

It can be seen that *on*, from prepositional verb *decide on*, is dropped before complementiser *for* in (2d), before *to* in (2d'), and also before *that* in (2b). In (2b) the *that* may be omitted but the *on* is still dropped. The *on* is retained before an -ING CoCl, as in (2c) and (2c'), and before an NP, as in (2a).

Note that no ambiguity arises as a result of this preposition dropping. There is no contrast between a simple verb *decide* and prepositional verb *decide on*. Thus, whether the *on* is retained—as in (2a), (2c), and (2c')— or dropped—as in (2b), (2d), and (2d')—it is clearly understood that in each instance the sentence involves the prepositional verb whose underlying form is *decide on*.

However, things are entirely different for phrasal verbs. As described in section 1.3, a phrasal verb consists of a simple verb, which may occur alone, plus one or two prepositions or adverbs. The meaning of a phrasal verb cannot be straightforwardly inferred from the basic meanings of its component words.

If the preposition were dropped from a phrasal verb, this could only be considered as the simple verb used on its own. The consequence of this is that a phrasal verb cannot be used with a THAT or with a (FOR) TO CoCl.

For a phrasal verb of the type 'Verb preposition X', the X slot may be filled by an NP or by an -ING CoCl, since the preposition does not drop before an -ING CoCl. This can be exemplified with phrasal verb *get over*:

Jason is <u>getting over</u> [his loss]$_{NP:O}$

Jason is <u>getting over</u> [Mary('s) having left him]$_{CoCl:O}$

But the X slot may not be filled by any of the other varieties of CoCl.

Simple verb *neglect* and phrasal verb *pass over* show an overlap of meanings. For example, each could be used to describe some oversight when cleaning a kitchen. For its O argument, *neglect* could have an NP or a TO CoCl:

Robin neglected [the stove]$_{NP:O}$

Robin neglected [to clean the stove]$_{CoCl:O}$

If *pass over* were substituted for *neglect* we would get (applying the 'dropping a preposition before complementiser *to*' rule):

Robin <u>passed over</u> [the stove]_{NP:O}
*Robin passed — [to clean the stove]

It is not acceptable to say *Robin <u>passed over</u> to clean the stove, with this involving the phrasal verb *pass over*. The *over* would have to be dropped, giving *Robin passed to clean the stove*. With no *over*, this sentence could only be interpreted as involving simple verb *pass*, with a linked clause (no CoCl): *Robin passed (in order) to clean the stove*. (Whereas *Robin* <u>passed over</u> *the stove* means that it didn't get cleaned, *Robin passed to clean the stove* indicates an intention to clean it.)

Simple verb *expect* and phrasal verb *count on* also have an overlap of meaning. *Expect* may take an NP or all three varieties of CoCl:

Jill had expected [a substantial bequest in her aunt's will]_{NP:O}
Jill had expected [being left a substantial bequest in her aunt's will]_{CoCl:O}
Jill had expected [that she would be left a substantial bequest in her aunt's will]_{CoCl:O}
Jill had expected [to be left a substantial bequest in her aunt's will]_{CoCl:O}

We can now try substituting *count on* for *expect* in the four sentences:

Jill had <u>counted on</u> [a substantial bequest in her aunt's will]_{NP:O}
Jill had <u>counted on</u> [being left a substantial bequest in her aunt's will]_{CoCl:O}
*Jill had counted — [that she would be left a substantial bequest in her aunt's will]
*Jill had counted — [to be left a substantial bequest in her aunt's will]

The *on* must be dropped before *that* and *to* in the last two sentences. Without its preposition, phrasal verb *count on* becomes simple verb *count* (with a quite different meaning) which is nonsensical in these two sentences.

Although there are hundreds of phrasal verbs, in fact only a handful have a meaning compatible with using a THAT or a FOR (TO) CoCl. Even when this would be semantically appropriate (as with *pass over* and *count on*), it is not syntactically admissible.

2.6 Modifying a preposition

There are limited possibilities for a modifier being added to a preposition when used in its basic sense. Compare modification of *inside* by *just* and *right* in:

> Jerry put the canister [just inside the room]
>> (implied: he put it by the door)
> Jerry put the canister [right inside the room]
>> (implied: he put it in the centre of the room)

Just may modify a preposition, as in this example, and it may also modify a sentence. Care must be taken to distinguish these uses:

SENTENCE ADVERB Kate just went [into the end house]
(she didn't go into any other houses)

PREPOSITIONAL MODIFIER Kate went [just into the end house]
(she hovered near the door)

The main prepositional modifiers include:

(a) *Just* can mean 'only this and no more'. For example *He went [just to the corner shop]* (and not further on to the supermarket). Another sense is 'to the minimal extent' as in *He hung the picture [just over the door]* (so that there was very little gap between the bottom of the picture and the top of the door). The other prepositions which *just* modifies include *in(to), out(-of), inside, outside, under, above, below, across, before, after,* and *past.*

(b) *Right* indicates 'definitely'. One can say *He went [right off the path]*, meaning a long way from the path, and *She stood [right under the mistletoe]* indicating that there was nothing approximate about it. *Right* modifies the largest array of prepositions. The few which do not take *right* include *to, toward(s), from, beyond,* and *near. Clear* has a related meaning as modifier but restricted use; it indicates 'all the way', as in *He jumped clear across the stream.*

(c) *Directly* means 'in a fixed direction'. *He ran [directly to the maypole]* indicates motion in a straight line, with no deviation. *Directly* may substitute for *right* in *She stood [right/directly under the mistletoe]*. In essence, it may modify any preposition indicating direction. *Straight* has a similar meaning but can also indicate 'without pausing' as in *The bull ran [straight at me].*

(d) *Close* indicates 'near position', and modifies just a few prepositions referring to position. For example *They marched [close behind the band]* and *He lives [close by the pub]*.

(e) *Way*, 'far position', is more-or-less the opposite of *close*. One can say *They marched [way behind the band]*. It can also be used with prepositions of vertical position and of distance, as in *It was hung [way above the door]* and *He lives [way beyond the mountains]*. Also with some temporal prepositions—*It was [way after six o'clock] when the meeting started*.

(f) *All* has the sense 'fully covered' and modifies prepositions indicating spatial or temporal extent. For example, *He searched [all over the place]*, *This shop is open [all around the clock]*, *The squire snored [all through the sermon]*, *She ran [all across the field]*, *He travelled [all along the mountain track]*, and *We forgot [all about him]*.

There is a rather special type of modification for prepositions indicating relative position in time or space. This involves adding a time or distance span. For instance, *Maria arrived [ten minutes after everyone else]*, *Mark ran [six miles past the church]*, and *The hermit lives [two days journey beyond the last village]*.

Note that this short account of how prepositions may be modified is far from exhaustive. The aim has been simply to outline the possibilities involved.

2.7 Prepositions which may follow their noun phrase

There appear to be just three prepositions which may either precede or follow the NP which they mark. These are *over*, *(a)round*, and *through*. For example:

She slept [through the night]	She slept [the night through]
He travelled [over the world]	He travelled [the world over]
They plant crops [round the year]	They plant crops [the year round]

Postposing the prepositions indicates that the activity did extend across the whole of the time or space indicated.

These prepositions belong to the set which may be modified with *all*. In fact, they typically occur with *all*. The interesting point is that when the preposition moves to follow the NP which it marks, *all* stays behind:

She slept [all through the night]	She slept [all the night through]
He travelled [all over the world]	He travelled [all the world over]
They plant crops [all round the year]	They plant crops [all the year round]

This shows that the pNP maintains is coherence, whether as *(all) through the night* or *(all) the night though*, etc.

It is interesting that *across* and *along*, the two other prepositions which we identified (in the last section) as being typically modified by *all*, do not undergo this right movement. I know of no explanation for this.

∗ ∗ ∗

Before embarking on examination of individual prepositions, in Part II, the next two chapters deal with particular kinds of complex verbs which include prepositions—phrasal verbs and prepositional verbs.

3

Phrasal verbs

English has many hundreds of complex verbs, each consisting of a simple verb (which can occur outside this combination) and one or two prepositions or adverbs. These are called 'phrasal verbs'. The meaning of a phrasal verb cannot be directly inferred from the basic meanings of its component words, so that each phrasal verb is, in effect, a separate lexeme and must be accorded its own entry in the dictionary.

However, the meanings of phrasal verbs are not arbitrary. To a greater or lesser extent, the meaning of almost every phrasal verb does relate to the meanings of the words making it up, albeit in an indirect way. Section 1.3 provided illustrations of how the meanings of phrasal verbs *hang onto*, *live on*, *hit on*, and *turn against* can be explained in terms of extensions from the basic meanings of the verb and preposition involved. We can now look further into their semantic make-up.

English Prepositions: Their Meanings and Uses. R. M. W. Dixon. Oxford University Press (2021). © R. M. W. Dixon.
DOI: 10.1093/oso/9780198868682.003.0003

3.1 Examining meanings

In some instances the meaning of a phrasal verb clearly relates to the basic meaning of the component simple verb; in some to the basic meaning of the preposition; in some to both; and in others to neither.

A. The meaning of the phrasal verb is a clear extension of the basic meaning of the component simple verb. Examples of this include (with the phrasal verb underlined in each example sentence):

(1)   Please don't <u>tell on</u> Fred!
         (that is, don't reveal Fred's misdeed to a person in authority)

(2)   The new manager <u>brought about</u> changes
         (that is, they re-organised the way the business is run)

Tell on, in (1), plainly involves an instance of telling. Simple verb *bring* refers to making something come, or come to be, which is reflected in the meaning of phrasal verb *bring about* in (2). The uses of prepositions *on* and *about* in these two sentences are not so clearly relatable to their basic meanings.

B. The meaning of the phrasal verb is a clear extension of the basic meaning of the component preposition. Examples of this include:

(3)   My brother is determined to <u>lay off</u> booze
         (that is, he won't drink it any more)

(4)   The manager has had to <u>lay off</u> one worker
         (that is, he has had to terminate the worker's employment due to adverse economic circumstances)

The basic meaning of *off* includes detachment (as in *He took off his hat*, and *Keep off the grass!*). This is clearly applicable to *lay off* in both sentences. In contrast, the phrasal verb does not easily relate to the basic meaning of simple verb *lay*.

(5)   The plane <u>took off</u> at noon
         (that is, the plane rose from the ground to fly through the air at noon)

Again, the sense of *off* is fairly basic (the plane became detached from the ground) but the phrasal verb has a quite different meaning (and transitivity) from that of simple verb *take*.

(6)   Uncle Sam <u>brought up</u> the twins after their parents died
          (that is, he reared them)

(7)   The corruption scandal has <u>brought down</u> the government
          (that is, the government has lost the confidence of parliament)

Bring up and *bring down* are clearly related to the basic meanings of *up* and *down*, describing something that is relatively higher/lower in height, age, or social standing. In contrast, the phrasal verbs are not obviously linked to the basic meaning of simple verb *bring*.

(8)   Annabelle felt a feeling of contentment <u>steal over</u> her
          (that is, she felt gradually more and more content)

This phrasal verb plainly relates to the basic 'covering' sense of preposition *over*, shown in *The blanket lies over the bed*. *Steal* is here being used in an extended sense.

C. The basic meanings of both verb and preposition can be perceived in the meaning of the phrasal verb. Examples include:

(9)   Mary <u>sat for</u> an examination in mathematics
(10)   Hannah <u>met with</u> a setback when her paper was rejected for publication

In (9), Mary's taking the examination would have involved sitting down, and one sense of *for* refers to the reason that something is undertaken. *Meet with* (for example, a setback) is just a slight abstraction from a basic sentence such as *Hannah met with a beggar*.

D. The meaning of the phrasal verb is rather different from the basic meanings of verb and of preposition. For example:

(11)   Aaron <u>took on</u> added responsibilities
          (that is, he undertook to be responsible for more things than before)

(12)   The Dean <u>held over</u> the final item of the agenda until the next meeting
          (that is, the final item would be delayed until the next meeting)

The judgements just given for sentences (1–12) are, to a degree, subjective. Nevertheless, they provide an indication of the semantic factors involved.

3.2 Two kinds of phrasal verb

All of the phrasal verbs just exemplified (except for *The plane took off*) have been presented in the form:

Verb-preposition-NP

However, this is deceptive. There are in fact two distinct grammatical types involved: (i) those in which the preposition must precede the NP, and (ii) those in which the preposition may either precede or follow the NP:

	PREPOSITION BEFORE NP	PREPOSITION AFTER NP
(i)	My brother is determined to lay off booze	*My brother is determined to lay booze off
	Please don't tell on Fred	*Please don't tell Fred on
(ii)	The manager has had to lay off one worker	The manager has had to lay one worker off
	Uncle Sam brought up the twins	Uncle Sam brought the twins up

For type (ii) the question now arises: which of the two possible structures should be taken as the primary one—that with the preposition before the NP, or that with it after the NP? This is decided for us by seeing what happens when the NP is a pronoun. We get:

*The manager has had to lay off him   The manager has had to lay him off
*Uncle Sam brought up them   Uncle Sam brought them up

This shows that, for type (ii) phrasal verbs, the underlying structure is that with the preposition following the NP. There is then a 'left movement rule':

> **For a phrasal verb of type (ii), the preposition may be moved leftwards to precede the NP so long as the NP is not a pronoun**

This is akin to the left movement described in section 2.1c in relation to an inner PP, with the preposition having its basic motion or location sense.

Why should there be this restriction against a preposition moving to the left over a pronoun? There is in fact a phonological explanation for it. As described in section 1.6, an object pronoun generally has the form of an enclitic and this attaches to the preceding verb. The verb makes up one phonological word with the pronoun enclitic, and this may not be interrupted. That is, neither a preposition nor anything else can intervene between verb and enclitic object pronoun.

We can thus recognise two kinds of phrasal verb, with underlying structures:

(i) Verb-preposition-NP   (ii) Verb-NP-preposition

However, there is a further difference. In structure (i) only a preposition may precede the NP. But in (ii) the NP can be followed by either a preposition or one of a limited set of adverbs, including *back* and *forth*, exemplified in:

WITH LEFT MOVEMENT

(13)   The general <u>cut</u> the rations <u>back</u>   The general <u>cut back</u> the rations

(14)   The new leader <u>set</u> her ideas <u>forth</u>   The new leader <u>set forth</u> her ideas

It will be convenient to employ abbreviations for types of phrasal verb through the remainder of this book. To this end, we will use:

p for what precedes the NP in a phrasal verb of type (i); this can only be a preposition

a for what follows the NP in a phrasal verb of type (i); this can be a preposition or an adverb

The phrasal verbs in example sentences (1–4) and (6–14) can now be characterised (using V for verb):

type (i), V-p-NP	type (ii), V-NP-a
tell on —, in (1)	bring — about, in (2)
lay off —, in (3)	lay — off, in (4)
steal over —, in (8)	bring — up, in (6)
sit for —, in (9)	bring — down, in (7)
meet with —, in (10)	take — on, in (11)
	hold — over, in (12)
	cut — back, in (13)
	set — forth, in (14)

There is a further restriction. Not every preposition can occur both in slot **p** and in slot **a**. Looking at the prepositions in examples given thus far, we find:

	only as **p**	as both **p** and **a**	only as **a**
PREPOSITIONS	for, with	on, off, over	up, down
ADVERBS	—	—	back, forth

(In addition *about* can be in both slots—occurrence in slot **a** is illustrated in example (2) and in slot **p** in *Jason is going about his business*.)

A full list is presented and discussed in section 3.7.

Having outlined the two most common types of phrasal verb, and identified elements **p** and **a**, we can now introduce the full inventory of phrasal verbs.

3.3 The six types of phrasal verb

There are in all six distinct types of phrasal verb:

	TYPE	EXAMPLE SENTENCES
I	V-a	The rain <u>set in</u>; The patient <u>passed out</u>; The plane <u>took off</u>
II	V-p-NP	Sentences above with tell on —, lay off —, steal over —, etc.
III	V-NP-a	Sentences above with bring — about, lay — off, bring — up, etc.
IV	V-NP-p-NP	James didn't <u>hold</u> Tim's rudeness <u>against</u> him That customer <u>took</u> you <u>for</u> a shop assistant
V	V-a-p-NP	Stella has <u>taken up with</u> a new boyfriend I don't <u>go in for</u> scuba diving
VI	V-NP-a-p-NP	The manager <u>put</u> Tom's loss <u>down to</u> inexperience She <u>tied</u> her holiday <u>in with</u> Mark's wedding

The same possibilities apply for all the **p** slots—in V-p-NP, V-NP-p-NP, V-a-p-NP, and V-NP-a-p-NP. And the same possibilities also apply for all the **a** slots—in V-a, V-NP-a, V-a-p-NP, and V-NP-a-p-NP.

The profiles of **p** and **a** are:

p is always directly followed by an NP

a is not directly followed by an NP, in its underlying structure

However, if preposition or adverb **a** immediately follows an NP (which is not a pronoun), **a** may be moved to the left of the NP. This was illustrated in the preceding section for type III. It also applies for type VI:

The manager <u>put down</u> Tom's loss <u>to</u> inexperience

She <u>tied in</u> her holiday <u>with</u> Mark's wedding

Some simple verbs may have either an NP or a complement clause (CoCl) in a core argument slot. This also applies to a limited extent for phrasal verbs. Just a few phrasal verbs may have an -ING CoCl in a slot identified above as 'NP', but only when it immediately follows a **p**. Examples include:

V-p-NP	You'll have to <u>deal with</u> [the accountant's resigning his post]$_{CoCl}$
V-a-p-NP	Martha <u>held out against</u> [Fred's taking the children away]$_{CoCl}$
V-NP-p-NP	Don't <u>read</u> too much <u>into</u> [the King's having fired the court jester]$_{CoCl}$
V-NP-a-p-NP	The board <u>put</u> the shortage <u>down to</u> [the manager's underestimating demand]$_{CoCl}$

As explained and illustrated in section 2.5c, the **p** of a phrasal verb may not be followed by a THAT or (FOR) TO CoCl. This is simply because a preposition drops from before a *that*, or *for,* or *to* complementiser; the phrasal verb would then lose its form, and become just the simple verb component.

No CoCl is encountered in any other 'NP' slot within a phrasal verb; that is, not in V-NP-a, nor in the first NP position in V-NP-p-NP or V-NP-a-p-NP.

Amongst the hundreds of phrasal verbs there are many examples of a verb and preposition/adverb constituting phrasal verbs of different types. We have seen that *lay* and *off* make up phrasal verbs of types V-NP-a and V-p-NP. Other examples include *give* and *out, put* and *up,* and *see* and *through*:

V-a   Jim's old car has finally <u>given out</u>
                (broken down for good)

V-NP-a   They won't <u>give</u> the results <u>out</u> until Monday
                (won't announce them until then)

V-NP-a   We <u>put</u> the cousins <u>up</u> for three nights
                (we let them stay with us)

V-p-NP   John <u>put up</u> a struggle

V-p-NP   She <u>saw through</u> his apparent bravado
                (and realised that he was actually a complete
                coward)

V-NP-p-NP   Her religious belief <u>saw</u> Mary <u>through</u> the crisis
                (it sustained her when things looked bad)

There are pairs of homonymous phrasal verbs, both of the same type. For instance:

V-p-NP   Thomas plans to <u>stand for</u> office
                (he'll put in a nomination)

V-p-NP   Lucy <u>stands for</u> decency, probity, and cleanliness
                (these are the qualities she values)

Which of the homophonous phrasal verbs *stand for* NP is involved, in each instance, can be inferred from the meaning of the NP following *for*. Another example is V-NP-a, *get — over*, discussed under (c) in section 3.5.

Verbs entering into phrasal verbs are almost exclusively monosyllable Germanic forms (those occurring in the largest number of phrasal verbs are *be, get, put, come, go, take, run,* and *bring*). Most are verbs which require NPs for their core arguments, rather than allowing complement clauses. The prepositions used in phrasal verbs are also virtually all Germanic—rare exceptions are *across* and *(a)round*—and predominantly monosyllabic—the exceptions here are *about, across, after, against, along, behind, over,* and *under* (plus the complex prepositions discussed in section 2.3 and again in section 3.7 below).

3.4 Transitivity

Recapitulating from section 2.5, there are three basic clause types:

- Intransitive, with one core argument, in S (intransitive subject) function.
- Transitive, with two core arguments, in A (transitive subject) and O (transitive object) functions.
- Copula with two core arguments, in CS (copula subject) and CC (copula complement) functions.

Besides copula verbs (basically, *be, become*) which can only occur in a copula clause, verbs divide into four classes:

(a) Strictly intransitive—may only occur in an intransitive clause; for example, *go, slip*.
(b) Strictly transitive—may only occur in a transitive clause; for example, *pick, cut*.
(c) Ambitransitive of type S = O—may occur in both transitive and intransitive clauses, with S corresponding to O; for example, *[The vase]$_S$ broke*, and *Jimmy$_A$ broke [the vase]$_O$*.
(d) Ambitransitive of type S = A—may occur in both transitive and intransitive clauses, with S corresponding to A; for example, *Jimmy$_S$ blew*, and *Jimmy$_A$ blew [his whistle]$_O$*.

Phrasal verbs may be categorised as:

- Transitive, where there is an NP immediately following the verb: types V-NP-a, V-NP-p-NP, and V-NP-a-p-NP.
- Intransitive, where there is not an NP immediately following the verb: types V-a, V-p-NP, and V-a-p-NP.

The great majority of transitive simple verbs may be passivised, with the original O argument becoming passive S, and the original A argument being either omitted or marked by preposition *by*. For example, *All the apples have been picked (by the gardener)*, and *The telephone lines have been cut (by the burglars)*.

Transitive phrasal verbs have similar properties to simple transitive verbs. They can generally be passivised and sometimes the original A argument may be omitted, as in: *One worker had to be laid off (by the manager)*, *The final item of the agenda was held over until the next meeting (by the Dean)*, *You were taken for a shop assistant (by that customer)*, and *Tom's loss was put down to inexperience (by the manager)*.

However, in many cases, the original A has to be retained, as a *by* phrase, to preserve the semantic content of the phrasal verb, as in:

(6') The twins were brought up by Uncle Sam after their parents died

(11') Added responsibilities were taken on by Aaron

Agentless passives *The twins were brought up after their parents died* and *Added responsibilities were taken on* would be incomplete and uninformative.

It is occasionally possible to passivise on an NP following a preposition—with a simple intransitive verb— in order to focus on something significant. It may be because the referent of the NP is cherished. An innkeeper could boast either *President Roosevelt slept on this bed* or *This bed was slept on by President Roosevelt*; here the *by* phrase is essential. Or it may be because the referent of the NP is despised. A dissatisfied guest could complain *Someone has drunk out of this glass* or else *This glass has been drunk out of*. Here a *by* phrase is not necessary; the point being made is that the glass is not clean, and it doesn't matter who had drunk from it before.

The final NP within a phrasal verb of types V-NP-p-NP, V-a-p-NP, and V-NP-a-p-NP may not become the S argument of a passive. However, there are just a few instances where an NP within a phrasal verb of type V-p-NP may become passive subject. For example:

The teachers are always picking on Tom

→ Tom is always being picked on (by the teachers)

The committee went through the document very carefully

→ The document was gone through very carefully (by the committee)

The possibilities here are very limited. For example, in the following phrasal verbs of type V-p-NP, the NP could not become passive subject: *tell on* — in (1), *lay off* — in (3), *steal over* — in (8), *sit for* — in (9), and *meet with* — in (10).

It is interesting to compare the transitivity of a phrasal verb with that of its component simple verb. These sometimes coincide, but often differ:

- All phrasal verbs involving intransitive verbs *come*, *go*, *fall*, and copula verb *be* are intransitive.
- All phrasal verbs involving transitive verbs *have* and *hand* are transitive.
- Many transitive simple verbs enter into both varieties of phrasal verb. For example, *get*, as in transitive V-NP-a, *The clever lawyer got the criminal off* and in intransitive V-a, *I'll get by somehow*. And *take*, as in transitive V-NP-a, *Sally took the company over*, and in intransitive V-a, *The plane took off*.
- Quite a few verbs which are ambitransitive of type S = O enter into phrasal verbs with the same ambitransitivity. For example:

	transitive: V-NP-a	intransitive: V-a
break	[The two parties]$_A$ broke negotiations$_O$ off	Negotiations$_S$ broke off
shut	They$_A$ shut [the factory]$_O$ down	[The factory]$_S$ shut down

3.5 Left movement

Dealing with prepositions in their basic meanings, section 2.1 described how an inner pNP may omit its NP when this is expected to be understood from context. For example, *He pulled the cloth off*, where the listener will assume that it was *off the table*. Following on from this, the preposition can be moved to the left of the preceding NP (provided that this is not a pronoun), giving *He pulled off the cloth*.

As described above, a phrasal verb of type V-NP-a or V-NP-a-p-NP may in many instances move the preposition (or adverb) **a** to the left over the preceding NP. There are a number of restrictions and tendencies associated with this left movement.

(a) As explained in section 3.2, a pronominal object is an enclitic which attaches to the preceding verb. A preposition cannot move to the left over the pronoun, since this would interrupt the verb-plus-clitic phonological word.

59

(b) Sometimes left movement of a V-NP-a phrasal verb leads to verb and preposition being understood in their basic senses.

Left movement is acceptable for:

The judge <u>let</u> the criminal <u>off</u>   →   The judge <u>let off</u> the criminal

However, left movement cannot apply to:

The lawyer <u>got</u> the criminal <u>off</u>

If one heard *The lawyer got off the criminal* one would infer that the lawyer had been sitting on or standing on the criminal and then moved away, similar to *John got off the horse*

Another example is:

The King <u>kept</u> the good work <u>up</u>   →   The king <u>kept up</u> the good work
The despot <u>kept</u> the serfs <u>under</u>   <no left movement>

The despot kept under the serfs would be understood as if *keep* and *under* had their basic meanings, as in *The despot kept under the bridge until the rain ceased.*

The interesting point here is that if a sentence should be ambiguous between the basic-senses and a phrasal verb interpretation, it seems that it is the basic-senses meaning which takes priority.

(c) There are some 'minimal pairs', where the same simple verb and preposition occur in both a V-p-NP and a V-NP-a phrasal verb. Sometimes there can be left movement of **a** over the NP in the second type and—due to the nature of the NPs involved—there would be no chance of confusion with the first type. For example:

V-NP-a   The manager <u>laid</u> one worker <u>off</u>   →   The manager <u>laid</u>
             (fired the worker)   <u>off</u> one worker

V-p-NP   My brother <u>laid off</u> booze
             (determined not to indulge
             in it any more)

The NP in the V-p-NP phrasal verb must refer to some deleterious habit, while the NP in the V-NP-a phrasal verb refers to people employed. The same NP could not be used in the two phrasal verbs; as a consequence, any sentence *X <u>laid off</u> Y* is unlikely to be ambiguous.

Another example of the same type is:

V-NP-a   The butler <u>knocked</u> the gold → The butler <u>knocked off</u>
            plate <u>off</u>   the gold plate
               (stole it)

V-p-NP   Jason has <u>knocked off</u> work
               (ceased working)

Once again, the possibilities for what can be NP for the two phrasal verbs are quite different, so that any sentence X *knocked off* Y is unlikely to be ambiguous.

In contrast, there are 'minimal pairs' of this type where the same NP could appear in each. As a consequence, left movement of **a** is blocked. For example:

V-NP-a   The preacher really <u>turned</u> the   \<no left movement>
            congregation <u>on</u>
               (got the congregation up to a
               fever pitch of excitement)

V-p-NP   John <u>turned on</u> the stranger
               (acted in a hostile manner, perhaps
               hitting or swearing at the stranger)

These two phrasal verbs can have NPs with the same reference. If the first sentence were to undergo left movement we would get *The preacher really turned on the congregation*, which could only have the V-p-NP interpretation, that the preacher became hostile towards the congregation,

We can see that if there should be competition between a V-p-NP phrasal verb and V-a-NP (derived by left movement from V-NP-a), it is the meaning of the former that prevails.

A further pair of the same type is:

V-NP-a   Basil <u>knocked</u> his partner <u>about</u>   \<no left movement>
            (treated his partner in a brutal
               manner)

V-p-NP   Basil <u>knocked about</u> the continent
               (travelled around the continent)

For each of these phrasal verbs the NP could be *the place. Basil knocked the place about* implies that he acted violently towards it, perhaps smashing it up. If one hears *Basil knocked about the place* it can only be the V-p-NP phrasal verb 'travel around'; that is, left movement from the V-NP-a structure is blocked.

A given simple verb and preposition may enter into more than two phrasal verbs, as with *get* and *over*:

| V-NP-a | Jane <u>got</u> the interview <u>over</u> quickly | <no left movement> |
| | (ensured that it was not protracted) | |

| V-NP-a | Jane <u>got</u> the message <u>over</u> | <no left movement> |
| | (made sure that people understand it) | |

| V-p-NP | Jane <u>got over</u> her sickness | |
| | (recovered from a bad experience) | |

There is here overlap between possible NPs in all three phrasal verbs. V-p-NP could be *Jane <u>got over</u> the interview* (if it was an unhappy experience) or *Jane <u>got over</u> the message* (if is contained bad and upsetting news). This blocks the possibility for left movement of **a** from the two V-NP-a structures.

Three restrictions on left movement have been enunciated. We can now look in the opposite direction, at circumstances under which left movement is highly desirable.

(d) When the NP preceding **a** in a phrasal verb is unusually lengthy, left movement of **a** is most likely. In its canonical form, a V-NP-a or V-NP-a-p-NP construction includes a discontinuous phrasal verb. Its parts are naturally split over an NP. But if the NP is too long, this will pose difficulties for listeners in processing the sentence. To avoid such an impediment, the elements in the phrasal verb should be kept close together, and this can be achieved by left movement.

Left movement is optional for the phrasal verb *hand — out*, of type V-NP-a, when the NP is short:

The mystic <u>handed</u> [books] <u>out</u>   →   The mystic <u>handed out</u> [books]

However, if the NP is long, there is a strong expectation of left movement:

The mystic <u>handed out</u> [books on all manner of esoteric and unusual topics]

Preposition *out* could have been marooned at the end of this sentence, a long way from *hand*, the simple verb component of the phrasal verb, but this would make the sentence hard to comprehend. Language is all about communicating meaning, and, to achieve this, the meaning should be easy to understand, which is here facilitated by left movement.

Another example involves phrasal verb *win — over*. Left movement is optional over a short NP:

We won [Timothy] <u>over</u>   → We <u>won over</u> [Timothy]

(got him on our side, persuaded him to agree with us)

Preposition *over* could follow a long NP, but is far more felicitous for it to be placed before, by left movement:

We <u>won over</u> [that cantankerous politician with a droopy face and a penchant for quoting from Kant]

An NP which includes a relative clause is particularly demanding of left movement. Compare phrasal verb *take — down* used with a short NP, with an NP featuring a relative clause, and with an NP including an abbreviated relative clause (where *that which* is replaced by *what*):

The policeman <u>took</u> [his statement]   → The policeman <u>took down</u>   down [his statement]

The policeman <u>took down</u> [the particulars which he wanted to tell the authorities]

The policeman <u>took down</u> [what he wanted to tell the authorities]

If none of the restrictions and preferences outlined above apply, whether or not left movement is applied can be a matter of whim. But it is frequently determined by the discourse context. Whichever of NP and preposition (or adverb) is in focus is likely to be placed in final position.

Consider the following conversation:

Who should we get rid of, the CEO or the chairman of the board?

Let's <u>bring down</u> the CEO

The CEO is in the spotlight, being contrasted with the chairman of the board, and is thus placed finally (by left movement), into focus position.

Now consider a different conversation:

I thought you supported the CEO

We used to, but now we want to <u>bring</u> the CEO <u>down</u>

The CEO is here old information. What is new in the second sentence is the negative meaning expressed by phrasal verb *bring — down*. The operative element of this is *down*, resulting in this preposition being maintained in final position.

There was discussion in section 2.7 of three prepositions—*over, (a)round,* and *through*—which in their basic sense may follow the NP within their pNP. The NP refers to space or time, and right placement of the preposition indicates 'across the whole extent' of that space or time; for example, *He roamed the island over.* This characteristic is generally restricted to the basic use of prepositions and does not extend to phrasal verbs.

3.6 Maintaining the integrity of a phrasal verb

As described in section 2.2, when the NP component of a pNP is replaced by a question word, this typically moves to the beginning of the clause. There are two alternatives: either (a) it leaves its preposition behind, or (b) it takes it with it. Thus:

Cecil complained to the manager

(a)   Who did Cecil complain to?

(b)   To whom did Cecil complain?

Four temporal prepositions (*since, until/till, after,* and *before*) only allow alternative (b). Most other prepositions readily accept alternative (a); a fair number also allow (b). (As shown in section 2.2, the same alternatives apply for questioning, for relative clause constructions and for other techniques for fronting all or part of a pNP.)

It is a characteristic—one might say 'a defining property'—of phrasal verbs that only alternative (a) is acceptable. That is, the preposition or adverb must remain in position after the simple verb component of the phrasal verb, rather then being moved to the beginning of the clause with the question word.

This can be illustrated with an example of each of the types of phrasal verb which involves a 'p-NP' sequence:

V-p-NP   The manager <u>laid off</u> one worker

(a)   Who did the manager <u>lay off</u>?

(b)   *Off whom did the manager lay?

V-a-p-NP		Jim <u>came up against</u> a problem
	(a)	What did Jim <u>come up against</u>?
	(b)	*<u>Against</u> what did Jim come up?
V-NP-p-NP		The customer <u>took</u> Tim <u>for</u> a shop assistant
	(a)	What did the customer <u>take</u> Tim <u>for</u>?
	(b)	*<u>For</u> what did the customer take Tim?
V-NP-a-p-NP		Janet <u>tied</u> her holiday <u>in with</u> Mark's wedding
	(a)	What did Janet <u>tie</u> her holiday <u>in with</u>?
	(b)	*<u>With</u> what did Janet tie in her holiday?

If there is an 'NP-a' element, left movement may convert it to 'a-NP'. The same restriction applies—the **a** element must remain in place when the NP is questioned. For example:

V-NP-a		Uncle Sam <u>brought</u> the twins <u>up</u>
→ V-a-NP		Uncle Sam <u>brought up</u> the twins`
	(a)	Who did Uncle Sam <u>bring up</u>?
	(b)	*<u>Up</u> whom did Uncle Sam bring?
V-NP-a-p-NP		Janet <u>tied</u> her holiday <u>in with</u> Mark's wedding
→ V-a-NP-p-NP		Janet <u>tied in</u> her holiday <u>with</u> Mark's wedding
	(a)	What did Janet <u>tie in with</u> Mark's wedding?
	(b)	*<u>In</u> what did Janet tie with Mark's wedding?

How do we recognise that something is a phrasal verb? There are basically two criteria. First, the meaning of a phrasal verb cannot be directly inferred from the basic meanings of its component words, And secondly, its components have a syntactic integrity: a prepositional or adverbial element must remain in position after the simple verb component and cannot be moved away (unlike many prepositions in pNPs). Neither of these criteria is, of course, cut-and-dried; there are always marginal cases, and a measure of subjectivity.

3.7 The prepositions and adverbs involved

Rather more than half of the simple and complex prepositions take part in phrasal verbs, either in slot **p**, or in slot **a**, or in both.

Those simple prepositions which do not feature in phrasal verbs are: *above, amid(st), among(st), before, below, beneath, beside(s), between, beyond, concerning, despite, during, except, inside, near, outside, past, since, till/until, toward(s), underneath, within,* and *without.* (Note that all of these have two syllables, except for *underneath* and *concerning* with three, and *since, till,* and *past* with one.) The complex prepositions which are realised as clitics all play a role—albeit a limited one—in phrasal verbs.

The occurrences of prepositions in phrasal verbs can be summarised—together with the adverbs in slot **a**— in a table. (Those in square brackets are exceptions, to be discussed soon.)

	as **p** in V-p-NP, V-NP-p-NP, V-a-p-NP, and V-NP-a-p-NP	as **a** in V-a, V-NP-a, V-a-p-NP, and V-NP-a-p-NP
A	of, for, with	
B	at, to, from	[to]
C	into, out-of [in]	in, out
D	on, onto, upon, off (off-of)	on, off
E	up-to [up]	up, down, along
F	against, after	
G	over, under, through, (a)round, about, across, by, behind, forth	
H		back, away, ahead, aside, apart, forward, together

Those which occur only in the **p** column are exclusively prepositions. Those which are restricted to the **a** column are basically adverbs. The forms which may be used in both slots combine properties of prepositions and of adverbs.

There is a difference between appearances in the **p** slot for different types of phrasal verbs. All of the forms in the **p** column appear in types V-p-NP and V-NP-p-NP. However, the occurrences at **p** in types V-a-p-NP and V-NP-a-p-NP—that is, after an **a** slot—are confined to *with, to, on, for, against,* and *at* (in that approximate order of frequency).

A number of prepositions are (save in contrastive contexts) pronounced as proclitics. They are thus more-or-less restricted to slot **p**, where there is a following NP to cliticise onto. As listed in section 1.6, the three relational prepositions in row A— *of, for,* and *with*—and the central spatial ones in row B—*at*, *to*, and *from*—are generally proclitics. So are the complex prepositions, described in section 2.3, which end in -*to* or -*of*. These are *into* and *out-of*, in row C, *onto* and *off-of*, in row D, and *up-to*, in row E. *Upon*, in row D, is also a proclitic.

The rows in the table will now be discussed in turn, examining the structural possibilities for each preposition. (Their semantics is studied at the appropriate section within chapters 5–14.)

Row A: *of, for, with*

These relational prepositions normally have proclitic form and are thus restricted to slot **p**, with a following NP. Each of *for* and *with* occur in several dozen phrasal verbs, while *of* is in just a handful. They include:

V-p-NP	The prince <u>fell for</u> Cinderella
	Please <u>bear with</u> me!
V-NP-p-NP	The new laws <u>deprive</u> people <u>of</u> their basic freedoms
	He <u>touched</u> John <u>for</u> a loan
V-a-p-NP	Tim isn't <u>cut out for</u> that role
	Rufus <u>got behind with</u> the payments
V-NP-a-p-NP	The party <u>put</u> John <u>up for</u> President
	John <u>has tied</u> the reunion <u>in with</u> Tim's wedding

By, which is sometimes pronounced as a proclitic, has spatial in addition to relational function. It features as both **p** and **a**, and is included in row G.

Row B: *at, to, from*

These are the central spatial prepositions; they are also proclitic and—in everyday use— require a following NP to attach to. There are many examples with *to*, fewer with *at*, and just a couple with *from*. They include:

V-p-NP	The cripple <u>took to</u> his bed
V-NP-p-NP	They <u>kept</u> the bad news <u>from</u> Mary
V-a-p-NP	The workers <u>kept on at</u> the boss
V-NP-a-p-NP	They <u>put</u> the shortage <u>down to</u> bad planning

To is perhaps the most versatile of all prepositions (and it is the second most frequent, after *of*). Although basically in slot **p**, there are a few phrasal verbs where it appears to be in slot **a**, and then takes stress, rather than being a clitic. *To* appears in slot **a** for the intransitive V-a phrasal verbs illustrated in *The men set to (and worked hard)*, and *The patient came to (after the operation)*. And also in slot **a** for the transitive V-NP-a phrasal verb in *The doctor brought the patient to*.

Row C: *in, into, out, out-of*

Section 2.3 showed how *into* and *out-of* each functions as a single complex preposition. They are proclitics—by virtue of the final elements *to* and *of*—and are thus restricted to slot **p** where there is a following NP for them to cliticise onto. *In* and *out* are the corresponding forms in slot **a**.

As illustrated in section 2.1, an inner pNP—with the preposition used in its basic sense—may omit the NP component if its identity should be understood from the context. For example, *The cashier passed the money over the counter* could, in appropriate circumstances, be shortened to *The cashier passed the money over*. The preposition may now be moved to the left over the NP, giving *The cashier passed over the money*.

We can see how this works with *in, into, out,* and *out-of*, used in their basic senses:

(1) (a) Mary let the cat into   (b) John took the garbage out of
            the house   the house

(2) (a) Mary let the cat in   (b) John took the garbage out

(3) (a) Mary let in the cat   (b) John took out the garbage

The interesting point here is that the complex prepositions *into* and *out-of* are used before an NP in (1a-b). Once the NP is omitted, in (2a-b), the proclitic forms *into* and *out-of* are not permitted, and have to be shortened to *in* and *out*. These may move to the left over the preceding NP, as in (3a-b).

(There is here a degree of difference between dialects. Some may use *in*, as an alternative to *into*, in (1a) giving *Mary let the cat in the house*. Others may use *out*, as an alternative to *out-of*, in (1b), giving *John put the garbage out the house*. These are simply variants on the basic scheme.)

Occurrence in phrasal verbs mirrors the structural possibilities for these prepositions when used in their basic senses.

Into and *out-of* appear in slot **p** for phrasal verb of type V-p-NP and V-NP-p-NP:

V-p-NP	Joe <u>came into</u> a fortune
	Try to <u>snap out-of</u> your depression!
V-NP-p-NP	<u>Sue</u> talked John <u>into</u> resigning
	We <u>screwed</u> some information <u>out-of</u> the spy

There appears to be no instance of *into* and *out-of* as **p** in phrasal verbs of types V-a-p-NP or V-NP-a-p-NP; that is, these complex prepositions are not found in slot **p** when this follows slot **a**.

In contrast, plain *in* and *out* occur only in slot **a**, in phrasal verbs of types V-a, V-NP-a, V-a-p-NP, V-NP-a-p-NP:

V-a	The rains <u>have set in</u>	We'll <u>hold out</u>
V-NP-a	Pam <u>packed</u> the job <u>in</u>	They <u>carried</u> the plan <u>out</u>
V-a-p-NP	We'll <u>fall in with</u> your plan	Tim <u>fell out with</u> Sam
V-NP-a-p-NP	<u>Fill</u> John <u>in on</u> the proposal!	Fred <u>took</u> his anger <u>out on</u> his wife

In each instance, the V-NP-a and V-NP-a-p-NP constructions may undergo left movement of the **a**, giving V-a-NP and V-a-NP-p-NP respectively; for example, *Pam <u>packed in</u> the job* and *He <u>took out</u> his anger <u>on</u> his wife*.

We saw that, in some dialects, either *into* or *in* is possible for (1a) and either *out-of* or *out* for (1b). No such variation is possible for phrasal verbs involving these prepositions; for example, *in* could not be used in place of *into* in *John <u>came into</u> a fortune*.

There is one irregularity—a sentence like *Little Rachel came out in spots* which could be regarded as involving a phrasal verb *come out in NP*, of type V-a-p-NP, with preposition *in* filling the **p** slot. Alternatively, *come out in NP* could be regarded as an idiom (the NP can only be *spots* or *a rash* or a hyponym of these).

Row D: *on, onto, upon, off, off-of*
These are some similarities, and also important differences, between the prepositions in row D and those in row C. Like *into* and *out-of*, complex prepositions *onto*, *upon*, and *off-of* are proclitics and require a following NP to attach to. They are thus restricted to slot **p** in phrasal verbs.

In contrast to *in* and *out*, which are restricted to slot **a**, we find that *on* and *off* appear in slot **a** and also in slot **p**. First, here are some examples of *on* and *off* in slot **a**:

V-a	Grandfather <u>lived on</u>	The rain is <u>holding off</u>
V-NP-a	David <u>took</u> Goliath <u>on</u>	He <u>called</u> the meeting <u>off</u>
V-a-p-NP	The duchess <u>kept on at</u> the maid	The burglar <u>made off with</u> the loot
V-NP-a-p-NP	\<no example known\>	He <u>played</u> Fred <u>off against</u> Mary

Onto or *upon* could not be substituted for *on* in slot **a** of these phrasal verbs, nor *off-of* for *off*.

The alternations between *on* and *upon*, and between *on* and *onto*, in their basic meanings, are subtle. In almost every instance, *on* may be used in place of *upon* or *onto*; the disyllabic prepositions simply provide further specification.

Onto may be used instead of *on* if some degree of motion is involved, as in:

> Tim got onto/on the bus
> Sally threw her money onto/on the table

And *upon* can be used instead of *on* if the reference is just to location, rather than motion:

> Prue sat upon/on the horse
> All eyes were upon/on me

Some sentences may have either a motion or a location interpretation so that all three prepositions are possible:

> Jane placed the cake on/upon/onto the table

There are just a few examples where only *onto* may be used, not *on* or *upon*:

> Grandfather lowered himself onto the bed

And also a few where only *on* is possible:

> The gadget turns on its axle

These alternatives extend over into phrasal verbs. We get the unusual circumstance of a phrasal verb allowing two possibilities. This can be illustrated by examining these at slot **p** in four types of phrasal verbs:

- V-p-NP

either *on* or *upon*:   Jessica <u>hit on/upon</u> a new idea

                                    You can <u>count upon/on</u> Jack for support

only *on*:   Please don't <u>tell on</u> Fred!

- V-NP-p-NP

either *on* or *upon*:   The boss <u>put</u> pressure <u>on/upon</u> Jill

either *on* or *onto*:   They've <u>slapped</u> another \$10 <u>on/onto</u> the price

only *onto*:   She <u>put</u> John <u>onto</u> the possibilities

- V-a-p-NP, V-NP-a-p-NP

For phrasal verbs of these types (where slot **p** follows slot **a**), there is
no alternative to *on*:

>   She <u>went back on</u> her promise
>
>   Mr Meggs has always <u>been down on</u> the workers
>
>   They <u>filled</u> me <u>in on</u> the new plan
>
>   We <u>let</u> Sally <u>in on</u> the secret
>
>   Algy <u>took</u> his anger <u>out on</u> the office boy

We thus see that the complex prepositions *onto* and *upon* do not occur
in slot **p** when it follows a slot **a**.

Discussion of possible (overlapping and contrasting) uses of *on*,
upon, and *onto* is one of the trickiest topics in English grammar. There
are gradations of judgement such that no really definite rules can be
presented, instead just tendencies.

Off is like *on* in occurring in slot **a** for phrasal verbs (illustrated above)
and also in slot **p**, as in:

V-p-NP   Let's <u>knock off</u> work!

V-NP-p-NP   The mayor <u>struck</u> the vicar <u>off</u> the list

I am not aware of any examples of *off* in slot **p** for phrasal verbs of types
V-a-p-NP and V-NP-a-p-NP.

In its basic sense, *off* may sometimes alternate with the complex
preposition *off-of*, as in *The policeman snatched the jewels off/off-of the
thief*. *Off-of* goes back several hundred years but today it is commonly
used only in American English. See sections 9.2b and 15.2d.

Row E: *up, up-to, down, along*

Up and *down* are primarily adverbs. They have secondary use as prepositions, but only with basic meanings. For example:

AS ADVERBS	AS PREPOSITIONS
The sailor looked up	The girl climbed up the mountain
The bird flew down	The boy walked down the hill

In their extended senses, *up* and *down* are almost exclusively adverbs. In keeping with this, they appear just in slot **a** for phrasal verbs. In fact, *up* is found in well over a hundred phrasal verbs (more than any other preposition or adverb), and *down* is in several dozen. Examples include:

V-a	The child <u>is acting up</u>	The car <u>broke down</u>
V-NP-a	The newlyweds <u>did</u> the house <u>up</u>	He <u>fought</u> his anger <u>down</u>
V-a-p-NP	We must <u>keep up with</u> our peer group	You need to <u>cut down on</u> whisky
V-NP-a-p-NP	Sam <u>took</u> Fred <u>up on</u> his offer	She <u>put</u> the error <u>down to</u> his illness

I know of no phrasal verb for which *down* fills slot **p**, and just one where *up* does—*put up NP*, illustrated in *John <u>put up</u> a struggle*.

Complex preposition *up-to* is a clitic and thus requires a following NP for it to attach to. For instance:

> Timothy loved Heather up-to three months ago

The fact that *up-to* is here one complex preposition, rather then being a sequence of two single prepositions is shown by the fact that *up* cannot be moved to the left of the preceding NP. That is, we cannot have **Timothy loved up Heather to three months ago*.

In keeping with this, *up-to* is found only in slot **p** for phrasal verbs, and is attested in two types:

V-p-NP	I don't <u>feel up-to</u> meeting your mother today
V-NP-p-NP	The committee <u>left</u> the decision <u>up-to</u> John

Since (with one exception) *up-to* and *up* occur in different slots, there is no possibility of one substituting for the other in phrasal verbs.

We have seen that each of the complex prepositions—*into, out-of, upon, onto,* and *up-to*—may be used in slot **p** only for phrasal verbs of types V-p-NP and V-NP-NP. That is, they cannot follow slot **a**, in types V-a-p-NP and V-NP-a-p-NP. (Information on the complex preposition *off-of* is slim; it is not known to feature in any phrasal verbs.)

Up is the major member of the pairing *up/down* and has far wider semantic and grammatical possibilities than the minor member *down*. For example, there is no complex preposition *down-to*. Every instance of *down to* involves two separate prepositions. From *Maggie took the basket down to the cellar* can be obtained *Maggie took down the basket to the cellar*, with *down* moving to the left over the preceding NP.

Along is, like *up* and *down*, primarily an adverb. Just in its basic sense, it may have secondary function as a preposition:

AS ADVERB	AS PREPOSITION
More along there!	Jason ran along the path

There are just a few instances of *along* in slot **a** for two types of phrasal verbs. For example:

V-NP-a	I <u>strung</u> the boss <u>along</u>
V-a-p-NP	He <u>scraped along on</u> his allowance

Row F: *against, after*
Although there is no phonological reason for it, *against* appears to always require a following NP; that is, it functions just as a preposition never as an adverb. In keeping with this, it occurs only in slot **p** for phrasal verbs:

V-p-NP	Xavier <u>acted against</u> the best advice
V-NP-p-NP	They <u>turned</u> the boy <u>against</u> his father
V-a-p-N	He <u>comes up against</u> the champion in the next bout
V-NP-a-p-NP	The King <u>played</u> the barons <u>off against</u> the politicians

After occurs in slot **p** for just a handful of phrasal verbs, all of type V-p-NP. For example, *Please <u>look after</u> the baby for me*, and *John <u>takes after</u> his father*.

Row G: *over, under, through, (a)round, about, across, by, behind, forth*
It is interesting that—apart from a handful of exceptions indicated in square brackets in the table—each of the items in rows A–C and E–F occurs in just one of the slots **p** and **a**. *On* and *off*, from row D, feature in both, as do those forms in row G.

Over is found in more than 40 phrasal verbs. For most it is in slot **a**; for example:

V-a	The scandal will soon <u>blow over</u>
V-NP-a	The cops <u>pulled</u> the car <u>over</u>
V-a-p-NP	They're <u>going over to</u> metric
V-NP-a-p-NP	The salesman tried to <u>put</u> a fast one <u>over on</u> the pensioner

But there are a dozen or so examples of *over* in slot **p** for two varieties of phrasal verbs, including:

V-p-NP	The criticism just <u>washed over</u> him
V-NP-p-NP	The boss <u>held</u> the threat of dismissal <u>over</u> her

Under, as the minor member of the pair *over/under*, occurs in far fewer phrasal verbs than the major member *over*, but still encompassing both slots **a** and **p**:

V-a	The firm has <u>gone under</u> (and thus all the employees are out of work)
V-NP-a	The despot <u>kept</u> the serfs <u>under</u>
V-NP-a-p-NP	The politicians <u>snowed</u> the people <u>under with</u> lies
V-p-NP	The cost of your lunches <u>falls under</u> the heading of 'miscellaneous expenses'
V-NP-p-NP	The king <u>brought</u> the rebels <u>under</u> control

The remaining forms in row G—*through, (a)round, about, across, by, behind, forth*—are each found in 20 or fewer phrasal verbs, but they do span both slots. They can be briefly exemplified, firstly in slot **p** for phrasal verbs of type V-p-NP:

He <u>came through</u> the ordeal alright
She tried to <u>get (a)round</u> John, and gain his confidence
He was just <u>going about</u> his business
I <u>came across</u> a lovely little stream on my walk this morning
How did you <u>come by</u> that painting?
The building work is <u>running behind</u> schedule
The baby <u>gave forth</u> a piercing scream

And in slot **a** for phrasal verbs of varying types:

V-NP-a	They <u>carried</u> the plan <u>through</u>
	The doctor <u>brought</u> the patient <u>(a)round</u>
	The new manager will <u>bring</u> changes <u>about</u>
	I'm trying to <u>get</u> the idea <u>across</u>
V-a	I'll <u>get by</u> somehow
V-a-p-NP	He <u>got behind with</u> the payments
V-NP-a	She <u>set</u> her ideas <u>forth</u>

Row H: *back, away, ahead, aside, apart, forward, together*
There are a number of adverbs which each occur in slot **a** for a few phrasal verbs. The most frequent are *back* and *away*, illustrated in:

V-a	They're always <u>hanging back</u>	The old fellow <u>passed away</u>
V-NP-a	She <u>knocked</u> the prize <u>back</u>	He <u>laughed</u> his failure <u>away</u>
V-a-p-NP	Joe <u>got back at</u> his tormentor	She can <u>get away with</u> anything

Brief illustrations of the others are:

ahead	in	V-a	We should <u>go ahead</u> (with the plan)
aside	in	V-NP-a	They <u>swept</u> the problems <u>aside</u>
apart	in	V-NP-a	Uncle Harry can <u>tell</u> the twins <u>apart</u>
forward	in	V-NP-a	Let's <u>bring</u> the meeting <u>forward</u>
together	in	V-a	That idea does <u>hang together</u>

Note that a number of these adverbs form a complex preposition by adding a relational preposition *of* or *with*, or the central spatial local preposition *from*—*back of, away from, ahead of, aside from, apart from, forward of,* and *together with*. None of these enters into phrasal verbs.

∗ ∗ ∗

The prepositions which feature in phrasal verbs—together with those that don't—are examined, group by group, in chapters 5–14. But, before that, the next chapter studies the nature and properties of prepositional verbs.

4

Prepositional verbs

Some verbs require a following preposition, so that verb-plus-preposition make up a single unit, a kind of transitive verb. We call these 'prepositional verbs'. For example:

allude to	as in	She alluded to my views on fashion
dispose of	as in	Please dispose of your cigarette butts properly!
rely on	as in	He is relying on support from his family
vouch for	as in	I can vouch for the accuracy of the report

Prepositional verbs are entirely different from phrasal verbs. Each phrasal verb includes a simple verb which may occur by itself. Its meaning when

English Prepositions: Their Meanings and Uses. R. M. W. Dixon. Oxford University Press (2021). © R. M. W. Dixon.
DOI: 10.1093/oso/9780198868682.003.0004

it is used alone is significantly different from the meaning of the phrasal verb—compare phrasal verb *pick on*, as in *That teacher is always picking on Aaron*, with simple verb *pick*; and phrasal verb *knock off* as in *We knock off work at five o'clock*, with simple verb *knock*.

In contrast, the simple verb within a prepositional verb does not occur alone (save sometimes in special circumstances; see section 4.1d below). A meaning attaches just to the combination.

A phrasal verb may involve one or two prepositions or adverbs, in six structural types, whereas a prepositional verb includes a single preposition. The most common prepositions which occur in prepositional verbs are *of*, *for*, and *with* (which have a purely relational basic meaning), *to*, *from*, and *at* (the three central spatial prepositions), *on* and *in* (major members of the pairings *on/off* and *in/out*).

Whereas the simple verb components of phrasal verbs are almost exclusively monosyllabic and Germanic, the simple verb components of prepositional verbs are predominantly polysyllabic and of Romance origin. Present-day English features many hundreds of phrasal verbs; there are rather fewer prepositional verbs, perhaps just a couple of hundred.

4.1 Properties

Accounts of English grammar typically state that *allude*, *dispose*, *rely*, and *vouch* are intransitive verbs which must take a pNP. There are several reasons why such an analysis should be rejected in favour of the one followed here, of regarding each of *allude to*, *dispose of*, *rely on*, and *vouch for* as a single unit—a prepositional verb—which is a type of transitive verb.

- A regular intransitive (or transitive) verb may be followed by a wide range of pNPs. For example *Sam ran* can co-occur with *towards Fred*, or *from the dog*, or *in the games*, or *after lunch*, or *for fun*, and many more. In contrast, *allude* only takes *to*, *dispose* only takes *of*, and so on.
- The NP which follows the preposition of a prepositional verb behaves in many respects like the object argument of a simple transitive verb. For instance, if semantically plausible, a passive derivation may apply, with this NP becoming intransitive subject for the passive. For example:

The accuracy of the report was vouched for by three of the managers

My views were not even alluded to

All the cigarette butts have been properly disposed of

However, there is one way in which a prepositional verb differs from a simple transitive verb. There are several positions within a clause where an adverb may be placed (initially, finally, after the first word of the auxiliary, immediately before the verb) but the one place from which it is barred is between a simple transitive verb and its object. One can say *She slyly mentioned my views on fashion* but not *She mentioned slyly my views on fashion*. However, an adverb can intrude between the verb and preposition of a prepositional verb. For example:

She alluded slyly to my views on fashion

Please dispose properly of your cigarette butts!

He is relying totally on support from his family

I can vouch absolutely for the accuracy of the report

It is appropriate to refer to the NP which follows a prepositional verb as being in object function, just like the NP which follows a regular transitive verb. However, the possibility for adverb insertion between verb and preposition indicates that there is a less strong semantic association between verb and object than for a simple transitive verb. This point is explored further in section 4.3.

4.1a Maintaining adjacency

In section 2.2 there was an account of how, when the NP portion of a pNP is replaced by a question word and this is moved to the beginning of the clause, the preposition may either (a) stay where it was, or (b) move with the question word. For example:

The burglar hid under a table

(a)　What did the burglar hide under?

(b)　Under what did the burglar hide?

For a plain pNP, alternative (a) is invariably alright, while (b) has varying degrees of acceptability, depending on the meanings of the lexical elements in the clause and the pragmatic context.

We saw, in section 3.6, that for a phrasal verb only option (a) is available. Prepositional verbs differ just a little. Alternative (a) is always to be preferred. For most prepositional verbs, (b) is quite unacceptable:

Maud disposed of the garbage
(a)   What did Maud dispose of?
(b)   *Of what did Maud dispose?

Tom grappled with the assassin
(a)   Who did Tom grapple with?
(b)   *With whom did Tom grapple?

Other prepositional verbs for which alternative (b) is not possible include *indulge in*, *wonder at*, and *partake of*, among many others.

There are, however, just a few prepositional verbs—typically, some of those with *to*—for which (b) is acceptable:

Eve alluded to my views on fashion
(a)   What did Eve allude to?
(b)   To what did Eve allude?

Adam referred to Shakespeare's Hamlet
(a)   What did Adam refer to?
(b)   To what did Adam refer?

Other prepositional verbs which accept alternative (b) are *pertain to* and *confess to*.

Two extremes have been illustrated. One is where alternative (b) is clearly acceptable; this applies in the case of *allude to*, *refer to*, and just a few others. The other is where (b) is not acceptable. Prepositional verbs in this class include, among very many others, *dispose of* and *grapple with*.

There are some prepositional verbs which fall between these two extremes; that is, where alternative (b) is marginally acceptable. For example:

The lawyer can vouch for the accuracy of the report
(a)   What can the lawyer vouch for?
(b)   ?For what can the lawyer vouch?

Henry is relying on support from his family

(a)   What is Henry relying on?

(b)   ?On what is Henry relying?

There is thus a scale of acceptability for alternative (b) in the case of prepositional verbs, with most of them falling at the 'unacceptable' end. Whether or not construction (b) is possible is thus indicative but not criterial for a prepositional verb.

4.1b Complement clause in object function

A complement clause may be used, in place of an NP, in transitive object function (and also, to a more limited extent, in transitive subject and intransitive subject functions). It may not replace the NP within a pNP involving a simple preposition. The object slot for a prepositional verb can be filled by a complement clause just like the object slot for a simple transitive verb. Compare:

She mentioned [John's having lost his job]$_{CoCl:O}$

She alluded to [John's having lost his job]$_{CoCl:O}$

This provides further support for treating a prepositional verb as a kind of transitive verb, rather than as an intransitive verb with an obligatory following pNP.

The three main varieties of complement clauses in English were outlined in section 2.5c—a THAT clause, referring to a fact, an -ING clause, referring to something extended in time, and a (FOR) TO clause, referring to a potentiality or intention. Whether a simple transitive verb, or a prepositional verb, occurs with a particular variety of complement clause depends on the compatibility of meaning between verb and complement clause.

A preposition must be dropped before complementiser *that, for,* or *to.* As a consequence, a phrasal verb may take an -ING complement clause but it cannot take a THAT or (FOR) TO clause; if it did the preposition of the phrasal verb would drop and it would just become the simple verb used on its own—this is discussed and exemplified in sections 2.5c and 3.3.

In contrast, a prepositional verb may have, as its O argument, any type of complement clause. This can be illustrated by repeating, from section 2.5c, sentences involving prepositional verb *decide on*. The O argument may be an NP or an -ING complement clause, in which case the preposition *on* is retained:

Father decided on [the inoculations]$_{NP:O}$

Father decided on [the children('s) being inoculated]$_{CoCl:O}$

Father decided on [being inoculated]$_{CoCl:O}$

If the O argument is a THAT or (FOR) TO complement clause, then preposition *on* drops:

Father decided — [(that) the children should be inoculated]$_{CoCl:O}$

Father decided — [for the children to be inoculated]$_{CoCl:O}$

Father decided — [to be inoculated]$_{CoCl:O}$

No ambiguity results from this preposition omission. Unlike the simple verb within a phrasal verb, the simple verb within a prepositional verb may not occur on its own and so these sentences are still regarded as involving the prepositional verb *decide on*.

A verb only takes a complement clause if there is a semantic association between the meaning of the verb and the meaning of the complement clause. A fair number of prepositional verbs may take an -ING complement clause. *Allude to* has just been illustrated. Others include *atone for* and *result from*:

You need to atone for [your son's having insulted the vicar]$_{CoCl:O}$

Much good may result from [the boss's having sacked the foul-mouthed foreman]$_{CoCl:O}$

Decide on is one of the few (perhaps the only) prepositional verb to accept all three kinds of complement clauses. Several take both -ING and THAT varieties:

The clerk confessed to [having stolen the money]$_{CoCl:O}$

The clerk confessed — [that he had stolen the money]$_{CoCl:O}$

Strive for takes a TO complement clause. Compare:

The athlete strove for [excellence]$_{NP:O}$

The athlete strove — [to achieve excellence]$_{CoCl:O}$

And *wish for* may take THAT and (FOR) TO complement clauses:

> I have often wished for [proper recognition]$_{NP:O}$
> I have often wished — [that my work should achieve proper recognition]$_{CoCl:O}$
> I have often wished — [to achieve proper recognition]$_{CoCl:O}$
> I have often wished — [for my work to achieve proper recognition]$_{CoCl:O}$

The *for* from the prepositional verb drops before complementiser *that*, *to*, and *for* in the last three examples. (Note that the *for* in the last example is the complementiser *for*, not the *for* from the prepositional verb.)

4.1c Nominalisations

From many prepositional verbs are derived nominalisations which describe activities. In almost every instance, the preposition stays with the simple verb. For example (underlining prepositional verb and its nominalisation):

AS PREPOSITIONAL VERB	AS NOMINALISATION
They <u>alluded to</u> the theft	Their <u>allusion to</u> the theft went unnoticed
They <u>disposed of</u> the refuse	Their <u>disposal of</u> the refuse is complete
He <u>referred to</u> Plato	He inserted a <u>reference to</u> Plato
They <u>participated in</u> the debate	I noted their <u>participation in</u> the debate
She <u>deviated from</u> the rules	<u>Deviation from</u> the rules is a serious business
He is <u>relying on</u> your support	His <u>reliance on</u> your support was commented on

This is a further demonstration that the two components of a prepositional verb comprise a single unit. The few adjectives derived from prepositional verbs preserve the same unity; for example, *He is <u>reliant on</u> your support*.

4.1d Omitting preposition plus noun phrase

One can, in the right circumstances, say *Father hasn't decided yet* or *Dirk has confessed*. Does this mean that the simple verb components from prepositional verbs *decide on* and *confess to* can be used on their own, as intransitive verbs? Not in the least. These are simply examples of the object argument of a transitive verb being omissible when its identity can be inferred from the context of use. In the case of a prepositional verb, the preposition is omitted together with the object NP or complement clause.

This can be illustrated first with regular transitive verbs. A conversation may go as follows:

A   The dog just bit the postman
B   I know

B's response is, in underlying form, *I know that the dog just bit the postman*. The complement clause in object function need not be stated since this is something already established by A's utterance.

Now consider another conversation:

A   One isn't allowed to walk on the grass in the quad
B   The boys understand (sc. that one isn't allowed to walk on the grass in the quad)

A conversation could not commence with a short utterance such as *I know* or *The boys understand*. These are transitive verbs and an object argument must either be stated or else understood, by textual anaphora, from what has gone before in the discourse.

Some prepositional verbs behave in a similar way. For example:

A   Which country are we going to for the summer holidays?
B   Father hasn't decided yet (sc. on which country we are going to for the summer holidays)

A   Have they found out who committed the murder?
B   Dirk has confessed (sc. to the murder)

Just as with *know* and *understand*, the object arguments of *decide on* and *confess to* may be left unstated if clear through textual anaphora. And in the case of prepositional verbs, such as these, the prepositional component is omitted along with the object. A conversation could not commence with *Father hasn't decided yet* or *Dirk has confessed*; there must be something preceding which indicates what it is which hasn't been decided on, or has been confessed to.

A limited number of other prepositional verbs may omit preposition plus object argument in similar circumstances; they include *object to*, *approve of*, and *disapprove of*. These are all fairly common verbs which describe an activity (*decide on, confess to*) or attitude (*object to, approve of, disapprove of*). The omission is not found with less common verbs, such as *allude to, vouch for*, and *aspire to*. Nor is it found with prepositional verbs describing a dependence (*rely on, count on*) or dissociation (*dispose of, refrain from*). That is, there are no circumstances in which one may hear just *I rely* or *Martha refrains*.

4.1e Two prepositional verbs involving the same simple verb

There are just a few instances of two prepositional verbs involving the same simple verb. We can examine two pairs, of quite different natures.

4.1e-1 *Wonder about* and *wonder at*

Prepositional verb *wonder about* expresses an enquiry. It can take as object argument an NP or an interrogative subordinate clause:

> I've often wondered about [Mary's true intentions]$_{NP:O}$
> We were wondering about [our next move]$_{NP:O}$
> We were wondering (about) [what our next move should be]$_{CoCl:O}$
> The general wondered (about) [where to go next]$_{CoCl:O}$

The prepositional component, *about*, may be either retained or omitted before an interrogative clause introduced by *what, where, which, who*, etc.

Prepositional verb *wonder at* indicates surprise. This can take either an NP or an -ING or THAT complement clause as O argument:

> We wondered at [grandfather's longevity]$_{NP:O}$
> We wondered at [grandfather's living so long]$_{CoCl:O}$
> We wondered — [that grandfather is still alive]$_{CoCl:O}$

As always, the preposition drops before complementiser *that*. But since *wonder about* does not accept a THAT complement clause as O argument, the last sentence above must unambiguously relate to prepositional verb *wonder at*.

(If someone makes an extravagant and scarcely believable claim, another person may respond with the idiomatic expression *I wonder!* This effectively combines the meanings of amazement and enquiry 'is that really so, surely not?')

4.1e-2 *Consist of* and *consist in*

For both of these prepositional verbs the referent of the object argument is involved in the make-up of the referent of the subject argument—but in quite different ways.

Consist of describes a set of physical components:

A jury consists of twelve citizens

The tea set consists of six plates, six mugs, one milk jug, and one sugar bowl

In contrast, *consist in* specifies the sort(s) of activity which are required for some pursuit or trait:

A lecturer's job consists in teaching students and conducting research

Patriotism consists in putting the interests of one's country first

There is no overlap between the kinds of referent of the O argument for the two verbs.

4.2 Meanings

Language is all about meaning, and if one encounters two phenomena which are basically similar but do demonstrate a structural difference, then it is appropriate to enquire whether this difference carries any semantic implication. Quite often, a prepositional verb has similar meaning to a plain transitive verb. Can we recognise any recurrent semantic difference?

Examination of a number of such pairs suggests that we can. For a prepositional verb, the referent of the argument in transitive subject (A) function is likely to be more in focus than the A argument of a corresponding plain transitive verb. By this is meant that it is likely to exercise more thought or emotion or control or effort.

Half-a-dozen sets of verbs will now be examined to illustrate this claim.

4.2a Dispose of *and* discard

There is an overlap of use; for example:

> We need to discard the unwanted materials
>
> We need to dispose of the unwanted materials

Discard indicates simply getting rid of something (just throwing it away) whereas *dispose of* implies doing something appropriate with it (putting it in a place where it will not offend or pollute).

Suppose that the thing no longer desired was a fur coat. If it were still in good condition, it could be disposed of, sold for money. But if it were full of holes then it should just be discarded, thrown into the rubbish bin.

A manager has serious doubts about some proposal. Then, next week, he allows it to go forward.

This can happen in either of two ways:

> He discarded his doubts
>> (he just adopted a more positive attitude)
>
> The committee disposed of his doubts
>> (they presented a set of reasoned arguments showing that his doubts had no foundation)

Discard is, basically, 'get rid of'. In contrast, *dispose of* implies mental (and/or physical) application, on the part of the referent of the A argument, relating to what happens to the referent of the O argument.

4.2b Object to, disapprove of, *and* dislike

The prepositional verbs *object to* and *disapprove of* may occur in the same syntactic frame as does regular transitive verb *dislike*, but with different overtones. For example:

> I dislike loud music
>> (being unable to avoid hearing it annoys me)
>
> I object to loud music
>> (I protest against its presence)
>
> I disapprove of loud music
>> (I think that it should not be allowed)

Note that here the prepositional verbs implicitly include the meaning of *dislike*. One could scarcely object to loud music or disapprove of loud music without being annoyed at its presence.

Dislike has a wide range of senses, relating to a person or place, or to some activity, or to an idea or principle. They are illustrated by:

(a)   Samantha dislikes John Brown
         (she finds distasteful his looks, or his manners, or some other
         aspect of him)

(b)   Samantha dislikes smoking
         (she doesn't enjoy doing this)

(c)   Samantha dislikes the habit of smoking
         (she thinks that it is an unhealthy habit)

The two prepositional verbs are mostly used in sense (c). *Disapprove* of describes how the referent of the subject argument considers that there should be a general prohibition:

   Samantha disapproves of smoking
      (she is of the opinion that the practice should be banned, at
      least in public places)

Interestingly, one can disapprove of some habit but still indulge in it (with sly satisfaction): *Samantha is loud in her disapproval of smoking, and enjoins her children never to embrace it, but has been known to smoke a sneaky cigarette in a moment of stress.* That is, there can be general disapproval but occasional personal indulgence.

Object to is quite different, indicating that the referent of the subject argument does not want the practice to involve them (without the suggestion of any general prohibition):

   Samantha objects to smoking
      (she doesn't want to have to do it herself, or have anyone
      smoking in her vicinity)

Object to is used when there is a formal protest; for example, against a proposal to chop down rainforest.

The contrasting meanings of the three verbs are neatly illustrated when they are used together in:

Irina's parents disliked her feckless boyfriend,
    and strongly disapproved of her marrying him,
    but decided not to formally object to it

Disapprove of and *object to* may have preposition-plus-object omitted under textual anaphora, as described in section 4.1d:

A: The committee has voted to permit smoking in the precinct
B: I object (sc. to the idea that smoking should be permitted in the precinct)
C: I disapprove (sc. of the proposal that smoking should be permitted in the precinct)

Dislike has a wider and less focused meaning, and cannot omit its object argument in this way.

Object to encapsulates the personal attitude of the referent of the subject argument, and for this reason it is the only one of the three verbs which may introduce direct speech. For example:

Chairperson: 'You're down to give the vote of thanks, Tom'
Tom objected: 'I don't want to do it'

Each of the prepositional verbs has narrower scope than the regular transitive verb *dislike*. For *disapprove of*, it is not just that the referent of the A argument has a general antipathy towards the referent of the O argument—they feel that it should not be allowed. For *object to* the focus is on the activity not impinging on the referent of the A argument.

4.2c Decide on *and* choose

The prepositional verb *decide on* and regular transitive verb *choose* appear in similar grammatical frames but with different nuances of meaning:

Isaac decided to go to town on Thursday
    (rather than doing something else on that day)
Isaac chose to go to town on Thursday
    (rather than on some other day of the week)

Choose has a rather specific meaning, indicating selection from one of a number of comparable possibilities. In contrast, *decide on* describes coming to a conclusion about something, after weighing up the potentialities:

> Veronica decided on buying a new car and then chose a Mercedes

As illustrated in sections 2.5c and 4.1b, *decide on* may take an NP or any variety of complement clause as O argument. So may *choose*. How they differ is in the possible meanings of the O argument. For *choose*, it must be something definite—*The party chose Tony as their new leader* (from the list of nominations), *They chose that they would go to Brighton for the annual outing* (rather than Margate or Hastings), *We chose to paint the front door red* (rather than blue or green).

Decide (on) can substitute for *choose* in each of these sentences. But the prepositional verb can also relate to an opinion, or an idea, or a plan, or a verdict. In none of the following could *choose* be used in place of *decide (on)*:

> Monica decided that she liked Florence best of all
>
> The Prime Minister decided that it would not be a good idea to recall parliament early
>
> Inspector Grant decided to investigate who had committed the crime
>
> The jury decided that Maurice was guilty

Decide (but not *choose*) can introduce direct speech, with this describing a considered decision. For example:

> 'The veterans' brass band will lead the parade', the mayor decided

And the meanings of nominalisations make clear the contrastive senses of the two verbs. A *choice* is what has been selected from a set of possibilities whereas a *decision* describes the result of careful thought.

Decide (but not *choose*) also has a causative sense. If a set of officials cannot come to an agreement about the merits of a certain course of action, they might decide to leave it to the President to decide the matter (that is, to make the decision). Suppose that Veronica could not at first decide what kind of car to buy. Then, the fact of being told that a Mercedes has more air-bags than any other brand decided her (made the decision for her).

In summary, *decide on* differs from *choose* in that the referent of the subject NP exercises thought and judgement, rather than just making a selection.

4.2d Aspire to *and* seek

Consider the following sentences which include the prepositional verb *aspire to*:

> Ragged Jimmy Smith aspired to the hand in marriage of the princess
>
> Molly Bloom aspired to fame which was quite beyond her reach
>
> He aspired to be considered a gentleman but forgot about his tattoos

In each case, *aspire to* could be replaced by *seek*, maintaining the same basic meaning but losing the overtone that the referent of the subject argument is being overly ambitious, reaching after something that is for them scarcely achievable.

The regular transitive verb *seek* can be directed towards a wide range of things. One can seek a rewarding job, a second opinion, to institute a ban on smoking, or to ease the pain of a dying man. For none of these would *aspire to* be appropriate.

The prepositional verb indicates that the referent of the subject argument is focusing on something which is unrealistic. Or it can be used to describe the unexpected, as in:

> My uncle never aspired to the job of manager and was surprised when he was appointed to it

Not only did the uncle not seek to be manager, he didn't imagine that he could be considered an appropriate person for the position.

Seeking is a realistic and matter-of-fact activity, with a good chance of success. In contrast, someone who *aspires to* a certain level of recognition or success is most probably succumbing to a dream concerning the unattainable.

4.2e Grapple with, struggle, *and* fight

The prepositional verb *grapple with* originated in the nautical sphere but is now firmly ensconced in everyday usage. It belongs to the same semantic set as regular transitive verbs *fight* and *struggle*.

The most frequent of these is *fight* and it has a wide range of uses. For example:

(a)   Sam fought with Tom

(b)   Sam and Tom fought

(c)   Sam fought Tom

(d)   Sam often fights

Fight may describe a spontaneous conflict or else something more organised—a boxing bout, or a war. The participants (here Sam and Tom) are of fairly equal standing.

Struggle is less common than *fight* and is more restricted in use; it is unlikely to describe anything which is planned. It may replace *fight* in frames (a) and (b) only. With *struggle*, the referent of the subject argument is accorded more prominence than the opponent, which is why one can only say *Sam struggled with Tom*, not **Sam struggled Tom*. But there should be a specific opponent—**Sam often struggles* sounds incomplete, one needs to add who or what it is that he struggles with; for example, with the bully, or to finish the assignment, or to make himself heard. *Sam has struggled all his life* implies that he has had to continuously contend with one specific thing (such as poverty or mental illness) which the addressee(s) are assumed to be familiar with.

People can fight or struggle for a purpose; for example, for control of the fort, or for the right to carry the flag, or to support their family. There are nouns *fight* and *struggle* describing a period of the activity.

Grapple with may only appear in frame (a). It implies serious and concentrated effort on the part of the proponent. This can be to overcome someone, perhaps as a matter of life of death, as in *Sam grappled with the knife-wielding intruder*. An episode of grappling is not an event; people do not 'have a grapple' in the way that they 'have a struggle' or 'have a fight'.

One can struggle with solving a mathematical problem or resolving a political impasse; this implies that the process of coming up with a solution is challenging but not out of reach. In contrast, one grapples with a problem which is of great difficulty and requires total absorption.

Summarising, the verb *fight* describes a balanced encounter on a recognised pattern. A participant is 'a fighter' (we do not have, in the same way, 'a struggler' or 'a grappler'). *Struggle* implies something more impulsive, focusing on the efforts of the protagonist. *Grapple with* takes this one notch further, where the referent of the subject argument puts in a desperate effort to achieve the desired end.

4.2f Allude to *and* mention

If one wishes to convey some piece of information in a matter-of-fact way, then the regular transitive verb *mention* may be used:

> Justine mentioned that Rufus was a hunchback

Prepositional verb *allude to* differs from *mention* in that it often conveys something that the speaker is apologetic about imparting, but considers it important that it be said. For example:

> Although any reference to Rufus's deformity annoyed him, Justine felt bound to allude to it
> (in order to explain why he needed assistance in certain basic tasks)

Being aware of the current climate of political correctness, some information may need to be conveyed in a discreet manner:

> The policeman described the assailant's height and build, and then alluded to his colour

Allude to appears on the surface to provide just a piece of background information. However, it is something which could be critically important, as in:

> When Morris asked Cynthia to marry him, he did allude to the fact that he was comfortably off

The essence of *allude to*—when compared with the more common and neutral verb *mention*—is that the speaker takes pains to convey some relevant information in a seemingly casual (and inoffensive) manner.

4.3 Analysis

A prepositional verb behaves in most ways like a regular transitive verb. But there are differences, both structural and semantic. What do these consist in?

The structure of a transitive clause which involves a simple transitive verb may be represented by:

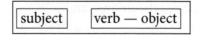

There is typically a close association between verb and object—a given verb typically occurs with a certain type of object, and vice versa. For example: eat a meal, tell a story, enter a room, spill some water, arrange the flowers, melt the ice, feel the heat, read a book, prove a theorem, answer a question, inspire the students. There is also, of course, a link between subject and verb—some types of verb may require a particular sort of subject. However, this is less developed than the connection between verb and object.

The structure of a transitive clause which involves a prepositional verb may be shown as follows:

subject — verb		preposition — object

We have seen that, with a prepositional verb, the referent of the subject argument plays a special role with respect to the activity described by the verb, more so than for a simple transitive verb of similar meaning. This is acknowledged by placing 'subject' and 'verb' together in a box.

The syntactic representations in the two diagrams explain the positioning of adverbs. An adverb may not intrude between a regular transitive verb and its object, but it may come between the verb and preposition of a prepositional verb (since they are in separate boxes).

The six examples discussed in the preceding section illustrate the distinctive roles played by the referent of the subject with a prepositional verb. This can involve extreme physical effort, as in the case of *grapple with* (as opposed to *fight*), and to both mental and physical application for *dispose of* (compared with *discard*). *Decide on* requires thought and judgement (less evident for *choose*), and *aspire to* describes a somewhat unrealistic ambition (compared to the straightforward verb *seek*). *Allude to* is used of a subtle technique for imparting relevant information in a seemingly casual manner (compared to *mention*). And while *dislike* just indicates a general lack of appreciation of something, *object to* focuses on the subject's desire not to be involved with it, and *disapprove of* the subject's opinion that it should be outlawed.

Other prepositional verbs illustrate further kinds of focus associated with the referent of the transitive subject argument. Compare *hanker after* and *hanker for* with *want*, *partake of* with *consume*, *confess to* with *admit*, *indulge in* with *enjoy*, and so on.

4.4 Hard to place

Verb *deprive* always occurs with preposition *of* and verb *subject* always with preposition *to*. Sample sentences are:

> The new laws deprive people of their basic freedoms
>
> The guards subjected the prisoners to ridicule

Deprive NP of NP and *subject NP to NP* do not accord with the usual profile of a prepositional verb since each requires an NP between verb and preposition. They have the structure of phrasal verbs of type V-NP-p-NP except that a characteristic of a phrasal verb is that the simple verb component may be used as a simple verb and this does not hold for *deprive* or *subject*.

However, there is a derived adjective *deprived* which can be used without an accompanying *of* (as in: *a deprived childhood*) which would be an unusual property for a prepositional verb. This suggests that *deprive of* should be treated as an aberrant phrasal verb, rather than as an aberrant prepositional verb.

Verb *subject NP to NP* is clearly related to adjectival form *subject to NP*, which can only occur in copula complement function; for example, *Prices may be subject to change* and *The scheme is subject to cabinet approval* (this can be extended to a reduced relative clause construction such as *He was one of those people (who are) subject to recurrent fits of anxiety*). That is, the preposition *to* is still firmly associated with *subject*.

These are in-between instances which do not accord with the typical character of either a prepositional verb or a phrasal verb. I propose to treat *deprive NP of NP* and *subject NP to NP* in the same way, as non-canonical phrasal verbs. (However, the alternative solution, to treat them as unusual prepositional verbs, would be equally acceptable.)

✷ ✷ ✷

Part I, which this chapter completes, has surveyed the main grammatical possibilities for prepositions. The basic kinds of structures, types of verbs, and so on, are clearly delineated. However, it must always be borne in mind that human language is not immutable. Speakers' judgements vary, habits of word behaviour ebb and flow. As a consequence, there are always fuzzy regions between the archetypes. It is generally a straightforward matter to decide whether something is a phrasal verb, or a prepositional verb, or just a productive sequence of verb plus preposition. However, competing criteria sometimes pull in different directions. It is this occasional element of fluidity which makes the study of grammar so intriguing.

We now move on to detailed discussion, taking the prepositions in groups. First, those that have a relational meaning—*of* and *for*, the kingpins, and then *by* and *with*. The following chapters discuss central spatial prepositions (*at, to, from*), then those dealing with enclosure (*in, out*), connection (*on, off*), superiority (*up, down*), position (*over, under*), and the rest.

Particular attention is paid to contrasting the meanings of prepositions which may be used in similar contexts; for instance, *arrive at the station* but *arrive on the goldfields*. *At* is discussed in chapter 7 and *on* in chapter 9; the comparative discussion of *at* and *on* then comes in chapter 9, after both prepositions have been dealt with.

The scene has been set. It is now time to introduce the players.

Part II
The Players

5

The mainstays

Of, for

English Prepositions: Their Meanings and Uses. R. M. W. Dixon. Oxford University Press (2021). © R. M. W. Dixon.
DOI: 10.1093/oso/9780198868682.003.0005

Unlike most prepositions, *of* /əv=/ and *for* /fər=/ have basic meanings which are relational rather than spatial and/or temporal. There are some spatial and temporal senses of *for* (for example, *They sailed for France, He's been sick for six months*) but these are of a secondary nature.

These two prepositions did have spatial origins. *For* developed out of a meaning 'earlier in time or space' (continued in preposition *before* and prefix *fore-*, as in *fore-shore* and *fore-word*). In Old English *for* was also used to indicate 'cause', 'reason', and 'purpose', anticipating the modern range of senses. The earliest meanings for *of* in Old English were 'away from', 'out of', 'from', and 'off', which are still reflected in a few modern senses. Some of its other meanings are thought to have developed in part through translation of French preposition *de*.

Today, *of* and *for* are the pre-eminent markers of grammatical relations. *Of* is far and away the most common preposition in modern English, and *for* the fourth most common. (The second is *to*, the third *in*, and the fifth *on*.) Both *of* and *for* are exclusively prepositions, never functioning as adverbs. They are generally pronounced as proclitic to the following NP.

At first blush, *of* and *for* might appear to show rather different grammatical proclivities. Indeed, around two-thirds of the occurrences for *of* are within an NP (for example, *a bottle of beer, his habit of spitting*) and only one-third in other grammatical contexts (for instance, *Simon repented of his misdeeds*). In contrast, only about one-sixth of the occurrences of *for* are within an NP (an example is *Anton's passion for music*), with the remainder being spread across a wide swathe of constructions (*Amelie posed for the artist, Harry was blamed for the crash*).

However, there are contexts in which they might seem to be interchangeable. When writing the preceding paragraph concerning how the two prepositions occur, there were alternative ways of phrasing available to me:

(1a)   the occurrences of *of*...   OR   (1b)   the occurrences for *of*...

(2a)   the occurrences of *for*...   OR   (2b)   the occurrences for *for*...

I chose to use (1b) and (2a) in order to avoid immediately repeating a preposition (which would be confusing for the reader, and also infelicitous). The implications of this are discussed in section 5.5, at the very end of the chapter.

One interesting context in which *of* and *for* appear to be substitutable is in the titles for ministers. In the Australian Federal Government (and also in the United Kingdom and in Papua New Guinea) every ministerial title uses *for*. In contrast, all ministerial titles in Canada (also in South Africa, India and Nigeria) have *of*. For example:

AUSTRALIA	CANADA
Minister for Health	Minister of Health
Minister for the Environment and Energy	Minister of Environment and Climate Change

New Zealand may be unique in employing *of* for some ministries and *for* in the case of others. For example:

NEW ZEALAND

Minister of Health

Minister for the Environment

Minister for Climate Change

In total, New Zealand has 28 'Ministers of' and 37 'Ministers for'. In section 5.4 there is discussion of the criteria for choice of preposition within ministerial titles in New Zealand.

However, in most contexts, *of* and *for* show quite different meanings. Compare:

The manager spoke of the athlete

The manager spoke for the athlete

The first sentence, with *of*, indicates the topic (or issue) that the manager was talking about—the athlete's fitness, or their achievements, or whatever. In contrast, the sentence with *for* states that the manager spoke on behalf of the athlete, in place of them. It gives the reason that the manager spoke but provides no information as to what was said.

Let us now compare NPs:

a house of worship

a house for worship

The first NP tells what sort of house it is; probably the building is sanctified, and all that happens there is worship. In contrast, *a house for worship* indicates a house—perhaps someone's private residence—which may be used for the purpose of worship.

In essence, an NP following *of* indicates the issue involved, while a comparable NP following *for* is likely to specify reason or purpose. This contrast in meaning can be illustrated with pairs of sentences. Note that *for* indicates reason in the first two, and purpose in the last two.

The judge acquitted Simon of murder
(*of* introduces the issue concerning which Simon was acquitted)
The judge punished Simon for murder
(*for* introduces the reason concerning which Simon was punished)

Samantha accused John of corruption
(*of* introduces the issue concerning which John was accused)
Samantha denounced John for corruption
(*for* introduces the reason concerning which John was denounced)

Ian is scared of meeting his girlfriend's parents
(*of* introduces the issue concerning which Ian is scared)
Ian is prepared for meeting his girlfriend's parents
(*for* introduces the purpose concerning which Ian is prepared)

Dr Smith is capable of helping the wounded
(*of* introduces the issue concerning which Dr Smith is capable)
Dr Jones is available for helping the wounded
(*for* introduces the purpose concerning which Dr Jones is available)

These examples provide an initial glimpse into the meanings of the two relational prepositions, ahead of the detailed discussions in sections 5.2 and 5.3. Before entering into these, it will be instructive to examine a couple of recurrent contexts in which they feature.

5.1 Contrastive uses

English often has alternative means of expression for a given concept, through cognate forms in different word classes. For example, *respect*, *desire*, and *scorn* each functions both as a verb and as a noun, with derived adjectives *respectful*, *desirous*, and *scornful*. There are three different forms in verb *appreciate*, noun *appreciation*, and adjective *appreciative*. From noun *contempt* is derived adjective *contemptuous*, and from adjective *fond* is derived noun *fondness*.

An interesting feature of English grammar is that, in a fair number of instances where there are related noun and adjective, the noun is followed by *for* and the adjective by *of*. For example:

> Luke showed respect for the family's customs
> Luke was respectful of the family's customs

> Mark exhibited contempt for John's paintings
> Mark was contemptuous of John's paintings

Further examples include:

NOUN + for	ADJECTIVE + of
show a desire for —	be desirous of —
demonstrate scorn for —	be scornful of —
have a fondness for —	be fond of —
display appreciation for —	be appreciative of —
have a capacity for —	be capable of —

In each instance, the adjective is used as copula complement and describes an attitude of the referent of the copula subject; the issue to which the adjective relates is introduced by preposition *of*. The corresponding noun functions—in these examples—as object of a transitive verb and takes an NP introduced by *for*, which states the reason for the mental attitude. If Mary says that she likes Fred's chocolate cake she is displaying appreciation for his cooking of this item. If she always thinks his cooking is good then she is appreciative of it. And similarly in other cases.

It must be noted that not all noun/adjective pairs behave like this. For some, *for* must be used in both cases. For example *show gratitude for* and *be grateful for*; this concept requires a reason to be stated, introduced by *for*. And for a few pairs both noun and adjective require *of*. For example, *show an awareness of* and *be aware of*; there can be no reason (or purpose) involved here, just a statement of which issue the awareness relates to, and this is introduced by *of*.

* * *

English has a goodly array of processes for deriving nouns from verbs. We can here focus on nominalisations which describe activities. A wide range of suffixes are found in these derivations, including *-ion/-ation/-tion/-ition, -ment, -ance/-ence, -ing, -al, -red*, and *-ure*.

The derivation goes as follows:

CLAUSE	X$_{\text{SUBJECT}}$	transitive.verb	Y$_{\text{OBJECT}}$	
→ NOUN PHRASE	X's	nominalised.verb	preposition	Y

In the majority of instances, the preposition is *of*. For example

> Oswald assassinated Kennedy
> Alan told me about [Oswald's assassination of Kennedy]

> The minister announced an enquiry
> We heard [the minister's announcement of an enquiry]

> Fiona demonstrated the new computer
> [Fiona's demonstration of the new computer] impressed the
>   committee

There are many other examples, covering verbs of almost every semantic type. They include:

transportation of	arrangement of	installation of	acceptance of
employment of	destruction of	seizure of	punishment of
development of	recognition of	management of	organisation of
understanding of	postponement of	prevention of	imitation of

Each of the nominalisations just quoted involves *of*, not *for*. However, there are a few nominalisations which most often take *for*, rather than *of*. For example:

> Frank prefers redheads
> Jason deplores [Frank's preference for redheads]

> Judy admires strong men
> [Judy's admiration for strong men] is well-known

It seems that nominalisations of verbs describing some positive aspect of liking generally take *for* rather than *of*; another example is *reverence for*. (Although not a nominalisation, *affection for* belongs in this set.) The nominalisation *liking* is found most often with *for*, although there are a few instances with *of*.

Interestingly, verbs describing negative correspondents to liking tend to prefer *of*. For example, *hatred of* is more common than *hatred for*. And *of* is greatly preferred after the nominalisations *detestation*, *abhorrence*, and *loathing*.

In summary, most activity nominalisations of transitive verbs mark the erstwhile object NP with *of*. There are just a few exceptions: positive verbs of liking show a strong preference for use of *for*.

This may be because such verbs express an affirmative mental outlook (similar to *wish for*, *long for*, *hope for*) which is associated with the purpose sense of preposition *for*.

There is another type of nominalisation, with opposite orientation. Recapitulating, we can have:

> Oswald assassinated Kennedy

(a)   Oswald's assassination of Kennedy

> (Oswald was the perpetrator; subject of the underlying transitive sentence)

Oswald's can be replaced with *the*, which then leads to a quite different nominalisation:

> The assassination of Kennedy (by Oswald)

(b)   Kennedy's assassination (by Oswald)

> (Kennedy was the victim, object of the underlying transitive sentence)

The following question might then be asked. How, on hearing talk of *X's assassination*, can one tell whether X was the villain, as in (a), or the victim, as in (b)? By the fact that in (a) '*of NP*' must be included whereas in (b) it cannot be included. (Here *by Oswald* is an optional extra.)

Many other transitive verbs allow two nominalisations in this way. For example: *Rome's destruction of Carthage* alongside *Carthage's destruction (by Rome)*, and *the chairman's postponement of the meeting*, together with *the meeting's postponement (by the chairman)*.

5.2 *Of*

The preposition *of* has a considerable range of uses, which will be discussed one by one.

5.2a Possession (in a wide sense)

We abbreviate the possessor as 'R' and the possessed as 'D' (based on the final letter of each). There are two ways of showing a possessive relationship—by an NP with the structure 'D of R' or by an NP with the structure 'R's D'. Sometimes only one of these is allowable, other times either.

5.2a-1 Ownership

Here the R owns the D, and may sell it or give it away.

> [The house of the manager] is up for sale
> [The manager's house] is up for sale

5.2a-2 Creatorship

Trotsky wrote (that is, created) his autobiography. One could then say:

> I just bought [the autobiography of Trotsky]
> I just bought [Trotsky's autobiography]

This is not in fact an instance of possession but it is included here since it is sometimes difficult to distinguish between Ownership and Creatorship. For instance *John's picture* could be a picture owned by John, or a picture painted by John.

5.2a-3 Association

This can involve kinship, or just a social relationship.

> [The sister of our neighbour] just walked by
> [Our neighbour's sister] just walked by

> [The best friend of Uncle Harry] just died
> [Uncle Harry's best friend] just died

Other nouns in this category include all kinship terms plus *relative, ally, disciple, enemy, opponent,* and *favourite.*

5.2a-4 Material part

This includes all body parts and parts of houses, artefacts, etc. Also *front, end, inside, piece, share, specimen, example,* and so on.

> [The injured foot of the bishop] is swollen
> [The bishop's injured foot] is swollen
>
> [The front tyre of the bicycle] needs to be repaired
> [The bicycle's front tyre] needs to be repaired

5.2a-5 Attribute

These include *taste, smell, sensation, height, width, texture, speed, age, health, history, temper, anger, kindness, generosity, luck, honesty, patience, opinion, idea,* and the like.

> I dislike [the bad smell of that youth]
> I dislike [that youth's bad smell]
>
> [The remarkable generosity of the king] was commented on
> [The king's remarkable generosity] was commented on

5.2a-6 Object nominalisations

There was description, at the end of the last section, of a type of nominalisation founded on the erstwhile object of a transitive verb. This has nothing to do with possession but it does employ the same alternatives, with *of* and *'s*. On the basis of *Cromwell executed King Charles*, we can get:

> [The execution of King Charles] was long overdue
> [King Charles's execution] was long overdue

From *Dr Smith organised the conference* there are nominalisations:

> [The organisation of the conference] was strongly criticised
> [The conference's organisation] was strongly criticised

* * *

Corresponding to the examples in sections 5.2a-1 and 5.2a-3–6, the verb *have* may be used to establish a possessive relationship. For instance *The manager has a house, The bicycle has a front tyre, That youth has a bad smell*. Note that *have* is typically used to draw attention to something significant; for example, one would be unlikely to hear *The bishop has feet*, whereas *The bishop has an injured foot* states something which is noteworthy.

5.2a-7 Contrasting *of* and *'s*

The example sentences just given were carefully chosen so that 'D of R' and 'R's D' would each be reasonably acceptable. However this is by no means always so. A number of general principles guide the use of these alternatives.

First, 'R's D' is generally preferred when R has human (or higher animate) reference. Thus, in a neutral context, one would be more likely to say *the manager's house* rather than *the house of the manager* (although the latter is perfectly acceptable). Similarly for the other examples with a human R.

Extending from this, when R is the proper name of a person, there is a very strong preference for 'R's D'. One would say *Mary's house* rather than *the house of Mary*; *Jim's sister* rather than *the sister of Jim*; and so on. The preference becomes absolute when a pronoun is used; one can only say *my house* and *your sister*, never **the house of me*, or **the sister of you*.

If you were enquiring about a book, you could use either alternative:

What is the title of the book? OR What is the book's title?

However, if you wanted to know how to address Uncle Jim (whether as *Doctor, Professor,* or just *Mr*), you could only ask:

What is Uncle Jim's title?

The alternative, **What is the title of Uncle Jim?*, is simply not felicitous.

The second condition on the use of 'R's D' relates to grammar. In the modifier slot within an NP in English we can have just one of the following: article, demonstrative, possessive phrase. Thus, one can say *a table, this table, Horace's table,* or *my table*, but not **a this table*, or **this Horace's table*, or **a my table*.

In all the examples given thus far the D has been specific and definite. In each 'D of R' construction, the statement of D preceding *of* begins with *the*. In the 'R's D' alternative, *the* cannot be included before D, since article and possessive NP are mutually exclusive. However, it is always implicit that D is definite (just as if *the* had been included).

Matters are quite different when D is indefinite, marked by article *a* in the 'D of R' construction.

We can first compare the possibilities when R is inanimate:

DEFINITE D   [The front tyre of the bicycle] needs to be repaired

INDEFINITE D   [A tyre of the bicycle] needs to be repaired

There is also a definite 'R's D' construction, where speaker and addressee know which tyre is being referred to:

DEFINITE D   [The bicycle's front tyre] needs to be repaired

However, there is no 'R's D' correspondent of the indefinite sentence with *of*. One cannot say *A bicycle's tyre needs to be repaired*. (One could say *A bicycle tyre needs to be repaired* but this just refers to some tyre of some bicycle, not a tyre of the bicycle which speaker and addressee are discussing.)

Matters are rather different when R is a person's name or a pronoun. We can compare the two ways of expressing possession for a definite D, and the single technique for an indefinite one:

DEFINITE D   the plays of Shakespeare   OR   Shakespeare's plays

INDEFINITE D   a play of Shakespeare's

For a definite construction one can use either *of* or *'s*, but not both. The indefinite construction combines these: 'a D of R's'. (*A play of Shakespeare* is not acceptable.) The D comes at the beginning of the NP and may be preceded by indefinite article *a* or by a demonstrative. One can say *a sister of Jim's*, or *that sister of Jim's*, or *this sister of Jim's*. Or the D, *sister*, could be preceded by a longer qualifier, as in:

[One of those sisters of Jim's] spread the gossip

[Any sister of Jim's] is welcome here

Yesterday I encountered [that same sister of Jim's]

The interesting point is that, in a neutral context, one can not use the definite article in this construction and say *the sister of Jim's*. It must be just *Jim's sister*.

(*The sister of Jim's* is only possible in special circumstances; for example, within a restricted relative clause construction such as *The sister of Jim's who was rude to you has just come into the room*.)

The combined construction is also used when the R is a pronoun, which then adopts possessive form; for example, *a friend of yours, that sister of mine* (not **a friend of you, *that sister of me*).

When R involves a common noun with human (or higher animate) reference, then the combined construction—using both *of* and *'s*—is possible and also optional. Both *a friend of my brother's* and *a friend of my brother* are acceptable; similarly with *that house of the manager's* and *that house of the manager*. Note that the combined construction is not allowed if the referent of R is inanimate; one cannot say **a tyre of the bicycle's*.

The third factor determining which possessive construction is to be used comes from discourse structure. Except in linguistics textbooks, a sentence seldom occurs in isolation, but rather as part of a flowing discourse built around a 'topic'. If R is the topic for that part of a discourse in which a possessive construction appears, then the 'R's D' alternative will be preferred; and if D is the topic, then the 'D of R' alternative is most suitable.

This can be illustrated for two stretches of discourse which both include a clause referring to *the management* as D and *the park* as R. In the first extract *the management* is the topic:

> The councillors began by discussing the management of the
>   orphanage, then they had a heated argument concerning
>   the management of the cemetery, and finally dwelt on the
>   management of the park.

It is *the management* which continues an established topic, with *the park* being the new information provided in the last clause. In this case, *the management of the park* is the preferred possessive construction. In the next extract it is *the park* which is the continuing topic, with the last clause introduction *management* as new information. Here, *the park's management* is the preferred possessive construction:

> The councillors discussed the park's development,
>   and the park's role as an oasis of quiet within the city,
>   before praising the park's management.

The topic running through a part of a discourse is far more often human than it is non-human. And it is more likely to be in R than in D function, leading to the 'R's D' construction being preferred. This correlates with the first principle, given a couple of pages back, that when R has human (or higher animate) reference then 'R's D' is generally preferred.

It is often pointed out that, when R is a very long NP, then the 'D of R' construction is preferred. It is easier for a listener to process something like *the gun of that evil character who lives in the tumbledown shack down the road* than an NP where the possessive marker *'s* is distant from the head of its NP, as in *that evil character who lives in the tumbledown shack down the road's gun.*

This is, in fact, covered by the discourse condition. Statement of a topic is likely to be short and succinct (indeed it is often just an anaphoric pronoun), whereas 'new information' may well be a lengthy NP. If a short D is the topic, then the 'D of R' alternative is the one to use.

The choice of possessive construction can have pragmatic implications. In 2018 I wrote a book intended for the general public and wanted to call it *The original languages of Australia*. The publisher was worried that this 'sounds a bit like an intimidating university press handbook' and suggested that *Australia's original languages* 'looks more user-friendly'. I agreed that the shorter title would be more likely to engage the interest of a bookshop browser.

5.2b Expansion

A rather different meaning for an NP 'X of Y' is where Y states what type of X is being referred to.

A: We're going to an exhibition
B: What sort of exhibition?
A: An exhibition of Indonesian tapestries

A: We're hoping to solve the mystery
B: The mystery of what?
A: The mystery of Agatha's disappearance

Among the many other examples illustrating this use for *of*, the following can be mentioned:

the island of Crete	a reward of $1000	a model of the Titanic
a house of cards	a house of worship	the idea of liberty

a cry of pain	the problems of the age	an outbreak of cholera
a habit of interrupting	a diagnosis of cancer	a theory of economics
men of science	activities of the army	reminiscences of the war
a tour of the state rooms	the sound of music	the picture of the castle

Generally, these *of* constructions cannot be rephrased with *'s*. However, this may sometimes be possible if the NP following *of* has human reference. If someone paints John, then this can be referred to as *the picture of John* or as *John's picture*. (Note that *the picture of the castle* would be unlikely to be rephrased as **the castle's picture*, since a castle is not human.)

It was mentioned earlier that *John's picture* has two other senses—Ownership and Creatorship. The three meanings clearly contrast:

	OWNERSHIP	CREATORSHIP	EXPANSION
underlying clause	John has the picture	John painted the picture	John sat for the picture
definite NP with *'s*	John's picture	John's picture	John's picture
definite NP with *of*	—	—	the picture of John
indefinite NP	a picture of John's	a picture of John's	a picture of John

Although all three form the same definite NP with *'s* (*John's picture*) only the Expansion sense can be in a definite NP with *of*. And while the indefinite NPs for Ownership and Creatorship are *a picture of John's*, that for the Expansion sense is *a picture of John*.

5.2c Quantifying

Another type of 'X of Y' NP involves X indicating the quantity or sort or nature of Y. Many number words can be used alone or followed by *of the*. Compare *three of the cats* which describes three chosen from an understood set of cats, with *three cats* which refers to any three cats. Apart from numbers, this type of quantifier includes:

many (of the)   most (of the)   several (of the)

plenty (of the)   a dozen (of the)   any (of the)   some (of the)

Other quantifiers always require *of*, and can also take *of the* to indicate selection from a specific set of items. For example:

> I bought a couple of horses
>
> I bought a couple of the horses (which Fiona had for sale)

Others in this set include:

hundreds of (the)   plenty of (the)   dozens of (the)

a lot of (the)   a number of (the)

And also epistemic terms such as *possibility of, probability of, chance of, prospect of,* and *risk of.*

This sense of the preposition *of* also includes an X which specifies the nature or organisation of the Y. For example:

a flood of tears   a dash of salt   a packet of biscuits

a bunch of flowers   a wave of enthusiasm   a stroke of luck

a chorus of angels   a trace of jealousy   a snatch of conversation

a school of fish   a slip of a girl   a brute of a man

a slab of cheese   a drop of water   a cup of water

Note this sense of the preposition can never be rephrased with *'s*. One can say *Please pass me the cup of water*, but not **Please pass me the water's cup*.

The prepositional verb *consist of* (see section 4.1e-2) relates to this sense of preposition *of*.

The distinction between senses (here, and elsewhere) is never watertight. For example, *a burst of laughter* could be characterised as Expansion—what sort of burst is it?—or as Quantification—what unit of laughter is it?

5.2d Relationship

A further type of 'X of Y' typically occurs in a copula construction—either '[X of Y] is Z' or 'Z is [X of Y]'. Here X indicates the relationship of Z to Y; this may refer to spatial orientation, to origin, or to reason.

The island is [(three miles) north of the harbour]

Sean is [a native of Canada]

This cheese is [a product of France]

[The purpose of the march] was to demonstrate our disapproval of the new law

The austerity proposals were [the cause of the riots]

Jaimie's success was [the result of hard work]

[The implication of that decision] is that half the workforce will be laid off

Constructions with a similar meaning may have a verb followed by *of*; for example, *Ming was born of Chinese parents* and *Dennis died of cancer*. Another kind of relationship is shown in *Jane and Bert are of the same age* and *Jim and Nell are of the same opinion*.

5.2e Focusing on a quality

We can compare the following pairs of sentences, one of which is another example of the 'X of Y' construction:

A valuable artefact	An artefact of value
A regrettable matter	A matter of regret
An interesting topic	A topic of interest
An amusing subject	A subject of amusement
A pitiful object	An object of pity

In the left-hard column there is a noun modified by an adjective. On the right-hand side we have the same head noun, but instead of a preceding adjective, it is now modified by *of* plus a noun corresponding to the adjective. This serves to focus attention on the quality involved—*value* or *regret* or *interest*, and so on.

A number of recurrent modifying phrases are on this pattern—*of merit, of the first water, of note, of no value, of no interest, of no concern, of no account, of no use*, extending to: *of necessity, of the opinion that...*, and *of a mind to...*.

5.2f Feelings, attitude, or competence

This sense of the preposition *of* relates to a clause, not just to an NP. It describes the feelings, or attitude, or competence of a person (referent of verbal subject or copula subject) towards an issue (which is stated after *of*). The nature of the feelings can be expressed by an adjective, a noun, or a verb, as in:

ADJECTIVE   Harry is afraid of snakes

NOUN   Harry has a horror of snakes

VERB   (You) beware of snakes!

    Beware (of) is an interesting verb in that it is only found in imperative form (or indirect imperative, as in: *Harry was told to beware of snakes*).
    There are a number of ways in which the feelings may eventuate.

5.2f-1 The issue arouses feelings in the subject

The three sentences just quoted illustrate this sense. It is also shown by a number of adjectives, as in:

    Jenny is ashamed of her rudeness

also *frightened of, scared of, wary of, terrified of, tired of, weary of*, and more. And by nouns *dread of* and *fear of*.

5.2f-2 The subject has a certain property with respect to the issue

This is shown by an adjective:

    George is guilty of the crime

    Hannah is worthy of the honour

Other adjectives with this property include *deserving of, innocent of, capable of*, and *incapable of*. There is also noun *knack*, as in *He has the knack of summing things up succinctly*. The idioms *have no hope of* and *make an example of* also relate to this sense.

5.2f-3 The subject has feelings (or an attitude) towards the issue

This can involve a verb or an adjective:

    Mavis boasts of her daughter's success

    Mavis is proud of her daughter's success

Other adjectives with this sense include:

confident of	hopeful of	convinced of	desirous of
optimistic of	certain of	sure of	unsure of
tolerant of	respectful of	critical of	contemptuous of
scornful of	jealous of	fond of	appreciative of

Verbs with this sense include *complain of, despair of, repent of*, plus prepositional verbs *approve of*, and *disapprove of*. Note also noun *love*, as in *The miser has a great love of money, The despot demonstrates a love of power*.

A related meaning is where the subject adopts an attitude towards someone else in relation to the issue. For example:

> Sally suspected Tim of having stolen the diamond necklace
> The police accused Tim of the theft

Or the verb may refer not to an attitude but to an activity:

> The judge convicted/acquitted Tim of theft

5.2f-4 The subject has a specialised competence with respect to the issue

> The duke is a collector of Ming china

Similar nouns include *connoisseur of, exponent of, judge of, proponent of*.

5.2g Knowledge

This again involves a clause, and it describes the subject having an awareness of the issue. It can involve adjective, noun, or verb:

> Mildred is aware of the decision
> Mildred has knowledge of the decision
> Mildred knows of the decision

There is a critical contrast between *Mildred knows the decision* (she knows what has been decided) and *Mildred knows of the decision* (she knows that a decision has been arrived at, but not what it is). Similarly for *read* and *read of, hear* and *hear of, approve* and *approve of*.

This meaning is also shown by adjectives *unaware of, ignorant of, conscious of,* and *mindful of,* by verbs *speak of, think of,* and *dream of,* and by nouns *impression of, memory of.*

Also within this sense, an *of* phrase may be added to a transitive clause, with the referent of the subject making the referent of the object become aware of the issue:

> Mildred informed father of the decision

Also *remind (someone) of, advise (someone) of, warn (someone) of, tell (someone) of, notify (someone) of.* Adjective *reminiscent of*—as in *The way Caroline smiles is reminiscent of her mother*—has similar meaning.

5.2h Dissociation

As mentioned at the beginning of this chapter, in Old English *of* meant 'away from', 'out of', 'from', or 'off'. This sense of the preposition comes through into modern usage.

A number of verbs refer to 'taking away'. For example:

> The trickster defrauded Paul of his life savings
>
> The policeman relieved Simon of his gun
>
> The court cleared Tina of any responsibility for the malfunction
>
> The corrupt politician demanded ten per cent of the profits

Also *rob (someone) of, divest (oneself/someone) of.* And prepositional verb *dispose of,* which was discussed in section 4.2a. Also *deprive (someone) of (something),* one of the few phrasal verbs which includes *of.* The idiom *ask a favour of* seems to belong here.

This sense of the preposition appears also to apply for a sentence such as:

> The doctors cured Andrew of his paranoid obsession

Prepositional verb *partake of* (for example, a share of the profits, the choicest dishes at a feast) involves 'taking from' and may also belong here.

A similar sense, of 'lacking' is found with a number of adjectives. For example:

> The burnt-out plains are now destitute of inhabitants
>
> After the spraying, the lawn is free of weeds
>
> He has a good salary and is now independent of his parents

Also *void of, irrespective of,* and idioms such as *hard of hearing.*

In British English a time of 8.55 would be stated as *five to nine.* However, in some parts of the USA it would be rendered as *five of nine;* literally 'five lacking from nine' (reflecting the meaning of preposition *of* in Old English). See sections 14.6b and 15.3a.

5.2i Special constructions with of

There are three special grammatical constructions for which *of* is an integral element.

(i) Derived adjective plus *of*. There was discussion in section 5.1 of activity nominalisations where the original object of the transitive verb is marked by *of* in most instances, by *for* in some, and *by* either in a few. A quite different process derives adjectives from transitive verbs describing a mental attitude, by the addition of *-ful* or *-ous;* the original object of the transitive verb is then marked by *of*. That is:

$$X_{\text{SUBJECT}} \text{ transitive.verb } Y_{\text{OBJECT}}$$
$$\rightarrow \quad X_{\text{COPULA.SUBJECT}} \text{ copula.verb [derived.adjective } of \text{ Y]}_{\text{COPULA.COMPLEMENT}}$$

For example:

Mary doubts the truth of his statement
→   Mary is doubtful of the truth of his statement

He envied her success
→   He was envious of her success

Similar adjectival derivations include:

forgetful of   resentful of   fearful of
respectful of   neglectful of   covetous of

(ii) *It was clever of Susan*. In each of the following pairs, the two sentences have essentially the same meaning:

Susan was clever in solving the problem
It was clever of Susan to solve the problem

The dean was generous in paying for the lunch
It was generous of the dean to pay for the lunch

The second sentence of each pair exemplifies a rather limited construction that begins with '*It is/was* ADJECTIVE' followed by *of* plus an NP with human reference. The adjective will belong to the semantic types human propensity (for example: *stupid, kind, cruel, honest*) or qualification (*correct, right, wrong, sensible*).

(iii) *A woman of experience*. A certain quality may be expressed through either adjective or noun (but with a slight difference of emphasis):

> Jane is an experienced woman
> Jane is a woman of experience

> Brutus is an honourable man
> Brutus is a man of honour

The second sentence of each pair exemplifies a special and rather limited construction: 'Z is an X of Y', such that:

- Z has human reference, typically being a personal name.
- X is generally restricted to *man, woman,* or *person* (perhaps also *boy, girl*).
- Y refers to a positive quality. For example: *honesty, intelligence, sense, wisdom, charm, grace, beauty, loyalty, generosity, mercy, strength*. (But not *dishonesty, foolishness, stupidity, ugliness, meanness, weakness,* or other negative terms.)

5.2j Of *repeated*

For several of the Possession senses there can be an *of* phrase within an *of* phrase within an *of* phrase, and so on. For example, *The red car of the friend of the brother of our neighbour*. Alternatively, '*s*-constructions could be employed: *Our neighbour's brother's friend's red car*.

For the Expansion sense, the following are all acceptable:

> The disappearance of Agatha
> Agatha's disappearance.
> The mystery of the disappearance of Agatha
> The mystery of Agatha's disappearance.

However, one would not hear *Agatha's disappearance's mystery* since an abstract NP such as *Agatha's disappearance* is not suitable as R in an 'R's D' construction.

Of course many types of NP can include either 'NP's' or 'of NP' as modifier to the head noun, producing many combinations which involve *of* in its varied senses. For example:

QUALIFYING within   [a couple of [horses of good breeding]]

QUANTIFYING   [a packet of [biscuits of dubious quality]]

And there are many other possible combinations.

5.2k Optional of

Complex prepositions *out-of, off-of, inside-of* and *outside-of* have *of* as the final element. *Of* is also by far the most frequent final component of phrasal prepositions. In each case the preposition is proclitic to the following NP.

It is interesting to compare the use of prepositions with and without a final *of* when referring to location or motion or time. First, *out* and *out-of* with sample examples of use:

LOCATION	Janet lives out-of town	final *of* is obligatory
MOTION	Mabel threw it out(-of) the window	final *of* may be omitted
TEMPORAL	The speaker ran out-of time	final *of* is obligatory

Now *inside* and *inside-of*:

LOCATION	You'll find the key inside(-of) the box	final *of* is optional
MOTION	Mark went inside the house	no final *of*
TEMPORAL	You must return inside(-of) an hour	final *of* is optional

From this we see that final *of* is associated with the location and temporal meanings, not with the motion meaning.

Another pair is *off* and *off-of*. As mentioned in sections 9.2b and 15.2d, I am unable to say much about when each of these two forms is to be preferred over the other. However, it does seem that *off-of* is more likely when referring to time, as in *The hurdler cut two seconds off-of his previous best time*; this agrees with the results for *out(-of)* and *inside(-of)*.

From the other observations above we might expect that *off-of* should be more common for location and plain *off* for motion. However, the investigations I have been able to conduct do not confirm this. Further study is needed.

5.21 Other uses

A number of adverbs take on the function of phrasal prepositions by adding *of*; they include *ahead-of*, and *in-front-of* (see section 11.2b–c). There are many more, which fall outside the scope of this book; for instance: *on-top-of, on-behalf-of, in-the-name-of, in-lieu-of, in-view-of, in-consequence-of, by-means-of, for fear-of, for-the-sake-of, for-want-of, in-spite-of, on-behalf-of, in-support-of,* and *on-condition-of.*

Because is a most interesting word. It is basically a conjunction with the meaning 'reason', linking two clauses:

> [Alex cancelled the barbecue]_{CLAUSE} because [rain was falling]_{CLAUSE}

However, the second component can be an NP, rather than a clause, and *because* then adds *of* to make itself into a phrasal preposition *because-of*:

> [Alex cancelled the barbecue]_{CLAUSE} because-of [the rain]_{NP}

Section 14.1c has further discussion of *because* and *because-of*, comparing them with the use of *since* as a conjunction indicating 'consequence'.

There are a number of other phrasal prepositions with similar meaning to *because-of*. They too must be followed by an NP—*by-reason-of, on-account-of, in-consequence-of,* and *as-a-consequence-of*.

Instead functions as a conjunction, either alone or following *but* or *and*:

> [The kitchen should have been cleaned yesterday]_{CLAUSE}, (but) instead [it was left dirty]_{CLAUSE}
> [Jim couldn't make a chocolate cake]_{CLAUSE} and instead [Maria prepared a pavlova]_{CLAUSE}

Similar to *because*, *instead* adds *of* to form a preposition, *instead-of*. This can link clause and NP, like *because*, and it can also link components within an NP:

[Denise will give the vote of thanks]$_{CLAUSE}$ instead-of [David]$_{NP}$

Next year I'm going to play [[hockey] instead-of [football]]$_{NP}$

The two most common prepositions, *of* and *to*, are gradually expanding their ranges of use. *Of* is moving in a rather surprising direction. The reduced form, *'ve*, of auxiliary *have* is being replaced by *of*. That is, some people have replaced *I would have done it* by *I would of done it*. The phonological form is the same: /'ai 'wud=əv 'dʌn=it/. Preposition *of*, generally a proclitic /əv=/ to the following word, is here an enclitic /=əv/ to the preceding word, being phonologically identical to *'ve*, /=əv/.

5.3 *For*

A range of senses can be distinguished for the preposition *for*; however, these do tend to merge together.

5.3a *Benefit*

Here, a peripheral NP 'for Y'—where Y has human (or higher animate) reference—indicates that the activity described by the core clause is for the benefit of Y.

It could be that Y comes to own something (this will be referent of the object NP of the clause):

Ursula knitted a pullover for Jules

(then Jules would own it)

The shopkeeper ordered a special item for Maria

(then Maria could buy it and own it)

The butcher gave the bone to Donald for his dog

(then Donald would give it to the dog and the dog would have it)

This scarf is for my wife

(I am intending to give it to her, then she will own it)

Or it could be that the referent of the subject argument does something on behalf of Y, which saves Y from having to do it:

Yvonne filled in the form for Algy

(then Algy didn't have to fill it in himself)

Or the referent of the subject may do something which benefits Y:

> John testified in court for his friend
>> (John spoke of the friend's good character, which might assist his acquittal)

> Adam posed for the artist
>> (so that the artist could paint him)

> Fiona devised a timetable for the new school
>> (so that the teachers and students of the school would know where to go and when)

> The theatre has designated spaces for wheelchairs
>> (where they can be placed, so that their occupants can watch the play)

5.3b Reason

Here 'for Y' provides an explanation concerning what is stated in the core clause. There are several possibilities.

5.3b-1 The reason for the subject's mental attitude

This can be expressed by verb, adjective, or noun. For example:

VERB	Mark apologised for being late
	Melinda thanked James for the flowers
ADJECTIVE	Melinda was grateful for the flowers
	Tom was anxious for his wife's safety
NOUN	Deidre felt shame for having been rude to Aunt Daphne
	Stella has a passion for dancing

5.3b-2 The reason for the subject's attitude towards someone

This is expressed by a transitive verb:

> We blamed Chris for the breakdown
> The general cited Clive for courage
> They congratulated Sam for doing so well
> The committee denounced Judas for treason

5.3b-3 The reason for the subject having a certain quality

This may involve an adjective or a noun:

ADJECTIVE   Rio is notorious for its high rate of murder
            Michael is famous for his jokes
NOUN   Paula received an award for bravery
            Robin has a reputation for honesty

5.3b-4 The reason for the subject undertaking some activity:

The surgeon operated on Judith for appendicitis
The policeman inspected the apartment for fingerprints
Isaac is studying for the examination

5.3b-5 The reason why the referent of an abstract noun is needed:

(She received) a prize for mathematics
(You'll need) a permit for the gun
(His adultery is) grounds for divorce
(It's certainly) an occasion for celebration

5.3b-6 The reason for a certain quality being ascribed to the subject:

The quality is shown by an adjective:

That tool is suitable for the task in hand
This fruit is ripe for eating
Your dress is perfect for the occasion

Other adjectives here include: *essential for, necessary for, satisfactory for, sufficient for, adequate for, appropriate for, available for, eligible for, good for, useful for.* Verbs *qualify for* and *suffice for* have a similar meaning, and so do the nouns as in: *be (good) value for, be an opportunity for.*

There are many semi-idiomatic adverbial phrases involving *for* which are associated with Reason. For example: *for effect, for a change, for no reason.*

5.3c Purpose

Here, 'for Y' describes a purpose or potentiality which the statement in the core clause is oriented towards. The subject predominantly has human reference.

5.3c-1 Ability to achieve a purpose

This is shown by adjectives and by nouns:

ADJECTIVE   Edmund is getting fit for the climb ahead

NOUN   Hilary has an aptitude for mathematics

Also: *ready for, prepared for, a flair for, a talent for, a facility for*, and *a capacity for*, among others.

5.3c-2 Attention directed towards a goal

This sense relates to verbs:

> We listened for a creaking sound
> They searched for the missing hiker
> I'm waiting for the postman

5.3c-3 An action directed towards a goal

This can involve speech:

> Johnny asked for a bow and arrow
> The people clamoured for justice
> He called for a doctor

Or some other social activity:

> They voted for change
> He appealed for mercy
> They sued for damages
> You need to report for duty

Other verbs here include: *beg for, petition for, apply for*, and *volunteer for*.

5.3c-4 A potentiality of the referent of a noun

The potentiality is marked by preposition *for* within a copula complement:

> Knives are for cutting
> This house is for sale
> These workers are for hire
> These supplies are intended for the army
> This ticket is for the concert tonight

Alternatively 'X for Y' may constitute an NP, as in: *Are there [any houses for sale]?* and *I've lost [the ticket for the concert tonight], [The house for worship] is on the next corner.* Another kind of 'X for Y' NP is illustrated by:

It's [time for work]

5.3c-5 Destination

Motion generally has a purpose and the place headed for may be identified by a *for* phrase after a suitable verb:

The ship sailed for the Indies
I'm heading for the stadium

Further examples of this sense include: *set out for, start for, embark for, steer for, make for,* and *leave for.*

5.3c-6 Mental aspiration

Three word classes have a role here:

VERB	Margaret had wished for a daughter, but she produced a son
	Charles has always aimed for the highest honours
ADJECTIVE	Max is eager for new challenges
NOUN	Martha has a mania for travelling

A number of prepositional verbs, with *for* as the inherent preposition, fall into this category; they include *wish for, long for, hanker for,* and *yearn for.*

Activity nominalisations were discussed in section 5.1. Most are followed by *of*; for example, *The court's punishment of the criminals.* However, *for* is preferred with positive verbs of liking—such as *admiration for* and *preference for.* They relate to this sense.

* * *

The recognition of senses for the preposition *for* (as for other prepositions) is subjective and far from watertight. For example, *His adultery is grounds for divorce* and *This fruit is ripe for eating* were listed under Reason but they are equally examples of Purpose—the grounds are for the purpose of divorce, and the fruit being ripe means that it can be eaten.

5.3d As complementiser

In section 2.5c, there was illustration of how some verbs may have a core argument slot filled either by an NP or by a complement clause. There are three main varieties of complement clause in English. A THAT clause refers to a fact, an -ING clause to an extended activity, while a (FOR) TO clause describes a potentiality or intention—this is linked to the Purpose sense of *for*.

A complement clause is most frequently found in transitive object slot:

I have arranged [for Mary to visit the dentist tomorrow]

The subject of the complement clause, plus the preceding *for*, will be omitted if it has the same reference as the subject of the main clause:

I have arranged [to visit the dentist tomorrow]

A few verbs may have a complement clause in transitive subject slot:

[For Bernard to threaten to reveal the secret code] annoyed Nick

In such constructions, the complement clause is typically extraposed to the end of the clause, its slot before the verb being filled by *it*:

It annoyed Nick [for Bernard to threaten to reveal the secret code]

A complement clause may function as subject of a copula construction:

[For John to solve the problem] was [easy]
[For you to remain here] would be [the correct course of action]

Extraposition of the complement clause to the end of the main clause produces a frequent and distinctive kind of *for* construction:

It was [easy] [for John to solve the problem]
It would be [the correct course of action] [for you to remain here]

5.3e Exchange

A basic construction here is:

subject - verb - X (object) - for Y

This describes how the referent of the subject undertakes some activity (described by the verb) in which X is replaced by Y. The most straightforward examples involve exchange of one item for another:

> I exchanged my pen for John's pencil
>
> They substituted a fake necklace for the real thing

Corresponding to verb *exchange* there is the phrasal preposition *in-exchange-for*, as in *I got John's pencil in-exchange-for my pen*. The phrasal preposition *in-return-for* has a similar meaning; for example, *I received a smile from Maria in-return-for loudly applauding her song*.

In a monetary economy, an object can be accorded a cash price:

> Prue sold the book to Chris for $10
>
> The dealer bid $100 for the painting
>
> Simon was ordered to pay compensation (of $500) for the damage he had caused

Other verbs which appear in this construction include *owe*, *buy*, *rent*, and *hire*.

A related construction is:

> X (copula.subject) - copula.verb - copula.complement - for Y

Here the copula complement specifies the way in which X is a replacement for Y:

> Margarine is a good substitute for butter
>
> Gujagay is the Dyirbal name for crocodile
>
> UK is an abbreviation for United Kingdom
>
> Dick is short for Richard

Another example of this sense is seen in: *For every ten conscientious workers, you'll find one lazy one.*

5.3f Time (and space)

Temporal duration can be specified with a peripheral NP marked by *for*, which follows the core of the clause (see sections 14.6c and 14.6f). For example:

We went without food [for a week]

Mary visited her parents [for Christmas]

Lucy loved Peter [for six months] and hated him [for five years]

English grammar allows a preposition sometimes to be omitted from an NP commencing with a number word and indicating time. For example, any or all of *from*, *on*, *from*, and *at* may be left out from:

The shop is open [(from) nine till five] [(on) weekdays],

and [(from) ten till two] [(at) weekends]

This omission applies in the case of *for* phrases which describe the temporal duration of some habitual activity. *For* can be included in or omitted from:

Felix works [(for) four hours] each day

Mavis sleeps [(for) two hours longer than her sister]

This omission can extend to statement of spatial extent, again for some habitual activity:

Susan walks [(for) ten miles] every morning

And the omission of *for* is also possible for an NP (commencing with a number word) referring to some significant length of time attached to a statement of location:

I have lived/been in London [(for) ten years]

There are a considerable number of semi-idiomatic peripheral NPs with *for*, referring to various aspects of time. Some examples of this are:

CURRENT TIME:	for the present, for the time being
SHORT TIME:	for a bit, for a moment, for (only) a while
LONG TIME:	for ages, for ever, for keeps, for life
PLACE IN SEQUENCE:	for the first time, for the last time

5.3g Special constructions with for

There are two special grammatical constructions where *for* is an integral element.

5.3g-1 Comparison with a norm

In this construction, the referent of the copula subject is compared with the referent of the NP following *for*, with respect to the quality expressed by the adjective in copula complement function:

> Sandra is tall for a girl
>
> Tom is short for his age
>
> The weather is cold for this time of year
>
> Jerry is clever for a Laputian

The last sentence implies that Jerry is cleverer that one would expect a Laputian to be (cleverer than most Laputians). And similarly for the other examples.

5.3g-2 Mistaken identity

The construction here is:

> subject - take - X (object) - for Y

This indicates that the referent of the subject erroneously thought X was Y. Instead of *take*, the verb can be *mistake*, which reinforces the implication of error. For example:

> The duchess took me for the vicar/for a doctor/for a burglar
>
> He must have taken you for a fool
>
> I took it for wool (when it is actually synthetic fibre)
>
> Sorry, I took you for your twin brother
>
> She mistook Tom for a ghost

5.3h For *in phrasal verbs and prepositional verbs*

Preposition *of* occurs in only a handful of phrasal verbs and in a smallish number of prepositional verbs; these were mentioned within the general discussion of section 5.2.

Several dozen phrasal verbs include *for*. In keeping with its role as a relational preposition (never used as an adverb) *for* occurs only in slot **p** (not **a**) in phrasal verbs of the four types: V-p-NP, V-NP-p-NP, V-a-p-NP, and V-NP-a-p-NP. Each relates to one of the senses which has been described. This can be illustrated with a selection (as before, phrasal verbs are underlined).

- **Benefit**

V-a-p-NP   John always <u>sticks up for</u> his sister

V-a-p-NP   The accountant <u>stood in for</u> the manager while he was sick

- **Reason for some activity**

V-a-p-NP   We must <u>stand up for</u> justice

- **Purpose**
  — **Attention directed towards a goal**

V-p- NP   Hilary is <u>standing for</u> president

V-NP-a-p-NP   We're going to <u>put</u> Major Coles <u>in for</u> the top job

  — **Action directed towards a goal**

V-a-p-NP   The workers <u>held out for</u> more pay

V-NP-p-NP   The drunken cousin <u>touched</u> Cecil <u>for</u> a loan

  — **Potentiality**

V-a-p-NP   I'm not <u>cut out for</u> that sort of work

  — **Mental aspiration**

V-p-NP   Sheila has a <u>thirst for</u> adventure

- **Exchange**

V-p-NP   Michael <u>passed for</u> white

V-p-NP   I suggest that we <u>settle for</u> half the fee

The phrasal verb *fall for*, as in *The handsome prince <u>fell for</u> the pretty milkmaid* can be linked to *have a liking for*, discussed in section 5.1.

There are also a number of prepositional verbs with *for*. Again, their meanings accord with those described above. For example:

Benefit   She <u>vouched for</u> his loyalty

Reason   Douglas <u>atoned for</u> his negligence

Purpose   You shouldn't <u>strive for</u> perfection

5.3i Combining instances of *for*

There are many ways in which a sentence may include two (or more) *for* phrases. Sometimes the *for* phrases can occur in either order, as in:

BENEFIT + TEMPORAL DURATION

Fiona devised a timetable for the new school for the third term

OR   Fiona devised a timetable for the third term for the new school

But most often there is a preferred order. This applies in:

BENEFIT + REASON FOR SOME ACTIVITY

This scarf is for my wife for Christmas

DESTINATION + PURPOSE: ACTION DIRECTED TOWARDS A GOAL

The ship sailed for the Indies for spices

If the order of *for* phases were to be reversed in the last two examples, we would expect juxtapositional intonation (shown in writing by a comma). Another example is (5) at the beginning of chapter 1, where we had the preferred order: BENEFIT + EXCHANGE.

There may also be dependence between *for* components, as in:

ACTION [DIRECTED TOWARDS A GOAL [BENEFIT OF GOAL]]

The salesman called [for a doctor [for the customer who had collapsed]]

The action of 'calling for' is directed towards 'a doctor' who will be the person of benefit for 'the customer'.

5.3j Other uses

5.3j-1 In phrasal prepositions

For is the final component of several phrasal prepositions; in each instance it is proclitic to the following word.

In-exchange-for and *in-return-for* were mentioned in section 5.3e. *But-for* and *save-for* are discussed together with *except (for)* in section 6.4.

The list of phrasal prepositions ending in *of* which introduce adverbial phrases, given in section 5.2l, includes three which commence with *for*—*for fear of, for the sake of,* and *for want of.*

5.3j-2 As a conjunction

For has a minor role as a conjunction of consequence. For example:

He begged to be allowed to return home, for he was desperately unhappy in the new land

This is rather high-flown usage, used more in writing than in speaking. The meanings and functions of conjunctions *since*, *because*, and *for* are contrasted in section 14.1c.

5.4 Prepositions used in New Zealand ministerial titles

The Government Minister in charge of education may, in speech, be referred to as the Education Minister, the Minister of Education, or the Minister for Education. Similarly, a colleague may be called the Health Minister, the Minister of Health, or the Minister for Health.

Which title is 'correct'—should one employ *for* or *of*? Which is the official designation, used in writing? Well, it depends on where you live. Each nation has its own convention. In some it is always 'Minister for'. In some it is always 'Minister of'. New Zealand is unusual in employing both designations. We will enquire concerning the conditions for choosing one preposition over the other in New Zealand.

5.4a Nations using for

In the Australian Federal Government, and also in the State Governments, every Ministerial title uses *for*. For example:

Minister for Finance   Minister for Defence

Minister for Women   Minister for Foreign Affairs

Note that *of* is always used after *Department*. The Minister for Education and Training heads the Department of Education and Training.

The same convention of using *for* applies for ministerial titles in the United Kingdom and in Papua New Guinea.

5.4b Nations using of

Every Ministerial title in the Canadian government uses *of*. For example:

Minister of Finance   Minister of National Defence

Minister of Status of Women   Minister of Foreign Affairs

Of is also used exclusively for ministerial titles in South Africa, India, and Nigeria.

5.4c New Zealand

As of 16 October 2017, the New Zealand government had 28 Ministers who between them spanned 65 portfolios. That is, each person had several responsibilities. For example:

Winston Peters was   Minister of Foreign Affairs
    Minister for State Owned Enterprises
    Minister for Racing

Andrew Little was   Minister of Justice
    Minister for Courts
    Minister for Treaty of Waitangi Negotiations

Tracey Martin was   Minister for Children
    Minister of Internal Affairs
    Minister for Seniors

Overall, there were 28 'Minister of' and 37 'Minister for'.

We can enquire concerning what principle is involved in choosing between the two prepositions. To an outside observer, it seems to go as follows.

(A) *Of* is used when Ministerial responsibilities cover a general area, basically an 'issue'. Thus:

of Agriculture	of Defence	of Education
of Employment	of Finance	of Fisheries
of Forestry	of Health	of Immigration
of Local Government	of Police	of Revenue
of Statistics	of Tourism	of Transport

(B) *For* is used where the Minister has a specific purpose, promoting some activity. These titles include:

for Arts, Culture and Heritage	for Biosecurity
for Building and Construction	for Food Safety
for Greater Christchurch Regeneration	for Infrastructure
for Māori Development	for Social Development
for Trade and Export Growth	for Workplace Relations and Safety

Sometimes the Minister's responsibility is for betterment of some community group:

for Disability Issues   for Ethnic Communities   for Pacific Peoples

for Rural Communities   for Small Business   for Veterans

for Women   for Youth

Or of a natural resource:

for the Environment

There are just a couple of instances where the preposition used is a little surprising. There is a Minister of Tourism and a Minister of Conservation. Surely Tourism and Conservation are areas to be promoted, justifying *for* rather than *of*.

* * *

The Secretary of the New Zealand Cabinet provided invaluable comment on this matter. First, the *Cabinet Manual* states: 'The Prime Minister decides on portfolio titles. There are no precise rules governing the application of portfolio titles; their use varies between administrations'.

It was explained that 'many of the older ministerial titles use the *of* style (for example, Health, Education, Finance, Defence), while a number of the newer titles use the *for* style (for instance, Crown/Māori Relations, Government Digital Services)'.

'Often *of* is used when the portfolio relates directly to a Ministry or Department (for example, the Minister of Conservation is responsible for the Department of Conservation). *For* may indicate responsibility for a broader area (for example, Minister for Sport and Recreation) or that the Minister has an overarching sectoral policy and/or coordination role across a number of other portfolios (for example, Minister for Child Poverty Reduction and Minister for Crown/Māori Relations)'.

'Minister of Tourism is an older title which probably dates back to a time when there was a Department of Tourism.'

A Prime Minister may choose to revise titles. 'For example, following the 2014 General Election, the then Prime Minister decided to modernise some ministerial titles—the former "Minister of Women's Affairs" title became "Minister for Women".'

'In summary, there are no overriding "rules" concerning the use of ministerial titles in New Zealand. A pragmatic and common sense approach is used, which reflects a combination of tradition and the Prime Minister of the day's preferences and priorities.'

Overall, one does rather gain the impression that *for* is gradually gaining ground over *of* in New Zealand ministerial titles.

5.5 Comparing the two prepositions *of* and *for*

It has been worthwhile to examine the New Zealand situation in some detail since it does nicely illustrate the contrastive meanings of *for* and *of*.

'Minister of Y' is regarded as the appropriate title when Y refers to an issue; that is, a general area of responsibility. In contrast, 'Minister for Y' is used when the minister's role is directed towards a goal (referred to by Y). This accords well with the semantic profiles described in this chapter.

When composing the first few paragraphs of this chapter, I had to make decisions concerning the use of the two prepositions. For example, should I say:

(1a) The meanings of *of*…   OR   (1b)   The meanings for *of*…

(2a) The meanings of *for*…   OR   (2b)   The meanings for *for*…

I selected (1b) and (2a) simply to avoid having 'of *of*' and 'for *for*'. But what are the implications of these decisions?

It is easiest to determine this by examining the use of *for* and *of* with another preposition, say *about*:

(3a) The meanings of   =   what the meanings are, how the
      about…   preposition *about* is used

(3b) The meanings   =   what the meaning potentialities are,
      for *about*…   how the preposition *about* can be used

Although *of* and *for* do exhibit a meaning difference, in the present context this is of only minor significance pragmatically. The (a) alternative is probably the most appropriate in each instance here. However, I preferred (1b) over (1a), ranking felicity over semantics.

* * *

The next chapter turns to two other major prepositions with predominantly relational meanings—*by* (there is here a secondary spatial/temporal sense) and *with*, plus the minor relational prepositions *together-with* (and adverb *together*), *except (-for)*, *but(-for)*, *despite* and *in-spite-of*.

6

Supporting artists

By, with, together, together-with, except(-for),
but(-for), despite, in-spite-of

This chapter completes the discussion of prepositions whose basic meanings are relational. The remaining eight chapters deal with those which are primarily spatial or temporal, although each one has an array of non-spatial/temporal extensions. *With* is fully relational, as are the

English Prepositions: Their Meanings and Uses. R. M. W. Dixon. Oxford University Press (2021). © R. M. W. Dixon.
DOI: 10.1093/oso/9780198868682.003.0006

more minor prepositions *together-with* (and the associated adverb *together*), *except (-for)*, *but (-for)*, *despite*, and *in-spite-of*. *By* does have a spatial/temporal sense, but this is secondary to the relational role.

With and *by* are the sixth and seventh most frequent prepositions. They do occur in superficially similar contexts but with quite different effect. For example:

(1)   Tom was hit with a stone

(2)   Tom was hit by a stone

Each of these is a passive derivation, but they are based upon rather different underlying constructions.

Transitive verb *hit* can have a human agent in subject slot, and there may then be a peripheral NP marked by preposition *with* indicating the instrument used by the agent to inflict the blow:

(1')   Someone hit Tom (with a stone)

Under a passive derivation, the underlying object argument becomes passive subject, and the underlying subject may be included, marked by preposition *by*; however, this is frequently omitted. The instrumental argument, marked by *with*, remains unchanged. The passive of (1') is thus:

(1")   Tom was hit (by someone) (with a stone)

This gives (1), which indicates that Tom was hit by some person wielding a stone.

Alternatively, *hit* may have an inanimate agent. Suppose that Tom is sitting at the base of cliff; a stone detaches itself from the cliff and falls on him. We could then use the transitive sentence:

(2')   A stone hit Tom

In this instance there can be no instrumental phrase, marked by *with*.

When (2') is passivised we get (2). Whereas (1) states that someone used a stone as a weapon to hit John, sentence (2) indicates that no human agency was involved—it was just the force of gravity which caused the collision of the stone with Tom.

Now consider another pair of sentences:

(3)   Maria was drenched by the rain

(4)   Maria was drenched with sweat

Sentence (3) is the passive derivation from:

(3')   The rain drenched Maria

As before, the underlying transitive subject, *the rain*, is marked with preposition *by* in the passive.

The rain can be in transitive subject function for *drench*, but *sweat* is unlikely to be; one would not hear *Sweat drenched Maria*. Whereas in (3) and (3') *drenched* is a verbal form, in (4) *drenched* is a derived adjective (a participle) in copula complement function after copula verb *was*. It is augmented by the peripheral NP *with sweat*, where *with* indicates the reason for a bodily state (as in *faint with hunger* and *bent with age*; see section 6.2d-1).

We can now discuss, in turn, the meanings of *by* and *with* before returning to comparison of the two prepositions, in 6.2h.

6.1 *By*

In Old English the preposition written as *be* and *bi* had a mainly spatial meaning, 'near, along, alongside, about'. It is an original component of the longer prepositions *beside(s)*, *below*, *beneath*, *behind*, *between*, *beyond*, and *before*. The simple preposition became *by* /bai/, developing its present-day range of relational senses in Middle English times. It is often realised as a clitic /bi=/ or /bə=/ or /bai=/ (see section 1.6). There is a related prefix *by-*, used with nouns, which is fairly productive; for example: *by-product* and *by-election*.

There are two overarching meanings. We will first deal with the minor one 'near to, not quite reaching' (which includes spatial and temporal uses) before investigating the predominant sense 'how something is done'.

6.1a 'Near to, not quite reaching'

This is a continuation of the Old English sense of the preposition. It may refer just to location, as in:

Grandpa sat by the fire
  (he sat near to the fire)

The shop by the police station is closing down

(the shop is located near to the police station)

They laid the two bodies out side by side

(one side of each body was near to one side of the other body)

Keep some brandy by you!

(have it near to you, readily available in case of emergencies)

A phrasal verb may involve a natural extension from a basic meaning of the preposition. Alongside *Sue stood by a pillar* (near to it) we can have *Sue stood by her friend*, with similar meaning. But there is also the phrasal verb *stand by*; if one hears *Sue stood by her friend* this implies that she offered support to the friend in time of trouble. Or one can *stand by a promise*, which means to be resolute and carry it through. Related to *Keep some brandy by you!* is the phrasal verb *lay* (e.g. some money) *by*, 'keep for future needs'.

Or this sense of the preposition may relate to motion, either past a place or along a linear path:

They walked by the school

(at one point their walk passed near to the school)

She ran by the river

(she ran along near to the river)

Compass directions need to be rather detailed. *Northeast* is half-way between *north* and *east*. *North-northeast* is half-way between *north* and *northeast*. Then *north by east* is half-way between *north* and *north-northeast*. The modifier *by east* indicates something close to north but to the east of it.

This sense of *by* is also found in temporal expressions such as:

You must be home by midnight!

This might be used when the speaker knows that the addressee has a tendency to stay out late and is saying that they can come home as close to midnight as they wish, but must not be later (see section 14.6b).

The NP following *by* may sometimes be omitted when its identity is clear from the preceding discourse, or from the context of speaking, as in:

The twins stood on the corner and Juan walked by [sc. the twins] without noticing them

There can be similar omission from:

> Why don't you <u>stop by</u> [sc. my house] for a drink on your way
> home from work

In terms of its meaning, *stop by* has here to be regarded as a phrasal verb. The meaning contribution of *by* is that the verb implies stopping at the house for just a short time (a temporal extension of the spatial 'closeness' of this sense of the preposition *by*).

It could be suggested that *by* is functioning as an adverb in the last two sentences quoted. However, it is more straightforward to treat it as a prepositional phrase with the NP component omitted when this could be understood from the context.

Other phrasal verbs relating to this sense of *by* include *stand by* (e.g. waiting for further orders), and *pass NP by*, as in *They <u>passed</u> me <u>by</u> for promotion*.

6.1b How something is done

Within this overall specification, seven sub-senses may be recognised.

6.1b-1 How something moves

There can be statement of the means of motion from one place to another, or the route, or the portal through which motion takes place:

> The students travelled by train/by camel
> The letter was sent by special messenger
> You go by the high road and I'll go by the low road
> The chief entered the house by the side door

6.1b-2 How something is organised physically

For example:

> The boxes are priced by weight/by size/by colour
> This picture is two metres long by one metre wide
> The width of this picture exceeds the width of that one by two
> centimetres
> We pay by the hour
> The applicants were listed by age

Two mathematical operations employ *by*:

> Seven multiplied by four is twenty-eight
>
> Twenty-eight divided by seven is four

And one can say: *Twenty-eight is divisible by seven*, meaning that twenty-eight divided by seven gives a whole number.

6.1b-3 The increments by which something progresses

Using the formula 'X by X', meaning '(one) X at a time'. This can relate to space or to time or just to numbers (generally of people):

> The enemy was pushed back, mile by mile, into the swamps
>
> Day by day his disillusion eased until he became more confident
>
> The choir entered the chapel two by two

A number of nouns referring to a discrete unit may occur in this construction:

> To assemble the model you must follow the instructions step by step
>
> The teacher dictated the hard words syllable by syllable
>
> Little by little the patient was becoming weaker

However, this pattern only has limited productivity, some of its manifestations (such as *little by little*) being idiomatic. Note the similarity of form with *(they laid the bodies out) side by side*, mentioned in the last section.

Idiomatic expressions such as *by leaps and bounds* and *better by far* relate to this sub-sense.

6.1b-4 How some activity is conducted

There can be specification of physical means, as in:

> This garment was sewn by hand/by machine
>
> I received the news by letter/by telephone
>
> The criminal was suspended by his heels
>
> Sir Jasper perished by the sword

Alternatively, the means may be an activity, or an intermediary:

> The blind man on the corner lives by begging
>
> She illustrated the plan by drawing a flow-chart on the whiteboard

He won the contest by working hard/by cheating

Those not attending can vote by proxy

Quite a few adverbial phrases belong in this category, including *by chance, by good fortune, by mistake, by accident, by guesswork, by (good) luck, by good thinking, by trickery.*

A *by* phrase may specify the authority for an activity, as in:

The executioner beheaded Anne Boleyn by order of the King

A further use of a *by* phrase is as an invocation to support some activity. *Swear by* will often be employed, as in the first verse by Macaulay's well-known poem from *The Lays of Ancient Rome*:

Lars Porsena of Clusium

By the nine gods he swore

That the great house of Tarquin

Should suffer wrong no more

The verb *swear* can be omitted from (but clearly understood in) an exclamation such as: *By the spirits of my ancestors, this affront will be revenged.* There is also *By Jove*, which is simply an exclamation of surprise (nothing to do with invoking a deity to support some resolve, despite including the name of a Roman god).

Or, a *by* phrase may specify how some activity was started, or continued, or finished:

The minister began his speech by telling a joke

Constance finished by thanking her parents

It may describe the means by which someone was able to see, or concerning the time of, an activity:

During the power outage, Jason worked by candlelight

The security guard works by day and sleeps by night

If a person does something unaided, one may say they did it *by themself.* If a door appeared to open spontaneously one could say:

The door opened by itself

An alternative way of describing this is *The door opened of itself*, employing a rather archaic sense of preposition *of*.

143

Also, a number of idioms fall under this sub-sense including *learn by heart* and *It's all done by mirrors.*

6.1b-5 How a mental condition or state is achieved

The mental activity can relate to the subject of the sentence:

> He was judged by his actions, not his words
>
> Jane tried to justify her bad temper by saying that she had a headache
>
> Max won Gloria's heart by promising to give up smoking

Or the *by* phrase may describe how a mental condition or proclivity was engendered in the referent of the object:

> Auntie frightened little Johnny by telling him ghost stories
>
> He insulted Felicity by not listening to her woes
>
> We persuaded/encouraged/convinced Ella to go by reminding her of her father's last words

Alternatively, the *by* phrase may describe how a people are affected by some activity:

> By leaving everything to his daughter, he had behaved badly by his son
>
> He did well by his children, so that they never wanted for anything

6.1b-6 How some knowledge or skill is obtained

There may be statement of the means for arriving at an inference:

> I recognised Jesse by her voice
>
> She could tell it was Hugh by the clumpy footsteps
>
> We knew him by his laugh

Or the means for improving some attribute:

> One always gains by experience
>
> Only by constant practice will you achieve an acceptable standard

6.1b-7 The reason for an attribute

Stating why a particular quality may be ascribed to a person (or thing):

Stella is generous by nature

Jack is a lawyer by profession

Maria is French by birth and German by residence

My brother is related to the Duke by marriage

This carving is of Roman origin by repute

6.1c By *as marker of the erstwhile agent in a passive construction*

Many transitive clauses may be converted into passive form. For example:

ACTIVE An infidel murdered the vicar

PASSIVE The vicar was murdered (by an infidel)

The transitive object becomes passive subject, often being topic for the stretch of discourse in which the sentence appears. The original transitive subject (in this case the agent) may optionally be stated. It is entirely appropriate that this should be marked by preposition *by* since it indicates the way in which the result was achieved. Someone might ask: *How was the vicar murdered?*, and the reply would be: *By an infidel.*

Many sentences which include a *by* phrase could be listed under the sense in section 6.1b-5, 'How a mental condition or state is achieved', but are in fact just regular passives. For example:

Anna was confused by so many conflicting instructions

The king was disgusted by the ambassador's bad manners

The Prime Minister was encouraged by media approbation

Nathan was sustained throughout the crisis by the love of Jesus

The passive version of a sentence describing how some eminent practitioner created a work of art may be shortened by omitting the passive verbal element. For example:

A play written by Shakespeare → A play by Shakespeare

A church designed by Wren → A church by Wren

Many verbs describing human emotions form an adjective (a participle) which functions as a copula complement and is typically followed by a prepositional phrase; we can call this 'construction (b)'. It has similar form to a passive construction, which may be labelled 'construction (a)'. We can compare:

(a) Tommy$_{\text{PASSIVE.SUBJECT}}$ [was terrified]$_{\text{PASSIVE.VERB}}$ [by the thunderstorm]$_{\text{UNDERLYING.AGENT}}$

(b) Tommy$_{\text{COPULA.SUBJECT}}$ was$_{\text{COPULA/VERB}}$ terrified$_{\text{COPULA.COMPLEMENT}}$ [of loud noises]

The first sentence is a passive stating that in this instance a particular thunderstorm terrified Tommy. The second sentence describes a characteristic of Tommy: his horror of loud noises.

The prepositions which are appropriate in construction (b), after a derived adjective, vary. Alongside *terrified of* we find *scared of*, *frightened of*, *tired of*, *surprised at*, *pleased with*, *satisfied with*, *annoyed with*, *delighted with*, *disappointed with*, *interested in*, *worried about*, and quite a few more. It is noteworthy that adjectives *impressed*, *inspired*, and *troubled* take *by*, the same preposition as in the passive.

There is a recurrent difference of meaning between the two construction types:

(a) BY PLUS NP IN PASSIVE	(b) PREPOSITION PLUS NP AFTER ADJECTIVE
NP refers to some definite happening (appropriate for the estwhile agent of a transtive verb)	NP refers to (i) a general prospect or (ii) the details of some activity

The examples given for *terrified* illustrate (a) *terrified by* a specific happening, here the thunderstorm, and (b-i) *terrified of* a general phenomenon, here loud noises.

Examples of (b-ii) include *surprised at* and *interested in*:

(a) He was surprised by Mary's winning the race

(b-ii) He was surprised at the ease with which Mary won the race

(a) She was interested by the news that Fred has resigned

(b-ii) She was interested in the reasons which Fred gave for resigning

Satisfied with and *pleased with* provide further examples of sense (b-i):

(a)   The rising demand for vehicles has been satisfied by increased production

(b-i)   We're satisfied with the sales prospects ahead

(a)   Mary was pleased by the view from the front window

(b-i)   Mary is pleased with life

The same NP may be included in constructions (a) and (b), with the identity of the preposition determining the meaning:

(a)   Hilda was pleased by his offer

                 (the fact that he made the offer pleased her)

(b-ii)   Hilda was pleased with his offer

                 (she was content with the details of what he offered)

These meaning characterisations just describe tendencies. As with most aspects of linguistic analysis, we do not encounter hard-and-fast 'rules'. There is always a good deal of fluidity but it can be explained in terms of variation from canonical patterns.

Some of these adjectival participles form negatives, which take the same preposition as the positive form. For example:

	IN VERBAL PASSIVE CONSTRUCTION	ADJECTIVAL PARTICIPLE IN COPULA CONSTRUCTION
satisfied	by	with
dissatisfied	—	with
interested	by	in
uninterested	—	in
impressed	by	by
unimpressed	—	by

The point to notice here is that only the derived adjectives may be negated, not the underlying verbs. We have adjectives *dissatisfied*, *uninterested*, and *unimpressed* but no verbs **dissatisfy*, **uninterest*, or **unimpress*.

It would be possible to include two *by* phrases in a sentence; for example, *Anne Boleyn was beheaded by the executioner by order of the King*, or *They travelled by car by the high road*. However this would normally be avoided, as infelicitous, and would be re-phrased. There is an

147

exception—combining the 'moving' and 'incremental' senses can be acceptable, as in *Two-by-two, the choir entered the chapel by the side door* (but note the first phrase, *two by two* has *by* in the middle, not at the beginning).

6.1d *By in phrasal verbs*

There are just a few phrasal verbs (and perhaps no prepositional verbs) which involve *by*. Some are of type V-a and V-NP-a, where *by* fills the **a** slot and others of type V-p-NP where *by* fills the **p** slot.

There was discussion in section 6.1a of phrasal verbs *stop by* (e.g. for a drink) and *stand by* (e.g. for further orders), both of type V-a, together-with *lay NP* (e.g. some money) *by*, of type V-NP-a and *stand by NP* (meaning 'support') of type V-p-NP.

Other phrasal verbs have meanings which are rather different from those of constituent verb and preposition (here *by*). For example:

type V-a	get by, 'succeed in a situation'
type V-p-NP	abide by, 'act in accordance with'
	come by, 'acquire'
	swear by (e.g. Tom's judgement), 'have great confidence in'

6.2 *With*

Old English had prepositions *mid* 'among, with, by means of' and *wiÞ* 'opposite, against, near'. In a somewhat unusual development, *mid* dropped out of use in the fifteenth century and *with* (as it was now spelt) expanded to take over its range of uses.

Today, the basic meanings of preposition *with* /wið/ are relational (rather then spatial or temporal). It is often pronounced as a clitic /wið=/ or /wi=/.

Five major senses can be recognised, some with a number of sub-divisions.

6.2a *The means by which something is achieved*

The basic sense here involves physical means, in 6.2a-1, which naturally extends to abstract means, in 6.2a-2.

6.2a-1 An instrument in a physical action

For example:

> The butcher sliced the meat with a sharp knife
> We should cover the child with a blanket
> They don't know how to eat with a knife and fork
> Uncle Will disguised himself with a false nose

Also belonging here would be: *The jester juggled with five balls at once,* and *The balloon was inflated with helium.* A speech event can be the instrument which affects a larger speech event:

> Bill punctuated Mark's speech with snide remarks

6.2a-2 Something abstract as the means to achieve a social ambience or a mental state

A *with* phrase may mark a type of social interaction:

> Mother greeted the visitors with a smile
> The Queen graced the occasion with her presence

Or the referent of the subject argument may engender a mental state in the referent of the object by means of their special attribute:

> The acrobat thrilled everyone with her daring
> Oscar charmed Amelia with his wit

A *with* phrase may describe what it was that created a mental state:

> He confused us with contradictory instructions
> She filled his mind with hatred

6.2a-3 How a phase of an activity is conducted

A *with* phrase is used to describe the way in which—or the reason why—some activity started, or continued, or finished:

> She concluded her speech with a warning
> The meeting opened with a prayer
> The riot started with a single stone thrown in anger
> That idea originated with Dr Jones

A similar meaning is found in *She persevered with the task.*

6.2b Association

There are eight sub-senses here.

6.2b-1 An inherent feature

This can be a physical feature, as in:

> Tim was born with six toes on his left foot
> Jerome is blessed with good eyesight
> Leila is endowed with soft, fair skin
> Anna speaks with a lisp

A *with* phrase having this meaning may occur within an NP; for example, *I saw [the man with six toes], [That girl with a lisp] is here to see you*, and *[A town with a cathedral] is always worth visiting.*

The *with* phrase may refer to a mental attitude, as when someone does something:

with spirit   with a heavy heart   with vengeance   with pleasure

Or their attitude may determine the way in which they act:

with care   with all one's might   with indifference   with tact

An extension from this is when the *with* phrase describes the effort required, or the consequences of the act:

with ease   with difficulty   with impunity   with success

6.2b-2 Knowledge

Here the referent of the subject argument is associated with some relevant information. For example:

> Mark is conversant with the basic principles of topography
> Judy is acquainted with the relevant rules and regulations
> You need to familiarise yourself with the new data processing system

6.2b-3 External features

The *with* phrase refers to something associated with—but not a part of—the referent of the subject:

The cellar is infested with rats

Your shirt is stained with gravy

The station is crowded with people

Her dress is adorned with tiny pearls

For this sense, the nature of the association is often coded in the verb, as exemplified by:

encumbered with	burdened with	equipped with	armed with
furnished with	shrouded with	surrounded with	inundated with
crawling with	swamped with	flooded with	infected with

6.2b-4 Association with a person (or animal)

A *with* phrase here may follow an intransitive verb referring to motion or rest, as the type of association:

Belinda went for a walk with her dog

He lives with his parents

You shouldn't consort/associate/mix with bad characters

This type of *with* phrase may occur within an NP; for *example [That man with a huge Labrador dog] just passed by.*

Other intransitive verbs with similar sense include:

co-operate with	collaborate with	trade with	mingle with

Nouns such as *an alliance with* and *a partnership with* belong here.

A *with* phrase with this meaning may follow a transitive verb. For example:

Rusty divided the booty with Sandy

You'll have to arrange your holidays with the boss

Mabel trusted Keith with her secret

Jim managed to solve the problem with Peter's help

This sense can be extended to temporal reference, as in: *Lucy gets up every morning with the sun.*

There is an interesting contrast between *meet* and *meet with*. Note that the *with* phrase implies a planned association:

> Jules met Jim
>> (unexpectedly, on the road)
>
> Jules met with Jim
>> (as arranged, in the coffee shop, at noon)

6.2b-5 Social interaction

This describes association involving interpersonal dealings:

> Please help Elia with his homework!
> Michael is talking/joking/arguing/conferring with his sister
> I enjoy bargaining with the locals
> Sir Basil has a tendency to quarrel with everyone

6.2b-6 Physical interaction

In contrast to the sense in 6.2b-5, there is here physical effect:

> The general engaged with the enemy
> The bus collided with a car
> Arthur struggled/fought/fenced with the champion
> Rome went to war with Carthage

Verbs which describe physical contact may have metaphorical extensions. For example: *The students wrestled with that problem in geometry.*

6.2b-7 Severing an association

With a suitable verb, *with* may mark the elimination of a previous or expected attachment:

> To pay off her husband's debts, Louise reluctantly parted with her
>> diamond bracelet
> Let's dispense with pretty platitudes and get down to business
> The President's obstinacy is likely to lead to a rupture in good
>> relations with our allies

There was mention in section 1.8 of a special imperative construction that is most used with three prepositions which are minor members (with negative meanings) of pairings: *off* from *on/off*, *out* from *in/out*, and *down* from *up/down*. The preposition effectively functions as predicate, followed by a *with* phrase indicating the association which is to be severed. Examples include:

> Off with his head!
>> (cut it off)

> Out with it!
>> (tell me the secret, don't keep it to yourself)

> Down with the monarchy!
>> (let's abolish it)

One also hears *up with* (which has a positive meaning) as when cheering on a sporting team; e.g. *Up with the Maroons!*

6.2b-8 Temporal association

The core clause describes something which is associated with what is stated in the *with* phrase, following on from it both causally and temporally (see also section 14.6b):

> With his father's death, Martin came into the dukedom
> With the passing of time, Aunt Agatha's attitude towards Martin mellowed

6.2c Agreement

This sense describes identity or equivalence. It can be shown with verb, adjective, or noun:

> Passover coincides with Easter this year
> The bishop agrees with his wife about most things
> I don't like being compared with his daughter
> You wait, I'll get even with that swindler
> Women are fighting [for equality with men in their pay]

A slightly different nuance relates to correlations, such as:

> The colour of the curtain harmonises with the colour of the carpet
> That tie doesn't go with that shirt, it clashes with it
> 'Ablution' rhymes with 'solution'
> Youth drunkenness correlates with lack of parental control

Or there may be substitution of one thing with something similar:

> Agatha alternates with Sandra in the lead role of the musical
> The old trees are being replaced with young ones

6.2d Explanation for a state

A *with* phrase is used to describe the cause for some physical or mental state.

6.2d-1 Physical state

The state is generally described by an adjective:

> The prisoner is faint with hunger
> Grandma is racked with pain
> She's worn out with anxiety
> Old Tommy is bent with age
> She was convulsed with laughter
> The beggar perished with cold

In extensions of this sense, the *with* phrase may have a more abstract reference, as in: *Martin was consumed with jealousy* and *Jean was assailed with doubts.*

6.2d-2 Mental state

Someone can experience an emotion or attitude concerning a person, or their behaviour, or just a happening:

> Don't be annoyed with Millie, it's her first day on the job
> The inspector was pleased with the way the dispute had been settled
> Inspector Grant is preoccupied with the disappearance of Agatha

Other adjectives taking a *with* phrase in this sense include:

angry with	disgusted with	exasperated with	impatient with
delighted with	satisfied with	happy with	impressed with
infatuated with	obsessed with	careful with	careless with

The *with* phrase may refer back to the subject of the clause, as in *Tom is content with his lot*, and *Sean became intoxicated with success.*

Or an adjective (or verb) can indicate an attitude towards someone, as in:

> The teacher was lenient with the latecomers
>
> We sympathised with Mary in her bereavement

Similar examples include:

friendly with   gentle with   firm with   honest with

Matters are reversed in the case of *Tim is popular with his schoolmates,* this describing the attitude of the schoolmates (referred to by the *with* phrase) towards Tim.

6.2e Activity directed towards something

Here the verb describes handling a task or situation; it often involves a sense of confrontation.

> Mavis would be unable to cope with looking after three extra children
>
> We're going to experiment with longer opening hours
>
> All her life, Jean fought with a sense of inferiority
>
> They are making good progress in the fight against malaria

Another example is one sense of *The lowlanders fought with the highlanders* (example (6) at the beginning of chapter 1), where *with* has similar import to *against.*

A further verb of this ilk is *manage with.* And there is adjective *busy with.*

6.2f With *in phrasal verbs and prepositional verbs*

Several dozen phrasal verbs include *with.* In keeping with its role as a relational preposition (never used as an adverb) *with* occurs only in slot **p** (not **a**) in phrasal verbs of types V-p-NP, V-NP-p-NP, V-NP-a-p-NP and, most frequently, in those of type V-a-p-NP. Each relates to one of the senses which has been described. This can be illustrated with a selection (as before, a phrasal verb within a sentence is underlined).

- Means: how a phase of an activity is conducted:

V-NP-a-p-NP The principal <u>wound</u> his speech <u>up with</u> a warning

V-a-p-NP   <u>Get on with/carry on with</u> the task

- Association: knowledge:

V-a-p-NP Edward <u>is up with</u> all the latest developments

This sense extends to: *Maria <u>came up with</u> a wonderful new idea.*

- Association with person:

V-a-p-NP Make sure that you <u>get in with/keep in with</u> the boss's wife

He <u>is hanging out with/has taken up with</u> some unfortunate friends

Uncle Fred has decided to <u>stay on with</u> the firm

- Severing an association:

V-a-p-NP Sue has <u>fallen out with</u> her brother

His ex-wife <u>made off with</u> all the antique furniture

A further extension leads to *Hannah <u>walked away with</u> the prize* (meaning that she won it with ease).

- Agreement:

V-a-p-NP We'll have to <u>fall/fit in with</u> his plans

They're trying to <u>keep up with</u> the Joneses

Their political view was <u>bound up with</u> their religious ideas

His evidence <u>ties in with</u> what the constable saw

V-p-NP   There's no alternative but to <u>go with</u> the general consensus

- Explanation for a state:

V-a-p-NP   Peggy has <u>gone down with</u> mumps

Jessica is <u>fed up with</u> Tom's infidelities

V-p-NP   The anarchists are a force to be <u>reckoned with</u>

There is a slight difference between phrasal verbs *reckon with NP* and *reckon for NP*. The former may refer to any sort of impediment (such as, *We hadn't <u>reckoned with</u> bad weather*), whereas the latter is likely to relate to something which had not been anticipated; for example, *I hadn't <u>reckoned for</u> a law to have been passed forbidding this.*

- Activity directed towards something:

V-p-NP   Boris will be able to <u>deal with</u> the situation

Please <u>bear with</u> me while I explain things

V-NP-p-NP   They <u>settled</u> the dispute <u>with</u> a handshake

V-a-p-NP   Let's <u>get through with</u> the formalities quickly

Get behind with (for example, his hire-purchase repayments) appears to be a substantial extension from the 'Severing of association' sense. There are a number of prepositional verbs which contain *with*. They include:

- **Inherent feature**. For example, *(Every word the king spoke was) imbued with (an aura of authority)*.
- **Physical interaction**. *Grapple with* was discussed in section 4.2e.
- **Action directed towards something**. For example, *toy with (the idea)*. A variation on this sense describes dealing with something in an inappropriate manner; for example, *tamper with* and *trifle with*.

6.2g Further points of interest

6.2g-1 Without

This preposition has two, rather different, senses. One is entirely spatial, the complement of *within*, roughly meaning 'outside of', as in *They live without the city walls*; this is discussed in section 8.3. The other is relational, the complement of *with*, meaning 'not with'.

In just a few of its senses *with* may be substituted by *without*, and then only when the lack of some feature can be considered relevant. For instance, one might hear *They ate without knives or forks* but one would be unlikely to encounter **He disguised himself without a false nose.*

Without may be used of an inherent feature—*Tim was born without any toes, Margaret speaks without an accent, [A town without a cathedral] is seldom interesting,* and *He did it without pleasure.* Then there are adverbial idioms such as: *without a care in the world, without prejudice,* and *without doubt.*

Other types of association are, in suitable circumstances, open to *without.* For example, *Today Mary went for a walk without her dog,* and *Mack did it without any help from anyone.* But most of the senses for *with* which were listed above are not susceptible to substitution by *without.*

6.2g-2 More than one *with* phrase

There are very few circumstances in which a clause may include two *with* phrases. When this is possible, it is generally regarded as infelicitous and avoided. For instance, *John cut up the meat with a knife* uses the 'instrument' sense of *with* and *John cut up the meat with Pete* employs the 'association' sense. These could be combined, giving *John cut up the meat with Pete with a knife* (or, having the *with* phrases reversed) but the result is ugly and would likely to be re-phrased (for example, using *together-with* rather than just *with* for 'association').

6.2g-3 Initial elements

It is interesting to note the etymologies of verbs (and adjectives) which are borrowed from Romance languages and typically take a *with* phrase.
—Well over a score of such verbs commence with *co-,* which goes back to Latin prefix *co(m)-,* meaning 'together'. Thirteen have been used in the examples above. Others include *combine with, communicate with, comply with, confront with, contend with,* and *contrast with.*
—A further batch of such verbs begin with *in-* or *im-* or *il-.* This relates to the Latin prefix *in-/im-/il-* 'into, onto'. Six were included in the discussion above. Others include *impregnate with, illustrate with, inscribe with, impress with,* and *inspire with.* Plus adjectives *impatient with, indignant with, intrigued with,* and *irritated with.*

6.2h Contrasting by and with

Many examples where these two prepositions contrast involve (a) a passive construction where the erstwhile agent is marked with *by,* and

(b) a derived adjective which is followed by *with*. This was illustrated at the beginning of the chapter with *drenched by* and *drenched with*. There was general discussion in section 6.1c where it was suggested that—in such pairs—the passive *by* phrase is likely to refer to some definite happening, and the post-adjectival phrase (marked by *with*, or some other preposition) will relate either to a general prospect or to the details of an activity. It was illustrated with *satisfied by/with* and *pleased by/with*. Other examples include *overcome by* (for example, fumes) and *overcome with* (remorse or doubts). Also, among others, *disgusted by/with, annoyed by/with, impressed by/with*, and *surrounded by/with*.

   The verb *replace* is of particular interest since it occurs in two differ-ent constructions. In November 1990, the British Conservative party voted to install John Major as its leader after Margaret Thatcher's resig-nation. One could say either:

ACTIVE   The party replaced Margaret Thatcher with John Major

PASSIVE   Margaret Thatcher was replaced with John Major (by the party)

Or else:

ACTIVE   John Major replaced Margaret Thatcher (as leader of the party)

PASSIVE   Margaret Thatcher was replaced by John Major (as leader of the party)

It can be seen that the *replaced with* and *replaced by* alternatives relate to different underlying active sentences.

   The contrast between *by* and *with* is nicely brought out by two ways of describing a single event:

   The Dean began by telling a joke
   The Dean began with a joke

The first sentence describes the way in which the activity was conducted (similar to *He won the contest by working hard*)—see section 6.1b-4—whereas the second one details the means used (*as in Mother greeted the visitors with a smile*)—see section 6.2a-2.

   The two idiom-like phrases *by your leave* and *with your permission* have similar pragmatic effect. Their uses overlap, as in:

159

By your leave, I'll reorganise the files today

With your permission, I'll reorganise the files today

The first sentence uses the 'how some activity is conducted' sense of *by* (similar to *By cheating he won the contest*). And the second employs the 'association' sense of *with* (similar to *With Peter's help, Jim managed to solve the problem*).

When comparing *of* and *for*, at the very end of chapter 5, there was discussion of how to avoid saying 'of *of* ' and 'for *for*'. A similar situation is encountered concerning *by* and *with*. There are the following alternatives:

(1a) This meaning is marked by *by*.

(1b) This meaning is marked by *with*.

(2a) This meaning is marked with *by*.

(2b) This meaning is marked with *with*.

Sentences (1a) and (1b) employ *by* for stating 'how something is done' (similar to *The motion was decided by a vote*) whereas (2a) and (2b) use *with* for 'the means by which something is done' (as in *The transaction was settled with a handshake*). The pragmatic effect is—in this case— similar, although there is a subtle difference of meaning. However, this is overruled by the desire for felicity of expression—(1b) and (2a) have been used, to avoid repetition of a preposition.

6.3 *Together* and *together-with*

Old English adverb *tōgæd(e)re* has become present-day *together* /tə'geðə/. It can function as an adverb, corresponding to preposition *with* in its 'association' sense. Compare:

(1a) Jane went to the market with Kate

(1b) Jane and Kate went to the market together

(2a) Michael built the house with Emily

(2b) Michael and Emily built the house together

(3a) The builder mixed sand with cement

(3b) The builder mixed sand and cement together

In each sentence the linked participants should be of equal status so that, for example, (1a) could alternatively be stated as *Kate went to the market with Jane*. In addition, the complex preposition *together-with* /tə'geðəwið=/ could be used here in place of *with*—*Kate went to the market together-with Jane*, and so on.

Together carries the meaning 'at the same time'. If *together* were omitted from (1b) we would get:

(1c)   Jane and Kate went to the market

This would be ambiguous between (i) they went separately, and (ii) they went in each other's company. Including *together*, in (1b), restricts the sentence to sense (ii).

The nature of the activities described in (2) and (3) is such that only sense (ii) is possible. Thus, adverb *together* may be omitted from (2b) and (3b) without any significant difference in meaning.

As mentioned, a *with*-construction may only be rephrased using *together* if the participants are of equal status. *Belinda went for a walk with Simon* (where they are both adults) could be restated as *Simon went for a walk with Belinda* or as *Belinda and Simon went for a walk (together)*. In *Belinda went for a walk with the dog*, Belinda is the main participant and the dog a secondary one. This would be unlikely to be restated as **The dog went for a walk with Belinda* or as **Belinda and the dog went for a walk (together)*.

There was discussion at the beginning of chapter 1 of how *The lowlanders fought with the highlanders* could have either (i) an 'association' sense, meaning that the lowlanders fought on the same side as the highlanders against a common enemy, or (ii) a 'physical interaction' sense, meaning that the lowlanders fought against the highlanders. Using *together-with* in place of *with*, so that we get *The highlanders fought together-with the lowlanders*, restricts the meaning to (i).

There are just a few other ways in which adverb *together* is linked to preposition *with*. One concerns the 'agreement' sense:

This colour goes well with that one

These two colours go well together

Together has several other senses. For example, *He worked for hours together* implies that there was no interruption. Then there are idioms such as *Pull yourself together!*, meaning 'control your emotions and try to behave purposefully!'. And it is found in a phrasal verb, as in *The two parts of his submission don't <u>hang together</u>*.

6.4 *Except (-for)* and *but (-for)*

Except (-for) has an unusual grammatical profile. It is basically a complex preposition which may occur in a peripheral phrase followed by an NP or any of the three main varieties of complement clause. For example:

(1) They didn't stop [except-for [a drink]]
(2) They didn't stop [except-for [(the driver's) having a drink]]
(3) They didn't stop [except [that they needed a drink]
(4) They didn't stop [except [(for the driver) to have a drink]]

It can be seen that the basic form of the preposition is *except-for* /ik'septfə/. As always a preposition—here *for*—is omitted before a complementiser *that, for,* or *to* (see section 2.5c). In each sentence the *except-(for)* constituent may be moved to the front, preceding *They didn't stop.*

An *except (-for)* phrase may also modify the head of a core NP. And it may be extraposed from there to the beginning, or to the end, of the clause.

(5) [Everyone [except John]] arrived on time
(6) [Except-for John] everyone arrived on time
(7) Everyone arrived on time [except (-for) John]

The *for* component of *except (-for)* would generally be omitted from (5) but included in (6). It could be included in or omitted from (7).

Another role for an *except (-for)* phrase is to modify a copula complement and here the *for* component cannot be omitted:

(8) Your letter of application is [alright [except-for a couple of mis-spellings]]

The phrasal preposition *but-for* /'bʌtfə=/ which may be followed by an NP or an -ING complement clause—overlaps in meaning with *except (-for),* and may substitute for it in (5–8). The difference is that *but (-for)* relates to an opposition, as in:

(9) Gordon would have won the race but for his horse's falling at the final fence

Except (-for) would be less appropriate in (9). In (1), (2), and (10), there is no idea of opposition, so that here *but-for* would be less appropriate.

(10)   I'm prepared to move anywhere except for Chicago

Save (-for) is another phrasal preposition with similar meaning to *except (-for)* but far less common than it.

6.5 *Despite* and *in-spite-of*

Despite was, like *except*, a loan from Old French into Middle English. *Despite* was shortened to *spite* (supported by *spijt* in Middle Dutch). Today, simple preposition *despite* /des'pait/ and phrasal preposition *in-spite-of* /ins'paitəv=/ have similar meanings, contrasting a negative with a positive.
    However, there is a significant difference:

(a)   If the factor is negative and the result is positive, then *despite* is
            preferred
(b)   If the factor is positive and the result is negative, then *in-spite-of*
            is preferred

For example:

(a)   Despite the bad reviews it received, William's book sold well
(b)   In-spite-of the good reviews it received, William's book sold badly

Further textual examples are:

(a)   Despite their money and house-hunting problems, the
            newly-married couple are happy
        Despite his spendthrift habits, Sinatra is also exceedingly generous
(b)   In-spite-of the description on the dust jacket, this is not really a
            book for the rank beginner
        In-spite-of further blood transfusions, he died in a coma the
            following day

* * *

This chapter and the previous one have examined those prepositions which have an exclusively or predominantly relational role. We can now move on to those whose basic meaning is spatial, commencing with the central set consisting of *at*, *to*, and *from* (plus *toward(s)*).

7

The central spatial prepositions

At, to, toward(s), from

English Prepositions: Their Meanings and Uses. R. M. W. Dixon. Oxford University Press (2021). © R. M. W. Dixon.
DOI: 10.1093/oso/9780198868682.003.0007

The chief spatial prepositions are *at* /ət=/, describing a position of rest, and the pair dealing with motion, consisting of major member *to* /tə=/ and minor member *from* /frəm=/. These three are exclusively prepositions, generally realised as proclitics; they are never used as adverbs and the NP which follows them may not be omitted. *To* is the second most frequent preposition in the language (behind *of*) with *at* and *from* being eighth and ninth most frequent. Their basic meanings are spatial (and secondarily temporal) with considerable extensions into more abstract senses.

All three prepositions were present in Old English with meanings similar to those which they display today. *Tō* could be followed by dative case, then meaning 'towards, to, at, near', or by genitive, then signifying temporal 'as', object of motion 'for', or degree 'to such an extent'. *Fram* was followed by dative case, indicating 'from' or agentive 'by'. And *æt* was followed by accusative, meaning 'as far as, until', or by dative, the sense then being 'at', or 'from', or agentive 'by'.

A special property of these prepositions, in the modern language, is that the definite article *the* may be omitted from a following NP with certain head nouns under certain conditions. Compare:

the NEEDED	*the* OMITTED
Joe is going to the studio	Joe is going to school
Joe is coming from the studio	Joe is coming from school
Joe is staying at the studio	Joe is staying at school

However, *Joe is going to school* (with no *the*) may only be used if Joe is a pupil or teacher and is going to the school to take part in the normal activity of a school. But if, say, Joe were a plumber going to fix some burst pipes, then one would have to include the article, saying *Joe is going to the school* (or *coming from the school*, or *staying at the school*).

Dialects vary somewhat as to which nouns allow the omission of *the* after *to*, *from*, or *at*. For British English, the list includes *college*, *university*, *class*, *prison*, *hospital*, and *theatre* (but only when referring to an operating theatre in a hospital).

Another noun with this property is *church*. A member of the congregation would say *I'm going to church*, whereas a plumber who was just visiting the building to do his job, and was not at all concerned with worshipping, would have to say *I'm going to the church*.

An interesting point is that while *the* may be omitted from before *church*, it must be retained before *cathedral*—one can only say *I'm going to the cathedral*, not **I'm going to cathedral*. It seems that *church*—like *school*, *prison*, and the rest—refers to both a place and the sort of activity it is intended for, whereas *cathedral* just denotes a building.

A similar contrast involves *town* and *city*. *Sue's going to town*—with no article *the*—specifies her destination and also that she will do there what one normally does in town. In contrast, *city* just refers to a place and requires the article—*Sue's going to the city*.

One other preposition shares this property with *at*, *to*, and *from*. This is *in* (discussed in chapter 8). The article *the* is deleted from *Robin is staying in school/church/class this evening*; and so on.

Another sort of deletion involves prepositions *at* and *to* before the noun *home*. One can say:

EITHER	Cecil stayed at home all yesterday	OR	Cecil stayed home all yesterday
NOT	*Cecil is going to home	ONLY	Cecil is going home
ONLY	Cecil is coming from home		

To, the major member of the pair *to/from*, has to be omitted before *home*, whereas *from*, the minor member, must be retained. If *Cecil is coming from home* were to be shortened to *Cecil is coming home*, it could only be understood as 'to home'.

However *at* can be either omitted or retained from before *home*, with significant difference of meaning. One may hear:

I wasn't feeling at all well, so I just stayed home today

Here *stay home* describes an activity. One could instead use *rest*, as *in I wasn't feeling at all well, so I just rested today*. This sentence answers the question *What did you do today?*

We can contrast this with a sentence including the *at*:

> There was a bad thunderstorm so we had no alternative but to
> stay at home today

This indicates location, similar to *There was so much work to get through that I stayed at the office late*. This sentence would answer the question *Where did you stay today?*

There is a similar, but slightly different, situation with *here* and *there*. *At* must be omitted after a verb of rest—*She stayed here/there*—and *to* after a verb of motion—*She walked here/there*. But *from* cannot be omitted—*She ran from here/there*.

We can now examine the meanings of *at*, *to*, and *from*, including contrasting their uses in similar frames. Discussion of the minor preposition *toward(s)* is interpolated between *to* and *from*.

7.1 At

This preposition, which is generally a proclitic, could be said to look in either of two directions:

- Some verbs and adjectives expect to be followed by a peripheral NP introduced by *at*; for example, *arrive at*, *aim at*, *marvel at*, and *clever at*.
- Some NPs expect to be introduced by *at*; for example, *at full speed*, and *at any price*. And a fair number of nouns are typically preceded by *at*; they include: *at sunset*, *at present*, *at war*, and *at fault*.

The overarching meaning of *at* is 'focus'. This can relate to a location, or a time, or a target, or the focus of some emotion or ability, or a quantity. The various senses and subsenses will now be addressed.

7.1a Focus on a spatial position

At provides a general statement of position. It can be compared to *in*, which indicates inclusion, and to *on*, which implies connection. This is illustrated by:

Pamela sat on a chair at the table

Ian stayed in a posh hotel at the seaside

Other examples are *The chamberlain lives at the palace* and *I'll meet you at the intersection*.

It may also be used with a verb which indicates 'getting into position', as in:

The plane landed at the main airport

The ghost appeared at the window

Josie arrived at the station ten minutes early

Abstract meanings extend from this sense. For example, one can *arrive at a conclusion*, or a jury can *arrive at a verdict*.

Nouns or NPs may be preceded by *at* in this sense. For example:

at close-quarters	at arm's length	at first hand	at anchor
at sea	at table	at its zenith	at full length

The sense may extend from location to an activity, either personal or general:

You can complete the assignment at your leisure

Rome and Carthage are at war again

Also *at play, at work, at rest, at ease, at attention*, and *at will*.

7.1b Focus on a temporal point, and on speed

Preposition *at* is used for reference to a point in time. Compare:

The result will be announced at noon

(precisely at that moment)

The result will be announced in the morning

(within that time span)

Sometime could be included before *in the morning* since this refers to a period of time—*The result will be announced sometime in the morning*—but not before *at noon*, since this refers to a specific time. (And see section 14.6a.)

Similar examples include: *at present, at that instant, at the age of forty, at the moment* (of her arrival), *at a time* (when you are free), *at your/someone's convenience*, *at the president's invitation*, and *all at once*. Relative time is shown by *at short notice*, *at (long) last*, and *at the latest*.

Temporal duration may be indicated, without paying attention to internal composition, as in:

> She ran for five hours at a stretch
> The minister spoke at great length

This leads into *at* as a sign of continuity, for example:

> Sarah toiled at the task day after day until she completed it

Also *labour at*, *work at*, plus phrasal verbs of type V-p-NP and V-a-p-NP: *stick at* (the job) *keep (on) at*, and *be on at*.

Someone may say:

> You will meet Margaret's new husband at dinner

This is treating at 'dinner' as a unit of time, without regard for its internal composition. Analogous phrases include:

at dawn   at daybreak   at sunrise   at dusk   at sunset   at night

One could say '(He told a few jokes) *at the beginning* (of his speech)' or *at the end* but only *in the middle* (not *at the middle*, since 'the middle' necessarily has internal composition).

The preposition *at* is used to refer to repeated points of time; for example, *at intervals*, *at times*, and *at random*. This extends to the speed at which an activity is conducted (which indicates the time taken to complete it):

> They worked at a steady pace

Also: *at a fast/slow tempo*, *at (full) speed*, *at a trot*, *at a gallop*, and *at full tilt*.

7.1c Focus on a target

We can here recognise four subsenses.

7.1c-1 Movement with respect to a target

This indicates quick movement focussing on some person or place:

> The attacker lunged at me, grabbing at my arm
> She came at me like a tiger

Other examples include *rush at, run at, spring at, fly at, jump at, lash out at*, and *hit back at*. There can be abstract extensions such as *They jumped at John's innovative new proposal*. And phrasal verbs *get at* (the essence of the matter), and *get back at* (the person who maligned you).

7.1c-2 Action with respect to a target

An activity can have a particular focus, as in:

> The marksman aimed at the centre of the bullseye
>
> The general ordered the cannon to be fired at the city walls

Other verbs which may be used in this sense include; *throw* (something) *at*, and *hurl* (something) *at* (see sections 1.1a and 7.2k-5).

In section 2.5a there was discussion of how a preposition (generally *on, onto*, or *at*) may be inserted before a transitive object NP to indicate that the object is not affected in the way that would be expected. For example *John kicked the ball* indicates that he sent it on its way. But inserting *at* and saying *John kicked at the ball* states that his action of kicking was with respect to a target (the ball) but was in this instance unfulfilled. Other transitive verbs which may insert *at* to indicate a non-usual effect on the object include *grab at*—as in a sentence quoted in section 7.1c-1—*clutch at, pull at, tug at, shoot at, hit (out) at*, and *nibble at*.

7.1c-3 Focus of speaking

Here *at* marks the target of some vocal activity (often of a negative nature):

> Charles swore at Diana

There is instructive comparison between *at* and *to* in this context, as illustrated in section 1.1a and in section 7.2k-5. Other verbs taking *at* in this sense include *snap at, nag at*, and *bark at*.

7.1c-4 Focus of looking and of facial or other gesture

There are many intransitive verbs describing kinds of visual activity and these expect an *at* phrase stating the target of attention, as in:

> They looked at the muddy swamp ahead

Others include: *gaze at, stare at, peer at, peep at, glance at*, and *gape at*. Along similar lines, there is *point at* (where the pointing may be by an extended hand or finger, or by pouted lips).

When people make a facial gesture this is often directed at some other person, the target:

Simon winked at me whenever Hure's name was mentioned

Also in this set are: *frown at*, *leer at*, and *grin at*. And phrases such as: *at a glance*, *at first sight*.

Smile at has a range of senses. One is similar to *wink at*:

Nigel smiled at Mary
(letting her know that he liked her and wanted to encourage her)

Another is as an expression of the subject's amusement:

Nigel smiled at Mary's antics/at the joke

One sense of *laugh at* is similar to that of *smile at* in the last sentence, showing amusement. A further sense is when exhibiting disdain or mockery:

Maria laughed at Monty's pathetic and unsuccessful efforts to mount the wild horse

7.1d Focus of an emotion

If some person experiences an emotion there must be a reason for it, and this is typically expressed with an *at* phrase:

Maria marvelled at Ken's feat in mounting the wild horse
They grumbled at the cost of Anne's trip
Chris was indignant at the suggestion that he should foot the bill

Other verbs and adjectives signifying emotion which take an *at* phrase include:

rejoice at	exult at	baulk at	fret at
shudder at	impatient at	frightened at	angry at

The phrase *at heart* relates to this sense, as in *She had his interests at heart*.

7.1e Focus of an ability

Many adjectives which describe an ability or quality take an *at* phrase stating what this concerns. For example:

Sandra is clever at solving mathematical problems

Ronald is quick at understanding new procedures

Others include:

good at	proficient at	skilful at	expert at
adept at	fast at	slow at	bad at
perfect at	honest at	lucky at	unlucky at

Related to these are verbs referring to achievements and the like, as in:

Kenneth usually wins at cards

Also: *lose at, cheat at, excel at, succeed at,* and *fail at.*

Fault has a range of uses. If a person does something in an unsatisfactory manner, you may notice a fault, fault the person for it, or say that the person *failed at* the task and is *at fault.*

7.1f Focus on quantity

Suppose that you request an expert to assess the value of some work of art. Their opinion could be one of the following:

It's worth five hundred dollars at the least/at the most/at a pinch/
at the outside

A trader could sell something *at a discount* or *at a loss* or *at a profit* or *at a premium.* A collector could want to buy an artefact *at any price.*

In these examples, *at* introduces a quantitative phrase. Other instances of this sense involve verbs such as *value* and *estimate*:

He valued the house at half a million

She estimated the likely cost of repairs at ten thousand

Guess can combine with *at* in two rather different ways: (*make a*) *guess at* and *at a guess.* It can relate to quantity or else to the nature of something:

I couldn't (make a) guess at what it might be worth/at what Joe
might be thinking

At a guess it's worth about ten dollars/it's from Tudor times

Extensions from this sense include: *(twenty thousand jobs are) at stake/ at risk, (the point) at issue (is whether you are prepared to sign)*, and *(you must avoid going there) at all costs.*

At scarcely features in prepositional verbs and is found in only a sprinkling of phrasal verbs, always in slot **p** (in keeping with the fact that it can only be a preposition). In section 7.1c-1 examples were given of types V-p-NP (*get at (the truth)*) and V-a-p-NP (*get back at (a critic)*).

7.1g Several occurrences in a sentence

At is more amenable than many prepositions to being included in several propositional phrases within a single sentence.

Most commonly, the spatial sense is combined with another sense. For example:

> Jim stood at the gate at noon
>
> At noon, Jim stood at the gate

Note that here the temporal phrase, *at noon*, can be placed initially or finally but could not intrude between *Jim stood* and the inner prepositional phrase *at the gate.*

In other examples, the spatial phrase is of the outer variety. It could follow an *at* phrase showing, say, a target sense but is most felicitously placed some way apart from it, at the beginning of the sentence:

> At the circus, we marvelled at the prowess of the acrobats

In informal speech there is no real limit on sequences of *at* phrases. For example:

> Edmund shouted at Meg at the party at the town hall

However, in the written register such a proliferation would likely be avoided by re-phrasing.

7.1h Contrasting at *with other prepositions*

We can now examine contexts where *at* may contrast with prepositions dealt with in the previous chapters.

7.1h-1 *Of* and *at*

We can compare:

> Jimmy is frightened of walking home (because of the ruffians on the streets)
>
> Jimmy was frightened at the suggestion that he should walk home

As explained in section 5.2f, *frightened of* relates to doing something, about which the subject has strong feelings (similar to *ashamed of* and *weary of*). In contrast, *be frightened at* relates to an unwelcome potentiality (similar to *be indignant at*); see section 7.1d.

7.1h-2 *For* and *at*

When the noun *present* is used with the article *the*, it refers to an extent of time and then takes *for* in this sense (section 5.3f):

> I'll stay in Italy for the present

Or *present* can be used without the article and then refers to a point in time, taking *at* in its 'focus on a temporal point' sense (section 7.1b):

> I'm living in Italy at present

7.1h-3 *By* and *at*

Section 6.1c compared (a) the passive form of a transitive verb describing human emotion, where the erstwhile subject always takes preposition *by*, and (b) a participial adjective derived from the verb which may be followed by a prepositional phrase introduced by one of a range of prepositions, including *at*. This can be illustrated by:

(a) Mike was astounded by Marcia's beauty

> (passive of: *Marcia's beauty astounded Mike*; Mike was affected by her beauty)

(b) Mike was astounded at the critical comments from the police

> (adjective *astounded* is functioning as copula complement; Mike has an emotional response to the comments—section 7.1d)

The pair *surprised by/surprised at* was illustrated in section 6.1c. Other verbs with similar behaviour include: *astonish, disgust, shock,* and *concern.*

7.1h-4 *With* and *at*

If someone's anger is directed at a particular person, then *angry with* is most likely to be used (section 6.2d-2), whereas *angry at* will be preferred when the anger is towards something more general (section 7.1d). Compare:

> James was angry with me for forgetting to switch the alarm on
>
> James was angry at the general incompetence of the financial section

However, these are only tendencies of use. As with many other pairs—contrasted throughout the book—there is a fair degree of overlap and substitutability.

Other adjectives of similar ilk include: *mad with/at, annoyed with/at, delighted with/at, disgusted with/at,* and *exasperated with/at.*

7.2 *To*

To 'approaching', which is the major member of the pairing *to/from*, is far more frequent than the minor member, *from* 'departing', and has a wider range of meanings. Both are generally pronounced as proclitics and they are strictly prepositional, occurring only in inner—not in outer—prepositional phrases (see section 2.1).

In some of their basic meanings, *to* and *from* operate in pairs. For example:

> Tim ran from Rochdale to Ramsbottom
>
> Edward works every day from noon to midnight
>
> Sue attached the trailer to the truck
>
> Meg detached the trailer from the truck

There is extension from the basic sense to abstract meanings such as *The situation went from bad to worse.*

Besides its regular prepositional uses, *to* also has the critical grammatical function of marking one type of complement clause (CoCl); this is a clause which may fill a core argument slot in the main clause, as an alternative to an NP in this slot. A (FOR) TO complement clause indicates 'potentiality' or 'intention'; for example (see also section 2.5c):

> Freda$_A$ arranged [a meeting]$_{NP:O}$
> Freda$_A$ arranged [for her husband to meet the counsellor]$_{CoCl:O}$

The subject of the complement clause is omitted (together with the preceding *for*) when it has the same reference as the subject of the main clause. Thus:

> Freda$_A$ arranged [to meet the counsellor]$_{CoCl:O}$

If there is a verb with opposite meaning to a verb which accepts a TO complement clause, this may take a variety of -ING complement clauses introduced by *from*. We can compare:

> They persuaded/encouraged [Mary to go]
> They dissuaded/discouraged [Mary from going]

* * *

The preposition *to* will first be discussed, drawing attention to parallel examples with *from*. However, the great majority of *to*'s meanings have no correspondent with *from*. In section 7.4 we will see that *from* also has a fair number of original senses, though not so many as *to*.

We begin with the basic spatial meanings of *to*, and then its more abstract senses, relating to similarity, beneficiary, attitude, mode, interaction, relevance, and potentiality and phase.

7.2a Basic meanings

These refer to spatial orientation.

7.2a-1 Motion with respect to a destination

To and *from* may be used in inner prepositional phrases with simple verbs of motion, both intransitive—*go, come, run, walk, crawl, drive, march*, and dozens more—and transitive—*move, send, fetch, take, bring, carry, throw*, and so on. *To* indicates 'approaching a destination' and *from* 'departing an origin'.

A number of verbs, by virtue of their meaning, only take *to* phrases; for example, *penetrate to the bone, retire to bed.* A similar meaning applies to idiomatic expressions such as *(bring the dog) to heel* and *(chilled) to the bone.*

There is extension of this sense to various facets of direction. They include the transmission of heat in *expose/exposure to* (the sun) and *radiation from* (a conflagration). A further extension is the directional sense of *apply* in *Jamie applied to the boss for a rise.*

Some temporal expressions mirror spatial ones. Alongside *That train goes from New Orleans to Memphis*, we get *That shop is open from nine to five* and *Samuel Johnson lived from 1709 to 1784.* This is dealt with in section 14.6d.

7.2a-2 Contiguity

Adjectives describing close spatial relations are typically followed by *to*, as in:

> The post office is adjacent to the church

Also: *next to.* This sense of *to* extends to phrasal prepositions *close-to* and *near-to*; see the discussion in section 11.3b.

With noun *cheek* we get the idiomatic expression *dancing cheek to cheek.*

The contiguity sense applies to nouns such as: *a preliminary to, a prelude to*, and *a sequel to.* Also, at a more abstract level: *an introduction to.*

7.2a-3 Attachment

This extends contiguity into contact. Examples with intransitive and transitive verbs are:

> The child clung to its mother
>
> They chained the dog to the post

Other verbs here include *adhere to, stick to, attach to, bind to, fasten to, add to*, and *link to.* Participial forms of transitive verbs behave in the same way: *attached to, linked to*, and so on. Verbs with converse meanings may take *from*; for example, *detach from*, and *unfasten from.*

Extensions of meaning away from a purely spatial sense include: *apprenticed to, married to* (and *marriage to*), *(have) an affiliation to*, and *(be) a delegate to.* And there are nouns indicating an attachment—*a preface to, a corollary to*, and *a postscript to.*

7.2a-4 Change

This describes one thing becoming another, and may overlap with the motion sense. Compare:

> Justin moved his office from Pitt Street to Martin Place
>
> Justin changed his address from Pitt Street to Martin Place

Also *transfer*, *divert*, and *turn*. Other verbs of change transcend the spatial sense—*convert*, *increase*, *decrease*, and *revert*. Generally, a *from* phrase is only likely in the presence of a *to* phrase:

> Gerald reverted (from Presbyterianism) to his original Catholic faith

Note that there is no *from* correspondent for *accommodate to the new circumstances*.

7.2a-5 Directing attention to the nature of something

With verbs such as *point to* and *listen to*, the preposition relates to the character of the referent of the NP which follows it:

> Tom pointed to the excellent articulation of Sue's plan
>
> Please listen to what he is saying

7.2b Similarity

The canonical adjectives here are *similar (to)* and *different (from)*.

> Wallace's ideas about evolution were similar to those of Darwin
>
> Tim's concept of social justice is significantly different from mine

Similar meanings attach to *akin to*, *tantamount to*, *analogous to*, *equivalent to*, *equal to*, *identical to*, *parallel to*, and *comparable to*. Note that for none of these is there a *from* equivalent. Further adjectives indicating a difference also take *to*—*opposite to*, *contrary to*, and *foreign to*.

Also in this sense group are nouns *resemblance to*, *likeness to*, and *similarity to*, plus verbs *correspond to*, *liken to*, and *conform to*. A judgemental difference is expressed by adjectives *superior to/inferior to*.

An extension of the similarity sense leads to *cut to shape/size* and *made to measure*.

7.2c Beneficiary

There are a number of syntactic frames involved with verbs showing the 'beneficiary' sense. The subject argument invariably has human reference.

7.2c-1 The transitive object has non-human reference

And the *to* phrase (which is here the beneficiary) will have generalised human reference with some verbs, but not with all. For example:

> Susie supplied socks to the soldiers
> I subscribed $100 to the relief fund

Other benefactive verbs of this type include:

give to	offer to	lend to	pay to
owe to	cede to	present to	throw to
bequest to	dedicate to	consecrate to	show to
reveal to	communicate to	impart to	explain to

Also *propose marriage to*. And after something has been given to someone, it *belongs to* them.

7.2c-2 The transitive object has human reference

Here it is the object which is the beneficiary.

> They appointed Tony to the position of manager
> Mother welcomed the guests to the party

Other verbs here are: *promote* (someone) *to*, *sentence* (someone) *to*, *relegate* (someone) *to*, *restore* (the king) *to* (the throne), *expose* (the children) *to* (danger), and *recall* (the reserves) *to* (duty).

7.2c-3 An intransitive verb where the *to* phrase has human reference

Here the *to* phrase refers to the beneficiary (sometimes it is a maleficiary):

> Emily apologised to the priest for falling asleep during his sermon
> We complained to the neighbours about their excessive noise

Also in this group are:

speak to	talk to	sing to	whisper to
pray to	minister to	pander to	surrender to
yield to	defer to	grumble to	protest to
appeal to	confess to	admit to	succumb to

The beneficence may be indirect. One can *reply to a person* or else *reply to a question*, in which case the reply is effectively to whoever posed the question. Similarly with *respond to*.

A set of adjectives describes how one person behaves towards other people (the beneficiaries):

> Marcia was kind/cruel to the prisoners

Also:

indulgent to	courteous to	discourteous to	loyal to
polite/rude to	considerate to	faithful to	generous to
mean to	hospitable to	sympathetic to	spiteful to

7.2d Attitude

This describes someone's mental orientation in relation to the referent of the *to* phrase.

It can first be illustrated with verb *agree*:

> The union agrees to the new workplace agreement

This sentiment may also be expressed with the adjective *agreeable*, in either of two ways:

(a) The union is agreeable to the new workplace agreement
(b) The new workplace agreement is agreeable to the union

Agreeable may be unique in allowing the arguments to be reversed and maintaining the same essential meaning. There are other adjectives which may be used just in frame (b), including:

acceptable to	pleasing to	satisfying to	repugnant to
distasteful to	abhorrent to	precious to	sacred to

And there are adjectives which occur just in frame (a). For example:

> Robin was alive to/oblivious to the new opportunities available

Also:

alert to	attentive to	awake to	blind to
deaf to	opposed to	indifferent to	averse to
insensitive to	amenable to	partial to	

There are many transitive verbs expressing mental attitude which can have a (FOR) TO complement clause—in place of a plain NP—as their O argument:

I like football$_{\text{NP:O}}$ I like [to watch/play football]$_{\text{CoCl;O}}$
I want [a dog]$_{\text{NP:O}}$ I want [to buy a dog]$_{\text{CoCl;O}}$

Verbs with this property are distributed across several semantic sets. We can just mention a selection.

(Those which employ a preposition with an NP drop this before complementiser *to*.)

LIKING:	love, like, hate, prefer, fear, dread
WANTING:	want, desire, crave, wish (for); also aspire to, hope (for), expect, need, require, pretend
TRYING	try, attempt, strive to, endeavour to, arrange, manage, fail
SAYING:	promise, decline, agree (to), assent (to), object (to)
DECIDING:	choose, decide on, resolve on
THINKING	remember, forget
SPEED:	hurry (with)

Related adjectives which take a (FOR) TO complement clause include: *happy, content, willing, reluctant, anxious,* and *eager*. For example:

I was happy (for Thea) to propose the vote of thanks

Another manifestation of attitude involves making a judgement, as in *They considered Lucy to be clever.*

7.2e Mode

A number of adjectives deal with the way in which something is done; for example, degree of difficulty. The adjective is used as copula complement (CC), with a (FOR) TO complement clause as copula subject (CS), and this may be extraposed to the end of the sentence:

[For Jane to solve the puzzle]$_{\text{CoCl:CS}}$ [was easy/difficult]$_{\text{CC}}$

It was [easy/difficult]$_{\text{CC}}$ [for Jane to solve the puzzle]$_{\text{CoCl:CS}}$

An alternative construction is:

The puzzle was easy/difficult (for Jane) to solve

Other adjectives here include *hard*, *tough*, and *simple*.

With adjectives of speed, the CS argument refers to a person, and the adjective is followed by a reduced TO clause:

Kate was quick/slow to solve the problem

7.2f Interaction

In *I want/would like Mary to apply for the position*, it is possible that Mary may not be aware of my attitude. Compare this with another set of verbs, also taking a (FOR) TO complement clause, exemplified by:

I encouraged/persuaded/convinced Mary to apply for the position

Here the speaker's attitude is communicated to the other person, so that they should undertake what would satisfy the speaker. Other verbs in this set include: *tell to, order to, command to, force to, allow to, permit to, provoke to, incite to, remind to, ask to, beg to*, and *invite to*.

7.2g Relevance

To can be used in establishing a connection which is described by an adjective:

Your costume is entirely appropriate to the occasion

That criticism is not applicable to all the staff

Also: *relevant to, immaterial to, pertinent to, related to*, and *germane to*. There may be a value judgement involved, as in: *detrimental to, beneficial to, (dis)advantageous to*, and *important to*. A number of prepositional verbs also fall under this sense, including: *refer to, pertain to, allude to*, and *relate to*.

A related meaning is when describing a person's experience; for example:

I was accustomed to her ways

He soon got used to the work

Or, putting things the other way around, stating perceptiveness and accessibility:

The correct course of action was obvious to Susie

Also: *visible to, apparent to, clear to,* and *evident to.*
   Another kind of relevance relates to obligation, as in:

You are responsible to the group manager

We are answerable to the stakeholders

Even priests are obliged to obey the rules

I am indebted to my first three wives for their financial support

7.2h Potentiality and phase

To is used with adjectives relating to the chance of something happening:

It is likely to rain today

Luca is apt to wave his hands around when explaining some
   critical point

Also: *certain to, liable to, tend to,* and *prone to.* Related to these are *doomed to (die)* and *lucky to (win).*
   A number of adverbial phrases introduced with *to* belong with this sense. For example:

To some extent, Donald must be held responsible for the
   breakdown of government

Others include: *to a great extent,* and *to a degree,* plus *(she enjoys life) to the full, (he drinks) to excess,* and *(he loves her) to distraction.*
   A related use of *to* is with verbs describing a phase of an activity:

Nicola started to/began to/continued to/ceased to work on her
   thesis

7.2i To *in phrasal verbs and prepositional verbs*

There are a couple of dozen prepositional verbs which include *to.* A number were mentioned in the last few sections—*adhere to, akin to, dedicate to, pander to, defer to, endeavour to, refer to, pertain to, allude to, apt to, liable to,* and *prone to*.

In keeping with its status as a preposition, *to* occurs in slot **p** for phrasal verbs of four types. A selection of those which relate to the meanings just described are:

SENSE	TYPE	
Motion	V-p-NP	The invalid has <u>taken to</u> his bed
	V-p-NP	She <u>turned to</u> Jim (for help)
Attachment	V-p-NP	My sister always <u>sticks to</u> the rules
Change	V-a-p-NP	When did they <u>change over to</u> metric?
	V-NP-a-p-NP	He needs to <u>bring</u> his work <u>up to</u> a decent standard
	V-NP-a-p-NP	We must <u>bring</u> him <u>round to</u> our way of thinking
Beneficiary	V-p-NP	Please <u>see to</u> the baby
	V-NP-p-NP	The soldiers <u>subjected</u> the prisoner <u>to</u> torture
Phase	V-a-p-NP	Let's <u>get down to</u> business

The meanings of phrasal verbs *talk down to NP* 'patronise' and *put NP down to NP* 'attribute to' (as in *She put the shortage down to bad planning*) do not accord with any of the meanings just listed for *to*. However, they do relate to the 'inferior position' sense of the **a** element, *down*; see section 10.3a.

To has one unexpected property. Despite the fact that it does not function as an adverb, there are just a few phrasal verbs where *to* fills the **a** slot:

SENSE	TYPE	
Attitude	V-a	The soldiers are <u>standing to</u> (awaiting orders to attack)
Phase	V-a	(There was a lot or work to be done and) Hannah <u>set to</u> at once
	V-a	(The driver lost consciousness in the accident and) <u>came to</u> in the hospital
	V-NP-a	The doctors <u>brought</u> the patient <u>to</u>

7.2j Other uses of to

The conjunction *in order to* is frequently shortened and becomes just *to*. For example, two intransitive clauses can be linked together as:

Meg went (in order) to swim

This is a quite different use of *to* from the plain preposition in *Meg went to the river*, and also from *to* in a (FOR) TO complement clause such as:

Meg hoped [(for Jill) to swim]$_{CoCl:O}$

The CoCl subject is not stated when it is identical with main clause subject. The two sentences

| with CONJUNCTION | Meg went to swim |
| including COMPLEMENT CLAUSE | Meg hoped to swim |

are superficially similar but in fact have quite distinct structures, involving different varieties of *to*.

A further use of *to* is as an intrinsic part of modal verbs *ought to* and *be to*, plus semi-modals *be going to*, *have (got) to*, *be able to*, *be about to*, *get to*, and *be bound to*.

When one examines whether a sentence may include several instances of a *to* constituent (in the senses covered in sections 7.2a–h) the obvious possibilities involve a complement clause within a complement clause within a complement clause and so on. Examples may be freely manufactured:

Stella ordered [Tom to tell [John to encourage [Mike to try [to remember [to hurry [to continue [to urge [the workmen to dig the ditch]]]]]]]]

However, only a pedantic school-teacher would attempt anything even a quarter as complex as this.

Otherwise, there are rather limited possibilities for a sentence including several *to* constituents.

7.2k Contrasting to with other prepositions

We can now examine contexts where *to* may contrast with prepositions dealt with earlier.

7.2k-1 *Of* and *to*

The following sentences may be used in the same circumstance, with similar meanings:

Jack was aware of the possibilities

Jack was alive to the possibilities

The first sentence exemplifies the 'knowledge' sense for *of* (section 5.2g); Jack is familiar with the possibilities, and he may or may not do something in connection with them. The second sentence is from the 'attitude' sense of *to* (section 7.2d). Jack not only knows about the possibilities, he realises their likely benefit for him.

Another contrast between these two prepositions is dialectal. In telling the time, many Americans would say *It's ten of nine* whereas in Standard British English it would be *It's ten to nine* (see sections 5.2h, 14.6b, and 15.3a).

7.2k-2 *For* and *to*

Either preposition can be used in:

Jill is the assistant for the project

Jill is the assistant to the boss

In the first sentence Jill would be assisting the whole project, which is the 'benefit' sense of *for* (section 5.3a) whereas in this second she would be closely associated with the boss, the 'attachment' sense of *to* in section 7.2a-3.

7.2k-3 *By* and *to*

It is difficult to distinguish between the meanings of the following two sentences:

Betty is standing close by the tree

Betty is standing close to the tree

They illustrate the 'near to, not quite reaching' sense of *by* (section 6.1a) and the 'contiguity' sense of *to* in section 7.2a-2. However, a difference does appear if a different verb is employed. *Betty walked close by the tree* would imply that she passed from one side of the tree to the other, whereas *Betty walked close to the tree* might be used if she just walked up to the tree, getting close to it.

7.2k-4 *With* and *to*

Either preposition can follow verb *correspond*:

> The results obtained correspond with projections set out in the plan
>> (what has transpired is similar to what was predicted to eventuate)
>
> These pins stuck in the map correspond to the enemy's munitions depots
>> (each pin indicates the position of one munitions depot)

The first of these sentences uses the 'agreement' sense of *with* (section 6.2c) and the second the 'similarity' sense of *to* (section 7.2b). Similar contrasts are found in *be identical with/to*, *be equal with/to*, and *have an affinity with/to*.

7.2k-5 *At* and *to*

There are a fair number of instances of contrast between these two prepositions. We can begin by recapitulating two examples from section 1.1a. First with *throw*:

> The fieldsman threw the ball at the wickets
>> (to hit the wickets)
>> 'Action with respect to a target' sense of *at*, section 7.1c-2.
>
> The fieldsman threw the ball to the wicketkeeper
>> (for the wicketkeeper to catch it)
>> 'Beneficiary' sense of *to*; section 7.2c-1.

Hyponyms of *throw* show different possibilities. One would say *hurl at*, but not *hurl to*, since *hurl* implies the use of force, which is not compatible with this sense of *to*. And the verb *toss* takes *to*, not *at*, since it implies a destination rather than a target.

Another contrast involves some verbs of speaking:

> Edmund shouted at Meg
>> (he was directing his annoyance at Meg)
>> 'Target as focus of speaking' sense of *at*; section 7.1c-3.
>
> Edmund shouted to Meg
>> (he was telling her something and had to raise his voice since she was far off)
>> 'Motion to destination' sense of *to*; section 7.2a-1.

There is a similar contrast between *talk at* and *talk to* (see section 1.1a). However, the meanings of other verbs of speaking restrict them to just one of these prepositions—*bawl* is only compatible with the 'target' sense of *at*, and *pray* only with the 'destination' sense of *to*.

A further contrast follows verb *point*:

> She pointed at Mack's home-made computer
>
> > (showing where it was located)
> >
> > 'Focus on gesture' sense of *at*; section 7.1c-4.
>
> She pointed to Mack's home-made computer
>
> > (as an example of what a clever boy can do)
> >
> > 'Directing attention to the nature of something' sense of *to*; section 7.2a-5.

There is an interesting contrast between the use of *at* with *look* and *to* with *listen*. *Look at* indicates directing the eyes to focus on a target (section 7.1c-4), whereas *listen to* provides another instance of the 'nature of the referent' sense of *to* in section 7.2a-5.

An instructive comparison involves *to*, *at*, and also *with*. The following three sentences may be used in similar circumstances, but with different orientations:

> Rita is familiar with this kind of work
>
> > (she has done it before)
> >
> > 'Knowledge' sub-sense of 'association' for *with*; section 6.2b-2.
>
> Rita is experienced at this kind of work
>
> > (she has the ability to do it)
> >
> > 'Focus of an ability' sense of *at*; section 7.1e.
>
> Rita is accustomed to this kind of work
>
> > (this is what she often does)
> >
> > 'Relevance' sense of *to*; section 7.2g.

The fairly subtle difference between phrasal verbs *get at NP* and *get to NP* is reflected in the senses of *at* and *to* involved here:

> The policeman wishes to <u>get at</u> the truth
>
> > (this is what his investigation is directed towards)
> >
> > Extension from the 'focus on a target' sense of *at*; section 7.1c-1.

The philosopher wishes to <u>get to</u> the heart of the controversy

    (he wants to find out the basic issues that are involved)

    'Attention to the nature of something' sense of *to*; section 7.2a-5.

Another pair of phrasal verbs illustrates a rather different contrast between *at* and *to*:

    I wish you'd <u>stick at</u> your work

        (keep doing it steadily, without interruption)

        'Focus on a target' sense of *at*; section 7.1c-2.

    I wish you'd <u>stick to</u> your own work

        (and stop bothering about what other people are doing)

        'Attitude' sense of *to*; section 7.2d.

7.3 *Towards* and *toward*

The Old English suffix-*weard(es)* 'in the direction of' was used in many adverbs including *norþ-weard(-es)* 'northward' and *hām-weard(es)* 'on the way home, homewards'. These have given rise to modern adverbs ending in -*ward(s)*, some of which may also function as adjectives. *Inward(s)* and *outward(s)* are mentioned in section 8.1h, *onward(s)*, *offward(s)*, *upward(s)*, and *downward(s)* at the beginnings of chapters 9 and 10. Generally, a final -*s* may be included when the word is used as an adverb—for example, *He went homewards*—and is omitted when employed as an adjective—*He set off in a homeward direction*. However, there is considerable variation concerning whether or not a final -*s* is included on adverbs.

    The OE suffix was added to preposition *tō*, creating a new preposition *tōweard(es)* 'in the direction of', which has come through into the modern language in two forms: *toward* /tə'wɔːd/ and *towards* /tə'wɔːdz/. There is no clear principle concerning when to use each form. In American English, *toward* is about five times more frequent than *towards*, whereas the reverse holds in Standard British English. Yet each dialect does utilise both forms. Which to use is essentially a matter of whim, perhaps involving considerations of euphony.

    In the basic spatial sense there is a clear contrast with *to*:

Samuel ran to the tower

(the implication is that he reaches the tower)

Samuel ran towards the tower

(this only specifies a direction, not a destination)

Beyond this, very few of the contexts in which *to* is used are available for *towards*, and vice versa.

The basic meaning of *toward(s)* is 'in a direction'. There are spatial and temporal senses, and extensions: in the direction of an achievement, feelings directed towards someone or something, and attitude directed at some act or state (but not quite getting there).

7.3a Spatial meaning

The most straightforward use is 'movement in the direction of a place', with verbs of motion, as in the example just given and in:

He made a move towards the lift, and then halted

She pushed the box towards the door

There can be the direction of attention, as in *point towards* and:

Look towards those far hills and you'll see a bright light

And there can be description of a location as being on the way to a place:

Mike's house is towards the top of the hill

7.3b Temporal meaning

This indicates a time which is moving in the direction of a specified temporal point, shown by a prepositional phrase introduced with *toward(s)*; see also section 14.6a.

People get into a bit of a panic towards the end of the financial year

There should be a few showers towards the end of the week

It was towards midnight when she returned

7.3c In the direction of an achievement

Getting something done may be a gradual process, and movement in the direction of the goal can be described using *toward(s)* with an NP describing the goal:

> We made some progress towards reaching agreement on the
>   plan for expansion
> They made efforts toward eliminating rampant corruption
> Pat and Sue put the bequest towards the deposit needed for
>   buying a house

7.3d Feelings directed at someone or something

This relates to a person having an emotional reaction to some other person or thing. It can involve a verb or a noun:

> How does Henry behave towards his parents?
> What are Jack's feelings towards Jill?

For some of the examples of this sense there is contrast with another preposition which conveys a similar but still slightly different meaning; typically, the *toward(s)* alternative implies greater involvement. With noun *affection* we can have:

> Maria showed a real affection towards the kitten
> Maria showed affection for the kitten

The *towards* sentence suggests that Maria is physically involved with the kitten—stroking it and talking to it. The *for* alternative is more measured; here Maria likes having the kitten around (whereas she can't stand the dog); see section 5.1.

With can alternate with *toward(s)* after adjective *gentle*:

> Anne is gentle towards dumb animals
>   (she shows consideration for their sensitivity)
>
> Anne was gentle with the fragile artefacts
>   (she took great care to handle them carefully so as to avoid
>   damage)
>   'Activity directed towards something' sense of *with*; section 6.2e.

As with *affection towards*, *gentle towards* implies involvement with the referent of the NP (here, dumb animals). When the NP has inanimate reference (fragile artefacts) a more detached attitude is shown by using *for*.

Adjective *hostile* may be followed by *to*, indicating a lack of appreciation of some general proposal or thing, or by *toward(s)* which may imply activity directed against what is unwanted:

> Leonardo is hostile to the idea of foreign intervention
> (and will vote against it)
> 'Attitude' sense of *to*; section 7.2d.

> Leonardo is hostile towards foreign immigrants
> (and will help man the barriers to keep them out)

7.3e Attitude directed at some act or state (but not quite getting there)

This sense is shown with verbs:

> She often verges towards despair
> They are leaning towards accepting the terms offered

And also with a noun such as *propensity* or *tendency*:

> He has a tendency towards self-destruction

7.4 From

In its spatial meaning, *from* 'departing an origin', the minor member of the pairing *to/from*, shows a number of correspondences with the major member *to* 'approaching a destination'. However, extensions from this basic meaning only occasionally relate to a sense of *to*. The extensions cover source, absence, difference, and prevention and lack of involvement.

7.4a Basic meanings

These refer to spatial orientation.

7.4a-1 Motion with respect to an origin

The great majority of verbs of motion—both intransitive and transitive—may occur with a *to* phrase, or with a *from* phrase, or with both. For example:

Brian walked from Oxford [sc. to here]

Brian walked to Oxford [sc. from here]

Brian walked from here to Oxford

An interesting property of *from* is that it not only patterns with *to*, in relating to motion, it also patterns with *at*, in relating to location. This can be seen in:

MOTION	LOCATION
Sam travelled from Paddington	Sam departed from Paddington
Sam travelled to Paddington	Sam arrived at Paddington

There are very few verbs of motion which may only take a *to* phrase, and not also a *from* phrase. In contrast, there are quite a few verbs of motion that are restricted to a *from* phrase. For example:

The tide receded from the shore

Valerie recoiled from the snake

For getting onto a horse there is a transitive verb, *mount—Mark mounted the horse*. The verb describing getting off a horse adds negative prefix *dis-* and becomes intransitive, requiring a *from* phrase:

Mark dismounted from the horse

Also *alight from* (e.g. a train).

The verb *escape* can have *to* and/or *from* qualification—*He escaped (from Nazi Germany) (to England)*. However the noun *fugitive* only takes a *from* phrase—*He was a fugitive from fascism*. Similarly with *refugee from*.

7.4a-2 Distance

Corresponding to the 'contiguity' sense of *to*, preposition *from* is used with an adjective describing a remote location, as in:

The post office is distant from the church.

This meaning of *from* is also found in the phrasal preposition *far-from*; see the discussion in section 11.3b.

7.4a-3 Change

Under this heading for *to* (section 7.2a-4), we saw that verbs of change can typically include a *to* phrase or a *from* phrase or both, as in:

They turned the statue (from facing north) (to facing south)

However, there are verbs describing change which may only take a *from* qualification:

Don't deviate from the script which you've been given!

7.4b Source

Extending from the spatial sense in *Sam departed from Paddington*, a *from* phrase can indicate the origin of something described by an intransitive verb:

All life forms evolved from amoebas
The plan stems from an idea of Dave's

Other verbs here include: *issue from, result from, derive from*, and *benefit from*.

A source phrase may also be added to a transitive verb:

From his father, Isaac inherited two newspapers and a gold mine
Hannah recited the poem from memory

Also *obtain from* and *steal from*.

A verb may describe some mental operation with the data base marked by *from*:

The detective drew his conclusions from the fingerprints on the whiskey bottle
Please don't judge his character from his unkempt appearance

A similar sense of the preposition is used with some nouns; for instance *Albert derived satisfaction from solving the problem*. Also, *pleasure, delight*, and *joy*.

A further sense of a *from* phrase is to state the nature of some physical condition:

Michael is suffering from gout
Joy awoke from a coma
Jim is recovering from a stroke

This meaning also involves verbs such as *recuperate from* and *rouse from*; plus adjectives like *tired from* and *exhausted from*.

7.4c Absence

A person or thing may not be in a place or position where they are expected to be, or where they were. This place may be shown through a *from* phrase. The absent item may simply be missing, or it could have been evicted, or separated off, or extracted. Subtraction also belongs to this sense.

7.4c-1 Missing

The absent item has simply gone, with no explanation provided. This sense can involve an intransitive verb or an adjective.

> The snake vanished from sight
>
> The diamond tiara disappeared without trace from the duchess's boudoir
>
> A rifle is missing from the rack
>
> Leonard was absent from class again today

7.4c-2 Eviction

Here a transitive verb describes the action of getting rid of some item:

> The principal has expelled Leonard from the school
>
> The king has banished Lord Jerrypot from the kingdom

Other verbs in this set include: *eliminate, eradicate, exclude, expel, evict, discharge, dismiss,* and *remove*. Also *release* in the context *Jack was released from jail today*.

7.4c-3 Separation

This meaning of *from* corresponds to the 'attachment' sense of *to* (section 7.2a-3).

Something can be attached to something and then separated from it. In a number of instances the 'separation' verb involves a negative prefix (*un-, de-,* or *dis-*) added to the 'attachment' verb. For instance, alongside *Kate tied the boat to its mooring*, we can have:

> Peter untied the boat from its mooring

Other pairs include: *attach to/detach from, fasten to/unfasten from, connect to/disconnect from,* and also *cede to/secede from*.

For some verbs of separation there is no corresponding verb of attachment. For example:

> You must separate the outer bark from the inner bark
>
> She just plucked the fruit from the tree

This sense is extended to mental states such as *freedom from fear/hunger*. And the general statement *I can't tell one person/thing from another.*

7.4c-4 Extraction

Here a transitive verb describes removing something which had been a part of something else:

> The surgeon extracted the bullet from my wound
>
> Please delete that reference to Whatmough from your thesis
>
> She removed the painting of her first husband from the dining room

There can be extension to more abstract senses:

> The new president extricated the nation from its financial crisis
>
> He quoted from Sapir's *Language*

We also get *The runner withdrew from the race* and *The trainer withdrew his star horse from the event*. Related nouns are *quotation from* and *withdrawal from*. And, at a more abstract level, there is *She was saved from false optimism*.

7.4c-5 Subtraction

There is correspondence with *to* in description of arithmetical operations. Alongside *She added two to five*, one could say:

> She subtracted/took two from seven

A related sense of *from* is seen in:

> The salesman deducted 20 per cent from the price of the coat

As mentioned at the end of section 7.2a-1, temporal and time expressions may mirror spatial ones, as in: *He was in jail from January to April.* When referring to time, *from* has a wider scope than *to*, and it combines temporal and source senses in:

> The west wing of the castle dates from the fourteenth century

7.4d Difference

Just as the adjective *similar* is followed by *to*, so adjective *different* most often takes *from*:

> The film was quite different from what I had expected

Although *different from* is the more frequent collocation, one also hears *different to*, patterned on *similar to*. (A third alternative, *different than*, was occasionally used in England in the eighteenth century and now has wide vogue in American English.) Note, however, that verb *differ* and noun *difference* may only be followed by *from*, not *to*.

7.4e Prevention and lack of involvement

In keeping with most of its non-spatial senses having negative overtones, *from* is used with verbs which describe stopping something happening and ceasing to do something.

7.4e-1 Prevention

A verb which describes someone making someone else do something will take a (FOR) TO complement clause and a verb with the opposite meaning will take a FROM -ING CoCl:

> I forced her to go
>
> I prevented her (from) going

The interesting point here is that the *from* may be omitted from the second sentence—and there is a difference of meaning. *I prevented her going* implies that direct means were employed (e. g. I blocked her path) whereas *I prevented her from going* could indicate indirect means (e.g. I used my influence to ensure that she wasn't issued with a passport).

Other verbs of prevention taking a FROM -ING CoCl include: *stop, save, spare, hinder, restrain, dissuade,* and *discourage*. (The last two were contrasted with *persuade* and *encourage* in section 7.2). *Forbid* is of particular interest in that it was first used with a TO clause (*I forbid you to go*), but as time went by, an increasing number of speakers came to prefer a FROM -ING clause (*I forbid you from going*), which accords better with the negative meaning of this verb.

7.4e-2 Lack of involvement

There are intransitive verbs which describe how someone ceases to take part—or doesn't take part—in an activity, which is shown by a *from* phrase.

> Jerome withdrew from the contest, with a leg injury
>
> Roland retired from the museum, having reached the age of 88
>
> Jennifer refrained from speaking during the debate

Also *abstain from* and *desist from*.

* * *

There are very few phrasal verbs involving *from*; under row B in section 3.7 *They <u>kept</u> the bad news <u>from</u> Mary* was quoted. Quite a number of prepositional verbs include *from*, including the following which were mentioned in the preceding sections: *deviate from, stem from, issue from, result from, derive from,* and *refrain from.*

7.4f Contrasting from with other prepositions

We can now examine contexts where *from* may contrast with prepositions dealt with earlier.

7.4f-1 Of and from

Once Julia's divorce has been finalised, one could say either of:

> Julia is now free of all marital responsibilities
>
> > 'Dissociation' sense for *of*; section 5.2h.
>
> Julia is now free from all marital responsibilities
>
> > 'Lack of involvement' sense of *from*; section 7.4e-2.

The *of* sentence focuses on the fact that she did have marital responsibilities and has been relieved of them. There is a subtle difference of meaning between this and the *from* alternative which simply states that she has removed herself from these responsibilities, and can direct her life in a new direction.

7.4f-2 *By* and *from*

A peripheral phrase accompanying verb *judge* can either use *by*, which relates to the way in which the judge thought, or else *from* which focuses on the information available to the judge:

> To judge by the evidence he gave, Simon did not even know the victim
>
> > 'How a mental condition or state is achieved'; section 6.1b-5.
>
> To judge from the evidence he gave, Simon did not even know the victim
>
> > 'Source' sense of *from*; section 7.4b.

7.4f-3 *With* and *from*

We can compare two ways of describing a tragedy:

> In the freezing conditions, six soldiers perished with cold
> > 'Physical state explanation' sense of *with*; section 6.2d-1.
>
> In the freezing conditions, six soldiers perished from cold
> > 'Source' sense of *from*; section 7.4b.

The *with* sentence states that the soldiers were cold and thus died, while the *from* one says that it was the cold conditions which caused the deaths.

*　*　*

Having dealt with the three central spatial prepositions, we can now turn to those with more specific meanings, commencing with *in, out,* and other prepositions relating to the notion of 'enclosure'.

8

Enclosure

In, into, out, out-of; within, without, inside(-of), outside(-of)

English Prepositions: Their Meanings and Uses. R. M. W. Dixon. Oxford University Press (2021). © R. M. W. Dixon.
DOI: 10.1093/oso/9780198868682.003.0008

At first glance, *in* and *out* might appear to be a straightforward pair of opposites. Compare:

(1) Jack stayed in last night   Jill went out last night
(2) We voted the new president in   We voted the old president out
(3) Bring the milk in!   Put the garbage out!

Similarly for *into* and *out-of*:

(4) Sam let the cat into the house   Sam put the cat out-of the house

(5) They talked John into resigning   They talked John out-of resigning

Alongside such congruences between the members of the pairs, there are also considerable differences—in etymology, and in form, meaning, and use.

In Early Old English there were prepositions *in* 'in, into' and *on* 'on'. Preposition *in* dropped out of use during Old English times, its meaning being added to that of *on*. The resultant ambiguity of *on* was resolved in Middle English, when *innan* 'inside' reduced its form to just *in* /in/ and enlarged its meaning to 'in', as *on* contracted its meaning to just 'on'. This effectively restored the original OE contrast between *in* and *on*. *In* also had adverbial function and could be followed by preposition *to*, the sequence developing into the complex preposition *into* /'intə=/.

The Old English adverbs *ūt* and *ūte* had similar meanings 'out, outside', and merged to give modern *out* /aut/. From the earliest times it could be followed by preposition *of* and there thus developed the complex preposition *out-of* /'autəv=/.

Section 2.3 provided justification for treating *into* /intə=/ and *out-of* /autəv=/ as unitary prepositions. (It should be *outof*, parallel to *into*, but English orthography is somewhat inconsistent; thus *out-of* is adopted here to show that it is a single word.) Each of *into* and *out-of* is, by virtue of the final element, generally a proclitic to the following word. They are purely prepositions and must be followed by an NP. In contrast, *in* /in/ and *out* /aut/ are always distinct words, never proclitics. Both function as adverbs although *in* is also used as a preposition (sometimes as an alternative to *into*) and *out* is sometimes so used (as a somewhat colloquial shortening of *out-of*). There is a fair amount of variation between dialects concerning the use of these forms. Their functions in Standard British English are described here.

In, which functions as both adverb and preposition, makes up a pairing with *out*, which is primarily an adverb and occasionally a preposition. The major member, *in*, has a basic meaning 'enclosed' while that of the minor member, *out*, is 'unenclosed, when something used to be enclosed or might be expected to be enclosed'. *In* has a wider range of meanings than *out* and is overall far more frequent. There are a number of prepositional verbs which include *in*—*participate in, consist in,* and *indulge in* were illustrated in chapter 4—but very few which involve *out*. However, perhaps rather surprisingly, we find about twice as many phrasal verbs with *out* or *out-of* as with *in* or *into*.

The basic functions of *in, into, out,* and *out-of* are:

	(a)	(b)
ADVERB	*in*	*out*
PREPOSITION OF LOCATION	*in*	*out-of*
PREPOSITION OF MOTION	*into* or *in*, for neutral spatial sentences	*out-of* may be reduced to *out* for pragmatic strength

Adverbial use is shown in:

The tide is coming in   The sun has just come out

The differences of function as prepositions can be illustrated with simple spatial sentences involving intransitive and transitive verbs with inner PPs:

			(a)	(b)
LOCATION		(6)	Sandra is sitting in the sun	Sandra is sitting out-of the sun
		(7)	Sandra placed her chair in the sun	Sandra placed her chair out-of the sun
MOTION		(8)	Bill went into the house	Bill came out-of the house
	OR	(8')	Bill went in the house	

(9)   Bill took the milk   Bill took the empties
into the house   out-of the house

OR   (9') Bill took the milk in
the house

For location meanings, in the (a) column we can only have preposition *in* and in the (b) column it must be *out-of*.

Looking now at motion, there is congruence between *into* in (a) and *out-of* in (b). But here there is a difference in that *in* may be used in the (a) sentences, as an alternative to *into*, with no significant difference in meaning. It appears that *in*, the preposition for location, is extended to be also a preposition for motion. However, using *in* rather than *into* is most likely if the verb has a fairly neutral meaning, just indicating motion (proto-typically *come, go, bring, take,* and *put*). We can compare:

	acceptability of replacing *into* by *in*
John came into the room	very high
John walked into the room	high
The ambulance turned into the driveway	medium
Charles rushed into the room	low

It seems that the extent to which the meaning of the verb exceeds straightforward 'entering', determines the likelihood of using just *in* rather than *into*.

There are limited circumstances in which *out-of* may be replaced by *out* in the (b) motion sentences, perhaps by analogy with *in* as an alternative to *into* in the (a) column. (See the discussion concerning 'optional *of*' in section 5.2k.) In Standard British English this occurs rather seldom, and predominantly in sentences which have pragmatic intensity; for example *Chuck it out the window!* and *She scurried out the door.* Using just *out* in a motion sentence is much more common in American English.

There was discussion in section 2.1b of how the NP component may be omitted from an inner PP when it could be understood from the context. For example, *Take the cloth off the table!* may be reduced to *Take the cloth off!* There can then be left-movement of the exposed preposition over a preceding NP (provided that it is not a pronoun), giving *Take off the cloth!*

With *into* and *out-of*, the following NP cannot simply be dropped since these prepositions require a following NP to cliticise onto. However, an NP can—in suitable circumstances—be omitted provided that *into* is replaced by *in* and *out-of* by *out*. Left movement may then apply for the *in* and *out*. This can be exemplified:

		(a)	(b)
MOTION	(8)	Bill went into/in the house	Bill came out-of the house
	(8r)	Bill went in	Bill came out
	(9)	Bill took the milk into/in the house	Bill took the empties out-of the house
	(9r)	Bill took the milk in	Bill took the empties out
	(9r-L)	Bill took in the milk	Bill took out the empties

In (8-a) and (9-a) the preposition may be *into* or *in*, but only *in* is permissible when *the house* is omitted, as in (8r-a) and (9r-a). In (8-b) and (9-b) the preposition can only be *out-of*, which must reduce to *out* when there is no following NP.

The location sentences, (10-a) and (11-a) may only use *in*, which remains after NP omission. But in (10-b) and (11-b) the preposition *out-of* has to be shortened to *out* when *the house* is deleted.

		(a)	(b)
LOCATION	(10)	James is staying in the house today	Jake is staying out-of the house tonight
	(10r)	James is staying in today	Jake is staying out tonight
	(11)	Mary left the map in her book	Jane left the map out-of her book
	(11r)	Mary left the map in	Jane left the map out
	(11r-L)	Mary left in the map	Jane left out the map

Sentences (11) describe Mary and Jane deciding whether or not to include a map in their respective new books. In the context of this discussion, *the book* would be understood if left unstated.

At the beginning of chapter 7 it was pointed out that *in* is one of four prepositions (with *at*, *to*, and *from*) which may omit *the* from a following NP before a limited set of nouns. One would say *Chris is in jail* if he were a prisoner, but *the* should be included, giving *Chris is in the jail today*, if he were a tradesman who paints public buildings. As mentioned in section 1.9, both *in* and *out* have cognate derivational prefixes, deriving both adjectives and nouns; for example, *an in-group joke* and *an out-patient*.

There are pairs of sentences with preposition *into* corresponding to *out-of*, as in (4), (8–9) and the phrasal verbs in (5). The are also pairs with adverbs *in* and *out*, as in (1–2). When we examine extensions from the basic spatial meanings, there is a frequent contrast between *in* and *out-of*. For example:

My son is still in danger	My son is now out-of danger
You're in luck today	You're out-of luck today
The film is in focus	The film is out-of focus

Section 8.1 deals with *in* and *into*, mentioning correspondences with *out* and *out-of* where these exist. This is followed, in section 8.2, by discussion of additional senses for *out* and *out-of*. We then turn to the related pairs *within* and *without*, and *inside(-of)* and *outside(-of)*, in section 8.3.

8.1 *In* and *into*

Similar to *at* (section 7.1), preposition *in* may be said to look in either of two directions:

(i) A fair number of verbs and a few adjectives expect to be followed by a peripheral NP marked by *in*; for example, *compete in*, *join in*, *share in*, *excel in*, and *(be) generous in*.

(ii) A large number of nominals are typically preceded by preposition *in*. The possibilities are:
- A single noun, such as: *in power*, *in public*, *in reality*, *in revenge*, *in prose*, *in uniform*, *in silence*, *in love*, *in difficulty*, *in conclusion*, and *in bulk*.
- A definite NP, such as: *in the affirmative*, *in the vernacular*, *in the news*, and *in the interval*.

- An indefinite NP, such as: *in an emergency, in a bad mood, in a fix*, and *in good hands*.

When we examine *into*, there are some examples of (i), following a verb—such as: *launch into, coax into*, and *inquire into*—but very few of (ii) preceding a nominal—the idiom *into the bargain* is a rare instance.

We sometimes encounter a verb or adjective being followed by an *in* phrase, and a related noun being preceded by *in*. Examples include:

(1)	The general triumphed in the battle	The general returned in triumph
(2)	I confided in John	I told John in confidence
(3)	The general was disgraced in the battle	The general returned in disgrace

In (1), *triumph* functions as both verb and noun; sentences (2) involve verb *confide* and derived noun *confidence*; and (3) links adjective *disgraced* with noun *disgrace*. For all three pairs the meanings are compatible. However, the meanings are different when verb *delight* is followed by *in* and noun *delight* is preceded by *in*.

James delighted in shouting
(shouting gave him delight)
James shouted in delight
(he was shouting because of his delight in something which is unstated)

Quite a number of verbs may be followed by an *in* (or an *into*) phrase and a derived noun follows the same pattern. For example:

René believes in miracles
We were surprised at René's belief in miracles

Also *persist in* and *persistence in*, *share in* and *a share in*, *indulge in* and *indulgence in*, *initiate into* and *initiation into*, *enquire into* and *an enquiry into*, *probe into* and *a probe into*.

The fact that *in* may mark either location or motion can lead to two possible interpretations as in:

Alan walked in the room
either (a) he entered the room by walking
or (b) he walked around within the room

The ambiguity can be resolved by using *into* in place of *in* for meaning (a), the motion sense, and *within* rather than *in* for (b), the location sense.

The basis meaning of *in* relates to enclosure and that of *to* involves reaching a destination. These are combined in the preposition *into*. The difference is brought out in:

> Juan walked in the door
>> (he walked through the doorway into the enclosed space beyond it)
>
> Juan walked into the door
>> (he collided with the door, as if trying to break into the space beyond it)

This relates to the fact that noun *door* can be used to refer just to a doorway (a space) or to the structure which fits into it, to close it off (a solid object).

The circumstances in which either *into* or *in* may be used, with no significant differences in meanings, are limited and are especially rare when the prepositions are extended from their basic spatial senses into more abstract meanings. For example, only *into* is acceptable in *divide into*, *bite into*, and *turn into*. And only *in* may be used for *in haste, in reply*, and *in love*, among very many others.

The following sections survey the senses of *in* and *into*, also noting corresponding senses for *out-of*.

8.1a Basic meanings

In its locational sense, *X (is) in Y* indicates that X is included within Y, and *X (is) out-of Y* states that X is not included within Y, when it used to be or might be expected to be. The motion senses shown by *X (went) into Y* and *X (came) out-of Y*, indicate movement of X to become included within Y or to become not included within Y. These are illustrated in:

MOTION	LOCATIONAL
The ball was put into the box	The ball is now in the box
The ball was taken out-of the box	The ball is now out-of the box

As mentioned, *in* can be an alternative for *into* in the motion sense only when the verb has a neutral meaning, indicating nothing more than directed motion (a verb like *go*, *come*, *bring*, *take*, or *put*). Thus, *The ball was put in the box* is acceptable and unambiguous.

The way this works can be seen by comparing:

> Geoff brought his bicycle into the garage
> Geoff rode his bicycle into the garage

In could be used in place of *into* in the *brought* sentence with no difference of meaning, since this verb only indicates directed motion. However, the substitution is scarcely possible for the *rode* sentence since here the verb has a wider meaning. *Geoff rode his bicycle in the garage* is most likely to be understood in a locational sense—he rode entirely within the garage (rather than from outside it to inside it).

The restriction to *into* is stronger with a verb describing impact. For instance, *Max crashed the car into a wall* could not use *in*. The nature of the object argument may also be relevant. *John drove the car into the garage* could use *in* rather than *into*; it is normal to drive from without a garage to within in it, whereas driving entirely within a garage is unusual. But with *John drove the car into a wall*, the *in* alternative is impermissible.

Although either *into* or *in* may be used after a neutral verb of motion, there is a slight difference of meaning. *Joe came in the room* may be used if he just entered it, whereas *Joe came into the room* suggests that he ventured some way in. One sense of the verb *duck* describes getting out of the way of something, as in *Dave ducked into his office to avoid being seen by Pamela*; this implies thorough entry and requires *into*, not *in*.

Some verbs of rest (including *sit*, *stand*, and *live*) are typically followed by a prepositional NP, which is likely to be introduced by *at*, *in*, or *on*. Corresponding to an *in* sentence there can be one with *out-of*, if this should be pragmatically plausible. For example:

- Alongside *Bill lives in town* we can have *Tom lives out-of town*, since this is a familiar contrast of residence.
- *Bill lives in the valley* is an acceptable sentence. However *Tom lives out-of the valley* would only be used with a particular contrast; for instance Tom also used to live in the valley but has now moved away.
- *The children are sitting in* class describes a normal occurrence whereas *The children are sitting out-of class* is difficult to contextualise.

There can be no *out-of* correspondent for the locational *in* phrases with verbs describing how something is completely within something else. These include: *immerse in, envelop in, include in, submerge in, enclose in, wrap in,* and *cover in.*

The motion sense may extend beyond physical position, as in *I put the cards into/in alphabetical order* [motion] *but you've messed them up and now they're all out-of order* [location].

We can now examine straightforward extensions from the basic sense. First, a number of verbs have a related noun such that an argument of the verb could be said to be included in the state described by the noun. There are examples where the argument is in S (intransitive subject) or O (transitive object) function:

The bird (S) is flying	→	The bird is in flight
The truant (S) is hiding	→	The truant is in hiding
The jailer chained the prisoner (O)	→	The prisoner is in chains
The teacher silenced the class (O)	→	The class sat in silence

One could say *The truant is out-of hiding*, meaning that he had been in hiding but has now emerged, and *The prisoner is out-of chains*, implying that he had been chained up but has now been released. However, **The bird is out-of flight* and **The class sat out-of silence* have little sense.

Verb *ambush* and noun *ambush* are particularly interesting with respect to the use of *in*. This is illustrated in:

The highwaymen ambushed the gold-diggers

The highwaymen waited in ambush for the gold-diggers

The gold-diggers were caught in an ambush by the highwaymen

In the second sentence *in ambush* (with no article) has adverbial function, indicating the way in which the highwaymen prepared to attack. *In an ambush* (with an article), in the third sentence, is a peripheral NP describing the trap the gold-diggers found themselves *in*.

The basic idea of inclusion is also shown by *in the news* and *in an emergency*.

Extensions from the basic sense of *into* maintain the focus on a destination, as in *look into, enquire into, jam (many objects) into (a small space)*, and *marry into*, as in:

Boris married into the Rockefeller family

In and *into* feature in a fair number of idiomatic expressions such as:

> I wouldn't want to be in his shoes
>> (this is a situation I wouldn't relish)
> We're all in the same boat
>> (all in the same unpleasant circumstance)
> She's got it in her to succeed
>> (if she tries hard, she will be able to succeed)
> This machine is quick and efficient, and it's compact into the bargain
>> (being compact is an extra, in addition to the features which were required)

Also *(be) in good hands, (be) in clover, (be) in one's blood,* and *(be) set in one's ways.*

8.1b Time and speed

Location within a period of time is marked by *in*, just like location in space (see section 14.6a). For example:

in the morning   in peace-time   in his youth   in the past
in one's sleep

And one can say *in the interval* (between Act one and Act two). Alongside *(this fruit is) in season*, there is *out-of season*.

There can be reference to some future period, starting from the present moment:

in a jiffy   in a minute   in a while   in due course   in the future

Relative time is shown by *(do it) in advance*, and *(there was) a delay in (implementing the plan)*. If some project is happening, it is *in progress* and the people responsible are *progressing in* its implementation. When there is a deadline one may hear *(the building must be completed) in time (for the official opening)*; see sections 14.6b and 14.6a. And a personal slant is expressed by *(he'll do it) in his own time.*

An *in* phrase may specify what is done during a period of time, such as *He spends his afternoons in gardening. Into* is appropriate when some activity moves forward, as in *We'll continue working at this task into the weekend.*

The speed at which something is done relates to the time taken to complete it. A high speed can be marked by *in*:

The tower was built in haste (and it fell down the following year)

Also *in a hurry*, *in a flash*, and *in a rush*.

8.1c A human in a certain state

This sense of preposition *in* covers physical state, mental or emotional attitude, and activity.

8.1c-1 Immersed in a physical state

This can be a bodily condition such as:

in bad health	in good health	in fine fettle	in pain
in agony	in a stupor	in a daze	in a trance
in a coma	in tears	in anguish	in heat

Or a social situation:

in danger	in a crisis	in need	in poverty
in luxury	in difficulty	in trouble	in a fix

There is an *out-of* correspondent for some of these. One can be *out-of pain* after being in pain and *out-of danger* after being in danger. A patient can come *out-of a coma*. But one would only be likely in special circumstances to hear *out-of agony*, *out-of a daze*, or *out-of luxury*.

This sense may also apply to plants. An extension of the motion sense of *into*—*The marigolds are just coming into flower*—is followed by an extension of the location sense if *in*—*The marigolds are in flower*. It may also apply to something in motion: *The spaceship is in orbit*, *The police are in pursuit*, *The champion is in the lead*, *The package is in transit*, and *The car is moving in reverse*. (For some of these there may be an *into* alternative, such as *The spaceship is now getting into orbit*.)

8.1c-2 Enveloped in a mental or emotional attitude

There are a number of verbs which exhibit this sense. For example:

Aaron gloried in his new-found freedom
Eve exulted in her win at the games

Also *delight in, rejoice in,* and *triumph in.* Plus adjectives *disappointed in, interested in,* and *happy/unhappy in.* Or someone else may express a mental judgement towards a person, as in *Jean is held in esteem by her colleagues.*

Some nouns describing emotional state are marked with *in*:

> You'll have to excuse them, they're in love
>
> He didn't know what he was doing, he was in a rage

Also *in a bad mood,* and the idioms *in a state of indecision* and *be in two minds* (about something).

An emotional state, marked by *in,* can be invoked as the reason for an action:

> The neighbours killed our dog in revenge

Also:

in anger	in fury	in fear	in terror	in fright
in joy	in delight	in triumph	in ecstasy	in shame

Similar sentiments can be expressed with *out-of,* including *out-of jealousy, out-of envy,* and *out-of fear.* The contrast between *in anger* and *out-of anger* is explained in sections 1.1c and 8.2b.

And there are verbs describing a mental attitude towards someone (or something):

> I trust in John's judgement AND I put trust in John's judgement

Also verb *believe in* and noun *belief in.* And nouns *(have) confidence* in and *(have) faith in.* As noted before, verb *confide in* goes with noun *(tell) in confidence* and adjective *be disgraced in* with noun *in disgrace.*

Nouns describing social position are typically marked with *in*:

> General Smithers is in command over the ninth battalion

Also *in power, in authority, in control, in bondage,* and *in subjection.*

8.1c-3 Displaying an attitude or an aptitude

An *in* phrase may explain the way in which someone exhibits a certain attitude:

> He was generous in giving up his share to a needy cousin
>
> She was kind in that she ministered to the needs of the crippled

Also *mean in, cruel in, brutal in, spiteful in,* and *merciless in.*

If a person displays a measure of ability, what this relates to may be shown through an *in* phrase, as in:

Judith is competent in basic book-keeping

Other adjectives of this type include: *proficient in, clever in, skilled in, skilful in, talented in, expert in,* and *experienced in.* There is also verb *excel in.*

An opposite sentiment is expressed by adjectives *lacking in* and *deficient in.* In fact, the meanings here extend further: a person may be lacking in brains or in common sense, a story may be lacking in plausibility, or a camp may be lacking in supplies.

A similar sense describes how something beneficial may engulf a person, essentially without their doing anything. *In luck*—with noun *luck*—and *lucky in*—with adjective *lucky*—can convey the same message:

Bill was in luck when he found the $100 note

Bill was lucky in finding the $100 note

And adjective *fortunate in.* Also, you can be *out-of luck* if everyone finds a $100 note except you.

8.1c-4 Engaged in an activity

For verbs dealing with an occupation, an *in* phrase may describe the occupation. For example:

June employed Max in the sales office

May is employed in the hospitality industry

Other verbs describing activities include: *work in, deal in, trade in, assist in, help in, dabble in, meddle in, indulge in,* and *compete in.* There are also adjectives *engaged in* and *occupied in.* Nouns which refer to proficiency in an activity include: *a specialist in* and *an expert in.*

Allied to this sense are *persist in* and *persevere in,* describing application to a task:

Adam persisted in selling off family heirlooms after he'd been told not to

April persevered in her attempt to buy the business

Also verbs describing the outcome of an activity—*succeed in* and *fail in*, together with derived nouns *success in* and *failure in*. For example:

Max has succeeded in revitalising the sales force

April eventually failed in her attempt to buy the business

And the verb of achievement *surpass* (others) *in*.

The *in* phrase for many of the verbs listed in this section may involve a plain NP or an *-ing* construction. One could say, for instance, either *Igor assists in the dictionary work* or *Igor assists in assembling a corpus*.

It is interesting to compare *intrude* and *intervene*, two verbs which are not dissimilar in meaning. *Intrude* bears unwelcome overtones, of entering a private domain, and takes the motion preposition *into*. In contrast, *intervene* has a more locational sense (like *stand in a queue*) and takes preposition *in*:

Please don't intrude into Monica's time of grief

Paul intervened in the argument, and settled the matter

8.1d Part of a group

Inclusion in a social unit is marked by *in*:

James is working in the civil service

Also: *in the army, in a union, in the work force, in good company*, and *in the family*. Verbs expecting such an *in* phrase include *enlist in*.

Rather than the name of an assemblage, there can be a noun referring to a kind of group membership, such as *in employment* and:

Jessie is in service and her brother is in uniform

Or there can just be description of some communal activity: *join in the singing* and *share in the fun*. Note also verbs *participate in* (the ceremony) and *involve* (someone) *in* (the decision-making), together with derived nouns *participation in* and *involvement in*. Allied to this sense is statement of composition such as *consist in* (see section 4.1e-2).

Preposition *into* is appropriate when the activity is dynamic, as in *They entered into a partnership* and *He went into the navy*.

For some of these examples there can be a matching sentence with *out-of*. For example *Joe is now out-of uniform* (locational sense, corresponding to *in*) and *Joe was invalided out-of the army* (motion sense, corresponding to *into*).

The 'part of' sense may also apply to abstract notions such as *an idea in philosophy* and *a theorem in geometry*.

8.1e In a certain form or condition

In can be used with a noun describing the way in which people or things are arranged or act:

in pairs	in a body	in unison	in bulk
in the lead	in single file	(keep) in step	

There can also be specification of a general ambience: *in public, in private,* and *in solitude.*
    Similar to these are descriptions of form:

in writing	in wax	in person	in the flesh	in profile
in miniature	in ruins	in a nutshell	in detail	in poetry
in prose	in silence	in a loud voice	in focus	in the vernacular

Only one of these can have an *out-of* correspondent; if an image is not in focus, it is *out-of focus.*
    A somewhat roundabout way of expressing agreement (or the reverse) is seen in *She replied in the affirmative* and *He answered in the negative.*

8.1f Engendering a happening

Partly by virtue of its *to* component, the preposition *into* relates to a goal. The following example sentences gradually extend from the simple spatial sense into more abstract domains:

The secretary put the letter into the mailbox	DESTINATION
The ringleader divided the booty into four portions	PRODUCT
The seamstress made the material into a gown	PRODUCT
Hugo translated the poem into Serbian	PRODUCT
The wizard turned Lancelot into a frog	TRANSFORMATION
Father talked John into accepting the job	HAPPENING

Transformation does not necessarily require a causer; one could hear *The wizard turned into a frog.*

There is an *out*-of correspondent for the destination and some of the product sentences—*The secretary took the letter out-of the mailbox* and *The seamstress made a gown out-of the material.* But for the reversal of a transformation *from* would be preferred over *out-of*—*The wizard turned Lancelot back from frog into prince.*

Corresponding to the happening sentence, we can have *Father talked John out-of accepting the job.* Some verbs are, by their meanings, restricted to one of the prepositional alternatives. One can say *His sisters laughed John out-of accepting the job*; the use of *laugh* here implies ridicule so that one cannot say *laugh into.* And *coax* generally relates to some positive happening. It can be used in *Father coaxed John into applying for the job*, but would be unlikely with *out-of.*

Into has a quasi-temporal sense in *Maria hastened into making a decision,* To this can be added an 'engendering a happening' meaning, as in *Father hastened Maria into making a decision.*

An extension from the motion sense of *into* is seen in:

> We voted Smithy into office

The NP *office* may be omitted if it is clear from the context, but then preposition *into* has to be reduced to *in*, giving: *We voted Smithy in.* (There are corresponding sentences with *out-of* and *out*.)

This sense of *into* is also found in *burst into* (tears/flames), *launch into* (for example, a stream of invective), and *initiate* (someone) *into* (say, a fraternity).

8.1g A specific property within a general field

A special construction involving *in* locates a property—described by an adjective—in terms of the conceptual sphere to which it belongs—shown by a noun. Examples include:

blue in colour	large in size	round in shape	rough in texture
light in weight	cheap in price	young in age	symmetrical in arrangement
sour in taste	loud in volume	ten in number	generous in nature

A similar construction has an adjective of comparison as the first element:

equal in length   similar in design   different in detail

8.1h Adverbial modifiers

There are a number of adverbial phrases commencing with *in*. For example:

> The president stated, in conclusion, that he was refusing to sign the treaty

The parenthetical *in conclusion* could, alternatively, be placed at the beginning of the sentence. Similar interpolations include *in addition* and *in reply*.

There are also adverbial phrases referring to manner, likelihood, phase, succinctness, practicality, and more:

in every way	in one way or another	in every respect
in any case	in most cases	in the circumstances
in all probability	in the main	in general
in my opinion	in the first place	in short
in brief	in outline	in turn
in theory	in practice	in reality
in principle	in part	in affirmation

There are also a number of complex adverbial-type phrases where *in* precedes a noun indicating a relationship, this being followed by *for* or *with* or *to* marking an NP which states what the relationship concerns. They include *in exchange for*, as in:

> In exchange for a bunch of bananas, Gertrude gave Irene a pineapple

Others include: *in return for, in reward for, in recompense for, in payment for, in contrast with*, and *in comparison with/to*.

Adverbs *inward(s)* /ˈinwəd(z)/ and *outward(s)* /ˈautwəd(z)/ go back to Old English and can sometimes be used in place of *in* and *out* when indicating direction. They may also function as adjectives. See section 7.3.

* * *

217

In is by far the most common simple preposition as first element of a phrasal preposition; for example, *in-spite-of*, *in-front-of*, *in-case-of*, *in-the-name-of*, and *in-lieu-of*.

* * *

It is possible to sprinkle a sentence with a fair number of instances of *in*. For example: *In the 'nineties, John had, in one way or another, in theory been in command in the factory in the city.* However, this is scarcely elegant, and a good stylist would find ways of rephrasing, in order to avoid such a superfluity of one preposition.

8.1i In *and* into *in phrasal verbs and prepositional verbs*

There are no prepositional verbs involving *into* and just a few with *in*. *Consist in* was discussed in section 4.1e-2. Others include *indulge in* (section 8.1), and *participate in* (section 8.1d).

In keeping with its function as a preposition, *into* is found just in slot **p** for phrasal verbs, and is attested in types V-p-NP and V-NP-p-NP. Many of the phrasal verbs with *into* are clear extensions from basic senses. (As before, phrasal verbs are underlined.)

SAMPLE BASIC SENTENCES	PHRASAL VERBS OF TYPE V-p-NP
Agatha came into the treasure cave	Agatha came into a fortune (she inherited it or was given it)
Joe smashed into the wall	Joe laid into the critic (he strongly criticised the critic)
The actress slipped into her gown	The actress slipped seamlessly into her role in the play (she took on the personality of the character she was portraying)
Fred got into university	Fred just scraped into university (he barely achieved the entry score)
Water is seeping into the attic Rust is eating into the metal roof	The legal fees are eating into John's capital (his capital is rapidly diminishing)

The car ran into a brick wall	I <u>ran into</u> an old friend at the market yesterday
	(I encountered him by chance)

SAMPLE BASIC SENTENCE	PHRASAL VERBS OF TYPE V-NP-p-NP
Jill put some of her secret fantasies into the story	Don't <u>read</u> any secret fantasies <u>into</u> Jill's story!

Several phrasal verbs with *into* relate to the 'Engendering a happening' sense of *into*, discussed in section 8.1f. *Turn into* can be of type V-p-NP or V-NP-p-NP, while *talk into* and *coax into* are solely V-NP-p-NP.

In can function as an adverb or as a preposition. However, its occurrence in phrasal verbs is almost exclusively in slot **a**. It occurs as **a** in all four types: V-a, V-NP-a, V-a-p-NP, and V-NP-a-p-NP. We can illustrate—for a selection of phrasal verbs—the ways in which they relate to the various senses of *in* (and *into*).

SENSE	TYPE	
Extension of basic meaning	V-NP-a	<u>Hand</u> the submission <u>in</u>!
	V-NP-a	<u>Have</u> the neighbours <u>in</u>
	V-NP-a-p-NP	They <u>fenced</u> the managers <u>in</u> <u>with</u> useless regulations
	V-a	The rain has <u>set in</u>
Time	V-a	Nicole <u>slept in</u> and missed her appointment
Enveloped in emotional attitude	V-NP-a	Donald couldn't <u>keep</u> his temper <u>in</u>
Displaying an attitude	V-NP-a	She <u>rubbed</u> his faults <u>in</u>
Engaged in an activity	V-a-p-NP	Eugene <u>goes in for</u> golf
	V-NP-a	Pam <u>packed</u> the job <u>in</u>
Part of a group	V-a-p-NP	Harold <u>got in with</u> the boss's wife
	V-NP-a	We can <u>count</u> Kate <u>in</u> (she'll vote for Muggins)

	V-a-p-NP	Jenny wants to <u>get in on</u> the scheme
	V-NP-a-p-NP	Please <u>fill</u> John <u>in on</u> the proposal
	V-a-p-NP	We'll <u>fall in with</u> your plans
Engineering a happening	V-a-p-NP	Jane <u>is in for</u> the top job
	V-NP-a	Jack <u>did</u> his wife <u>in</u> (and collected the insurance)

Left movement is generally possible for an *in* (as **a**) which follows a non-pronominal NP. For example, *They <u>fenced in</u> the managers <u>with</u> useless regulations*, *Donald couldn't <u>keep in</u> his temper*, and *Jack <u>did in</u> his wife*.

Examples of phrasal verbs with *in* filling a **p** slot are hard to find. A rare example—of type V-a-p-NP—is *Samantha <u>came out in</u> spots*.

8.1j *Contrasting* in *and* into *with other prepositions*

We can now examine contexts where *in* and *into* may contrast with prepositions dealt with in the previous chapters.

8.1j-1 *Of and* in

The contrast between prepositional verbs *consist in* and *consist of* was explained in section 4.1e-2. Another pair is illustrated in:

Alex partook generously of the cake
(he ate lots of it; see section 5.2h)
Joshua partook in the general celebrations of victory
(he joined others in the rejoicing; see section 8.1d)

8.1j-2 *By and* in

There are two ways of stating that someone naturally shows a certain propensity (for example, being kind or cruel, generous or mean, or jealous):

Charlotte is generous by nature
Charlotte is generous in nature

The first sentence relates to the 'reason for an attribute' sense of *by*, discussed in section 6.1b-7 (alongside *a lawyer by profession* and *French by birth*). The second sentence uses the *in* construction whereby an adjective describing a general property is linked to a noun for the general field to which the property belongs (similar to *rough in texture*); see section 8.1g.

There is little difference of meaning between these sentences. It is just that—in this instance—the richness of the grammar provides alternative windows for expressing a certain idea.

As described in section 6.1c, many transitive verbs describing human emotions form a derived adjective which is homonymous with the passive form of the verb. Within the passive construction the erstwhile transitive subject takes *by*. The derived adjective is followed by a peripheral NP marked by one of a variety of prepositions. These include *in*, used after adjective *interested*. A pair of sentences with *interested by* and *interested in* were contrasted in section 6.1c. A further pair is:

> Greta was interested by the offer of a cheap mortgage
>> (passive of: The offer of a cheap mortgage interested Greta)
> Bertha is interested in geometry
>> ('immersed in a mental attitude' sense of *in*, after adjective *interested*; see section 8.1c-2)

8.1j-3 *With* and *in*

Here we can compare:

> The rank-and-file were disappointed with the electoral loss
> The rank-and-file were disappointed in the leader

In the first sentence, *with* is used in its 'mental state' sense (section 6.2d-2), the dismay of the rank-and-file is directed towards the event (the loss). By contrast, the second employs the 'mental attitude' sense of *in* (section 8.1c-2), describing a lack of satisfaction concerning the performance of the leader.

A different example of the contrast between *with* and *in* is:

> There is little progress with the reconstruction project
> We are making significant progress in the fight against malaria

The first sentence uses the 'activity directed towards' sense of *with* (section 6.2e), indicating how far off the completion of the project may be.

The other sentence illustrates the temporal sense of *in* (section 8.1b), describing how things are moving along.

8.1j-4 *At* and *in*

Using the basic senses of these prepositions, one would say *Edgar arrived at the town hall* but *Edgar arrived in the city*. Preposition *at* is used with *the town hall* since this is just a spatial position (Edgar could be meeting a friend there). And *in* is the preposition which it is appropriate to use with *the city* since it refers to a considerable area and Edgar will be immersed in it.

Another example of contrast between *at* and *in* is:

> Eva rejoiced at the news that France had been liberated
>
> Eva rejoiced in her love for Antonio

The first sentence uses the 'focus of an emotion' sense of *at* (section 7.1d), indicating Eva's happiness when she hears this news. For the second sentence, *in* has its 'enveloped in an emotional attitude' sense (section 8.1c-2)—Eva is simply immersed in adoration of her lover.

Either preposition may also be employed after verb *excel*:

> Julia excels at planning excursions
>
> Catherine excels in mathematics

At is used to describe a person's competence at doing something, the 'focus of an ability' sense of this preposition (section 7.1e) whereas the *in* sentence indicates an aptitude for some field of endeavour (section 8.1c-3).

There are a number of instances where *at* may introduce an NP consisting just of a noun, while *in* marks an NP where the same noun is modified by *the*. For example:

> Rome and Carthage are at war again
>> ('focus on an activity' sense of *at*; section 7.1a)
>
> Eric drove an ambulance in the war
>> ('period of time' sense of *in*; section 8.1b)

Or *at* and *in* may both refer to time, but with a different orientation:

> Ghosts tend to prowl around at night
>
> The chimney collapsed in the night

The first sentence, with *at*, indicates an habitual activity which may take place on any night (section 7.1b) whereas the second sentence describes something which happened during one night. (It is a convention of English that *in the night* refers to the night immediately prior to the time of speaking.)

There is also a contrast between *at present* (focusing on the moment of speaking) and *in the present*, which refers to a period of time including the moment of speaking (and contrasts with *in the past* and *in the future*).

8.1j-5 *At* and *into*

Suppose that someone has an apple and engages it with their teeth. There are several possibilities:

> Ted bit the apple
> Ted bit into the apple
> Ted nibbled the apple
> Ted nibbled at the apple

The first and third sentences just employ transitive verbs, *bite* and *nibble*. In each instance a preposition may be inserted between verb and object NP (see section 2.5a) but the choice of and effect of the preposition depends on the meaning of the verb. *Bite an apple* typically implies 'take a piece out-of it'. Adding *into* modifies the meaning, just stating that Ted's teeth were inserted well within the apple (see section 8.1a). *Nibble* describes biting small pieces off something; adding *at* suggests that even this was scarcely accomplished (compare *kick the ball* and *kick at the ball*, discussed in section 2.5a).

8.1j-6 *To* and *in*

At first glance, *to* and *in* contrast in:

> Michael drinks whiskey to excess
>> (he drinks more of it than is good for him)
> We have whiskey in excess
>> (we have more than is needed for our requirements)

However, the two sentences have rather different grammatical structure. In the first, *to excess* functions as an adverbial modifier (section 7.2h). In the second, *in excess* is the abbreviation of a peripheral NP along the lines of *in excess of our requirements* (section 8.1e).

8.2 *Out-of* and *out*

In and *into* are the major member of the pairing *in(to)/out(-of)* and they have the independent meaning of 'enclosure' or 'inclusion'. The meaning of the minor member—combining *out-of* and *out*—is essentially relative to that of the major member. It indicates that something is not enclosed or not included when either it used to be or it might be expected to be. For example:

Meg is in town today but Jack is out-of town
(we expected to find Jack in town today, as he was yesterday)

This applies for the basic senses of the prepositions and also for many of the extended senses. If one hears *Joe is now out-of training*, it presupposes that at one time he was *in training*. Someone can be said to be *out-of work* if they had previously been (and hope again to be) *in work*. If one hears *Jenny has fallen out-of love with Jim*, there is a clear understanding that earlier on *Jenny fell in love with Jim*. A politician may be *in office* and then, after a ministerial reshuffle, find themself *out-of office*.

In sections 8.1a–f, a fair number of examples were given for each of the senses of *in* and *into*. If there are corresponding examples involving *out-of*, these were mentioned; but there are generally only a few of them. For instance, discussion of the sense 'in a certain form or condition' (section 8.1e) listed twenty or so instances with *in* (*in writing*, *in miniature*, *in ruins*, etc.) and there are many more. For only one of the examples mentioned is there a regular *out-of* correspondent—a camera may be said to be *out-of focus* (the clear message being that it should be *in focus*).

Besides sharing—often in small degree—in some of the meanings associated with *in* and *into*, *out-of* and *out* show a number of senses of their own. Each of them is related to a basic sense.

8.2a Lacking

The following sentences show the natural progression from the basic sense for *out-of* 'not included in' to the more abstract sense of 'lacking'.

There are dogs in the pet store
(all are for sale)
The dogs are out-of the pet store
(they've run away)

The pet shop is out-of dogs

> (it lacks dogs, but there are kittens, goldfish, and canaries
> available for sale)

The village store is out-of sugar

> (it lacks sugar)

Note that there is no *in* correspondent for the last two sentences. *Out-of* has here moved apart from the major member of the pairing.

An abstract quality may also be marked as lacking through use of *out-of*:

> The boss came to be out-of patience with George's erratic
> behaviour

> I'm totally out-of sympathy with Robin's idea about nationalism

This sense also features in *out-of one's mind*, *out-of proportion*, and *out-of guarantee*.

If a speaker is allocated a certain number of minutes and exceeds these, the chairperson may point to the lack of remaining time by saying:

> Please stop now, you are out-of time

It is possible to say *in time* but this has a rather different meaning, describing how something was achieved to meet a deadline (see section 8.1b):

> We ran and were just in time to catch the train

There can be more complex 'lacking' constructions. For example, *Roger cheated James out-of his lawful inheritance* states that James came to lack that which should be his by right. The idiom *out-of sorts* also belongs here.

When a fire has finished burning—that is, when the flames (the actual fire) have died away—one can say *The fire has gone out*, or just *The fire is out* (there is here no equivalent using *in*). Also *The light is out* (meaning that the light-globe is kaput).

8.2b *Arising from*

If X arises from Y, this may be expressed by *X out-of Y*. What is referred to by X may be some idea or attitude. The progression from a basic sense 'not included' to the abstract one 'arising from' is shown through:

> Mike picked a silver dollar out-of the ashes left by the fire
>
> Hector acquired a sense of who he was out-of the ruins of his marriage
>
> (Hector's sense of who he was arose from the ruins of his marriage)
>
> Hamish voted for Peggy out-of loyalty to her
>
> (Hamish's voting for Peggy arose from his loyalty to her)

It was pointed out, in section 1.1c, that the following sentences both describe Bill hitting Fred, with the reason being anger.

1 Bill hit Fred in anger

2 Bill hit Fred out-of anger

However, the circumstances would be different. Sentence 1 employs the 'enveloped in an emotional attitude' sense of *in* (section 8.1c-2). Bill hit Fred impetuously *in a fit of anger*. He was in a state, got carried away, acted in the heat of the moment, and perhaps regretted it afterwards. In contrast, sentence 2 features the 'arising from' sense of *out-of*. Bill had been getting increasingly angry with Fred and because of this he hit him deliberately, in full realisation of what he was doing.

Other abstract nouns which may be preceded by *out-of* in its 'arising from' sense include: *kindness, compassion, humanity, conviction,* and *despair*.

Another interesting pair of sentences is:

3 In every class there is one very bright student

(with the rest being pretty average)

4 Out-of every class there is one very bright student

(who is likely to go on to achieve great things in life)

Superficially, these have similar meanings, but their orientations are quite different. Sentence 3 uses *in* with the basic sense of 'inclusion', as in: *One in twenty of the students is very bright*. For sentence 4, *out-of* has the 'arising from' sense; the focus is here on the bright student, picking them out from the rest of the class.

The meaning of *out-of love* depends on the preposition which follows. *Out-of love with* has the 'lacking' meaning, while *out-of-love for* is the 'arising from' sense:

Jenny has fallen out-of love with Jim

    (she now lacks any love with him)

Jenny nursed Jim out-of love for him

    (arising from her love for Jim, Jenny nursed him)

A similar pair could involve *out-of sympathy with* and *out-of sympathy for*.

8.2c Adverb function

Out is primarily an adverb and it encompasses a spectrum of meanings. Only for a minority of these is there a correspondent with *in*.

8.2c-1 Direction

The most straightforward examples are with verb *breathe*. Here the adverbs simply state how air is being expelled from, and being taken into, the mouth:

The patient breathed out   The patient breathed in

Sometimes an adverb could be expanded into a peripheral NP:

    The tide is coming in (towards the shore)

    The tide is going out (away from the shore)

    The sun has come out (from behind the clouds)

Corresponding to these, the adverb can function as copula complement: *The tide is in*, *The tide is out*, and *The sun is out*. For the sun going out of vision one could say *The sun has gone (in) behind the clouds*, but never *The sun is in*.

There is a notable contrast between *out* used in its 'lacking' sense—section 8.2a—in *The light is out* (there is no illumination) and in its 'direction' sense in *The sun is out* (illumination has increased).

Once the examination grades have been announced, it is appropriate to say *The results are out*.

8.2c-2 Release

When a fire alarm goes off, there are two ways in which people may react. These can be described by using the prepositions in their basic meanings:

They stayed in the building   LOCATION SENSE OF *in*

They ran out-of the building   MOTION SENSE OF *out-of*

The second sentence may be reduced to just *They ran out*, especially if the action was energetic. This sense can be extended to anything emanating from a source with vigour, such as:

> The victim cried/shouted out
> The noise blasted out

He hit out implies that significant force was involved, and *She reached out* that her arm was extended as far as it would go. When Muggins' latest novel reaches the bookstores, the message *goes out* that:

> Muggins' new book is out

That is, it has been released. Also showing this sense is: *The secret is out*.

Note that there are no adverbial *in* correspondents for *out* in the release sense, or in the next sense, that of 'done fully'.

8.2c-3 Done fully

Using the basic sense of preposition *out-of*, one can say: *Emile took the cake out-of the oven*, which may be reduced to: *Emile took the cake out*. Here *out* signifies that the taking from the oven has been completed. This sense of *out* can be extended to the completion of other kinds of activities, as in:

> The boatyard has fitted the ship out for a long voyage
> The food has just lasted out for the duration of the voyage
> They have now served the dinner out

If there is an altercation, the protagonists may *fight it out*, meaning that they fight on until a conclusion is reached.

As mentioned under (iv) in section 1.8, *out* has limited use as the predicate of an imperative sentence, followed by *with*—*Out with it!* meaning 'Don't keep the information to yourself'. A recent use as verb is when exposing someone's homosexuality (against their wishes), as in *They outed the candidate a week before the election*.

8.2d Out *and* out-of *in phrasal verbs*

There are probably no prepositional verbs with *out* or *out-of*. Just a few phrasal verbs include *out-of* while several dozen involve *out*.

In keeping with its function as a preposition, *out-of* is found just in slot **p** for phrasal verbs, and—like *into*—is attested in types V-p-NP and V-NP-p-NP.

SENSE	TYPE	
Extension of basic meaning	V-p-NP	Anna <u>swept out-of</u> the meeting
Immersed in a mental state	V-p-NP	You need to <u>snap out-of</u> this self-pity
Engendering a happening	V-NP-p-NP	We <u>talked/laughed</u> Jim <u>out-of</u> buying a jet-ski
Release	V-NP-p-NP	The auditors <u>did</u> me <u>out-of</u> my bonus
	V-NP-p-NP	The guards <u>screwed</u> vital information <u>out-of</u> the captive

In keeping with its primary function as an adverb, *out* is only found in slot **a** within phrasal verbs. It occurs in all four types: V-a, V-NP-a, V-a-p-NP, and V-NP-a-p-NP. We can illustrate with a selection:

SENSE	TYPE	
Immersed in a physical state	V-a	The poor old fellow's heart <u>gave out</u>
	V-NP-a	We <u>wore</u> old Joe <u>out</u> (with all that walking)
Immersed in a mental state	V-NP-a-p-NP	The boss <u>took</u> her anger <u>out on</u> the cleaner
Part of a group	V-NP-a	We can <u>count</u> Cecil <u>out</u> (he won't come)
	V-a-p-NP	Dorothy <u>fell out with</u> Jim
Engendering a happening	V-NP-a	The tough guy <u>laid</u> the security guard <u>out</u>
	V-NP-a	The renegades <u>carried</u> the plan <u>out</u>
Lacking	V-NP-a	I should soon be able to <u>wipe</u> the debt <u>out</u>
Direction	V-a	The advance party is just <u>setting out</u>

Release	V-a	The blossoms <u>are out</u> (on the apple tree)
	V-NP-a	That pulp writer certainly <u>churns</u> books <u>out</u>
	V-a-p-NP	Timothy has <u>come out in</u> spots
Done fully	V-a	We <u>held out</u> (until reinforcements arrived)
	V-NP-a	Hannah has <u>worked</u> the problem <u>out</u>

Left movement is generally possible for an *out* (as **a**) which follows an NP. For example, *The boss <u>took out</u> her anger <u>on</u> the cleaner, I should soon be able to <u>wipe out</u> the debt*, and *That pulp writer certainly <u>churns</u> <u>out</u> books.*

8.2e *Contrasting* from *and* out-of

In its basic sense, preposition *from* has a wider range of meaning than the motion sense of *out-of*. Consider:

Tom ran from the house

can be used if (a) Tom had been inside the house then ran through the door and away or (b) Tom was standing just outside the door then ran away.

Tom ran out-of the house only has sense (a) since it presupposes that Tom was in the house. Alongside *Tom ran from the bull* we cannot say **Tom ran out-of the bull*, since he wasn't inside it.

In a few instances, either *from* or *out-of* may be used with little significant difference in meaning. For instance, *He took the milk from the fridge* and *He took the milk out-of the fridge*. Also, *They drew a confession from John* and *They drew a confession out-of John*.

A statement involving *from*, which always indicates motion, may lead into one with *out-of* in its locational sense:

John resigned from the company and is now out-of the company

8.3 *Within* and *without*, *inside(-of)* and *outside(-of)*

Prepositions *within* and *without*, and *inside(-of)* and *outside(-of)*, are further specialisations of the more general pair *in(to)* and *out(-of)*. They may sometimes be interchanged but more often show similar but significantly different meanings.

Late Old English combined the preposition *wiþ* 'opposite, against, near' with adverbs *innan* 'inside' and *ūtan* 'outside' to create complex adverbs, later prepositions, which developed into modern *within* /wi'ðin/ and *without* /wi'ðaut/. These refer to location, rather than to motion.

Within relates to a boundary and contrasts with *in* which can just refer to a space. This is illustrated in:

1   Gavin stayed within the garden   Gavin stayed in the garden
2   Gavin stayed within the walls   *Gavin stayed in the walls
3   *The smell of spring is within the air   The smell of spring is in the air

A garden is a bounded space and so both *within* and *in* are acceptable in 1. But in 2, *the walls* represent a boundary and so *within* is used. (*Gavin stayed in the walls* would imply that he was in chamber built into the walls, not in an area bounded by the walls.) In 3, the air is an unbounded space, making *within* impermissible here.

Without is a most unusual preposition, having two totally different meanings (each of which goes back a thousand years):

- *Without* can be the opposite of *within*, meaning 'beyond a boundary' and often contrasts with it within a sentence:

  The officers camped within the walls of the city and the rank-and-file without

Today, the use of *without* in this spatial sense appears archaic and perhaps a trifle pretentious.

- The far more common use of *without* is as the opposite of *with*, now meaning 'not having'; see section 6.2g-1. For instance:

  Stella went for a walk without her stick but with the dog

Just the first meaning of *without* is relevant for the discussion of this chapter.

Inside /ˌin'said/ and *outside* /ˌaut'said/ began, in Middle English, as nouns and it is likely that they evolved through combining prefixes *in-* and *out-* (see section 1.9) with noun *side*. *The in-side/out-side of the vessel* would have become *The inside/outside of the vessel*. During Middle English and Early Modern English times, these nouns enlarged their grammatical scope to become also used as adjectives, as adverbs and finally—in the eighteenth century—as prepositions (referring to both location and motion). The development is illustrated in:

NOUN	the inside/outside of the house
ADJECTIVE	the inside/outside wall of the house
ADVERB	She stayed inside/outside (during the storm)
PREPOSITION	They stood/walked inside/outside the church

During the early nineteenth century, the form of the prepositions—when indicating location or time—came to be optionally expanded by adding *of*—*inside/outside of the church* as an alternative to *inside/outside the church*. This was probably by analogy with the *of* required after *inside/outside* when used as a noun. (The habit of including *of* in the prepositions tends to be denigrated by prescriptivists and lexicographers; nevertheless, it is a feature of the language.)

As pointed out in section 5.2k, *inside* (and *outside*) are most likely to include the *of* when used in a temporal or location sense:

LOCATION	You'll find the key inside(-of) the box	final *of* is optional
MOTION	Mark went inside the house	no final *of*
TEMPORAL	You must return inside(-of) an hour	final *of* is optional.

It is interesting that *inside* and *outside* each still functions as noun, adjective, adverb, and preposition, whereas *within* and *without* are primarily prepositions. They do also have adverb-type functions but these can be treated as reductions from prepositional phrases. For example:

Frank stood by the car window watching the strange antics within (sc. the car)

The man had been asleep within the room and now lay dead without (sc. the room)

These pairs of prepositions may be linked:

The stranger wandered all around, within and without the village

He painted all the walls, inside and outside the hospital

The last sentence can be rephrased, with adverbs rather than prepositions. *He painted all the hospital walls, inside and outside.* Or this could be shortened to *He painted all the hospital walls, inside and out.*

When what was intended to be the inside of a garment is placed on the outside there is a nifty idiom to use: *This shirt is inside out.*

8.3a Within *and* inside(-of)

Both of these prepositions refer to boundedness and there are some contexts in which either may be used. For example, *inside* behaves like *within* for sentences 1–3—one can say *Gavin stayed inside the garden* and *Gavin stayed inside the walls*, but not **The smell of spring is inside the air.*

In sentence 2, *Gavin stayed within/inside the walls*, the shorter preposition *in* could not be used (while retaining the same meaning). However, for most of the examples quoted in the remainder of this section, *in* is a (less specific) alternative. Where this is so, *within* or *inside* is marked with †. If there is no †, then *in* is not a viable option.

The difference between them is that *inside* suggests a closer or cosier fit, and *within* a more generous one. *He put the book inside† the box* is likely to be used when it just fitted; the book was touching—or close to touching—the sides of the box. In contrast, *He put the book within† the box* might be used if the box were commodious, holding many objects including the book. The contrast between *inside* and *within* is brought out in:

> Mollie placed the money inside† an envelope and hid the
> envelope somewhere within† the house

The money fit snugly into the envelope but the envelope could have been placed anywhere within the considerable interior of the house. We can also compare:

> The statue stands within† a thicket of trees
> (as it were part of the thicket)
> The statue stands inside† a thicket of trees
> (this is its physical position, entirely surrounded by trees)

The meaning of *within* extends to 'being a part of' in a general sense:

> Queensland is a state within† Australia
> (it is a political part of the nation)

> I worked within† the telecommunications industry for thirty years
> (I was a part of that industry)

Inside implies physical location and could scarcely be used in these sentences. Neither could *inside* be substituted for *within* in: *It was a story within† a story,* or *Please keep this secret within† the family.*

When dealing with relative spatial position, only *within* is appropriate (not *inside*):

> All professors are required to reside within fifteen miles of the university

Interestingly, when referring to relative time (of short duration), either preposition is acceptable:

> The messenger has promised to return within/inside(-of) twenty minutes

(This implies 'before twenty minutes has elapsed'. If one said *return in twenty minutes* it would mean 'when twenty minutes has elapsed'.)

But when the duration is extended, only *within* is likely to be used:

> I doubt if we shall see a world state within† our lifetimes

In fact the longer the period (ten hours, a day, year, a generation,…) the more likely it is for *within* to be preferred over *inside-of*. This correlates with the *inside* being used for a cosy fit in a small space (money inside an envelope) and *within* for placement in a larger space (the envelope being somewhere within the house).

Sometimes either *within* or *in* is acceptable, but *in* is sufficient:

> Walter lives in an ivy-decked cottage
> Walter lives in the village of Much Bumbling

In either of these sentences, *within* could have been used. but it would be unnecessary. The sense of *within* is already conveyed by the words used. However, if the two statements should be combined into one sentence, then *within* might be preferred in place of the second *in*:

> Walter lives in an ivy-decked cottage within† the village of Much Bumbling

This is simply for felicity. Either *in* or *within* is appropriate, and using one of each is preferable to having a rather ugly sequence of two *in*'s.

There are a number of extensions of *within* from its spatial meaning. *Within one's grasp* can refer to something physical which may be clutched, or to some scientific reasoning which can be understood. If someone says *It is within Sam's power to cancel the contract,* they are stating that this is included as a part of the actions that are allocated to Sam. And *Not providing adequate clothing counts as negligence within the meaning of the Act,* states that this action is regarded by the Act as negligence.

8.3a-1 Three opposites for *within*

The preposition *without* can have a spatial meaning 'not within' (which does sound rather archaic) but this is swamped by the predominant sense 'not with'. The upshot is that *within* needs to find something else as its opposite. There are basically three possibilities.

(i) **Within and out-of.** In its spatial sense, *within* has *out-of* as its opposite:

> Maria is within sight/earshot of Simon
> Maria is out-of sight/earshot of Simon
> That apple should be just within your reach
> That apple is just out-of my reach

There are also *within bounds* and *out-of bounds*.

Both *within* and *out-of* may follow *from*, so that *from within* and *from out-of* could each be regarded as a complex preposition. For example:

> That noise is coming from within the shed
> The policeman seemed to appear from out-of nowhere

(ii) **Within and outside(-of).** There is an extended sense of *within*, relating to adhering to the bounds of some social convention, and here its opposite is *outside(-of)*, as in:

> Dennis operates strictly within the letter of the law
> Dennis operates way outside(-of) the law
> This matter falls within the scope of the enquiry
> This matter falls outside the scope of the enquiry

From can also be involved here, as in *They appointed a new manager from within/from outside the company.*

(iii) **Within** and **beyond.** There is an extension from the basic meaning of *within* which describes how a person is careful not to attempt more than is feasible for them. Its opposite here is *beyond* (see also section 11.3a). For example:

> Jasper spends carefully and lives within his means
> Joseph spends extravagantly and lives beyond his means
> Jenkinson operated within his capabilities (and the business thrived)
> Jones operated beyond his capabilities (and the business folded)

8.3b Outside(-of)

Outside is like *inside* in functioning as noun, adjective, adverb, and preposition. As the opposite of *inside(-of)*, the preposition *outside(-of)* describes something not being circumscribed by a boundary. If it is not the case that *Charles is inside† the castle*, then it must be that *Charles is outside the castle*.

The difference between *out-of* and *outside(-of)* is illustrated by:

1   Jeff put the chair out-of the house
2   Jeff put the chair outside(-of) the house

Sentence 1 implies that the chair had been inside the house and Jeff has taken it out. There is no such suggestion for sentence 2; Jeff could have unloaded the chair from a truck and placed it in its permanent position, outside the house. Whereas *out-of* means 'not enclosed, when it either used to be or might be expected to be', *outside(-of)* merely indicates position with respect to a boundary.

We saw that *within* and *inside* carry a subtle difference of meaning. *The statue stands within the thicket* regards the statue as part of the thicket whereas *The statue stands inside the thicket* just deals with its physical location. If neither of these statements is applicable, then it must be that *The statue stands outside the thicket*. That is, the semantic contrast between *inside* and *within* is neutralised, with *outside* the opposite for both.

The basic meaning for *outside(-of)*, 'beyond a physical boundary', can be extended to refer to whatever there is beyond a collection of people or things or ideas:

> Outside(-of) members of the cabinet, who else knows about the proposal?
>
> Outside of an apartment in London and a cottage in Tuscany, Max has two yachts
>
> Outside of Pythagoras' theorem and Newton's laws, what else does Sue know?

Besides or *aside from* or *apart from* could be used in place of *outside(-of)* here.

Another extension of meaning relates to what is beyond some personal or social limit. For example: *That fur coat is outside my price range,* and *Such a happening is entirely outside my experience.*

* * *

The next chapter focuses on the pairing *on/off,* together with *onto, upon* and *off-of,* Just as with *in* and *out,* there are intriguing differences between the meanings and uses of major member *on* and minor member *off.*

9

Connection and adjacency

On, upon, onto, off, off-of; against; beside(s)

English Prepositions: Their Meanings and Uses. R. M. W. Dixon. Oxford University Press (2021). © R. M. W. Dixon.
DOI: 10.1093/oso/9780198868682.003.0009

When one hears *X is on Y* this often indicates that X is above Y and touching it, as in:

(1)   The cat is sitting on the mat

However, this is only one aspect of the meaning of *on*. One may also hear:

(2)   The beetle is crawling on the ceiling
(3)   They fixed the undercarriage on the plane
(4)   Max has gravy on his chin
(5)   The dog is on a leash

The full meaning of preposition *on* is 'connection'. The beetle adheres to the ceiling by its claws. The undercarriage has been screwed to the underbelly of the plane. The gravy is running down Max's chin. The leash is clipped onto the dog's collar. Then there are a wide range of extensions from this basic spatial sense; for example, *Susanne appeared on TV*, *The black horse is gaining on the white one*, *Jim relies on his wife*.

On is the major member of the pairing *on/off*. As is usual with these pairings, *on* is far more common than *off* and has a wider range of meaning. *Off* may refer to a 'disconnection', typically when there was a connection but this has been discontinued, or when a connection would be expected. For example:

(3')   They took the undercarriage off the plane
(4')   Max has wiped the gravy off his chin
(5')   The dog is off its leash

Sometimes the *off* correspondent for an *on* sentence requires a little contextualisation, as in:

(1')   (The cat had been on the mat but Aunt Agatha pushed it off and)
        The cat is now off the mat

An *off* correspondent for (2) would require even more contextualisation. There are also some uses of *off* for which there is no direct counterpart with *on* (although there may be an indirect link). For example: *The red-light district is off limits*, and *If the fulcrum is off centre, results are likely to be unreliable*.

In Old English, *on* functioned as both preposition and adverb with a meaning similar to that which it has today. As mentioned at the beginning of chapter 8, during OE times preposition *in* dropped out of use with *on* taking over its meaning. Then, in Middle English, *innan* 'inside' reduced its form and enlarged its sense to become modern-day *in*, allowing *on* /ɔn/ to contract to its original meaning.

Off has an interesting history. The OE preposition *of* 'of, out of, from' developed in two directions. A reduced form became modern preposition *of*, which is generally a clitic /əv=/; see chapter 5. And there developed modern adverb *off* /ɔːf/, which is also used as a preposition. Like *on* /ɔn/, *off* is never a clitic. (As mentioned in section 1.9, both *on* and *off* have cognate derivational prefixes, deriving both adjectives and nouns; for example, *an on-looker* and *an off-key vocalist*.)

There are complex prepositions relating to *on* and *off*. *Upon* /ɔpən=/ goes back to OE times while *onto* /ɔntə=/ (sometimes written *on to*) came into use in the late sixteenth century. As explained in section 2.3, each of these is a clitic (*on* and *off* themselves are never clitics). The complex prepositions are followed by an NP, for them to cliticise onto, and can only be prepositions, never adverbs. The same applies for *off-of* /ɔfəv=/ which—although almost uniformly disparaged— is a much-used alternative for preposition *off* in American English; a little more is said about this in section 9.2b. (As is the case throughout this volume, I am here attempting to describe Standard British English.)

Adverb *onward(s)* /ˈɔnwəd(z)/ may be used in place of *on* when indicating direction; for example, *From the age of sixteen onward, Jason led a happy life*. Whereas *inward(s)*, *outward(s)*, *upward(s)*, *downward(s)*, *homeward(s)*, *northward(s)*, and so on, go back to OE, *onward(s)* only came into use in ME times. *Offward(s)* /ˈɔːfwəd(z)/ is attested from the sixteenth century, but is today rare and esoteric.

The basic functions of *on*, *upon*, *onto*, and *off* are:

	(a)	(b)
ADVERB	*on*	*off*
PREPOSITION OF OF LOCATION	*on, upon*	*off*
PREPOSITION OF MOTION	*on, onto*	*off*

Examples of adverbial use are: *The inspector just talked on* and *Did you see him run off?*

Preposition *upon* refers to location, and *onto* to motion (this relates to the motion meaning of its second component, *to*). *On* has a very general meaning and in most cases can be used instead of *upon* or *onto*. Thus:

location (6) Sam sat upon/on the horse

motion (7) Julie turned the package onto/on its side

Sentences (1–5) were given just with *on*. But *upon* could be substituted in (1) and (4), and *onto* could be in (3). Note that some uses of *on* could not be replaced by either *upon* or *onto*; these include (2) *The beetle is crawling on the ceiling* and (5) *The dog is on a leash*.

Some happenings could be described by using either *upon* or *onto*. For example:

(8) Mollie put the cake upon/onto/on the counter

If *upon* were used, this would focus on the location to which Mollie consigned the cake. With *onto* it would be describing the path of motion for the cake. There is little difference in effect.

But in other circumstances *upon* and *onto* would be describing different happenings:

(9) Jim ran upon/on the platform

　　　 (he was located on the platform for all of the act of running)

(10) Jim ran onto/on the platform

　　　 (his running moved him from being off the platform to being on it)

A nifty example of the contrast between *on* and *off* is shown in:

(11) Mike is building a house on the main road and Phil is building one off the main road

Taking account of what people normally do, one would infer that Phil's house is to be some way off the main road, and Mike's adjacent to the road (that is, beside it).

On has a fair breadth of meaning; in (11) it indicates contiguity with the main road rather than contact with it. In contrast, *upon* is rather more specific. Substituting *upon* for *on* in the first clause of (11) may describe a quite different event:

(11') Mike is building a house upon the main road

Hearing this, one might understand that the house will be built within the borders of the main road. (Alternatively, one could say *actually **on** the road* where *on* is stressed.) This is a possible meaning for (11) but it is likely to be rejected on grounds of common sense, since it is not usual to build a house in the middle of a main road. However, employing *upon*—or stressing *on*—may indicate that the unexpected is happening.

In essence, preposition *upon* indicates location above and touching (that is, on top of). This is why it could not be used in place of *on* in (2), (3), or (5), or in a temporal expression such as *on Monday* or *on time*. *Upon* can alternate with *on* in some more abstract uses—for example *She dotes on/upon her puppy*—but not in others—*He's mad on dancing*. (The interchangeability of *on* and *upon* in phrasal verbs is discussed in section 9.1h.) Approaching it from the opposite direction, there are very few uses of *upon* for which the more general *on* could not be substituted.

Preposition *onto* is more limited, being only possible when motion is involved, as in (7), in (3), where the undercarriage was moved into position below the plane and connected to it, and in:

(12) Anne got onto/on the bus at the Town Hall

Note that if *upon* were used instead of *onto* in (12) it is likely to be understood as meaning that Anne climbed onto the roof of the bus.

Onto can almost always be substituted by the more general *on*. There are just a few instances where *on* would scarcely be felicitous:

(13) They lowered the patient onto the bed
(14) The corner gate leads onto the road

In (13) the verb *lower* demands a preposition of motion. And in (14), preposition *onto* could be substituted by *to*, indicating that the second component of the complex preposition is operative here. (*Onto* also has a specialised use in mathematics; for example, *mapping one field onto another*.)

There are rather few instances where only *on* is possible—(2), (5), and also:

(15) The machine rotates on its axle

The NP component may be omitted from an inner prepositional phrase when—since the activity described is familiar—its identity would be understood. The exposed preposition can then be moved to the left over a preceding non-pronominal object NP. Thus, expanding on the examples quoted in section 2.1c:

	(a)	(b)
(16)	She put the cloth upon/ onto/on the table	She took the cloth off/ off-of the table
(17)	She put the cloth on	She took the cloth off
(18)	She put on the cloth	She took off the cloth

In (16a) there is a choice of prepositions possible before NP *the table*. However, in (17a) only *on* is possible since there is no following NP for the clitic prepositions *upon* and *onto* to attach themselves to. It is thus *on* which is available for left movement in (18a). Similarly, *off-of* could be used in (16b) but not in (17b) or (18b).

* * *

Section 9.1 surveys the range of meanings for *on, upon,* and *onto,* also mentioning correspondent senses for *off.* This is followed, in section 9.2, by discussion of additional meanings for *off.* Sections 9.3 and 9.4 deal with *against,* which extends the idea of 'connection' to 'opposition', and *beside(s),* which describes adjacency, an adjunct of connection.

9.1 *On, upon,* and *onto*

There are several contexts in which preposition *on* is expected:

(i) Quite a few verbs are typically followed by a peripheral NP introduced by *on* or *upon.* For example: *agree (up)on, comment (up) on, border (up)on, embark (up)on, gaze (up)on, reflect (up) on.* Many of these derive a nominalisation which takes the same *(up)on* phrase—*agreement (up)on, bordering (up)on,* and so on.

(ii) A number of adjectives expect an *(up)on* phrase: *(be) contingent (up)on* and *(be) reticent (up)on*; others expect just an *on* phrase: *(be) keen on* and *(be) mad on.* These refer to 'a feeling directed towards something'. *(Be) drunk on (e.g. vodka)* differs in that it describes 'a state resulting from something'.

(iii) Some nouns require an *on* phrase to explain their scope. For example: *an inquest on, an authority on, (put) the blame on.* Some may also use *upon*—*(bring) discredit (up)on, (have) mercy (up)on.*

(iv) Many nominals are typically preceded by preposition *on* (never *upon*). The possibilities are:

- A single noun, such as *on stilts, on trust, on approval, on leave, on strike, on business, on fire.*
- A definite NP, such as *on the phone, on the agenda, on the alert, on the side, on the prowl.*
- An indefinite NP, such as *on a diet, on a spree, on an adventure, on a high, on an impulse.*

Note that there are no instances of *into* in these lists.

The following sections survey the senses of *on* (plus *upon* and *onto*) and also of *off(-of)* where these correspond.

9.1a Basic meanings

There are several kinds of connection which are described with *on*.

When *upon* is a fully acceptable alternative for an example quoted, this is shown as *up(on)*. *Upon* may also be used—within an appropriate context—in some other examples, except for those where the *on* is chosen by a following noun or NP (set (iv) from just above). *Onto*, expressing motion, is a less common alternative for *on*.

9.1a-1 Physical connection

On can here relate a person or an animal or an artefact to some location:

The queen is sitting (up)on the throne
Rebecca is lying (up)on the sofa
The boat is floating (up)on the lagoon
The bird perched on the branch
Janes lives on a boat

If motion is involved, then *onto* is appropriate:

The messenger jumped on(to) his horse

The preposition may link together two locations:

> Finland borders on Sweden

Or *on* may introduce a body-part NP:

> She has a ring (up)on her finger
> He kissed her on the lips
> Tim was lying on his back
> He followed on foot
> Harry had a furtive look on his face

Also: *on one's knees, on all fours, on tiptoe, (the bird is) on the wing.* And idioms such as *(She has chess) on the brain,* and *(The murderer now has two deaths) on his conscience,* extending to *Do you have any money on you?*

On (but scarcely *upon*) may refer to the projection of an image, as in:

> John is on the photograph, at the far right
> I saw it on TV
> You'll find it on my website

This extends to the idea of 'inclusion' involving something written on paper:

> What's on the menu?
> Jim's name is on the list (of committee members)

And it extends further to membership:

> Jim is on the committee

There may be a connection of location, shown by *on*, between any two physical entities. For example: *The cross is on the church steeple,* and *That hotel is on the coast.*

9.1a-2 Activated connection

A connection may be achieved through movement. For example:

> We arrived on the scene after the body had been removed
> The two groups of hikers simultaneously converged (up)on the inn
> The yacht was cast (up)on the rocks by the storm

> The tiger pounced (up)on its prey
>
> He turned his back on the disaster scene
>
> He put his shoes on his feet

From the last example one would normally omit *his feet* (after all, on what else would he be likely to put his shoes) giving *He put his shoes on.* The preposition *on* may then be moved to the left over the preceding object NP, producing *He put on his shoes.* (Note that there are *off* correspondents for these sentences: *He took his shoes off* and *He took off his shoes.*)

A connection engendered by movement may be unlawful or unwelcome. For example:

> The boys were trespassing (up)on private property
>
> The street fighting scarcely impinged (up)on our suburban lives
>
> The sea is encroaching (up)on the cliffs

There can be metaphorical extensions here; for example, *I am sorry to encroach (up)on your valuable time.*

Alternatively to a connection being established through movement, movement may involve a connection, as in:

> The operator pushed on the lever

Or there may some more complex activity, with *on* used to mark what is affected by the activity:

> The general pinned a medal on(to) the hero
>
> The lovers carved their initials on the tree
>
> The surgeon operated on my right leg

A general verb of activity will employ an *on* phrase to indicate what the activity concerns, as in:

> James is working on the problem/computer/garden

9.1a-3 Detached connection

On may indicate that two items are linked by vision or smell or talk:

> Never had I gazed (up)on such splendour
>
> Mother just went to check on what the children are doing

The light is shining on his face

The bloodhound is on the scent

I call on Thea to propose the vote of thanks

This can extend metaphorically, as in *You must look (up)on Pete as a friend*, and *Please concentrate/focus on the task in hand.*

9.1b Prolongation

When *He put his shoes on his feet* is shortened to *He put his shoes on*, preposition *on* adopts an adverb-like function. This sense is extended to *She switched the lights on* and *She switched on the lights* (the verb could instead be *turned* or *put*). There is no underlying NP (along the lines of *his feet* in the previous example) so that here *on* must be considered an adverb. It can be seen that preposition and adverb merge in meaning. Adverb *on* can then function as copula complement in *The lights are on*. This meaning 'it is happening' may then be extended to *The concert is on (at the Town Hall tonight)*. (Note that there are *off* correspondents for these sentences: *She switched the lights off* and *She switched off the lights*, *The lights are off* and *The concert is off* (it has been cancelled).)

This adverbial use of *on* carries an implication of continuity—once switched on, the lights will offer sustained illumination. Adverb *on* carries a similar sense of prolongation when it follows a variety of intransitive verbs:

The mourners walked on in silence

He was too infirm to take part in the games and could only sit and look on

She's fit and healthy and will live on for a good while yet

Indeed extensive prolongation may be shown by coordinating *on*'s (almost without limit):

She ran on and on

The bishop talked on and on and on...

As illustrated in section 1.2, preposition *onto* can also indicate prolonged action, as in *Hang onto the other end of the rope, so that we don't get separated in the dark!*

9.1c Mental links

There are several ways in which a mental connection is marked with *on*.

9.1c-1 Mental activity

Preposition *on* marks the topic with which the referent of the subject NP is concerned. This can involve thinking or deciding:

> The leader speculated on what might happen next
>
> We had planned on a trip to Futuna
>
> They decided on a July wedding
>
> Mel's team are intent on winning the championship

Also: *ponder on, meditate on, think on, reflect on, dwell on, brood on, determine on.*

Or speech (or writing) may be involved:

> The president commented on the poor rate of progress
>
> The two parties agreed on a joint course of action

Other verbs here include: *remark on, speak on, lecture on, confer on.*

The activity may be directed toward a person, as in:

> We advised Mary on the best course of action
>
> They congratulated Jane upon her promotion

Also: *enlighten (someone) on, bestow (something) on.*

Some verbs may switch functions of the person experiencing a mental state, and what the state involves. For example, alongside *Marcia pondered on the difficulty of the situation* we can have:

> The difficulty of the situation gradually dawned on Marcia

When a verb selects an *on* phrase, a cognate noun may do likewise:

> Julia lectured on clitics
>
> Julia published [her lectures on clitics]

Nouns of similar import behave in the same way (even though there may be no underlying verb); for example: a *textbook on chemistry*, a *disquisition on sobriety*. And a noun referring to a learned person may be followed by an *on* phrase explaining what their learning relates to:

Silvia is an authority/expert on Hittite

9.1c-2 Mental attitude

A person may have feelings about someone or something, stated through an *on* phrase. This can involve a verb, an adjective, or a noun:

Margaret dotes (up)on her new-born baby

Tom is keen on badminton

Jill took pity on the waif

Please have mercy on me!

Also: *fawn (up)on, be mad on, be gone on* (meaning 'be infatuated with'), *take vengeance on, have compassion on, put the blame on.*
    An interesting construction here involves a reflexive:

Maxine revenged herself on the man who insulted her grandfather

Alternatively, the corresponding noun could be used, still taking an *on* phrase:

Maxine took revenge on the man who insulted her grandfather

In this example the emotion is directed towards someone else. However, it could be self-directed, as in:

Albert prides himself on his achievements

Here the corresponding noun requires an *in* phrase, not an *on* phrase: *Albert takes pride in his achievements*; this is the 'enveloped in a mental or emotional attitude' senses of *in*, described in section 8.1c-2.

9.1c-3 Manner, outlook, and stance

An *on* phrase may state how a person conducts some activity.
One type describes the way in which something is done or the mental outlook involved, and has adverbial function:

She was meeting her lover on the sly

On an impulse he smashed the idol

She would never visit a dictatorship on principle

Others of this ilk include: *on the quiet, on the spur of the moment, on second thoughts, on reflection*, extending to *on purpose*.

A second type describe a mental stance. These *on* phrases function principally as copula complement; for example:

Simon was on the defensive all through the interview

Also: *on the alert, on edge, on tenterhooks, on a high, on a spree, on top of the world, on one's best behaviour, on guard,* and *on the make.*

9.1d State

Moving away from mental links, there is a wide range of *on* phrases which essentially describe states. One group, predominantly functioning as copula complement, have inanimate reference:

Those books are on order
The milk is on the boil

Others include: *on display, on view, on fire, on loan, on sale, on the latch,* and *on ration.*

Some phrases of this type may also have adverbial function, such as *He bought it on credit* and *I got it on the cheap.*

Another group, also used as copula complement, relate to humans:

Uncle Jack is on parole
Aunt Mary is still on the phone

Also: *on the dole, on probation, on trial, on bail, on strike, on duty, on guard, on parade, on leave,* and *on the mend.*

For a third group the *on* phrase describes an activity:

Aunt Ada is in town on business

And: *on a picnic, on a visit, on holiday, on a vacation, on an adventure, on the job.*

There is a further group, concerned with movement, which typically follow *be* or *go*:

The soldiers are on the march
He went/was on the prowl

Amongst other phrases in this set are: *on the move, on the run, on the go, on the loose, on the warpath.*

9.1e Dependence

In its basic senses, *on* implies a dependency. Consider: *The cat is sitting on the mat.* The mat was there anyway and the cat needs it for something to sit on; the mat does not need the cat. Similarly if one hears *There's a piece of used chewing gum stuck on the underside of the table,* the gum requires the table as a place to be stuck on. This sense of the preposition is extended in various ways.

9.1e-1 General dependency

On can be used to mark something which the referent of the subject is dependent (up)on in non-spatial circumstances. This sense occurs in a number of prepositional verbs; for example:

> The neophytes relied (up)on the advice of their professional mentors
>
> The plan hinges (up)on a deal being struck with the producers
>
> Our business is founded (up)on truth, trust, and sincerity

Other verbs in this set include: *depend (up)on, count (up)on, base (something) (up)on, model (your behaviour) (up)on;* also *sponge (up)on and draw (up)on.* And there are adjectives which take *on* in the same sense:

> Growth is contingent (up)on improved efficiency

Also: *conditional (up)on* and, bringing in a temporal nuance, *consequent up(on).*

Nouns indicating a dependency may expect a preceding *on,* as in:

> You can go to the party on condition that you are home before ten o'clock
>
> I'm writing on behalf of the minister

There are also self-contained *on* phrases which convey a dependency, such as: *(Don't change the date) on my account.* Now consider:

> These decisions bear on the happiness of everyone

Bear (up)on effectively reverses syntactic functions. As an alternative to *The happiness of everyone depends on these decisions,* one could say: *These decisions bear on the happiness of everyone.*

9.1e-2 Material dependency

An *on* phrase may introduce an NP describing what is needed to fulfil the activity described by a verb, or by verb plus object:

> She subsists on a small pension
>
> The duke thrives on steak and potatoes
>
> He wastes time/money/energy on worthless pursuits

Also: *live on, feed on, dine on.*

An *on* phrase may supply the reason for a state described by an adjective, as in *The pantrymaid is drunk on cooking sherry*. And a noun referring to some habit may be introduced by *on*; for example: *on drugs, on antibiotics, on a diet.*

9.1f Quantitative

On and *off* can have their meanings extended from spatial objects (*put the book on the table, take the book off the table*) to monetary addition and subtraction:

> They've put twenty per cent on the price of blankets
>
> Customers, take another thirty per cent off the sale price!

Also: *They've imposed a tax on/taken the tax off prescription drugs.* And:

> Karl made a considerable profit/loss on potato futures

The positive or negative sense is here encapsulated in the nouns *profit* and *loss*, so that just *on* (the unmarked member of the pairing *on/off*) is used for both circumstances. Similar remarks apply for the phrases *on the increase* and *on the wane*.

A pharmacy was cutting prices on fragrances. The notice outside read *Up to 70% off fragrances*, which was straightforward, being an elliptical form of *off the price of fragrances*. But when one entered the shop there was a different notice, using preposition *on* rather than *off*. It read: *Save up to 70% on fragrances*. This can be explained as being an elliptical vision of a clause:

> On buying fragrances, save up to 70%

The word *buying* had been omitted as understood (what else would one do with fragrances in a pharmacy?) and the clauses reversed to highlight the discount.

The 'increase' sense of *on* extends to anything measurable. For example, *elaborate on*, *improve (up)on*, and *improvement on*, as in:

> Monica elaborated on the plan (by providing detailed costings)
>
> Your second draft is a big improvement on the first draft
> (in quality of argumentation)

Or it may relate to speed or distance:

> The chestnut is putting on a spurt and gaining on the leading horse
>
> General Windrush's troops are advancing on the enemy

In the last example, the troops are moving towards making a connection with the enemy.

An *on* phrase may also be used as an assessment:

> On balance, I slightly prefer the green-space proposal
>
> On average, Indian printers are the most competitive in Asia

9.1g Temporal

Chapter 14 describes how prepositions are used to refer to time. Basically, *at* pinpoints a particular point of time (*at midnight*), and *in* places something within a span of time (*in the morning*) whereas *on* has the special property of referring to anything relating to 'day'. The rationale for this is explored in section 14.6a. For example:

> Ellalene always has her hair done on a Friday
>
> We'll see Dorothy again on her birthday
>
> We always celebrate on June 20th, our first date

On is also used in set phrases such as:

> I liked him on first acquaintance

The 'connection' sense of *on* is employed in:

> Donald always arrives on time
>
> The work is proceeding on schedule

There is further discussion in section 14.6a.

9.1g-1 Temporal clause

There may be an -ING clause specifying a temporal event, this being introduced by *on*; it generally precedes the main clause. For example:

> On Basil's agreeing to contribute, Fiona finalised the program
>
> On hearing the police siren, Joe hid under the bed

9.1h On, upon, *and* onto *in phrasal verbs and prepositional verbs*

Quite a few prepositional verbs which include *on* or *upon* have already been mentioned—*impinge (up)on, encroach (up)on, decide (up)on, dote (up)on, rely (up)on, hinge (up)on, sponge (up)on,* and *bear (up)on*. There appear to be none with *onto*.

   On may function as preposition or adverb and is, accordingly, found in both slot **p** and slot **a** for phrasal verbs. *Upon* and *onto*, which are only prepositions, are solely in slot **p**. The prepositions occur in all four **p** slots, in V-p-NP, V-NP-p-NP, V-a-p-NP, and V-NP-a-p-NP. We can illustrate with just a sample:

SENSE	TYPE	
Activated connection	V-p-NP	By chance we <u>happened (up)on</u> the vicar in the supermarket
	V-NP-p-NP	Mother <u>turned</u> the dog <u>on</u> the intruder
	V-NP-a-p-NP	Why don't we <u>let</u> Sally <u>in on</u> the secret
	V-NP-p-NP	Jim <u>put</u> me <u>onto</u> a cheap mortgage scheme
	V-NP-p-NP	The boss <u>put</u> pressure <u>(up)on</u> Jack
Prolongation	V-p-NP	You'd better <u>hang onto</u> that job
Mental activity	V-p-NP	He's <u>bent on</u> an early start tomorrow
	V-p-NP	Clarissa has just <u>hit (up)on</u> a wonderful idea
	V-p-NP	That teacher always <u>picks on</u> Tommy

	V-p-NP	Please don't <u>tell on</u> Fred (help cover up his misdeeds)
Dependency	V-p-NP	You can always <u>bank (up)on</u> Uncle Jack for support
	V-a-p-NP	I'll have to <u>fall back on</u> my savings
Quantitative	V-NP-p-NP	They've just <u>slapped</u> $2 <u>on(to)</u> the price of a pineapple

It can be seen that some phrasal verbs only employ *on*, some *on* or *upon*, some *on* or *onto*, and some just *onto*.

It is hard to relate the phrasal verb in the V-p-NP construction *My car <u>died on</u> me* to any of the senses for *on* that have been listed.

Relating to its adverbial function, *on* is in slot **a** for phrasal verbs types V-a, V-NP-a, and V-a-p-NP. (I have not encountered *on* in type V-NP-a-p-NP.) Here is a selection:

SENSE	TYPE	
Activated connection	V-NP-a	'<u>Bring</u> the battle <u>on</u>!', the cavaliers cried
	V-NP-a	David <u>took</u> Goliath <u>on</u>
	V-NP-a	The organisers have <u>laid</u> drinks <u>on</u> for all the contestants
Prolongation	V-a	<u>Carry on</u>!
	V-a	It seems that Grandma will <u>live on</u> for ever
	V-a	<u>Hold on</u>, I'll be with you shortly
	V-a-p-NP	Jim <u>stayed on in</u> the job for thirty years
Mental activity	V-a-p-NP	Why are you always <u>getting on at</u> Emily!
	V-NP-a	He's always <u>putting</u> a performance <u>on</u>

It is generally possible to move *on*, as **a** element, to the left over a preceding object NP; thus: *Bring on the battle!*, *They have laid on drinks*, and *He's always putting on a performance*.

9.1i Contrasting on and upon with other prepositions

We can now examine contexts in which *on* and *upon* may contrast with prepositions discussed in the previous chapters.

9.1i-1 Of and on

Although adjectives *dependent* and *independent* have complementary meanings they select different prepositions, *on* and *of* respectively:

> Tim is still dependent on his parents for financial support
>
> As the result of his new contract, Joe is now financially
>   independent of his parents

With adjective *dependent*, *on* is used in its 'dependency' sense (section 9.1e) whereas, with *independent*, *of* has its 'dissociation' or 'lacking' sense (section 5.2h).

Of and *on* may be used after the same verb, *think*, as in:

> You need to think of the consequences of your decision to resign
>
> You know what the consequences will be of your decision to
>   resign, and now you need to think on what the loss of status
>   in the community will mean for your family

Think of employs the 'knowledge' sense for *of* (section 5.2g) whereas *think on*—like *reflect on* and *meditate on*—has the 'mental activity' sense of *on* (section 9.1c-1).

9.1i-2 For and on

A house may be described as *On sale* ('state' sense of *on*; section 9.1d) or advertised as *For sale* ('potentiality' sense for *of*; section 5.3c-4). The pragmatic effect is similar but the semantics differs. *For sale* indicates that it is intended that the house should be sold, whereas *On sale* merely states that it is available for sale.

9.1i-3 By and on

There are complementary ways of describing how something came about, and they involve different prepositions:

> Simon upset the fish tank by accident
>
> Simon upset the fish tank on purpose

On purpose is related to the 'outlook' sense of *on* (section 9.1c-3). *By accident* involves the 'how an activity is conducted' sense of *by* (section 6.1b-4); *by chance* and *by mistake* have similar meaning and function.

Suppose that Tom walks to a rendezvous. One could say either *He came on foot* or *He came by foot*. These describe the same activity but from different viewpoints:

- *On foot* uses the 'physical connection' sense of *on* (section 9.1a-1), stating what body part was used for the locomotion; it contrasts with *on his hands and knees* and *on tiptoe*.
- *By foot* uses the 'how something moves' sense of *by* (section 6.1b-1). Tom could arrive by car, or by train, or by camel; it is by analogy with these that we get *by foot*.

9.1i-4 *At, in,* and *on*

These three prepositions relate to different kinds of location: *at* for a position of rest, *in* for inclusion, and *on* for connection. Phrases introduced by them may occur in variable order; typically, one phrase is included within another. We can compare:

Ingrid lives [at the seaside][in a villa [on Beach Road]]

Jim sat [at the head of the table [in the kitchen]][on a stool]

In each sentence the phrases occur in the order *at–in–on*. But in the first sentence the *on* phrase modifies the head noun of the *in* phrase, and in the second the *in* phrase modifies the head of the *at* phrase. Many similar examples can be constructed, with the prepositions in all possible orders and showing varied constituency.

9.1i-5 *At* and *on*

If someone arrives somewhere, the place where they arrive may be shown by *at* or *on*, depending on the nature of the place. For example:

Jack arrived at the gold-mine

Jack arrived on the goldfields

The gold-mine is a specific establishment, and *at* is here used in its 'focus on spatial position' sense (section 7.1a) whereas the goldfields is a region, and it selects *on* in its 'activated connection' sense (section 9.1a-2). *Jack arrived on the gold-mine* sounds odd; one might infer that he had climbed on top of the building.

9.1i-6 *To* and *on*

When providing instructions on how to find the bathroom one could equally well say either of:

> The bathroom is the second door to the right
>
> The bathroom is the second door on the right

The first sentence focuses on the direction, using *to* in its basic sense (section 7.2a)—go to the right, then it's the second door. In contrast, the second sentence operates in terms of the location, using *on* in its 'physical connection' sense (section 9.1a-1)—the place you are looking for is behind the second door on the right-hand side.

The verb *agree* can be followed by a *to* phrase or an *in* phrase, with a difference of meaning:

> The union agreed to a new workplace agreement which the employers had put forward
>
> The union and the employers agreed on a new workplace agreement

The first sentence uses the 'attitude' sense of *to* (section 7.2d), showing that the union agreed to something presented to it. The 'mental activity' sense of *on* (section 9.1c-1) is employed in the second sentence; here the new workplace agreement was worked out jointly between the two parties involved.

9.1i-7 *Towards* and *(up)on*

The verb *verge* has two slightly different uses. It can mean 'getting near to', and then takes *towards* in its sense 'attitude directed at some state (but not quite getting there)'; see section 7.3e. Or it can mean 'getting associated with', and then takes *(up)on* in its 'activated connection' sense; see section 9.1a-2.

> His feelings were verging towards despair
>
>   (they were getting closer and closer to despair)
>
> His feelings were verging (up)on despair
>
>   (they were coming into contact with despair)

9.1i-8 *In* and *on*

The contrasting meanings of these two important prepositions, 'enclosure' and 'connection', are illustrated in many ways. For example one would arrive *in a car* (*in* because enclosed) but *on a bicycle* (*on* because of connection, no enclosure involved).

The preposition appropriate to describe hitting someone depends on the body part involved:

> Brenda hit Martin in the stomach
>
> Brenda hit Martin on the head

The stomach is flexible and a fist impacted on it will force it in, making it concave so that the fist is effectively within its scope; thus, *in* is appropriate here. But the head is hard and here only *on* can be used, indicating contact.

Another contrast is between *That spot is in the fabric* (it is part of the design) and *That spot is on the fabric* (it is a dirty mark which can be removed).

9.1i-9 *Into* and *(up)on*

The verb *enter* describes going into something. In its extended meanings it may be followed by *into* or *(up)on*:

> Richard entered into a series of complex negotiations
>
> Rebecca entered (up)on a new phase of her life

The first sentence shows an abstract sense of the basic meaning of *into*, extending from sentences like *Richard walked into the room* (section 8.1a). In the second sentence, Rebecca advances from one stage of her life to another; it is appropriate here to use *(up)on* in its 'activated connection' sense (section 9.1a-2).

9.2 *Off* and *off-of*

The meaning of *off* is complementary to that of *on*. While *on* refers to 'connection', *off* relates to 'disconnection', typically of something which had been connected but no longer is so, or of something which might be expected to be connected but isn't.

Quite a number of the occurrences of *off* parallel those of *on*, particularly when dealing with basic meanings concerning concrete objects.

For example, a thing which can be *put on* may be *taken off*. However, the correspondence does not extend to more abstract senses; a vain person may *put on airs and graces* but there is no expression which describes taking them off.

Sometimes an *off* sentence is straightforward, if Max *gets gravy on his chin*, he can later *wipe the gravy off his chin*. Someone could remark *John has a cheeky look on his face*, and a supervisor might demand: *Take that cheeky look off your face!* Here the *off* sentence could stand alone. But sometimes an *off* statement requires a contextualising *on* statement. For example:

> Basil and Sybil danced together on the platform and then kissed off the platform

Basil and Sybil kissed off the platform, all on its own, sounds odd. But, within a sentence which also includes an *on* clause, it is perfectly felicitous.

Only a rather small proportion of the *on* sentences and phrases quoted in section 9.1 have an *off* correspondent, although there are often independent *off* items for the senses listed. These can be briefly surveyed.

Physical connection. *Off* may typically relate to distance, as in:

> Fred's house is a long way off the road

This can be shortened to *Fred's house is a long way off* (that is, from here). This adverbial sense of *off* is extended to *He ran off* (that is, ran some distance away from here). Also *She cleared off* and colloquial directives such as *Be off!*, *Buzz off!*, *Piss off!*, *Bugger off!*, and others.

Alongside a notice *Only college fellows may walk on the grass* there may be a warning: *Students must keep off the grass*. This leads into the *off* phrase in *The grass is off limits for students*.

For many sentences using *off* in a basic sense, there is implicit contrast with an *on* sentence. For example, *Moses is driving off the road* implies that one can also *drive on the road*. If one hears *Joan is off the committee*, it is to be inferred that she was previously *on the committee*.

Alongside specifications of spatial distance, such as *The town is still five miles off*, adverb *off* may be used for 'deferred time' (see section 14.6c), as in *The conference is still three months off*. (There is here nothing corresponding with *on*.)

Activated connection. Some of the most straightforward sentences contrast *on* and *off*; for example, *He got on(to)/off the train*, *She jumped on(to)/(up)on/off the horse*, and *Put the dog on a leash/Take the dog off the leash*. However, for others quoted in section 9.1a-2, there is no *off* correspondent; for example, *converge (up)on*, *turn one's back on*, and *trespass (up)on*.

Detached connection. Only a few of the on sentences may have an *off* counterpart. One is:

> Monica took her eyes off the screen (when confronting images appeared)

Alongside *The bloodhound is on the scent*, it is possible to say *The bloodhound is off the scent*; however, *The bloodhound has lost the scent* is likely to be preferred.

Prolongation. As mentioned in section 9.1b, we do have adverbial use of *off* in *The lights are off* and *The concert is off*; also *The deal is off*. This indicates permanent disconnection.

Stance. There are far more *on* phrases than *off* phrases here (for example, *on the alert* and *on the sly*). However we do find *(he is) off his food*.

State. There are here quite a few *off* phrases. Some have *on* counterparts, including:

> If you're going to be home late, I'll leave the door off the latch
> What time do you come off duty tonight, sweetie?

Also *off ration*, *off the phone*, *off probation*, *off guard*.

When the boss is enraged one might say: *She is boiling with anger*. And then advise: *Wait a few minutes until her anger's gone off the boil*.

Quantitative. As illustrated in section 9.1f, the *put/take* pairing applies again here. One can *put 20% on the price* or *take 20% off the price*.

A work schedule may be described as: *five weeks on and two weeks off*.

9.2a Removal and deprivation

Off has a basic meaning 'disconnect' which is extended in several directions. Beyond the straightforward *take off (something)* there are such verb-plus-preposition combinations as:

Maria cut a button off the coat

Alan broke the handle off the cup

In a context where listeners know what is being talked about, the NP following *off* may be omitted, and the bare preposition moved to the left over a non-pronominal object NP. Thus: *Maria cut a button off* and *Maria cut off a button*, *Alan broke the handle off* and *Alan broke off the handle*.

This sense of 'removal' extends to adverbial use of *off* after an intransitive verb, as in:

A button fell off

The handle broke off

The weather has cooled off

With the economic downturn, profits have fallen off

Also after the object of a transitive verb, such as:

John has paid the debt off AND John has paid off the debt

Verb *finish* can indicate 'complete removal', as in *Luke has finished the grapes*, this meaning may be accentuated by including *off*, giving *Luke has finished off the grapes*. (As mentioned in section 1.8, *off* can be used as the predicate of an imperative sentence, followed by a *with* phrase; it then has the sense of complete removal, as in *Off with his head!* and *Off with you!*)

Off is also used for 'deprivation', as in:

The larrikin stole off his mother

Verb *sponge* can be followed either by an *on* phrase or by an *off* phrase with similar effect but different underlying semantics:

The larrikin sponged on his mother

The larrikin sponged off his mother

The first sentence employs the 'general dependency' sense of *on* (section 9.1e-1), similar *to depend (up)on* and *draw (up)on*; it focuses on the relationship between the larrikin and his mother. The second sentence has the 'deprivation' sense of *off*, similar to *steal off*, it focuses on the mother being divested of what the larrikin extracts from her.

One can also say *Joan lives off the land*, meaning that she takes what she needs to eat from the land, thus depriving the land of this. (*Joan lives on the land* is quite different, having a straightforward locational sense.)

9.2b Off-of

It is interesting that *off* and *of*, which developed from the same OE form, have combined to form a complex preposition *off-of* /ˈɔfəv=/. *Off-of* made its first appearance in the mid-fifteenth century and since then has been used in British England as an occasional alternative for preposition *off*. Across the Atlantic, *off-of* is much used in place of preposition *off*.

It is likely that, in American English, prepositions *off* and *off-of* are not absolutely equivalent. One would expect that one would be preferred in certain circumstances and the other in different circumstances, just as we were able to distinguish between *out* and *out-of* at the beginning of chapter 8.

Dictionaries are unhelpful; their treatment is summarised in section 15.2d. As a speaker of British/Australian English, I lack appropriate intuitions concerning this American usage. However, it does seem that *off-of* may be preferred for temporal statements, as in *The swimmer cut half a second off-of her record*. The discussion of 'optional *of*' in section 5.2k suggests that *off-of* might be preferred for location and plain *off* for motion. However, evidence to support this speculation is not at present available.

Just *off* has been employed in the examples of this chapter; *off-of* could undoubtedly be substituted for many of the prepositional uses (not of course for the adverbial ones).

9.2c Off in phrasal verbs and prepositional verbs

Just a few prepositional verbs include *off*; one of these is *reel off*, as in *Michael can reel off the names of all the presidents*. *Off* is a component of several dozen phrasal verbs. Like *on*, it functions as both adverb and preposition; and accordingly occurs in both slot **a** and slot **p** for phrasal verbs.

Off is only encountered in slot **p** for a handful of phrasal verbs of two types. Type V-NP-p-NP is illustrated by *The Duke* <u>struck</u> *the vicar* <u>off</u> *the list of invitees*, which relates to the 'activated connection' sense.

Phrasal verbs of type V-p-NP which include *off* mostly relate to 'removal' or 'deprivation'; for example:

> My brother <u>laid off</u> booze after his dismissal for drunkenness
> Jason <u>knocked off</u> work early today
> Mother has <u>gone off</u> Archie/chocolates
> (she doesn't like him/them any more)

There are many phrasal verbs of types V-a, V-NP-a with *off* in slot **a**, and just a few of types V-a-p-NP and V-NP-a-p-NP. We can illustrate with a selection:

SENSE	TYPE	
Physical connection	V-a	The plane has <u>taken off</u>
Activated connection	V-NP-a	He changed direction to <u>head</u> the pursuers <u>off</u>
	V-NP-a	The rebels have <u>pulled</u> a victory <u>off</u>
	V-a	Has the experiment <u>come off</u>?
Detached connection	V-NP-a	That rotting carcass <u>gives</u> a bad smell <u>off</u>
Prolongation	V-NP a	They have <u>called</u> the meeting <u>off</u>
Mental activity	V-NP-a	The bishop has promised to <u>kick</u> the discussion <u>off</u>
	V-NP-a	He was able to <u>carry</u> the impersonation <u>off</u>
	V-NP-a	He was able to <u>take</u> Winston Churchill <u>off</u>
	V-NP-a	Don't keep <u>telling</u> Sarah <u>off</u>!
	V-NP-a	The judge <u>let</u> the assailant <u>off</u>

	V-a-p-NP	The captain's enthusiasm <u>rubbed off on</u> the rest of the team
	V-NP-a-p-NP	Max <u>played</u> Fred <u>off against</u> Mary
Removal	V-NP-a	The manager was forced to <u>lay</u> half the work-force <u>off</u>
	V-a	The milk has <u>gone off</u>, it's sour
	V-a	Peter's sense of loneliness has <u>worn off</u>
	V-a	The old codger had seemed so healthy, but he's just <u>popped off</u>
Deprivation	V-NP-a	It was the butler who <u>knocked</u> the gold plate <u>off</u>

We also get the phrasal verbs of types V-a and V-NP-a in *The bomb <u>went off</u>* and *They <u>let</u> the bomb <u>off</u>.* These can be regarded as extensions from the 'removal and deprivation' sense.

When *off*, in slot **a**, follows an NP (which is not a pronoun) it can generally be moved to the left over it; this is especially prevalent when the NP is lengthy. Indeed, such movement is often preferred; for example, *The rotting carcass <u>gives off</u> a bad smell, He was able to <u>carry off</u> the impersonation.*

9.2d Contrasting off with other prepositions

There are a couple of interesting contrasts between *off* and prepositions discussed earlier.

9.2d-1 From, out-of, and off

Consider the following sentences involving the three prepositions, each in its basic sense:

1 Archie jumped out-of the plane
2 Archie jumped off the plane
3 Archie jumped from the plane

Sentence 1, with *out-of*, implies that Archie was within the plane and then exited from it. Sentence 2, with *off*, could describe the same happening but it also has a wider meaning and could be used when Archie had been standing on top of the plane. *From*, which is vaguer, could be used instead of *out-of* in 1 or instead of *off* in 2. But when *from* is used there is generally an expectation that, alongside a place of departure marked by *from*, there will also be a destination marked by *to*; for example, *Archie jumped from the plane to the truck which was standing alongside it.*

Another instructive pair of sentences is:

4   Robin tore a page out-of the book

5   Robin tore a corner off the sheet of paper

In sentence 4, the page was included within the book and has now been extracted; *from* would be alternative preposition here (but *off* could not be used). In the second sentence, the corner has been disconnected, shown by *off*. The corner was a part of the sheet but was not included within it, so that using *out-of* would be inappropriate.

In sentences 1–3, the intransitive subject *Archie* refers to a person, who is likely to journey from one place to another. In contrast, in sentence 5 *a corner* is transitive object whose referent is being detached. There is no expectation of a journey (from X to Y), and it would not be felicitous here to use *from* in place of *off*.

(Note that, just occasionally, one encounters a compound preposition *from off*. For example: *He jumped from off the plane*, which would have essentially the same meaning as sentence 2.)

9.2d-2 *Out* and *off*

These two prepositions can be used in the same frame but carry different meanings:

> Those elm trees have died off
>
> Those elm trees have died out

The first sentence uses the 'deprivation' sense of *off* (section 9.2a) implying that the elm trees have temporarily 'died' because of weather conditions but are expected to regenerate. (This is similar to *The weather has cooled off*.) In the second sentence we find that 'done fully' sense of *out* (section 8.2c-3); describing the irreversible demise of the trees.

9.3 *Against*

The present-day preposition *against*, /ə'geinst/ or /ə'genst/, goes back to the Old English preposition *on-gēan* or *on-gegn* 'opposite, in front of, against'. The final *-st* was added in late Middle English, perhaps to distinguish this preposition from the adverb *again*, which came from the same source but had developed a quite different meaning. (See section 1.10.)

In its basic meaning, *against* indicates contact between two entities, there also being physical opposition between them. For example:

> Jim swam against the tide
>
> Jim pushed against the door

In each of these sentences, Jim is exerting force against an opposing impediment. A milder situation is described by:

> Jim leaned against the wall

Jim and the wall are not simply in contact here. Jim may be tired or injured so that he is unable to stand on his own, and is supported by leaning on the wall. One could say that the wall 'opposes' Jim's propensity to fall down.

A different slant on 'opposition' was illustrated in section 1.2. The normal procedure with a picture is *hang it on a wall* with the front of the picture facing outwards so that it can be seen. But if someone took an aversion to the picture and didn't want it to be seen, they could *turn the picture against the wall*, so that it is the opposite way to what one would expect it to be.

Against is used for a variety of types of 'opposition' and also extends to 'contrast' and 'balance'. These will be discussed in turn.

9.3a *Opposition*

Against may introduce an NP with physical or abstract reference. We can begin with the former.

Fight is a straightforward transitive verb which describes a reciprocal activity. One could say either *Bill is fighting Tom* or *Tom is fighting Bill*. The verb may also be used where the referent of the subject is a person or a human group who use force in opposition to their adversary, and then *against* is included:

> The patriots fought against the oligarchy

One can also fight against injustice or discrimination or apathy.

There are verbs describing types of opposition which expect an *against* phrase:

> They rebelled against totalitarian rule/the unfair tax system
>
> The soldiers defended the castle against assault/the workers

Also *strive against, struggle against,* and *arm (oneself) against.*

This sense of *against* is also found after nouns which refer to a type of opposition, as in:

> We plan to wage war against the highlanders/poverty

Also *(plan) a campaign against* and *(lead) an attack against.*

One may take steps to avoid some unwelcome happening, referred to by an *against* phrase:

> We must be on our guard/take precautions against interlopers

Similar meanings attach to *protect (oneself) against, insure against,* and *guarantee against.*

The verb *compete* implies opposition (albeit of a non-violent variety) and may take an *against* phrase, as in:

> Julie is competing against the best athletes in the world

Others here are *race against* and *win against.* And there can be a metaphorical extension when what one is trying to match is not the speed of a person but the rate of movement of the hands of a clock (that is, the immutable forward movement of time):

> It'll be a race against the clock/time to get this work completed on
> schedule

Against patterns with *for* in describing the casting of ballots:

> Seven people voted for Ian as editor and three (people) voted
> against (Ian as editor)

The portions in parentheses may be omitted. However, it is not the case that *against* is then functioning as an adverb; it is simply a preposition with its following NP anaphorically omitted. Similar remarks apply for a bookmaker's call: *Pegasus—five to one against* (that is, against Pegasus winning the race).

9.3a-1 Involving social acts

Speech acts can be used to indicate non-physical opposition, as in:

> The forger is going to appeal against such a lengthy sentence
>
> We voted against re-introduction of the death penalty
>
> Jason testified against his brother
>
> We cautioned Sandra against speaking her mind

When someone considers a potentiality and then comes to a negative ('opposing') decision concerning it, this may be expressed with verb *decide* followed by *against* introducing an -ING clause. Thus:

> Mother Ursula decided against letting the children see *Jaws*

Or simply: *We decided against going.* (If positive decisions were made, *on* would replace *against*. That is: *Mother Ursula decided on letting the children see Jaws* and *We decided on going.* This is the 'mental activity' sense of *on*, described in section 9.1c-1.)

Mental attitudes which describe opposition may employ an adjective or a noun plus an *against* phrase. For example:

> Tony is prejudiced/has a prejudice against homosexuals
>
> There is a lot of discrimination here against atheists
>
> Lisa bears a grudge against those people who ruined her
> father's business

9.3a-2 Contrary acts

Against may also be used to indicate contravention of something which is sensible or lawful, as in:

> Donald acted against the best advice
>
> The government has gone against the will of the people
>
> You know that's against the law

Others here are: *against her better judgement, against his parent's wishes, against the grain, against the rules,* and *(a crime) against society.*

This sense extends to *The neophyte cut the wood against the grain* (when the normal—and easier—practice is to cut wood with the grain).

9.3b Contrast

Against may join two entities which are linked in an aesthetic sense; that is, they show a contrast (which is often pleasing). For example:

> The yellow sunflowers go well against the blue sky in Stella's painting
> The red roofs stand out against the grey mist
> The potted plant looks good against the background of the Chinese screen

This sense extends to contrast on a more abstract level, such as: *The dollar fell against a background of fiscal uncertainty.*

At the beginning of this section, *Jim leaned against the wall* was quoted as an example of the 'opposition' sense of the preposition. *Jim stood against the wall* (not in contact with it) is quite different. This must be regarded as an example of the 'contrast' sense, similar to the potted plant standing against the Chinese screen.

9.3c Balance

The sense of *against* dealing with 'contrast' between two entities naturally extends to a comparative assessment of them. This 'balance' meaning is illustrated in:

> In deciding whether to promote Charles we'll have to weigh his skills against his bad temper
> It is necessary to balance expenditure against revenue

Alternatively, *against* may introduce a negative factor, which produces an imbalance:

> The odds against him winning are considerable
> Dick's previous disloyalty counts against him
> He won't get that job, his age is against him
> That profit can be set off against the total debt

9.3d Against *in phrasal verbs*

There appear to be no prepositional verbs involving *against* and just a handful of phrasal verbs. In keeping with its function as a preposition (not as an adverb) *against* is in slot **p** for phrasal verbs of all four types: V-p-NP, V-NP-p-NP, V-a-p-NP, and V-NP-a-p-NP.

SENSE	TYPE	
Opposition	V-a-p-NP	Now you've <u>come up against</u> a serious rival
Involving social acts	V-p-NP	The boy <u>turned against</u> his father
	V-NP-p-NP	The wicked stepmother <u>turned</u> the boy <u>against</u> his father
Contrary acts	V-p-NP	You mustn't <u>go against</u> social conventions
Balance	V-NP-a-p-NP	Max <u>played</u> Fred <u>off against</u> Mary
	V-NP-p-NP	I don't <u>hold</u> his youthful misdemeanours <u>against</u> him

9.3e *Contrasting* against *with other prepositions*

There are a number of contexts where *against* contrasts with some of the prepositions dealt with earlier.

9.3e-1 *With* and *against*

These two prepositions were compared at the very beginning of chapter 1. The following sentence is ambiguous:

> We fought with the lowlanders

This can be either (a) the 'association' sense of *with* (section 6.2b-4), as in *We co-operated with the lowlanders* (against a common enemy); or (b) the 'physical interaction' sense of *with* (section 6.2b-6) as in *Tom grappled with Jim*. The meaning of *with* is clarified by changing the NP in the *with* phrase. If *the enemy* were used instead of the *lowlanders*, then sense (b) would be indicated. If *our allies* were used this strongly suggests sense (a).

We fought against the lowlanders has a similar meaning to the sentence with sense (b) of *with*; this is the 'opposition' sense of *against*. The difference is that sense (b) of *with* merely indicates engagement, whereas *against* implies strongly directed force, most likely fuelled by opprobrium.

9.3e-2 *From* and *against*

These two prepositions may be used in similar circumstances but with different implications:

> We must protect the castle from attack
> We must protect the castle against attack

The first sentence uses the 'prevention' sense of *from* (section 7.4e-1), suggesting that the possibility of an attack should be avoided, perhaps by signing a pact of non-aggression with the enemy. The second sentence has the 'opposition' sense of *against* and may refer to the need to strengthen the defences of the castle to repel any possible attack.

9.3e-3 *On* and *against*

We can compare:

> Jim pushed on the door
> Jim pushed against the door

The second sentence with the 'opposition' sense of *against* implies that the door is stuck and that force is needed to overcome this hindrance to its opening. In contrast, the first sentence, with the 'activated connection' sense of *on* (section 9.1a-2) would be used when there was nothing to prevent the door opening freely.

In similar fashion, *Jim is leaning on the wall* simply indicates contact whereas, as explained above, *Jim is leaning against the wall* implies that the wall provides an opposition to his falling over.

9.4 *Beside(s)*

Beside /bəˈsaid/ and *besides* /bəˈsaidz/ are alternative forms of a preposition which goes back to the Old English combination of preposition *be* 'near, along, alongside, about' (see section 6.1) and *sīdan*, the dative form of noun *sīde* 'side'. (See section 1.10 on the addition of the *-s*.) *Beside(s)* does not enter into any prepositional verbs or phrasal verbs.

The basic meaning is spatial, 'in proximity to'. It is interesting to compare *beside* with *against*:

> Jim stood against the pillar
>
> Jim stood beside the pillar

The location of Jim with respect to the pillar could be the same for the two sentences but the relation between the two entities differs. The first sentence picks out Jim against the background of the pillar (this is the 'contrast' sense of *against*, in section 9.3b), whereas the second sentence just indicates relative position.

9.4a Basic meaning

In its spatial sense, *beside* could often be replaced with *by the side of*. For instance, it could be so replaced in each of the following:

> Jim walked beside the river
>
> > (he walked along the path by the side of the river)
>
> Jim walked beside the doctor
>
> > (he was by the side of the doctor as they walked)
>
> Jim sat beside the invalid's bed
>
> > (he sat by the side of the invalid's bed)

However, *beside* transcends its etymology in that it can be used for a position near to any part of an object, not necessarily its side, as in *John stood beside the back of the car.*

Following a noun or adjective describing a gradable quality, the basic meaning of *beside* is extended to mean 'compared with'. For example:

> Edward is a genius/an idiot beside Harry
>
> Chloe looks tall/tiny beside Rosie

There is a similar sense in: *Ibsen can be placed beside Shakespeare as a top-quality dramatist.*

Another abstract extension is to say that something is *beside the point*, meaning that it is irrelevant to what is being discussed. The idiomatic expression *be beside oneself with* (rage, joy, etc.) is a relic from an earlier sense of the preposition.

9.4b Addition

A somewhat different sense of *besides* could often be replaced by *as well as* or *in addition to*. There are a number of syntactic possibilities here. First, the preposition can mark an NP within an NP. In the following example either *besides* or *in addition to* could be used:

> Several departments [besides/in addition to marketing] have
> expressed their unease with the proposal

A *besides* phrase can be extracted from its syntactic context and moved to the front of the clause:

> [Besides/in addition to marketing] several departments have
> expressed their unease with the proposal

This fronting is motivated by the fact that the 'addition' sense of *besides* carries a contrastive focus. In keeping with this, the head of the NP from which the *besides* phrase was extracted may be questioned, and then *besides* is greatly preferred over *in addition to*:

> [Besides marketing] which departments have expressed their
> unease with the proposal?

We can now examine sentences where the *besides*-type constituent is in object function in the clause (rather than being in subject function, as in the last examples).

> Nick hates custard [as well as prunes]
> [Besides prunes] what does Nick hate?

It would be unacceptable to use *besides* rather than *as well as* in the first sentence, and infelicitous to use *as well as* (or *in addition to*) instead of *besides* in the second. This further illustrated the 'contrastive focus' nuance of the 'addition' sense of *besides*.

A second function of *besides* is to introduce a clause:

> Julie is a fine athlete [as well as/in addition to/besides being a top
> scholar]

Again, if the *besides*-type clause is moved to sentence-initial position (in contrastive focus), preposition *besides* is preferred (rather than *as well as* or *in addition to*):

[Besides being a top scholar], Julie is a fine athlete

The unusual grammatical properties of *besides* extend further. It sometimes seems to function as an adverb (or perhaps as a conjunction). However, these can be accounted for as elliptical versions of the prepositional use. Here are some examples:

He has seven dogs and three cats besides (the seven dogs)

I don't want to go, and besides (not wanting to go) I'm tired

The new house is too big and expensive, and besides (it being too big and expensive) I've grown fond of the old one

By anaphorically omitting the parenthesised portions, we obtain surface structures in which *besides* might give the appearance of being an adverb or a conjunction.

For the spatial sense and its extensions, illustrated in section 9.4a, only the form *beside* is likely to be used (although *besides* is sometimes encountered here). *Besides* is generally preferred for the 'addition' sense, as in the examples presented here, but *beside* is often employed instead (except, perhaps in the quasi-adverbial examples just given).

9.4c Contrasting by with beside

In its basic sense 'near to and not quite reaching' (section 6.1a), *by* can have similar import to *beside* in its basic meaning 'in proximity to'. Consider sentences with a verb of rest describing location with respect to an object:

Jim stood beside the pillar

Jim stood by the pillar

These are equivalent; and so too would be sentences with verb of motion and an NP referring to a long entity:

Jim walked beside the river

Jim walked by the river

However, when the prepositions are followed by an NP referring to a unit entity, with a verb of motion, they convey quite different meanings.

Compare:

> Jim walked beside the doctor
> Jim walked by the doctor

The *beside* sentence states that Jim was by the side of the doctor as they walked along together. In contrast, the *by* sentence indicates that Jim's walking commenced on one side of the doctor, passed the doctor, and progressed to the other side.

* * *

Having in this and previous chapters dealt with the major prepositions *in* and *on* (plus allies relating to enclosure, connection, and adjacency), we next consider *up* and *down*, whose prepositional use is secondary to their main function as adverbs.

10

Superiority

Up, up-to, down

Up and *down* are basically adverbs, with secondary function—just in their spatial and closely related senses—as prepositions.

They have contrasting origins. In Old English there were two adverbs, *ūp, upp* 'upward', indicating motion, and *uppe* 'on high', describing location. These merged into modern adverb *up* /ʌp/ 'to or at a high place'.

English Prepositions: Their Meanings and Uses. R. M. W. Dixon. Oxford University Press (2021). © R. M. W. Dixon.
DOI: 10.1093/oso/9780198868682.003.0010

OE had noun *dūn* 'hill' (this continues as the modern-day noun *down* 'rolling, grassy land', typically used in the plural e.g. *the Hampshire Downs*). The OE adverb *of-done* 'downwards' involved the combination of preposition *of* (which, as mentioned at the beginning of chapter 5, then meant 'away from') with the dative form, *dūne*, of *dūn* 'hill' (literally 'away from hill'). This gave rise to adverb *adown* (which survives today but is rather rare) and thence to modern-day *down* /daun/ 'to or at a low place'.

During late Middle English times, both *up* and *down* extended their scope to also function as prepositions. More recently they came to be used as adjectives (for example: *He was up all night* and *Meet me on the down platform!*), as verbs (*Tom upped his offer for the company* and *Jan downed the beer*), and also as nouns:

> Life is full of ups and downs; you have to enjoy the ups and
> weather the downs

Up and *down* may be paired in idioms. A successful person can be described as *up and coming* and someone who has fallen on hard times as *down and out* (this is the 'lacking' sense of *out*; see section 8.2a).

Up and *down* have a long history as prefixes and this continues to burgeon; they can be added to nouns and verbs, deriving nouns (*up-draught, down-turn,* and *up-rising, down-pour*), verbs (*up-root* and *down-grade*) and adjectives (*up-river, down-hill,* and *up-lifted, down-trodden*). In recent times, there has been a tendency for the adverb *up* following a verb to develop into a suffix—*break-up* and *clean-up* (both the 'completion' sense of *up*), *hold-up* (the 'cessation' sense), and very many more.

Adverbs *upward(s)* /ˈʌpwəd(z)/ and *downward(s)* /ˈdaunwəd(z)/ (see section 7.3) go back to OE times, and can be used in place of *up* and *down* when indicating a direction; for example *She looked up/upwards* and *He looked down/downwards*. They may also function as adjectives—*an upwards/downwards trend in profits*.

Up—as the major member of the pairing *up/down*—is more frequent and has a wider range of meanings than the minor member *down*. It appears that these two forms do not feature in prepositional verbs. They do, however, play a significant role in phrasal verbs. *Up* is found in more than a hundred phrasal verbs (far more than any other preposition or adverb) and *down* in several dozen. In keeping with their main function as adverbs, they occur almost exclusively in slot **a** (not in slot **p**) of phrasal verbs.

The complex preposition *up-to* /ˈʌptə=/ came into being in the late eighteenth century. As explained in section 2.3, this is a clitic, by virtue of its final element *to* /tə=/ (*up*, and also *down*, are never clitics). *Up-to* is followed by an NP for it to cliticise onto and can only function as a preposition. It is found in slot **p** for a number of phrasal verbs. See section 10.2.

In their basic senses, *up* 'to or at a high place' and *down* 'to or at a low place' are antonyms. Their reference may just be spatial. An adverbial example is:

The bird flew up   The rickety tower fell down

And for a prepositional example we can have (here the same verb is employed):

The monkey ran up the tree   The monkey ran down the tree

As is often the case with an inner prepositional phrase the NP component, *the tree*, can be omitted when its reference may be understood, giving just *The monkey ran up/down*.

It is interesting to examine the use of *up* and *down* with the basic stance verbs, *lie*, *sit*, and *stand*, according as they describe movement from one posture to another. *Up* is used for movement to a higher plane and *down* for movement to a lower one:

TO POSTURE → FROM POSTURE ↓	lying	sitting	standing
lying	—	sit up	stand up
sitting	lie down	sit up (straight)	stand up
standing	lie down	sit down	stand up straight

The antonymic contrast is maintained with extensions from the basic senses. For instance, high and low speed, as in:

You'd better speed up, Maurice, or we'll be late for the ceremony!

You'd better slow down, Maurice, this is a school zone!

Interesting examples involve one adverb being substituted for the other so that the meaning of the sentence is radically changed. This involves *up* and *down* being employed in quite different senses. For example:

Jeremy drank the beer up
(it was all gone; the 'completion' sense of *up*)

Jeremy drank the beer down
(it descended from mouth to stomach; the basic spatial sense of *down*)

Interestingly, although one can say *Jeremy ate the apple up* (he consumed all of it) one cannot say **Jeremy ate the apple down*. It is true that after the apple is bitten, chewed, and swallowed, it does descend to the stomach but this is a complex process, whereas there is a perception that the beer just flows down.

Another kind of contrast is shown in:

The meeting broke up in mid-afternoon
(all business had been satisfactorily completed; the 'completion' sense of *up*)

The meeting broke down in mid-afternoon
(the participants could not agree on anything; the detrimental 'finishing' sense of *down*)

There are further examples of contrasts between *up* and *down* in section 10.3e.

We can first survey the range of meanings for *up*, mentioning correspondences with *down* where they occur. Section 10.2 has an account of *up-to*. The final section describes additional senses for *down*. Since there are so many phrasal verbs involving *up* and *down*, these will often be included in the general semantic review, rather than being reserved for a later section. As elsewhere in the book, phrasal verbs are generally underlined.

10.1 *Up*

Five major senses can be recognised for *up*—superior position, maintenance, creation, completion, and cessation.

10.1a Superior position

In its most basic sense, *up* may indicate a greater height, a greater value, or a greater intensity, and *down* the reverse.

10.1a-1 Spatial

Up and *down* may be used productively to introduce prepositional phrases. These can refer to location, as in:

> Sue is up a ladder pruning the apple trees
>
> Harold is down the mine blasting out coal

Or they can refer to movement:

> The steeplejack is climbing up/down (the tower)

The NP may be omitted from such a prepositional phrase—as in the last example—if its reference is clear from the context.

Many spatial uses are purely adverbial, as in:

> The sun comes up in the east and goes down in the west

When the adverb is used after a transitive verb, it may be moved to the left over the preceding object NP (if this is not a pronoun). For instance:

> Jason picked a cup up from the floor and put the cup down on the table
>
> Jason picked up a cup from the floor and put down the cup on the table

Up is used to describe the achievement of a height, as in *build the wall up*, and *pile up*, *heap up*. The directional sense of both adverbs may be used with a verb of attention: *look up* and *look down*.

For the idiomatic combination with *up* shown in *Emily threw up (her dinner)*, meaning that she vomited it up, there is a corresponding expression with *down*—*Emily kept her dinner down*, meaning that she retained it in her stomach rather than vomiting it up.

Up is used in relation to rest and sleep. One *lies down* on a bed and then *gets up* from a bed. In the morning, a person simply *gets up*, or someone else may *get them up*. *Up* is used in a different sense when saying that someone *wakes up*, or that some other person *wakes them up*; here the adverb describes emerging from a state of sleep into one of awareness. Note also:

> Last night I waited up until three o'clock for Belinda to return from the ball

Here *wait up* indicates both the physical state (as in *get up*) 'not in bed', and also the mental one (as in *wake up*) 'not asleep'.

10.1a-2 Value

There is a natural extension from spatial height to social eminence; for example, *Dr Smithers keeps getting promoted up the academic hierarchy.* And also to price and age:

> The price of eggs has gone right up
> Greedy shopkeepers have put the price of eggs up
> → Greedy shopkeepers have put up the price of eggs
> The age for retirement has gone up from 65 to 67

There are *down* equivalents for all of these.

10.1a-3 Intensity

Increase or decrease in speed may be shown by *up* or *down*. *Speed up* and *slow down* were exemplified a few pages back. And someone may be urged to *Hurry up!* (there is no *down* counterpart for this).

The adverbs are also used to describe alteration in noise level:

> Please turn the radio up/down!

Someone who is mumbling may be requested to *Speak up!* (There is no *down* correspondent here; all one could say is: *Speak more quietly!*)

Up can also describe an increase in emotion, as in the phrasal verb:

> The evangelist/politician <u>stirred</u> the crowd <u>up</u> to a fever pitch of hysteria

(In most cases when an adverb follows a non-pronominal NP in object function, it can be moved to the left over it, e.g. <u>*stirred up*</u> the crowd. This will generally not be remarked on below. When the object NP is lengthy, left movement of the adverb may be preferred, and it will be quoted in this way.)

Both adverbs may relate to mental well-being, as when a person is said to have *cheered up*, or be encouraged to *bear up*, in order to get out of *being down in the dumps.*

10.1b Maintenance

Up may be used to describe just continuing something, not necessarily improving it. For example:

> <u>Keep</u> the good work <u>up</u>, Johnny-boy!

My husband always tries to <u>keep up with</u> the Jones, so we've
   had to buy a bigger TV

You need to <u>follow up</u> that good idea

Or *up* can relate to supporting some person or ideal:

Henry always <u>sticks up for</u> his sister whenever she's being criticised

We must all <u>stand up for</u> our basic rights

Whereas *up* is used for offering support, the antonym *down* is appropriate for when support is withheld:

Jim <u>backed</u> John <u>up</u>, by corroborating his alibi

Tom <u>let</u> John <u>down</u>, by refusing to corroborate his alibi

A further sense of *up* describes a redress, restoring equilibrium after there has been a break:

You need to <u>make up for</u> your previous rudeness by being nice
   to Auntie Meg

Kate and Joan used to be friends and then fell out but now
   they've <u>made up</u>

Jasper <u>put up</u> a struggle to retain his job

10.1c Creation

Another sense of *up* relates to when someone makes something happen. The 'something' may be material, as in *John is putting a house up* (this also has a tinge of the spatial sense, since the house is going up). Or the 'something' may be abstract:

James <u>put</u> a solid argument <u>up</u> for why we should not hire Tonkins

Thomas <u>came up with</u> a new idea

Melinda <u>set</u> a meeting <u>up</u> between the warring factions

Andy <u>made</u> a story <u>up</u> about Ian crashing the car

The storyteller <u>conjured up</u> a vision of opulence and sloth

Also: *<u>draw</u> a plan <u>up</u>, <u>scrape</u> the deposit <u>up</u>, <u>put</u> the house <u>up</u> for sale*, and
<u>set</u> Tom <u>up in</u> business.
   Or the 'something' may just happen, as in:

An irritating new problem has just <u>cropped up</u>

The whole family <u>rolled up</u> to see the daughter's stage debut

The computer system <u>is up</u> again

'Something' from the past may be reactivated, as in:

The prosecutors <u>dug up</u> Boris's criminal past

I propose to <u>take</u> Fred <u>up on</u> his promise

Alternatively, it may be human feelings which are activated:

Archibald <u>plucked up</u> courage and asked the duke for his daughter's hand in marriage

The duke's face <u>lit up</u>

You took a long time to <u>make</u> your mind <u>up</u>

A further example is: *The kids are <u>playing up</u> again.*

10.1d Completion

This is a pervasive meaning of *up* (interestingly, there is no corresponding sense of *down*). The adverb *up* may be an optional addition to a sentence, indicating that something has been done fully, or that a purpose has been attained:

Harry filled the tank (up) with water

Join the pieces (up) to complete the puzzle!

I just called John (up) on the outside line

There are many other possibilities, including:

drink the milk (up)   eat your dinner (up)   finish the cake (up)
gather the eggs (up)   tidy the apartment (up)   weigh the advantages (up)
trip Fred (up)   beat the prisoner (up)   the child grew (up)

With the same meaning, *up* is an integral component of a number of phrasal verbs:

Harry <u>topped</u> the tank <u>up</u> (with water)

The exam's tomorrow, I need to <u>swot up</u> on physics

They've <u>called</u> John <u>up</u> into the army

The clown <u>made</u> his face <u>up</u>

The dishonest clerk tried to <u>cover up</u> the discrepancies in the accounts

Others include:

<u>polish</u> my speech <u>up</u>	<u>do</u> the house <u>up</u>	<u>round</u> the cattle <u>up</u>
<u>wrap</u> the meeting <u>up</u>	<u>tie</u> the final details <u>up</u>	<u>write</u> the proposal <u>up</u>
<u>bring</u> the child <u>up</u>	<u>settle up</u>	your time <u>is up</u>
<u>touch</u> the paintwork <u>up</u>	<u>put</u> the visitors <u>up</u>	<u>sum</u> the recommendations <u>up</u>

10.1e Cessation

With an intransitive verb, the inclusion of *up* can indicate that something has terminated:

School <u>has broken up</u> for the holidays

The game's <u>up</u>, Doubtful Donny has told everything

The machine has <u>seized up</u>, something must have jammed inside it

Or, with a transitive verb, an agent may cause something to stop:

The highwaymen <u>held</u> the stagecoach <u>up</u>

Horatio <u>pulled</u> the horse <u>up</u> outside the front gate of the castle

We'd better <u>shut</u> John <u>up</u>, or he may spill the beans

One could also order John to hold his tongue by telling him: *Shut up!*

In a modification of this sense, *up* indicates a gradual diminution. For example: *You'd better <u>ease up</u> or you'll have a breakdown*, and *He's beginning to <u>sober up</u> now*.

The cessation sense of *up* often intensifies some negative happening. It is an adverb in:

The rebels smashed the machine up

And there are many phrasal verbs relating to this meaning; for instance:

The demonstration <u>snarled</u> the traffic <u>up</u>

Also:

blow the building up   mess the arrangements up

throw the job up   pass the opportunity up

Up may be used, in a variant of this sense, to show that some possibility has not been utilised:

Julian passed up a fine opportunity to better himself

10.1f Up in phrasal verbs

As noted before, up does not feature in any prepositional verbs but it occurs in a multitude of phrasal verbs. In keeping with its main function as an adverb, up is found almost exclusively in slot **a**, for phrasal verbs of all four types: V-a, V-NP-a, V-a-p-NP, and V-NP-a-p-NP. A limited selection of phrasal verbs were quoted in previous sections. Illustrations of the types are:

TYPE	SENSE	
V-a	cessation	The game is up
	creation	A problem cropped up
V-NP-a	intensity	He stirred the crowd up
	maintenance	Keep the good work up!
V-a-p-NP	creation	Thomas came up with a good idea
	maintenance	Henry always sticks up for his sister
V-NP-a-p-NP	creation	His father set Tom up in business
	creation	I propose to take Fred up on his promise

There are just a couple of phrasal verbs, of type V-p-NP, with up in slot p:

V-p-NP	maintenance	Jasper put up a struggle to retain his job
	creation	Archibald plucked up courage

10.1g *Contrasting* up *with other prepositions and adverbs*

There are just a couple of interesting contrasts between *up* and items discussed in the previous chapters.

10.1g-1 *In and* up

The following sentences offer different angles on an activity:

> Martha is gathering the eggs in
> (picking them up from the nesting boxes and bringing them into the house)

> Martha is gathering the eggs up
> (making sure that she has them all)

The first sentence uses the basic spatial sense of *in* (section 8.1a); Martha is simply bringing the eggs into the house. In contrast, the second sentence has *up* in its 'completion' sense (section 10.1d).

There is a similar contrast with phrasal verbs <u>lay</u> NP <u>in</u> and <u>lay</u> NP <u>up</u>:

> We need to <u>lay</u> supplies <u>in</u> for the snow-bound months
> (making sure that what we may need is in the house)

> We need to <u>lay</u> supplies <u>up</u> for the snow-bound months
> (checking that every item is there)

A rather different contrast between *in* and *up* is shown with two other phrasal verbs:

> Don't <u>throw</u> that job <u>in</u>!
> (abandoning the effort to do it satisfactorily)

> Don't <u>throw</u> that job <u>up</u>!
> (deciding not to do it anymore)

The first sentence uses an extension from the basic meaning of *in* (section 8.1a; compare with *She threw the certificate in the garbage*), and the second sentence employs the 'cessation' sense of *up* (section 10.1e).

10.1g-2 *By and* up

We can here compare the phrasal verbs in:

Kevin <u>passed</u> several good opportunities <u>by</u>
(he was aware of them but didn't act quickly enough)

Kevin <u>passed</u> several good opportunities <u>up</u>
(he decided not to apply for any of them)

The first sentence employs the 'near to, not quite reaching' sense of *by* (section 6.1a) while the second sentence uses *up* in its 'not utilised' sense (section 10.1e).

10.2 *Up-to*

We can have adverb *up* followed by a peripheral NP introduced by *to*, as in:

Maria is looking up [to her father, who was standing on the top of the hill]

Contrasting with this sequence of *up* and *to*, there is a complex preposition *up-to*. This has limited use as a preposition in spatial and related senses, and appears in slot **p** for phrasal verbs of types V-p-NP and V-NP-p-NP. By virtue of its final element, *up-to* is a clitic which must attach to a following NP (it can thus never function as an adverb).

It is instructive to contrast the sequence of *up* and *to*, in the sentence just quoted, with the complex preposition *up-to* in a phrasal verb of type V-p-NP:

Martin <u>looks up-to</u> his father
(he respects and admires him)

We can now contrast a transitive clause with adverb *up* plus a peripheral clause marked by *to*, with a phrasal verb of type V-NP-p-NP where the **p** is *up-to*:

John took the package up [to Jenny]
John <u>left</u> the decision <u>up-to</u> Jenny

In the first sentence, adverb *up* can be moved to the left over the preceding object NP, giving: *John took up the package to Jenny*. No such movement is possible for the second sentence, since here *up* is an integral part of the complex preposition *up-to*.

The meaning of *up-to* blends several senses of *up* (not 'completion' or 'cessation') with the basic meaning of *to* 'approaching'. These can now be exemplified.

10.2a Superior position, value, or time

Up-to may function as a preposition when it has a straightforward sense referring to a spatial upper limit, as in:

> We stood up-to our knees in muddy water
>
> They immersed the patient up-to his neck in saline solution

An extension from this sense, relating to attitudinal stature, is the phrasal verb *look up-to*, illustrated above.

Preposition *up-to* may indicate a limit of money or of number:

> The entrepreneur said that he would pay up-to $500,000 for the property
>
> You can change your preferences up-to three times

Up-to is also used for a limit of time:

> It will take up-to three years to complete the project
>
> The champion practises up-to six hours a day

10.2b Maintenance

Here *up-to* is used to show that something is approaching a desired state:

> Her performance <u>came up-to</u> expectations
>
> He tries to <u>live up-to</u> the high standards of his ancient family
>
> The brochure has been <u>brought up-to</u> date

The sense of redress is shown in:

> David decided to <u>stand up-to</u> the bully

10.2c Creation

A gradual approach to some creative act can use *up-to*. For example:

He spent a long time <u>working up-to</u> a statement of the actual
proposal

And *up-to* can be employed for transferred creation, as in *John left the
decision up-to Jenny*.

Human feelings often involve 'approaching' in various ways:

He says that he <u>feels up-to</u> the challenge
We'd better <u>face up-to</u> the danger ahead
Lancelot is <u>making up-to</u> the boss's wife
Your brother-in-law is <u>getting up-to</u> his old tricks again

10.3 Down

The range of senses shown by *down* is similar to that for *up*, simply
reversing the meanings. A number of examples were quoted in section 10.1; these can now be augmented. As with *up*, phrasal verbs will be
included in the general discussion.

10.3a Inferior position

Down has limited use as a preposition—an example is *Sheila lives down
the hill*—and more as an adverb:

Shoot the plane down!
Put your ideas down on paper
Hold the dog down!
    (restrain it in a low position so that it does not run away)

There is metaphorical extension of the last sentence to <u>hold</u> the job <u>down</u>
(make sure you don't get fired; literally, don't let the job get away).

Interestingly, *down* functions as an adverb in *fall down* (one could say
just *John fell*, or expand it to *John fell down*) but the complementary
expression, *get up*, is a phrasal verb (one could not say just **John got*).

Down has the meaning 'to a low place' in *She drank the beer down*,
and 'at a low place' in *He kept his dinner down* (didn't throw it up). The

counterpart for *Martin looks up-to his father* (with the complex preposition *up-to*) is:

> Martin's father <u>looks down on</u> him
> (he considers him a lazy layabout)

If a manager *talks down to* a cleaner it means that they regard them as an inferior being and adjust the way they speak accordingly. You can *put a person down* or *do a person down* by criticising them publicly and making them feel discomfited.

Down patterns with *up* in referring to value (*The price has gone down*) and intensity (*Slow the process down!* and *Calm the crowd down!*). It can refer to a lower number, as in *Charles <u>cut down on</u> how many cigarettes he smokes each day.* And there is a temporal sense, with *down* referring to 'a later time' (see section 14.6f), as in:

> That diamond necklace has been handed down from mother to
> daughter for generations

One can build up something material, such as a shed, or something more abstract, as in:

> They carefully built up a five-year plan for expansion

What can be put together (with *up*) may be taken apart (with *down*):

> I want you to break this plan down, and cost every component of it

Section 10.1b illustrated how *up* may have a 'support' sense, and contrasted *back John up* with *let John down*. *Down* is also used for a lack of continuation, as in *Fiona stepped down from the board* and *Jim backed down and withdrew his criticism.*

The reason for some unwelcome happening can be introduced with *down*, this indicating that the critical factor was of inferior quality:

> She <u>put</u> the shortage <u>down</u> to bad planning
> They <u>put</u> the error <u>down</u> to his inexperience

10.3b Personal feelings

An unfortunate happening may reduce someone's morale, this being marked by *down*:

Her mother's illness <u>got</u> Mary <u>down</u>

Indeed, a person can just *be down in the dumps* for any of a variety of reasons.

Someone's physical state will be diminished by illness, leading to the inclusion of *down*:

Jocelyn <u>is down with</u> measles

Alternatively, some unwelcome emotion may be suppressed, this being shown by *down*:

Sidney <u>fought</u> his anger <u>down</u>

Modesty may lead to restraining pride to a low level, shown by *down*:

The champion <u>played</u> his success <u>down</u>

Down may also describe some embarrassment fading over time:

Don't worry, you'll <u>live</u> the scandal <u>down</u>

10.3c Finishing

A further sense of *down* relates to something being brought to an end (generally, with a detrimental overtone):

They've <u>shut</u> the factory <u>down</u>
The sex scandal <u>brought</u> the government <u>down</u>
The army <u>put</u> the peasants' uprising <u>down</u>
When an animal reaches the end of its useful life, it is generally
  <u>put down</u>
We <u>voted</u> the proposal <u>down</u>
Thomas <u>broke</u> the door <u>down</u>

There need be no agent specified, as in:

The computer system <u>is down</u>
The air-conditioner has <u>broken down</u>

Or it may just be an opportunity which is dismissed:

The duchess <u>turned</u> the invitation <u>down</u>

10.3d Down *in phrasal verbs*

Down is like *up* in not being encountered as part of a prepositional verb. In keeping with its main function as an adverb, *up* is found only in slot **a** for phrasal verbs, of all four types: V-a, V-NP-a, V-a-p-NP, and V-NP-a-p-NP. A limited selection of phrasal verbs were quoted in previous sections. Illustrations of the types are:

TYPE	SENSE	
V-a	finishing	The machine <u>broke down</u>
V-NP-a	suppression	Sidney <u>fought</u> his anger <u>down</u>
V-a-p-NP	inferior position	The manager <u>looks down on</u> the cleaners
V-NP-a-p-NP	inferior quality	She <u>put</u> the shortage <u>down to</u> bad planning

Note that we get opposing attitudes expressed through different means. *Martin looks up-to his father* involves complex preposition *up-to*, whereas *The manager <u>looks down on</u> the cleaners* uses phrasal verb *look down on NP*.

10.3e *Contrasting* up *and* down; *plus* off *and* out

The difference between the 'cessation' sense of *up* and the 'finishing' sense of *down* is illustrated by the following pairs of examples:

> The factory is shut up
> (just for the one month's annual holiday; the 'cessation' sense of *up*; section 10.1e)
> The factory has been shut down
> (closed permanently; the detrimental 'finishing' sense of *down*; section 10.3c)

Note the contrasting verb forms here—*is* for a temporary closure and *has been* for one that is final.

> The plane broke up in mid-flight
> (it lost its coherence and split into several parts; the 'cessation' sense of *up*)
> The plane broke down
> (the engine conked out and the plane couldn't fly; the detrimental 'finishing' sense of *down*)

For the following pair *down* has a spatial sense and *up* again denotes 'cessation':

> The rebels blew the building up
>> (it no longer exists; the 'cessation' sense of *up*)
>
> The wind blew the building down
>> (it is now lying on the ground; the 'inferior position' sense of *down*; section 10.3a)

There is a clear contrast between *speeding up* and *slowing down*, where both adverbs directly refer to velocity. But the language also allows for subtleties, as shown by the pair:

> I'm slowing down
>> (diminishing speed; the 'reduced intensity' sense of *down*; section 10.3a)
>
> I'm slowing up
>> (completing the process of slowing down to the allowed speed; the 'completion' sense of *up*)

The 'removal and deprivation' meaning for *off* was described in section 9.2a. It is interesting that in some contexts *off* can have a similar meaning to *up*, while in other contexts it can have a similar meaning to *down*. Thus:

> Egbert finished the cake up
>> ('completion' sense of *up*; section 10.1d)
>
> Egbert finished the cake off
>> ('removal' sense of *off*; section 9.2a)

In the first sentence *up* indicates that the eating of the cake has been completed while in the second sentence *off* states that the cake is no more.

> The weather has cooled down
>> ('low intensity' sense of *down*; section 10.3a)
>
> The weather has cooled off
>> ('removal' sense of *off*; section 9.2a)

Down is used in the first sentence to indicate that the temperature has dropped to a relatively low level. In the second sentence, *off* is used to state that the temperature has moved away from a higher level.

One sense of *out* is 'done fully' (section 8.2c-3) and this can be used in a similar context to the 'completion' sense of *up*:

> The waiters have served the dinner up
>
> The waiters have served the dinner out

In the first sentence *up* is used to state that the serving of the dinner has been completed, and in the second sentence *out* indicates that all the dishes making up the dinner have been placed on the table.

* * *

In the next chapter we turn again to items which are primarily prepositional—*over, under, above, below,* and others of the sizeable set dealing with position.

11

Position

Over, under, above, below, beneath, underneath; behind, ahead(-of), in-front(-of), back, forth, forward(s), backward(s); beyond, near(-to), close-to, far-from; along, alongside, across, through, throughout

English Prepositions: Their Meanings and Uses. R. M. W. Dixon. Oxford University Press (2021). © R. M. W. Dixon.
DOI: 10.1093/oso/9780198868682.003.0011

Prepositions relating to position fall into four sets, each fairly distinct from the others:

- Vertical position: *over, under, above, below, beneath, underneath*; discussed in section 11.1.
- Horizontal position and orientation: *behind, ahead (-of), in-front (-of), back, forth, forward(s), backward(s)*; discussed in section 11.2.
- Distance: *beyond, near(-to), close-to, far-from*; discussed in section 11.3.
- Passage: *along, alongside, across, through, throughout*; discussed in section 11.4.

11.1 Vertical position: *Over, under, above, below, beneath, underneath*

The pairs of prepositions *over/under* and *above/below* can be substituted one for the other in some circumstances. For example:

(1)   Samantha hung the picture over/above the fireplace

(2)   Simon placed the table under/below the window

There is no difference in effect according to whether *over* or *above* is used in sentence (1), and whether *under* or *below* is used in (2). The meanings are—very roughly—equivalent; 'higher than/lower than'. However, these characterisations will soon be refined.

In many contexts of use the meanings can be rather different. For example:

(3)   The giant stood above the bridge

(4)   The giant stood over the bridge

The meaning of (3) is that the giant stood on, say, a platform which was higher than the bridge. (If his feet were touching the bridge then preposition *on* would be appropriate.) Sentence (4) could have this meanings but it could, alternatively, be used to describe the giant standing with one foot on either side of the bridge, his crotch being higher than the centre of the bridge.

Another example is:

(5)   The warrior had a wound below the knee

(6)   The warrior had a wound under the knee

Hearing (5) one would infer that the wound was on the shin, vertically lower than the knee. In contrast, (6) most likely indicates that the wound was on the backside of the knee.

In fact, the pairs *over/under* and *above/below* have rather different etymologies, grammatical possibilities, and meanings.

Over /'ouvə/ comes from preposition *ofer* 'over, above' in Old English, while *under* /'ʌndə/ relates to OE preposition *under* 'under, among'. In the modern language, *over* and *under* function primarily as prepositions. The NP may be omitted—when it could be understood from the context—from an inner prepositional phase with *over* (or, less readily, from one with *under*); for example *Jasper came to the ditch and jumped over (the ditch/it)*. As exemplified in section 2.1c, such a bare preposition may be moved to the left over a non-pronominal object NP; for example, *The cashier passed over the money*. *Over*, at least, has limited function as an adverb; for example, *Fold the blanket over!*, and also as an adjective in copula complement function (*The war is over*). And, as described in section 2.5b, *over* may be omitted when a significant activity is being described; for example, *Stella jumped (over) the perimeter fence*.

Both *over* and *under* have considerable metaphorical extensions from their basic spatial senses. *Over* features in some prepositional verbs and also in a couple of score phrasal verbs (in both **p** and **a** slots), while *under* is in a handful of phrasal verbs (again in both slots). From OE times, both *under-* and *over-* have also functioned as prefixes and remain productive with every kind of word; for example, nouns *under-world* and *over-coat*, verbs *under-pay* and *over-use*, adjectives *under-privileged* and *over-sensitive*.

Above /ə'bʌv/ and *below* /bi'lou/ were later additions to the language. Both entered first as adverbs: *above* from prefix *a-* plus adverb *bufan* 'above' in early Middle English, and *below* from *be* (see section 6.1) plus *loghe* 'low' a couple of centuries later. They soon developed prepositional functions, and *above* also functions as an adjective (for example *The above instructions*).

Above and *below* are much less frequent than *over* and *under*. They have rather few metaphorical extensions from the basic senses, and they do not enter into prepositional verbs or phrasal verbs. Nor do they have much function as prefixes (*above-board* and *below-stairs* are possible exceptions). Also, their meanings are quite different from those of *over* and *under*.

Above and *below* have, essentially, a unilinear reference, relating to something which is (either physically or metaphorically) vertical. For example:

> Please fix the horseshoe above the doorway
>> (it should be higher than the middle of the doorway, in a straight line with it)

If the average mark for an assignment is fifty, then one might hear:

> Samantha scored sixty, ten above the average, and Simon scored thirty, twenty below it

In contrast, *over* and *under* relate to a two- or three-dimensional space and typically refer to extension or motion from one side of it to the other side. We can compare:

> The plane flew over the mountain
> The plane flew above the mountain

The first sentence could describe the plane taking off from an airfield on one side of the mountain, rising higher than the peak of the mountain and then landing on the far side. In contrast, the second sentence simply states that the plane's height was greater than the top of the mountain. Another instructive pair is:

> Jack jumped above the cliff edge
> Jack jumped over the cliff edge

On hearing the sentence with *above*, one might have an image of Jack jumping up and down on a platform erected over the cliff edge. The second sentence indicates that he jumped from the cliff, across the edge, and onto the ground below.

We can compare the use of the two prepositions with the verb *look*:

> Sally looked above the fence
>> (to see what there was which was vertically higher than it; perhaps a bird in a tree)

> Sally looked over the fence
>   (to see what was on the other side of it)

And also sitting with respect to a fire:

> Mabel is sitting over the fire
> Mabel is sitting above the fire

The first sentence describes Mabel crouching down to warm herself, a leg and an arm on either side of the blaze. The second sentence might describe Mabel sitting on a hillside higher than the place where the fire was burning, and unaffected by it.

Suppose that in some organisation there is a hierarchy of levels of responsibility. If Alice is level 2 and Xavier level 6, then we would say that, in rank, *Alice is above Xavier*. They may work in different divisions of the company and never have any contact; this is immaterial. The preposition *above* merely indicates their relative positions on the linear hierarchy.

However, the statement *Greta is over Nigel* implies that Greta has a higher rank than Nigel (probably that immediately above his) but also that they work in the same part of the company and that Greta is Nigel's immediate boss, telling him what to do and checking up on his work. Preposition *over* indicates an envelopment of authority between the higher and lower entities.

Below functions like *above*, and *under* like *over*. One would say that, in rank, *Xavier is below Alice*. And also that *Nigel is under Greta*, having to do as she directs.

Over and *above* do have overlapping meanings and the two prepositions are sometimes coordinated to indicate an extreme state. For instance, *Over and above all else, I value my marriage to Ermintrude*, and *Over and above an inflated salary, Frank receives a generous annual bonus*.

The next section explores the meanings and uses of *over* and *under*. *Above* and *below* are dealt with in section 11.1b. The long-established prepositions *beneath* and *underneath* are the topic of section 11.1c.

11.1a *Over and* under

The major member of the pairing, *over*, is more frequent than the minor member, *under*. And *over* has a wider range of extensions from the basic spatial sense. We can discuss the range of meanings for *over*, mentioning corresponding senses of *under*. Additional meanings for *under* are in section 11.1a-4.

'X is over Y' can describe X being at a higher level than Y, extending from one side of it to the other, or moving from one side to the other, or just being on the far side. 'Y is under X' is similar, but at a lower level.

11.1a-1 X extends from one side to the other of Y

There may be contact between X and Y or there might be a distance between them. Thus, *The giant stood over the bridge* and:

> Mist lay over the valley
>
> The race started under a leaden sky

Often, 'X is over Y' will imply 'Y is under X' as in:

The blanket is over the child	The child is under the blanket
There is a covering of snow over the valley	The valley is under a covering of snow

Over may be modified with *all* to indicate 'in every part of'. For example: *We searched all over the garden for the missing key* and *She has travelled all over the world*. It is also much used in non-spatial expressions such as *He was all over her with protestations of love*.

As described in section 2.7, *over* is one of only three prepositions which may—in limited circumstances—follow rather than precede their NP (the others are *through* and *(a)round*). For example, *He searched the garden over*. Postposing *over* indicates that the activity covers the whole of the area specified. Note that when *all* is included it stays put and does not move with *over*; thus: He *searched all the garden over*.

Relative height is contrasted in: *Kim carried the sack over her shoulder* and *Tom carried the sack under his arm*. There is an extension of the meaning of *under* to agriculture: for example, *These five acres are under cultivation/are under rice*.

A range of extensions reach out from this basic spatial sense. Y can refer to an extent of time rather than of space (see section 14.6f):

> The castle has been gradually decaying over the years
>
> Sue always works over the weekend
>
> Max lingered over the dessert

In metaphorical extension, space or time is replaced by thought, or by mental attitude, or by vision, as in:

> Janet pondered over what to do next
>
> They are raving over the agility of the new goalkeeper
>
> The builder looked over the architect's drawings
>
> The quality of the air-bags is under investigation

There is an *over/under* pair involving the same noun, *watch*:

Barnabas has watch over the factory   The factory is under the watch of Barnabas

Another extension of meaning for *over* relates to preference, as in *I would always choose apples over pears*. It is used in a description of happiness concerning some glad event:

> The team triumphed over their old rivals, and they then exulted over the victory

Also *have a win over, achieve victory over, rejoice over, gloat over*, and *crow over*. Or a description of dismay concerning a sad event, with *grieve over, cry over, mourn over, lament over*, and *feel sad over*.

Over may introduce the reason for an activity, typically a dispute involving several people; for example:

> They are haggling over the price

Also *fight over, struggle over, argue over, quarrel over, differ over*, and *disagree over*. There are fewer verbs indicating coincidence of opinion which take *over*; they include *agree over* and *concur over*.

There is an *over/under* pair in similar vein:

They debated over the best policy   The best policy was under debate

There is a fairly productive derivation:

> L verb M → M is under nominalisation-of-verb (by L)

For instance:

> The committee is considering the new proposal
>
> The new proposal is under consideration (by the committee)

This also applies for *discuss, cultivate, treat, suspect, review*, and *guard*.

There may be an aura of authority or power or importance which X extends over Y. For example:

> The minister presided over the meeting
>
> The king rules over a wide empire
>
> Seniors take precedence over juniors in seat assignment

Here again we find *over/under* pairs:

> General Joos has command over the army
>
> The army is under the command of General Joos

> Professor Smith has influence over Jimmy
>
> Jimmy is under the influence of Professor Smith

Control or *authority* could be substituted for *influence* here.

In the examples just given, with *over*, X has had human reference. When X is non-human, an *under* construction is appropriate:

> Simon crashed the car when under the influence of alcohol
>
> He only signed the confession under duress

The *under* construction may be used when focus is on Y. For instance:

> Mary Haas studied under Edward Sapir

Also: *be under the doctor, be under an obligation, be under orders, be under arms*, and *do it under protest*. *Under* may, in addition, indicate a state in which a person finds themselves: *under attack, under arrest, under suspicion, under a handicap*, and *under threat (from)*. And it may specify a situation; for example, *under the circumstances, under certain conditions*, and *under one's own volition*.

11.1a-2 X moves from one side to the other of Y

Again, there may be contact between X and Y or there might be a distance between them. Thus *The plane flew over the mountain*, and:

> Kim walked over the bridge
>
> Larry swam under the bridge
>
> The duke ran over the drunken beggar
>
> The Dutchman painted over the picture
>
> A happy feeling <u>stole over</u> Mary

There may be at transitive verb 'make X move from one side to the other of Y':

> Captain Johns flew the plane over the mountain
> Please spread the cloth over the table!

A number of phrasal verbs of type V-NP-a belong here. For example *hand* the money <u>over</u>, *get* the ordeal <u>over</u>, and:

> The big multi-nationals are <u>taking over</u> many small family businesses

The Y element may have abstract reference:

> It's not easy to <u>get</u> a complex idea <u>over</u> to a bunch of dull students

Or Y may refer a person who could be enticed to switch allegiance:

> We'll have to <u>get</u> Mary <u>over</u> to our side

As an adverb, *over* is used to indicate repetition:

> You haven't cleaned the kitchen very well, better do it over!

One often hears: *They did it over and over again.*

11.1a-3 X is on the far side of Y

For example:

> My parents live over the mountain (that is, on the other side of the mountain from here)

In this sense, *over* can extend its prepositional role to function as an adverb:

> Sam works over in America (that is, on the other side of the ocean)
> I'll go over tonight and see what is happening on the other side of the tracks

Indeed, the adverb *over* may relate to either going or coming:

> Why don't you <u>come over</u> for dinner tonight?
> Let's <u>invite</u> the neighbours <u>over</u>

A variant of this sense involves change of orientation:

> We turned the mattress over
>
> Susan folded the blanket over
>
> Pamela fell over

Also *roll over* and *bend over*.

Y may be a number, or a sum of money, which X extends to the far side of:

> His weight is just over the limit allowed
>
> I wouldn't bid over one million for a rundown place like that
>
> How much is left over after you've taken what you need

Under shows a complementary meaning:

> She got it for under two thousand
>
> He solved the problem in under twenty minutes

Also *under age*.

Over can indicate that some activity is finished; that is, we are 'on the far side of it'. In this sense, *over* may function as an adjective:

> The strike/war/recession/meeting/storm <u>is over</u>

This can be used for the ending of something unwelcome, or else of something which was pleasant, as in: *The good times <u>are over</u>*. To emphasise the finality of something being finished, *over* may be modified with *all*; for example, *It's all <u>over</u> now, you can come out of hiding.*

Interestingly, there is an expression with *under* which has similar import, but through a different semantic path. *Under* is in its spatial sense when describing a vessel which has sunk: *The boat has gone under (the water)*. This has metaphorical extension when the subject is an enterprise, indicating that it has failed, akin to the 'finished' sense of *over*. Thus:

> It's all <u>over</u> with the Cumfy Shoe Company, I'm afraid that firm
>   has <u>gone under</u>

11.1a-4 *Under* in hiding

The spatial sense of *under* may describe something which is not visible by virtue of being under something else. For example, *The robbers hid the loot under a rock*. This can be extended to several techniques for obscuring the identity of a person or the nature of some enterprise:

> Professor Stewart publishes novels under a pseudonym
>
> The robber gained entry to the house under disguise as a repairman
>
> Sandra went to the ball under the guise of a white rabbit
>
> They lured John away under the pretence that there was a phone call for him
>
> In thinking that he might get the prize, Bill was labouring under a delusion/misapprehension

Or natural resource may be utilised in order for something to be done clandestinely:

> They painted the graffiti under cover of darkness
>
> I told Brenda the password under my breath so that no one else should hear it

There are related idiomatic expressions: *under a cloud* (in disgrace), and *under the weather* (ill). With *over* we get: *She is over the moon* (that is, extremely happy).

11.1a-5 *Over* and *under* in prepositional verbs and phrasal verbs

There are just a few prepositional verbs which include *over* (none, it appears, with *under*); they include *gloss over* (a little like *paint over*) and *puzzle over* (akin to *ponder over*). *Over* occurs in a fair number of phrasal verbs and *under* in just a few. The interesting point is that they are found in both slot **a** and slot **p** of a phrasal verb. This is in contrast to the items surveyed in previous chapters which may feature in slot **a** or in slot **p** but—save for a few rare exceptions—not in both.

Most instances are in slot **a**. *Over* is attested in phrasal verbs of all four types: V-a, V-NP-a, V-a-p-NP, and V-NP-a-p-NP, and *under* in all except V-a-p-NP. Some examples were given above (phrasal verbs are always underlined) and in section 3.7, row G. Others include:

TYPE	SENSE	
V-a	**extending**	Monica was <u>bubbling over</u> (with enthusiasm)
	far side	If one company <u>goes under</u>, others tend to follow

V-NP-a	**extending**	The Tsars <u>held</u> the serfs <u>under</u> (for thousands of years)
	moving	Let's <u>hold</u> the final item on the agenda <u>over</u> (until the next meeting)
	moving	They <u>carried</u> the surplus <u>over</u> (into the next financial year)
V-a-p-NP	**moving**	America has not yet <u>gone over to</u> metric
V-NP-a-p-NP	**moving**	The wicked stepfather <u>put</u> a deception <u>over on</u> Paula
	moving	Politicians <u>snow</u> the people <u>under with</u> lies

And the prepositions appear in slot **p** for phrasal verbs of types V-p-NP and V-NP-p-NP. For example:

TYPE	SENSE	
V-p-NP	**extending**	The boss's whiskey <u>falls under</u> the heading of 'incidentals'
	extending	The need to write that report is <u>hanging over</u> me
	moving	That criticism seems to have <u>washed over</u> Andrew
	moving	A feeling of utter despair <u>stole over</u> Donald
V-NP-p-NP	**extending**	They <u>held</u> the threat of dismissal <u>over</u> Boris
	extending	Your authority is needed to <u>bring</u> the youths <u>under</u> control

There are many homonymic sets of phrasal verbs. *Get-NP-over* and *get-over-NP* were mentioned in section 3.5. These can now be revisited, with a 'minimal pair':

| V-NP-a | **moving** | Jennifer <u>got</u> the ordeal <u>over</u> (made sure that it happened without delay) |
| V-p-NP | **far side** | Jennifer <u>got over</u> the ordeal (recovered from the horror of it) |

11.1a-6 Contesting *over* with other prepositions

We can now examine contexts in which *over* may contrast with prepositions discussed in the previous chapters.

11.1a-6a *Of* and *over*

One could say either *Pete has surveillance of the factory* or *Pete has surveillance over the factory*. However, these two sentences have different grammatical structure and thus meanings:

> Pete$_{\text{NP:A}}$ has [surveillance of the factory]$_{\text{NP:O}}$
>
> Pete$_{\text{NP:A}}$ has [surveillance]$_{\text{NP:O}}$ [over the factory]$_{\text{PERIPHERAL PHRASE}}$

In the first sentence, *surveillance of the factory* is the object NP of verb *have*; this describes Pete's job. In contrast, the second sentence states that Pete's job is surveillance, and the peripheral NP *over the factory* indicates the extent of the surveillance.

11.1a-6b *For* and *over*

A verb describing a mental attitude may be followed by either *for* or *over*:

> They mourned over Jill's untimely death
>
> They mourned for Jill's unfulfilled potential

The second sentence uses the 'reason for mental attitude' sense of *for* (section 5.3b-1), lamenting about all the things which Jill might have achieved. The sentence with *over* simply states how their sorrow extended over Jill's death (section 11.1a-1).

11.1a-6c *On* and *over*

Noun *influence* has a range of meanings. We can compare:

> This medication has an influence on cholesterol levels (it raises them)
>
> I had no influence over the way it was done (my influence didn't extend this far)

In the first sentence, *on* shows its 'general dependency' sense (section 9.1e-1) and in the second *over* relates to how far the influence extends (section 11.1a-1).

On and *over* also alternate in a quite different way. The following are equivalent ways of saying how you got to know something:

I heard that piece of news on the radio

I heard that piece of news over the radio

Moving pictures were introduced around 1900 and people would naturally say *I saw that on the screen*, using the 'physical connection' sense of *on* (section 9.1a-1). When broadcasting followed, there was an analogic extension to *I heard that on the radio*. The second sentence uses *over* in its 'moving from one side to the other' sense (section 11.1a-2); the news item travels from the announcer in the studio via radio waves to the listener's receiver.

11.1a-6d *Against* and *over*

These two prepositions can have similar effect but with different implications. Consider:

Righteousness will always triumph against evil

Righteousness will always triumph over evil

The first sentence employs the 'opposition' sense of *against* (section 9.3a); this implies that there is often a struggle between the contrary forces but that righteousness eventually prevails. The second sentence, with *over*, simply declares that righteousness will extend across evil, smothering it (section 11.1a-1).

   A quite different matter is that *over* and *against* may co-occur as in *Jane stood over against the tower*. This is not a complex preposition, but rather a sequence of adverb *over*, in its 'on the far side' sense (section 11.1a-3), and a prepositional phrase introduced by *against* in its basic sense (section 9.3).

11.1b Above *and* below

As explained above, prepositions *above* 'higher than' and *below* 'lower than' have linear reference whereas *over* and *under* relate at a spatial entity. This is bought out in:

There was a wisp of smoke above the fire
   (vertically higher than the fire)

There was a cloud of smoke over the fire
   (a mass of smoke, extending from one side of the fire to the other, and perhaps beyond)

Above and *below* also refer to north/south orientation, or upriver/down-river:

> Along the east cost, New York is below Boston and above Atlantic City
>
> On the Thames, Teddington is above Gravesend and below Oxford

They can relate to numbers, or to ranks on a hierarchy:

> Seniors' discount is available for those aged sixty and above
>
> Major is above Captain and below Colonel

Over and *under* would not be felicitous in any of the four sentences just given. But, as exemplified at the beginning of this chapter, there are contexts in which either *over/under* or *above/below* may be used. For example:

(1a)   Samantha hung the picture above the fireplace

(1b)   Samantha hung the picture over the fireplace

As explained earlier, *above* and *below* have one-dimensional reference, whereas *over* and *under* provide a multi-dimensional description. Sentence (1a) effectively draws a vertical line from the picture to the fireplace, with the picture being higher on it. Sentence (1b) treats the picture as a rectangle with its whole extent, from one side to the other, being higher than the fireplace. In this instance, (1a) and (1b) have equivalent effect. (Similarly for *Simon placed the table under/below the window.*)

However, this is not always the case. The contrast between the linear reference of *above* and the areal reference of *over* is brought out in:

> Jim hung his jacket above the back of the chair
>   (the bottom, of the jacket was higher than the top of the chair)

> Jim hung his jacket over the back of the chair
>   (the jacket enveloped the back of the chair)

There is one situation where *above* and *under* pattern together:

> Father O'Leary is above suspicion
>
> Bazza Tompkins is under suspicion

For the first sentence it is as if there is a straight line leading up to Father O'Leary. In contrast, the second sentence suggests that there is a tangle of clues linking Bazza Tompkins to the crime; preposition *under* spans this spatial conglomeration. (Similar uses of *above* are in *above reproach* and *above criticism*.)

An NP following *above* or *below* may undergo anaphoric omission, as in:

> They inspected the garage, the bedroom (which is) above (the garage) and the basement (which is) below (the garage)

The portions in parentheses may be omitted. *Above* and *below* are not then adverbs, or post-head adjectives; they are simply prepositions with the NP they mark being anaphorically understood.

There is another use of *above* and *below* which is confined to the written mode. Suppose that there is a picture in the middle of a page. The text at the top of the page may refer to *the picture below* and the text at the bottom of the page may refer to *the picture above*. It would be misleading to suggest that *below* and *above* are here functioning as adverbs, or as post-noun adjectives. Rather, they should be analysed in the same way as in the sentence quoted above about the garage—as prepositions; in this instance the understood following NP is, in effect, *here*.

(Instead of *the picture above*, one could say *the above picture*; *above* is then functioning as an adjective. Interestingly, this function is only occasionally employed for *below*; many speakers would consider it scarcely felicitous to say **the below picture*.)

As a relic of the time when a manuscript might consist of one long sheet (which would be rolled up, rather than folded over) *above* may refer to something quite a bit earlier in the document. For example, the first sentence of this section began: *As explained above....* We also find *As mentioned above...*, *As described above...*, *As referred to above...*, and so on. Or there may be listed a set of rules with an injunction below (the list): *The rules above must be strictly adhered to.* In each of these instances, the NP understood to be marked by *above* would be *here*.

There are instances where *above* makes up, with article *the*, a full NP. Someone might discuss courses taught elsewhere and conclude with:

> I recommend that we should consider introducing here courses similar to the above

Is *above* functioning here as a noun, in *the above*? Superficially, perhaps, but not if afforded a perceptive grammatical analysis. *The above* is elliptical from *the (courses listed) above (here)*.

Returning now to discussion of spoken (as well as written) language, omission of an NP following *above* or *below* may depend on the context of speaking. For instance, in a cold climate someone might declare:

> It's been ten degrees below today but the forecast is for two above tomorrow

Listeners will understand that the reference is to above or below zero degrees (freezing point).

Above is the major member of the pairing *above/below*. It is more frequent than the minor member, *below*, and has a wider range of disparate senses. If someone considers themself to be *above the law* this means that they disregard legal requirements (and hope not to get caught). A quite different meaning is associated with *Sir Jasper is above politics*; this implies that he is only involved with matters deemed less mundane than politics. When someone remarks that a certain person is *getting above himself/herself* this implies that they are behaving in a way appropriate to a higher station of life than that which they hold.

A frequent use of *above* is in the adverbial phase *above all* or *above all things*, meaning 'more than anything else'. For example:

> Above all, we need more efficiency and economy in our effort
>
> I wish above all things to secure the hand of Sofia in marriage

11.1c Beneath *and* underneath

Old English had preposition *neoþan* 'below' and also two complex prepositions made up of *under-* plus *neoþan* and *be-* (the ancestor of modern *by*, see section 6.1) plus *neoþan*. Only the latter have come down to us, as *underneath* /ˌʌndəˈniːθ/ and *beneath* /biˈniːθ/.

These prepositions are not common, and may be encountered more often in literary than in colloquial style. They do not occur in prepositional or in phrasal verbs, and only *beneath* has metaphorical extensions. Nevertheless, their spatial senses are noteworthy.

In sentences where either *under* or *below* may be used, *beneath* and *underneath* are also acceptable:

> Simon placed the table under/beneath/underneath/below the window

Beneath and *underneath* are more similar in meaning to *under* than to *below*, referring to 'lower than' spatially rather than just linearly. They can be used in place of *under* in:

The race started under/beneath/underneath a leaden sky

Below would be less felicitous here; and it would be unacceptable in:

I fell with my foot beneath/underneath/under me

I fell with my foot below me would somehow imply that the foot had become detached.

The following sentences contrast in meaning:

The nuns sat underneath the trees

The nuns sat beneath the trees

The first sentence implies that the nuns were fully covered by the trees, so that anyone flying above in a plane would not be able to see that they were there. The second sentence indicates that they sat around, in the shade of the trees but not out of view to anyone above.

A similar meaning is found in:

Beneath the castle is a fir tree
(that is, the tree is beside the castle, at a lower level than it)

If *underneath* were used here it would imply that the fir tree was fully covered by the castle, perhaps growing in a basement.

Unlike *beneath*, *underneath* may be used as an adjective, as in:

The underneath (part) of the boat needs to be painted

The noun following *underneath* may be omitted making *underneath* appear—on the surface—to be functioning as a noun.

We see that *underneath* means 'fully covered by' or 'over the whole bottom surface of'. In contrast, 'X is beneath Y' indicates that X occupies a region that is at a lower level than Y and adjacent to it. Suppose that a victorious general returns home and rides past a major landmark:

He was greeted by cheers from beneath the triumphal arches

This doesn't mean that the people cheering were precisely below the arches (that would be *underneath*), simply that they were grouped around there.

This expansive meaning of *beneath* naturally leads to metaphoric uses. It may be employed to draw attention to some underlying trouble which is in contrast to a superficially tranquil exterior. For example:

> The psychologist perceived undercurrents of opposition beneath the apparent calm
>
> Beneath her straight-faced facade, she was seething with anger
>
> Beneath his cloak of cooperation, General Joos was planning a coup

There are also idiomatic uses such as *It was beneath his dignity to polish his own shoes*, and *Their drunken invective was beneath contempt*.

11.2 Horizontal position and orientation: *Behind, ahead(-of), in-front(-of), back, forth, forward(s), backward(s)*

Horizontal position and orientation are marked by a conglomeration of forms: preposition *behind*, phrasal prepositions *ahead-of* and *in-front-of*, their associated adverbs *behind*, *ahead*, and *in-front*, plus adverbs *back*, *forth*, *forward(s)*, and *backward(s)*. Note that the phrasal prepositions end in *of*, which is a clitic to a following NP; the *of* is thus dropped when no NP follows.

The meanings and their markings can be summarised in a table, with corresponding columns for (a) ahead/in-front/forward, and (b) behind/back/backward:

		a		b	
		PREPOSITION	ADVERB	PREPOSITION	ADVERB
1	SPATIAL MOTION	ahead-of	ahead	behind	behind
2	TEMPORAL MOTION	ahead-of	ahead	behind	behind
3	SPATIAL LOCATION	in-front-of	in-front	behind	behind
4	FLOWING		forth		back
5	SPATIAL DIRECTION		forward(s)		back

6 TEMPORAL DIRECTION	forward(s)	back
7 ORIENTATION	forward(s)	backward(s)

Each row can be briefly illustrated, before we embark on discussion of the individual prepositions and adverbs. For rows 1–3, prepositional examples are given first, then adverbial ones.

1a/b   Danny's horse is two lengths ahead-of/behind the favourite
        Look ahead/behind!

2a/b   The building work is ahead-of/behind schedule
        Roger is ahead/behind with his repayments

3a/b   Mollie is standing in-front-of/behind the statue
        Jill went in-front/stayed behind

4a/b   The tourists streamed forth from the cruise ship/went back to the cruise ship

5a/b   The army moved forward/back

6a/b   Ken looked forward to a lazy retirement/back on an unhappy childhood

7a/b   Jane could recite the alphabet forwards/backwards

11.2a Behind

This is a continuation of the Old English preposition/adverb *behindan*, which had the same meaning; it was a combination of *be-* (see section 6.1) and adverb *hindan* 'from behind'.

Behind /bɪˈhaɪnd/ is today primarily a preposition. It refers to someone or something either located or moving 'at the rear of' something else. For example:

Nurse Angela put a pillow behind the patient's head
The newly-weds are pulling a trailer behind their car

When *behind* does not have an NP following this may still be understood, as in:

Winston caught up with the procession and followed behind

This is plainly a shortening of *Winston caught up with the procession and followed behind the procession*, with the second occurrence of *the procession* being anaphorically omitted. That is, *behind* still has its prepositional function here.

However, in a few instances, *behind* plainly is an adverb. Consider (*ahead* is also an adverb here):

You walk ahead and I'll come behind!

It would be tortuous to try to relate this to an underlying *You walk ahead-of me and I'll come behind you!* Another adverbial use is: *I left it behind*.

The preposition *behind* is also used of temporal movement (see section 14.6b):

Those hard years in prison are behind you now

I regret to say that your ideas on design are quite behind the times

Behind has various metaphorical extensions. First, for being 'in the rear' in terms of achievement:

Ben is behind the rest of the class in algebra

America is lagging behind Russia in missile power

Or to describe something 'at the rear of' a misleading exterior:

Behind Lord Jones' gruff behaviour lies a heart of gold

What is the reality behind her facade of easy-going optimism?

There must be some hidden purpose behind his
    uncharacteristic generosity

A further sense of *behind* is almost the reverse of the last, the preposition marking what the referent of the subject was 'at the rear of' in the sense of being responsible for.

General Joos was the man behind the coup

Or *behind* can indicate support:

The whole province is behind the Motion for Independence

We must really get behind the President in his hour of need

There are just a few phrasal verbs which include *behind*. It is in slot **p** for *You must <u>put</u> that disappointment <u>behind</u> you (and get on with the rest of your life)*, a phrasal verb of type V-NP-p-NP, and for *The building work is <u>running behind</u> schedule*, of type V-p-NP. And it is in slot **a** for *He <u>fell/got behind with</u> the repayments*, which is of type V-a-p-NP.

316

11.2a-1 *Beneath* and *behind* converging

Although emanating from different basic meanings, *beneath* and *behind* converge on a similar sense, relating some underlying negative state or activity to a superficially calm exterior. Three examples with *beneath* were given at the very end of section 11.1c and three with *behind* were quoted just above. Both are typically found with *facade*:

> He harbours deep ambitions beneath/behind a facade of
>   unflappability
> The business was a hidden mess behind/beneath the facade of
>   normalcy

Behind in this sense is about ten times more common than *beneath*. Each preposition is generally substitutable for the other. Nevertheless, there does appear to be a tendency to prefer *beneath* when the underlying item refers to a nefarious activity, as in:

> His violence was concealed beneath a facade of unthreatening
>   ordinariness
> A trauma which threatens to destroy our lives simmers beneath
>   the facade of propriety

For special effect, the two prepositions may be combined, as in an account of Germany in the 1930s:

> The party purge was conducted beneath and behind the facade of
>   martial parades and election campaigns

11.2b Ahead(-of)

It was not until about 1600 that the adverb *ahead* /əˈhed/ and phrasal preposition *ahead-of* /əˈhedəv=/ entered the language; they were, literally 'on head'.

We have seen how *ahead-of* is used to mark spatial or temporal motion (the converse of *behind*) with the meaning 'in advance of'. Further examples are:

> The drum-major always marches ahead-of the band
> That form has to be submitted at least six weeks ahead-of the
>   day of departure
> Stella has a bright future ahead-of her

There are rather more examples of adverb *ahead* than there are of the adverb function of *behind*. These include:

> There's danger ahead
>
> The Liberals are ahead in the voting
>
> In the years ahead you will come to appreciate all that your
> father has done for you
>
> He's ahead-of his time, putting forward ideas for which the
> world is not yet ready

A few metaphoric extensions of *ahead(-of)* mirror those for *behind*. Thus: *Ben is ahead-of the rest of the class in algebra*, and *America is ahead-of Russia in missile power*.

Ahead features in slot **a** for a few phrasal verbs of type V-a. For example: *She forged ahead in her profession* and *We're pushing ahead with the project*.

11.2c In-front(-of) *and* back

When used as nouns or adjectives, *front* and *back* form a cosy pair of opposites:

> Hazel sat in the front (part) of the bus and Henry sat in the back
> (part) (of the bus)

However, when employed in other functions they are entirely different.

Noun (and adjective) *front* was a loan from Old French into Middle English in the thirteenth century. It originally meant 'forehead' but the more general meaning 'advance part of' soon developed. The phrasal preposition *in-front-of* /ɪnˈfrʌntəv=/ followed a few centuries later.

In-front-of is most used to describe spatial location, as in row 3 of the table at the beginning of section 11.2 where it patterns with preposition *behind*. An NP marked with *in-front-of* may modify a verb or the head of an NP, as in:

> The house in-front-of the church is for sale
>   and the cottage behind the church is being demolished

In-front-of is a—less preferred but perfectly acceptable—alternative to *ahead-of* for describing spatial motion (row 1 of the table); that is, one might hear *Danny's horse is two lengths in-front-of the favourite*. However *in-front-of* does not have a temporal sense; it would not be felicitous to replace *ahead-of* by *in-front-of* in *The building work is ahead-of schedule* from row 2. (And note that *ahead-of* could not replace *in-front-of* for the spatial location sense in row 3, *Mollie is standing in front of the statue*.)

Like *ahead-of*, *in-front-of* may occur without a following NP and then necessarily drops the *of*. Indeed, it then has the character of an adverb, as in:

> Don't drive too close-to the car in-front
>
> General Joos drove to church with a guard of mounted police
> in-front and behind

In-front(-of) has an entirely spatial meaning, with no metaphorical extensions.

Bæc was a noun in Old English with the same meaning as its modern descendent *back*. In OE it combined with *on* (see the beginning of chapter 9) to create adverb *onbæc* 'back, backwards', which reduced to *aback* and then modern adverb *back* /bak/ (having the same form as the noun/adjective/verb).

Basically, adverb *back* means 'in a rearwards direction', and it sometimes partners with *forward* in both spatial and temporal direction senses; for example:

> Janice leaned back/forward in the chair
>
> We need to put the clock back/forward one hour

However, *back* often carries the additional meaning of 'return towards a point of origin', again in either a spatial or a temporal:direction sense:

> Jimmy ran back (towards where he had come from)
>
> Jane looked back (towards the home she would never see again)
>
> Frank went back to bed
>
> Please think back to the day of the accident and tell me exactly
> what happened

With a transitive verb, it is the referent of the O argument which is returned:

> Kate took six books back to the library
>
> Give me my money back!
>
> Tom put the vase back on the mantelpiece

There is a natural extension of *back* to more abstract meanings, referring to breathing, or speaking, or many kinds of activities or happenings:

> That man who you left for dead has come back to life
>
> The Professor kept referring back to Neil's sparsity of publications
>
> Meg grew disgusted with the computer's malfunction and reverted back to her old method of bookkeeping
>
> Short skirts have come back into fashion

There is a further extension to 'redress', getting one's own back for some perceived affront, as in:

> Take that insult back at once!
>
> This unruly student always answers back
>
> Molly hit Joe and then he hit her back in return

Back appears in slot **a** for a number of phrasal verbs of types V-a, V-NP-a, and V-a-p-NP, including:

SENSE	TYPE	
direction	V-a	The troops <u>fell back</u>
	V-a	The lazy boys <u>hung back</u> from volunteering
return	V-a-p-NP	John <u>went back on</u> his promise to lend us the deposit
	V-a-p-NP	We had to <u>fall back on</u> our own resources
	V-NP-a	Losing that contract <u>set</u> the firm <u>back</u> a good deal
	V-NP-a	Supplies were low and they had to <u>cut</u> the rations <u>back</u>
redress	V-a-p-NP	I want to <u>get back at</u> the bully

11.2d Forth

In Old English *forþ* 'out, forwards, onwards' was a prominent adverb which entered into several dozen combinations. Only a sprinkling of these have survived; they include *forthright* and *forthcome* (now generally in the form *forthcoming*).

Modern adverb *forth* /fɔ:θ/ sometimes sounds a trifle archaic and is not too common. But it is useful, having a rather special semantic character. Its basic meaning is describing something emanating from a source in a rush, or in a flow (it can be in any direction):

> Oil gushed forth from the well
> The tide surged forth through the blow-hole
> The music welled forth from the concert hall
> The wind sent forth a blast that knocked me over

Forth is also used when a point of origin is particularly significant:

> They sailed forth on a voyage of exploration
> From that day forth he never again touched a drop of alcohol

Forth features in just a few phrasal verbs. It is in slot **p** for one of type V-p-NP: *The monster gave forth a frightful stench*. And it is in slot **a** for:

type V-NP-a   The new director set his ideas forth
      V-a-p-NP Father O'Rourke held forth on the virtue of
                abstinence

Forth appears in column a of the table at the beginning of section 11.2. There is no item in column b with similar meaning; *back*—in its 'return' sense—would have to be used, as in *The tourists streamed forth from the cruise ship* and *The tourists went back to the cruise ship*. Indeed, there is a coordinated adverb *back and forth*:

> The ants kept taking things back and forth along the plank

The common phrase *and so forth* indicates 'and other items of a similar nature'.

11.2e Forward(s) *and* backward(s)

Adverb *forward* /ˈfɔwəd/ is a continuation of Old English *forweard* or *forþwaerd* with similar meaning. The OE adverb *onbæc* became *aback* and then, around 1300, added suffix *-ward* to create adverb *abackward*. At about the same time as *aback* dropped its initial vowel to become *back*, so *abackward* reduced to become *backward* /ˈbakwəd/.

Today, *forward* and *backward* function as adjectives and as adverbs. Just in the latter use, their form may be *forward* or *forwards* and *backward* or *backwards*. The final -*s* has been an optional addition since the fifteenth century. Its use today varies from dialect to dialect but appears to carry no difference of sense. (Overall, the -*s* is more common on adverb *backward* than on *forward*.)

Forward is many times more frequent than *backward* and has a far wider range of senses. Both *forward* and *backward* function as adjectives and they then pattern together, as in:

> Jim took a forward glance and Sue a backward glance

However, in adverbial use *forward* 'in an advancing direction' has as its opposite *back* 'in a rearwards direction'. The example just above used adjectives; the corresponding sentence with adverbs is:

> Jim looked forward and Sue looked back

Besides referring to spatial movement, adverb *forward* can refer to the advancement of some project, or to advancing a nomination, or the improvement of a social index. Examples of these are:

> We need to move forward with construction of the new town hall
>
> Have you put forward a candidate for the presidency?
>
> The country is inching forward in its economic growth

Forward has a directional meaning, quite different from *forth*. It could not be substituted for *forth* in most of the sentences quoted in the last section. An exception is the temporal sense; either adverb may be employed in:

> From that day forth/forward he never again touched a drop of alcohol

Forward appears in slot **a** for a phrasal verb of type V-NP-a: *They have <u>brought</u> the meeting <u>forward</u>.*

Adverb *backward(s)* has a quite different and rather special meaning 'someone or something moves in the direction that their back is facing'. Compare:

> Diana walked back to the statue
>   (she turned to face the statue and walked towards it)
> Diana walked backwards to the statue
>   (she had her back to the statue, so that she could not see it, and walked towards it)

Joe drove back to the station
>
> (he turned the car round and drove in forward gear towards the station)

Joe drove backwards to the station
>
> (he backed the car, in reverse gear, towards the station)

The adverb can be extended to describe some activity being undertaken in a direction opposite to the normal one, as in *Jane can recite the alphabet backwards*. A further extension is seen in:

Our new manager knows the hotel business backwards

This means that he knows the business through and through, whichever way you fancy.

11.3 Distance: *Beyond, near(-to), close-to, far-from*

Reference to distance uses prepositions *beyond* and *near*, and also phrasal prepositions *near-to*, *close-to*, and *far-from*.

11.3a Beyond

The Old English preposition *begeondan* has become modern *beyond* /bi'ɔnd/, maintaining the same meaning. If one hears 'X is beyond Y', this means that X is a goodly distance on the far side of Y. We can compare this with *over* used in its 'on the far side of' sense (section 11.1a-3):

My parents live over the mountain

My parents live beyond the mountain

The *over* sentence simply states that they live on the other side of the mountain. Using *beyond* adds more: they live a considerable distance from the mountain, on the far side of it.

It is significant that *beyond* may be modified by *way* (see section 2.6) to magnify the distance involved: *My parents live way beyond the mountain*. In contrast, *over* simply specifies a place; and it would not often take *way*.

The spatial sense of *beyond* is illustrated by:

The high shelf was beyond his reach

Eliza was gazing beyond me into space

An NP following *beyond* may be omitted when it would be anaphorically understood, as in: *Fred travelled to India and beyond* (that is, beyond India).

There is also a temporal sense, as in *Stephen worked beyond midnight* (see section 14.6b).

The spatial sense is extended to indicate 'a lot more than':

His interests extend beyond linguistics

William's donation goes way beyond the sum originally promised

She was wise beyond her years

Interestingly, when *beyond* is used in a negative sentence it simply means 'no more than', as in:

I have no horses beyond those twenty

The leader's bravado didn't impress anyone beyond the party faithful

Moving into a more abstract sense, *beyond* can indicate that something exceeds a mental or fiscal competence:

Joan's exposition of the proof was beyond my understanding/
beyond me

Buying that house would be beyond my means

Just for the last sentence, the opposite situation would be described using *within*: *Buying that house would be within my means*. Similar examples include: *beyond one's control* and *beyond one's powers*. (And see (iii) in section 8.3a-1.)

Beyond may be used when something cannot be achieved because of the circumstances:

This broken machine is beyond repair

Your drunken brother is beyond salvation

What happened fifty years ago is beyond recall

Similar situations are described by: *beyond recognition* and *beyond redemption*.

A further sense of 'X is beyond Y' states that X is in a region which is outside the scope of Y. For example:

That the President should behave in this manner is beyond belief

The donor's generosity was beyond expectation

Mildred is lovely beyond description

When a British prince admitted fraternising with a convicted sexual predator, the populace was outraged. But the Prime Minister commented:

> The Royal Family is beyond reproach

If he had said *above reproach* this would imply that the royal family's behaviour was impeccable, which was plainly untrue. By using *beyond reproach* he was implying that they were accorded a special status where the idea of reproach was not permitted to apply.

Beyond is also used in parenthetical expressions such as *She had, beyond any doubt, a touch of genius.* And *the back of beyond* is a humorous phrase for referring to a really remote place.

11.3b Near(-to), close-to, far-from

There are three phrasal prepositions which refer to distance: *near-to* /'niətə=/, *close-to* /'kloustə=/ and *far-from* /'fa:frəm=/. Through the final *to* or *from*, each ends in a clitic, which is attached to a following NP.

These are the only phrasal prepositions whose lexical elements are adjectives (*near* and *far* are of Germanic and *close* of Romance origin). They have comparative and superlative forms which carry over into the prepositions. Example sentences are:

> Tim sat near-to/close-to/far-from the stage
> Tim sat nearer-to/closer-to/further-from the stage than Jane
> Tim's chair is nearest-to/closest-to/furthest-from the stage

Alongside phrasal preposition *near-to* there is also a simple preposition *near* (which is much commoner than *near-to*). *Near* also has comparative and superlative forms—*nearer* and *nearest*—and is the only simple preposition to do so. *Near-to* may be replaced by *near* in each of the three sentences just quoted.

Near and *near-to* have similar but not identical meanings. In essence, *near-to* may be preferred when motion is involved (thus reflecting the meaning component supplied by *to*) with *near* being preferred when describing a static situation. Thus:

> Tim moved his chair near-to the stage
> Tim's chair is near the stage

The basic meaning of *near* and *near-to* is spatial 'in the vicinity of'. It is extended to cover physical and mental conditions. We can illustrate a contrast:

> The calamity caused Agatha to come near-to despair
>
> Agatha was near despair all winter

The first sentence describes how Agatha moved towards despair while the second one deals with a static situation, which lasted for a goodly time.

In some contexts the *to* alternative is most common. For instance, *Robin was near-to suicide, Mother was near-to tears*. Only *near-to* is possible when followed by an *-ing* phrase, as in: *He is near-to making a decision*.

Near-to or *near* may be used to describe something in the vicinity of a quantitative measure:

> There were near(-to) a hundred people present
>
> That is near(-to) the ideal temperature for storing cheese

Note that *near* also functions as a verb. For example, *The children always get excited when Christmas nears* (and see (iii) in section 1.8).

The range of meaning for *close-to* is similar to that of *near-to*; it may be substituted for *near-to* in each of the examples quoted above. When this happens, the contrast between *near*, for a static situation, and *near-to*, for a non-static one, is lost.

In spatial uses, *near(-to)* indicates 'at a short distance from' and *close-to* 'at a very short distance from'. As the precursor to a kiss, one might say *She moved her lips close-to his*; note that *near-to* would be less felicitous here.

Close-to is also preferred to describe emotional associations, as in:

> Lydia is very close-to her father
> (they love each other, and there is an empathy between them)

Near-to is possible here, but would again be less felicitous.

Overall, *close-to* is typically preferred for non-spatial expressions. *Near-to tears* is fine, but one would more often hear *close-to tears*. Further examples of *close-to* with an abstract sense are:

> Many prisoners are close-to starvation
>
> We are close-to solving the problem

Far-from has a spatial sense indicating 'a long distance away' and is the antonym of *near(-to)* and *close-to*:

> The farmers live far-from their gardens

Like *near(-to)* and *close-to*, *far-from* has considerable extension to abstract statements, as in:

> Far-from wanting to help Hector, Jane was close-to incriminating him
> Far-from being less frightened than before, Johnny started
> screaming in terror
> The police are far-from solving the murder mystery

Note also: *He is far-from clever/sad/satisfied* and *The announcement was far-from pleasing/comprehensible/expected*.

Near, close, and *far* have extensive use as adjectives; it is sometimes not easy—especially with *near*—to distinguish these functions. *Close* and *far* may also be followed by a variety of other prepositions; they include: *close by, close on, close upon, close behind, far off*; there is also the phrasal preposition *as-far-as*.

There are in addition the widely used derived adverbs *nearly* and *closely*, which have quite different meanings.

11.4 Passage: *Along, alongside, across, through, throughout*

There are five prepositions which describe linear movement, in space or time: *along, alongside, across, through,* and *throughout*.

11.4a Along

Old English preposition *andlang* 'along, alongside' developed into present-day *along* /ə'lɔŋ/. Adverbial use followed in the fourteenth century.

As a preposition *along* introduces an NP with the meaning 'move from one part of the referent of the NP to another part, always maintaining contact with it'. For example:

> Garry ran along the road
> Robin danced along the verandah

In its basic sense, *along* is often modified by *all*, which indicates 'maintaining contact with every part of it', as in: *Robin danced all along the verandah*.

It is instructive to examine the use of *along* and *on* in:

1 Jack walked along the path   (from one point of the path to another)

2 Jack walked on the path   (the path was the place where he walked)

3 Jack walked along on the path   (combining the above two)

On functions as a preposition in 2 and 3. *Along* is a preposition in 1, but an adverb in 3. Indeed, one will often hear just:

4 Jack walked along

Here the context of speaking will indicate what track Jack was walking along.

Preposition *along* is also used for describing items located between one point and another:

There's a row of houses along the riverbank

Note that in this sense, *along* cannot be used as an adverb; that is, one cannot say: **There's a row of houses along*. The preposition can also be used for directing attention: *Look along the shelf!* Again, the NP following *along* may not be omitted.

Adverb *along* is often used in commands. If people are gawping at a crime scene, a policeman may instruct them: *Move along there, please!* A teacher may say to a student: *Run along now!* (that is, to your next class). (If she just wanted the student to go away, she would say: *Run off!*) Other recurrent instructions include *Come along!* and *Hurry along!*

Abstract uses of *along*—as adverb or as preposition—are generally small variations on the basic sense. For example:

The child is dragging along (behind its mother)
Negotiations for a peace treaty are dragging along

The search party is proceeding along the railway line
The committee will proceed along the lines you suggested

Adverb *along* may be followed by NPs introduced by *on*, *behind* (as in examples above), *by*, *to*, *from*, *in*, *through*, *after*, and *past*, among many others. *Along* is often used before *with*:

> Jason escaped (along) with two other prisoners
>
> Hannah gets a good salary (along) with generous fringe benefits

Along is optional in the two sentences above. But it cannot be omitted from:

> Two city offices were closed down along-with one in the country

It appears that we have here a complex preposition *along-with*, meaning 'in addition to'.

There are a handful of phrasal verbs which feature *along* in slot **a**:

| type | V-a-p-NP | Tom doesn't <u>get along with</u> his mother (they're always arguing) |
| type | V-NP-a | Let's <u>string</u> the boss <u>along</u> (and tell him that we're all resigning) |

There are two phrasal verbs (of type V-a-p-NP), with similar meaning, differing only in that one uses *by* and the other *along*:

> I'm just able to <u>scrape by on</u> the pension
>
> I'm just able to <u>scrape along on</u> the pension

The first sentence, with *by*, describes the situation in general terms (see section 6.1b-4), In the second, *along* implies just being able to live from one day to the next.

11.4a-1 *Alongside*

Prepositions *along* and *beside(s)*—see section 9.4—go back to OE. In the early eighteenth century they spawned a new preposition *alongside* /əˈlɒŋˌsaɪd/. This began in nautical speech but soon expanded into general usage.

Alongside can be used in similar circumstances to its progenitors:

Tommy Tar walked beside the river	preposition *beside*
Tommy Tar walked along the river	preposition *along*
Tommy Tar walked along beside the river	adverb *along*, preposition *beside*

Tommy Tar walked alongside the river	preposition *alongside*

The basic meaning of *alongside* is 'at the side of and parallel to', as in the location sentence:

> The boat is moored alongside the pier

Alongside has some non-spatial senses, and these are more similar to those of *beside(s)* than to those of *along*. It may indicate 'in addition to' or 'in the company of', as in:

> Alongside diligence and honesty, we value loyalty
> Betty has been working alongside her cousins, picking raspberries

11.4b Across

Middle English borrowed *across* /əˈkrɔs/ from Old French; it began as an adverb and soon added prepositional function.

The basic meaning of preposition *across* is 'moving from one extremity of an object to another, maintaining a level path', as in *Mary cycled across the bridge*.

It is instructive to compare the possibilities for using *over* and *across* after the verb *jump*:

Max jumped over the patch of mud	Max jumped across the patch of mud
Max jumped over the ditch	Max jumped across the ditch
Max jumped over the fence	<no corresponding sentence with across>

Whereas *over* implies 'a greater height', *across* requires 'a level path'; hence one cannot say **Max jumped across the fence*.

If the verb of the clause describes a continuing activity, then *across* implies 'maintaining contact'. This explains another instance of the difference between *over* and *across*:

Judy flew across the lake	Judy flew over the lake
Judy swam across the lake	<no corresponding sentence with over>

The 'greater height' sense of *over* is incompatible with the meaning of *swim* which requires constant contact with the water.

Other examples of the basic spatial motion sense of *across* are:

> Kate moved across the room
>
> Joe walked across the border between France and Spain

There is extension to time (see section 14.6f):

> Across the years, I've learnt a great deal from Professor Penkinsnaffer

Across may also have locational reference, as in:

> Houses have been built right across the beach (from one side to
>   the other)

The preposition may relate to two things on opposite sides of an object:

> The interrogator sat across the desk from the suspect
>
> Eliza sat across the bench (with one leg on either side of it)

Or it can describe relative position, as in *Tom lives across the road (from Lucy)*. Note that the *from* phrase may be omitted when it would be understood from the context of speaking.

Across may also refer to sight, as in *Jan looked across (the room) at her boy-friend*; here the NP following *across* may be omitted when its reference would be understood.

An adverbial sense of *across* appears in:

> This plate is ten centimetres across
>   (that is, ten centimetres from one extremity across to the other)

Some abstract senses of *across* are straightforward extensions from the spatial sense. Compare:

> Jane took the parcel across (the city) to Joe
>
> Jane got the idea across to Joe

A related example is: *The con-man put the scam across on the trusting pensioner*.

Another instance of an abstract sense being linked to a spatial one is:

> The knife cut across the slab of meat
>   (cut it from one side to the other, dividing it into two)

The vote cut across party lines
(each party was divided in the way its members voted)

A special sense is exhibited in phrasal verbs—of type V-p-NP— such as *come across* and *run across*, which means 'encounter by chance'. For example:

I <u>came across</u> an interesting old manuscript in the attic

The phrasal verbs *run into* (see section 8.1i) and *run across* have similar meanings. They are interchangeable in:

Tom <u>ran across</u> an old school friend in the market
Tom <u>ran into</u> an old school friend in the market

There is, however a difference. In its 'encounter by chance' sense, *run into* may only refer to encountering a human. In contrast, there are virtually no restrictions on the NP following *run across*:

Tom <u>ran across</u> a ruined church/a little waterfall/a crocodile

There is also an intransitive phrasal verb *come across*, of type V-a:

The minister spoke at length but I'm afraid his meaning didn't
<u>come across</u>
Cindy <u>came across</u> as a complete idiot/a skilled mediator

A similar example is *Sue <u>came across</u> with a great idea.*

It will be seen that *across* occurs in slot **a** for phrasal verbs of types V-a and in slot **p** for phrasal verbs of type V-p-NP.

11.4c Through

The Old English preposition *þurh* had a similar range of meanings to its modern descendent *through* /θruː/. There was an early alternation of spellings between *through* and *thorough*; the former became the form of the preposition, and the latter of an adjective with similar meaning. The preposition *through* had developed an adverbial function by early Middle English times. And there is a related prefix *through-*; for example a *through-passenger* will buy a *through-ticket* for a *through-train* which enables them to get to their destination without having to change trains.

Preposition *through* has a similar meaning to *across*, but there is an important difference. Essentially, *across* has a two-dimensional reference, and *through* a three-dimensional one. This can be seen by comparing:

Cynthia ran across the field

Cynthia ran through the long grass (in the field)

In the first sentence, the field is regarded as flat and Cynthia moves from one end to the other. In contrast, the second sentence refers to movement from one side to the other within the long grass growing in the field.

11.4c-1 Three-dimensional space

A common use of *through* is to describe motion from one end to the other of an enclosed space, as in:

The bank-robbers crawled through the sewer pipe

Belinda drove through the tunnel

Substituting *across* here would give a quite different meaning. If one heard *The bank-robbers crawled across the sewer pipe*, this would imply crawling from one side to the other of the pipe, width-wise, being on top of it, whereas *crawled through the sewer pipe* implies crawling from one end of the pipe to the other, length-wise, being within it. Similarly for the second sentence.

The three-dimensional space need not be enclosed; that is, it need not have a top. Examples include *through the long grass* and:

Terry waded through the water

The police chased the robbers through the alleyways of the old town

An NP following *through* may be anaphorically omitted when it would be repeated from earlier in the sentence, as in:

Belinda didn't fully inspect the house but just walked through (the house)

Tom ran to the tunnel and then just strolled through (the tunnel)

Through may also be used for direction of vision:

Sir Eustace looked through the telescope

Lady Ruth glanced through the pile of invoices

A further sense is temporal; that is, 'progress from one end to the other of a period of time'. For example (see also sections 11.4c-6, 14.6f, and 15.3a):

Aunt Marcia has certainly lived through hard times

The dean hurried through the agenda

The duchess dozed through the sermon

As described in section 2.7, *through* is one of only three prepositions which may—in limited circumstances—follow rather than precede their NP (the others are *over* and *(a)round*). This is found most often with temporal reference. Thus:

The baby slept (all) through the night

The baby slept (all) the night through

Postposing *through* emphasises that the activity really did extend over the whole of the period of time specified. Note that when *through* is extraposed, the modifier *all* does not move.

There are some examples of *through* following its NP when the preposition is used in its spatial sense. Suppose that Joe has lost something and ransacks the house to try to find it. One could say either of:

Joe has searched through the house

Joe has searched the house through

The second sentence emphasises how thorough the search has been. (Note that the related adjective *thorough* has just been used to explain this use of preposition *through*.) Or with verb *read*, there can be:

Samuel read through the book

Samuel read the book through

The first sentence may be used when Samuel has undertaken a casual reading of the book (perhaps skimming over boring bits). In contest, the second sentence states that he read every part of it most carefully.

Through has further uses—to describe the passage of a noise, or the extent of some activity, as in:

His piercing whistle went right through my head

The nail is half-way through the board

Harry cut through the wrapping to reveal a sacred icon lying
    on a bed of velvet

11.4c-2 A gap

The idea of three-dimensional space, typical for the basic use of *through*, may reduce to just a gap, as in:

> The plumber entered through the back door
> The cat jumped through the window
> The maid peeped through the keyhole

In the following sentence, the action of the truck simultaneously made a hole in the fence and proceeded through it:

> The truck drove through the fence

11.4c-3 Completion

Consider a sentence employing *through* in its basic sense:

> The carer guided the blind man through the streets of the city

There is a natural metaphorical extension:

> The minister guided the bill through the various legislative processes

This could be abbreviated to just: *The minister guided the bill through.* We now have *through* functioning as an adverb, meaning 'completely, from one end to the other'.
Other examples of this adverbial use include:

> The postman was drenched (through)
> Yuri has learned the poem (through)

Each of these may be used without the adverb. Adding *through* to the first sentence indicates that the postman was soaked from top to toe. And adding it to the second sentence indicates that Yuri knows the poem absolutely by heart, from beginning to end, and can recite it verbatim.

There are a fair number of phrasal verbs involving this meaning; see section 11.4c-6.

11.4c-4 Through an intermediary

Preposition *þurh* had a range of meanings in OE including this one, stating what something was (or is) achieved by means of:

The ambassador could only communicate through an interpreter

I am related to Mrs Mopp through marriage

You can talk to me through email

11.4c-5 By reason of

A further sense of the OE preposition, which is retained in the modern language, involves identifying a cause or reason, as in:

She succeeded simply through hard work

He lost his job through carelessness

Peter found the corpse through curiosity about a fetid smell
   from the basement

11.4c-6 *Through* in phrasal verbs

There are a couple of dozen phrasal verbs which include *through*, some having it in slot **p**, others in slot **a**.

Most of those with *through* in slot **p** have a straightforward relation to the basic sense of the preposition. Compare (as before, phrasal verbs are underlined):

Meg saw through the window the pine trees behind it

Sue <u>saw through</u> the specious proposal (to the deception behind it)

Harry cut through the wrapping on the icon

Tommy <u>cut through</u> the red tape

Other phrasal verbs of type V-p-NP are:

Kate <u>came through</u> the ordeal unscathed

I just <u>scraped through</u> the Latin exam

The boss <u>ran through</u> the reasons for his decision to close down
   the cycle works

One verb of this type does have a rather unusual meaning

Dick soon <u>ran through</u> his inheritance (he spent it all, from first
   cent to last)

There are also a number of phrasal verbs of type V-NP-p-NP:

They managed to <u>pull</u> the patient <u>through</u> the operation

The teacher <u>took</u> the students <u>through</u> the proof

Her mother's love helped <u>see</u> Mary <u>through</u> the crisis

Phrasal verbs where *through* is in slot **a** naturally relates to the adverbial sense of *through* (section 11.4c-3) where it indicates 'completion'. Types V-a, V-NP-a, and V-a-p-NP feature here:

V-a	John was able to <u>win through</u>, by dint of determination and hard work
	The plan <u>fell through</u>, because of lack of high-level support
V-NP-a	We've got to <u>carry</u> this plan <u>through</u>
	Jim <u>skimmed</u> the document <u>through</u>
V-a-p-NP	She <u>was through with</u> trying to pretend that she loved him
	You've got to <u>get through to</u> the voters, if you want to win the election

There are a few phrasal verbs with *through* which mirror those with *across*. For example, two of the sentences given in section 11.4b can use *through* in place of *across*:

The minister spoke at length but I'm afraid his meaning didn't <u>come across/through</u>

Cindy <u>came across/through</u> as a complete idiot/a skilled mediator

It is difficult here to perceive any difference in meaning between the *across* and *through* alternatives. It may be that the difference which is apparent in spatial use becomes neutralised when the sense becomes more abstract.

11.4c-7 Contrasting *through* with other prepositions

The contrast between *across* and *through* was illustrated at the beginning of section 11.4c. We can now examine contrasts with other prepositions.

11.4c-7a *By* and *through*

In some contexts, *through* and *by* appear to be substitutable:

1   Jenkins' business is run through his agent

2   Jenkins' business is run by his agent

In fact, the meanings are rather different. Sentence 1 states that Jenkins issues orders to his agent who passes them on to the workers. In contrast, sentence 2 states that Jenkins gives authority to his agent to issue the orders. Rephrasing the sentences:

3   Jenkins runs his business through his agent

4   Jenkins' agent runs his business

Sentence 2 is the passive derivation from 4 (see section 6.1c). The passive of 3 is *Jenkins' business is run by Jenkins through his agent*, which can be shortened to 1.

11.4c-7b *Over* and *through*

Both *over* (section 11.1a-1) and *through* can relate to temporal duration (see section 14.6f):

> Over the past twenty years, Marcel has stayed calm
>
> Through all the pitfalls and triumphs of the past twenty years, Marcel has stayed calm

Over, in the first sentence, simply indicates 'from one side to the other' of the past twenty years. In contrast, *through* treats the time period as having internal structure; this is akin to walking through long grass or chasing through alleyways.

11.4c-7c *Above* and *through*

Both *above* and *through* can be used in connection with noise, but to different effect. Consider:

> Nigel had to shout to make himself heard above the noise
>
> Nigel could scarcely be heard through the noise

To be heard, Nigel was forced to make his voice louder (a greater count in decibels) to rise above the general hubbub (see section 11.1b). If he could not achieve this, the only hope was that his voice should be somehow distinctive (for example, high-pitched), in order to cut through the racket; an analogy might be a bulldozer cutting a path through a dense jungle.

11.4d Throughout

In Old English *þurhut* 'quite through' functioned as preposition and adverb. It has developed into present-day *throughout* /ˌθruːˈaut/.

Preposition *throughout* indicates 'in every part of'. It can refer to space or to time:

> Stan travelled throughout Europe
>
> Mavis worked throughout the night

In these sentences, *throughout* could be replaced by *all through* without significant difference in meaning.

The contrast with *through* is illustrated in:

> Janet walked through London
> (from one side to the other)
>
> Janet walked throughout London
> (in every part of it)

Another instructive contrast is shown in (see also section 14.6f):

> Pelé began to dominate through the second half
>
> Pelé dominated throughout the game

Through indicates progress from one item to another within some spatial or temporal extent. The first sentence states that Pelé's domination was incremental, gradually increasing as the second half progressed. In contrast, *throughout* indicates a constant quality, domination from kick-off until the final whistle.

The NP following *throughout* may be omitted if it would repeat an NP from earlier in the sentence or it would be understood from the context:

> Many ministers resigned during the crisis but Smithers stayed
> loyal throughout
>
> Pelé dominated throughout

Throughout also has limited function as an adverb. A sentence in which it is a preposition may be more succinctly cast with *throughout* as an adverb:

> Everything is in good condition throughout the property
>
> The property is in good condition throughout

Throughout is confined to basic spatial or temporal senses. It cannot follow its NP in the way that *through* may, as in *She slept the night through*. And *throughout* does not have metaphorical extensions, nor is it found in phrasal verbs.

* * *

Having in this chapter dealt with a profusion of prepositions and adverbs describing position, we next consider six prepositions concerned with distribution.

12

Distribution

Among(st), amid(st), between, in-between;
(a)round; about, concerning

This group of prepositions naturally divides into three sets: (1) *among(st)*, *amid(st)*, *between*, and *in-between*, which refer to distributive inclusion; (2) *(a)round*; and (3) *about*, plus *concerning* which has a similar meaning to one sense of *about*.

12.1 *Among(st), amid(st), between, in-between*

In their basic senses, each of these four prepositions introduces an NP with plural reference. For example:

English Prepositions: Their Meanings and Uses. R. M. W. Dixon. Oxford University Press (2021). © R. M. W. Dixon.
DOI: 10.1093/oso/9780198868682.003.0012

> Luke owns three buildings among that sea of skyscrapers
>
> Mark lives in a tiny house amid that sea of skyscrapers
>
> John lives in a tiny house between/in-between two skyscrapers

The sentence with *among* states that Luke's buildings are surrounded by skyscrapers, the sentence with *amid* that Mark's house is in the middle of a collection of skyscrapers, and the sentence with *(in-)between* that John's house is flanked by skyscrapers.

The three prepositions all go back to Old English. *Among* /əˈmʌŋ/ developed out of *on-gemang* 'in a crowd or assemblage', and *amid* /əˈmid/ from *on-middan* 'in the middle of'. Each of these added an optional final *-st* in the fourteenth century (see section 1.10). OE included a number of prepositions each with a meaning similar to 'between'—*betwēonan* or *betwinan, betweox, betwux, betwix*. These have given rise to modern-day *between* /bəˈtwiːn/ and the now moribund *betwixt* /bəˈtwikst/. (The latter still has currency in the phrase *betwixt and between* 'neither one thing nor another, an uncertain position between two alternatives'.) The complex preposition *in-between* evolved about 1600.

Among(st), amid(st), between, and *in-between* function only as prepositions (never as adverbs). They do not enter into prepositional verbs or phrasal verbs, and show limited possibilities for extension from spatial meanings. We can now discuss them in turn.

12.1a Among(st)

We may have a peripheral phrase referring to Y, and introduced by *among(st)*, following a copula or intransitive clause whose subject argument refers to X. There are a number of possible meanings associated with this.

First: X is one of Y, a group of similar people or things, as in:

> Jennie likes to be among her friends
>
> I noticed that Frank was among the people who abstained
>
> Apples are among the fruits which can be grown in this climate
>
> Fred counts himself among the great man's followers

A reciprocal construction may include *among(st)* used in this sense. For example: *They quarrelled amongst themselves.*

An alternative meaning is that X is surrounded by Y, a group of similar people or things. Thus:

Edward strolled among the pines and cedars

The king walked among the cheering crowds

Freda fell among thieves

Or 'among Y' may specify a population, Y, within which a certain state prevails, as in:

Bullying is the leading cause of suicide among teenagers

The vicar has a reputation for honesty amongst his parishioners

That kind of music is popular among teenagers nowadays

When a phrase *among(st)* Y follows a verb of giving, whose O argument refers to the gift, X, this states that X is distributed across the members of Y:

Deadeye Dave divided the booty amongst members of the gang

Other verbs here include *split*, *share*, *distribute*, and *apportion*. See the further discussion of this in section 12.1c-5.

The meaning of the preposition is extended to cover more abstract groupings. For example:

Among other hobbies, I collect stamps

Among other things, you have swindled Mary

Physics is among the subjects which I like best

In most cases either *among* or *amongst* may be employed with no real difference in meaning. However, there may be a tendency to prefer *among* for the extended, more abstract, sense illustrated in the last three examples.

12.1a-1 Contrasting *with* and *among(st)*

We can compare:

John hid the Will with the other documents

John hid the Will among the other documents

On hearing the first sentence, one would understand that the other documents were hidden in some place and that John hid the Will in the same place. This is the 'association' sense of *with* (section 6.2b), as in *He lives with his parents*. In contrast, the sentence with *among* states that John thrust the Will into a pile of other documents ('a group of similar things') as a way of hiding it. Interestingly, if the verb were changed, so that we had *John put the Will with/among the other documents*, there would be no obvious difference in meaning between use of the two prepositions.

12.1b Amid(st)

The NP following *amid(st)* may be the plural form of a count noun or else a mass noun. *X is amid(st) Y* indicates that Y is all around X. For example:

> George died amidst a circle of friends
> Joan stood alone amid the flames
> I could hardly see anything amid the cloud of tobacco fumes

Amid(st) is often used where Y describes some noise:

> Her words were lost amidst the clatter of machinery

Or the NP marked by *amid(st)* may have abstract reference:

> Helen maintained her position amid a storm of dissent
> Jock did say a few sensible things amidst all that nonsense

This can be extended to a situation where Y relates to a potentiality:

> The minister postponed his visit to the colony amid signs of
>   political upheaval

Either *amid* or *amidst* may be used in most contexts, with no difference of sense. An exception is the last example quoted (with abstract reference), where *amid* should perhaps be preferred. In place of *amidst* it is generally possible to use *in the midst of*, with similar meaning.

Despite their similar meanings, *among(st)* and, *amid(st)* are substitutable one for the other in only a few of the most basic spatial contexts. For example, *Edward strolled among/amid the pines and cedars* and *George died amidst/amongst a circle of friends*

12.1c Between *and* in-between

The most typical use of *between* is to introduce an NP referring to two entities:

> John lives in a tiny house between two skyscrapers
>
> The river descends between two high cliffs

The referent of the subject of the sentence is said to be located, or to be moving, within a space bordered by the two entities—here, the skyscrapers and the cliffs.

However, an NP following *between* can refer to more than two entities. Consider a row of ten equi-spaced pillars. One could say:

> There is a gap of six feet between each pillar and the next

Or else:

> There is a gap of six feet between the pillars

Here the NP marked with *between* refers to more than two things. But the underlying meaning is 'between each two of the pillars'.

We can consider another example. Suppose that three nations (let us call them A, B, and C) meet together for trade talks, and afterwards there is an announcement:

> The three nations have agreed between themselves on trade pacts

The use of *between* here implies three one-to-one sets of pacts— A and B sign one set, B and C another set, while A and C sign a further set.

This contrasts with:

> The three nations have agreed among themselves on trade pacts

The use of *among* here, in place of *between*, implies that all three nations signed a single set of trade pacts which apply to them all.

In essence, *between* always indicates a relation between two things, but can be expressed through a number of grammatical strategies. We can distinguish five senses: spatial or temporal separation, joining across a gap, creation of a gap, division, and choice. There is also the intriguing matter of the complex preposition *in-between*, and how this fits into the overall picture.

12.1c-1 Spatial or temporal separation

In the basic spatial sense, *between Y and Z* relates to location or movement within the space bounded by the referents of Y and Z:

> Max stood between the fireplace and the window
>
> Eugene kicked the ball between the goalposts

There is a related temporal sense, dealing with a period of time demarcated by Y and Z (see section 14.6e):

> We plan to arrive between two and three o'clock
>
> There was a ten-year gap between his first and second marriages

Alternatively, a *between* phrase may indicate a spatial or temporal range:

> Ursula lives somewhere between Reading and Oxford
>
> The building will take between six and twelve months to complete

There may be a more abstract range, as in *The colour is somewhere between green and blue*.

12.1c-2 The complex preposition *in-between*

In its basic meaning, preposition *in* describes a location of inclusion, as in *The ball is in the box* (see section 8.1a). A phrase introduced by *in* may combine with a phrase introduced by *between*:

> Max stood [in the space [between the fireplace and the window]]

This can be reduced to:

> Max stood [in-between the fireplace and the window]

The two components of *in-between* /inbəˈtwiːn/ are closely linked, indicating that it is a single word, a complex preposition; this is shown by writing it with a hyphen.

Preposition *in-between* came into use about 1600. In certain contexts it may be used as an alternative to plain *between*, emphasising the sense of 'enclosure'. (This complex preposition is a quite different word from adjective/noun *in-between* 'intermediary', which dates from the early nineteenth century.)

In its basic sense, preposition *in* refers to location (the corresponding preposition for motion is *into*; see the beginning of chapter 8). In keeping with this, *in-between* is pretty well confined to statements of location. For example:

John lives in a tiny house (in-)between two skyscrapers

Here, either *between* or *in-between* is allowable. In contrast, *in-between* would be unlikely for a sentence describing motion, such as *The river descends between two high cliffs*.

With a verb of motion, *between* and *in-between* may convey different meanings. Consider

Peter ran between the goalposts

Peter ran in-between the goalposts

Hearing the first sentence, one would be most likely to understand that Peter ran off or on the football field through the space between the goalposts; this is the 'motion' sense of *between*. In contrast, the second sentence, with *in-between*, demands a locational meaning: Peter ran back and forth in the space between the goalposts.

Temporal uses of *between* may also employ *in-between*; for example: *There was a ten-year gap (in-)between his first and second marriages*.

When referring to a spatial or temporal range, only *between* is possible; for instance: *The journey takes (*in-)between ten and twelve hours*.

An NP following *(in-)between* may be anaphorically omitted when its referents have been stated earlier in the sentence. For example:

(a) John stood on one bank, and Mary on the other, with a raging torrent (in-)between them

(b) John stood on one bank, and Mary on the other, with a raging torrent (in-)between

(a) I had two interviews with a three-hour gap (in-)between them

(b) I had two interviews with a three-hour gap (in-)between

For the (a) sentence of each pair, *between* would be most common, although *in-between* is perfectly acceptable. In contrast, *in-between* would be much preferred for the (b) sentences, where the NP is anaphorically omitted. That is, when the preposition is exposed, lacking a following NP, then *in-between*, the stronger alternative, is most likely to be employed.

347

In-between is confined to spatial locational and to temporal meaning. It would be unlikely to be used —instead of *between*—for the extended senses described in the following sections.

12.1c-3 Joining across a gap

With an appropriate verb, *between Y and Z* can refer to establishing a link across the space separating these two entities:

> Jasper tied a rope between the two trees
>
> They are building a network of roads between all the major cities

This extends to linkings of a more abstract nature:

> A marriage has been arranged between the Montagues and Capulets
>
> We are hoping for a smooth transition between governments
>
> There is a connection between hard work and good results

Others of this type are: *an affinity between, a resemblance between, an equality between*, and *a coalition between*.

Sometimes a sentence involving *between* may be ambiguous between two senses of the preposition. For example:

> They are building a road between Little Middling and Much Binding

This could be interpreted as:

- Either the 'spatial separation' sense. The road is being built across the region separating the two towns (but not touching either of them).
- Or the 'joining across a gap' sense. The road is being built to link the two towns.

Note that *in-between* may replace *between* only for the 'spatial separation' sense. Thus *They are building a road in-between Little Middling and Much Binding* is unambiguous.

Another kind of 'joining' involves the amalgamation of the same feature between two individuals, as in:

> Jim and Sue have five million between them
>
> Between Dr Meggs and Mr Sims there are sixty-three years of devoted service to the school

12.1c-4 Creation of a gap

Rather than linking across an existing gap, *between* can refer to the emergence of a gap:

> Rivalry/a rift/a quarrel developed between the two brothers
>
> A sense of duty came between Hilda and her enjoyment of life
>
> A disparity arose between the views of the sisters concerning the appropriate course of action
>
> An argument erupted between mother and father concerning where to go for their vacation

Between may also describe an intrusion which leads to the interruption of some social bonding:

> The evil step-mother came between Angela and the father

12.1c-5 Division

This use of *between* is similar to one of the senses of *among(st)*, described in section 12.1a. However, there is a difference. We can compare:

> Deadeye Dave divided the booty between members of the gang
>
> Deadeye Dave divided the booty among(st) members of the gang

The sentence with *between* is more likely to be used if each member of the gang received an equal share (the 'one-to-one' underlying meaning of *between*). If each member of the gang did receive a share but there was a different amount for each person, then *among(st)* should be preferred.

Another instance of this sense is:

> We'll split the bill between the three of us

This implies that the three diners each pay an equal share.

12.1c-6 Choice

Here *between* introduces two alternatives only one of which can be pursued. For example:

> You must choose between a career in football and one in the church
>
> I had to decide between staying unhappily married and losing the children

There are a number of ways of expressing this sense of *between*, including:

> We had to compromise between being fully honest and losing the contract
>
> I can't tell the difference between haddock and cod
>
> You mustn't discriminate between the sexes
>
> For Alex there is no clear line between fact and fancy

12.2 *(A)round*

In the early fourteenth century, Middle English borrowed, from *rund* in French, the word *round* /raund/. This functioned as adjective, noun, verb, and adverb. Prefix *a*- was then added within ME to create a variant form of the adverb: *around* /ə'raund/ (literally 'on round'). In the fifteenth century, both *round* and *around* extended their use to also function as prepositions. Today, the two forms are in most contexts substitutable; however, it appears that *round* is more often preferred in British and *around* in American English (see section 15.3a).

A basic meaning of an NP *(a)round X* relates to that of the adjective *round*: 'to move (or be) in a circle which encloses the referent of X'. For example:

> Sam ran round the obelisk
>
> The earth circles round the sun

There is a similar temporal sense (see section 14.6f):

> Mollie worked round the clock
>
> Payday comes around each Friday

There need not be a full circle—just a part of a circle will do, or anything involving a 'turn':

> Sally ran round the house from the front door to the back door
>
> Algy dodged around the corner to avoid the debt-collector
>
> The fans crowded around the pop star
>
> All his friends rallied around Jim, to comfort him after the rejection

Alternatively *(a)round X* may just have a general meaning 'here and there with respect to X':

> Hugh travels around the country on business
>
> There is forest around the castle
>
> The agent showed the buyer around the house

The NP following preposition *(a)round* may be omitted when it could be understood from the context:

> Hugh travels around on business
>
> There is forest around
>
> The agent showed the buyer around

When such an isolated preposition follows a (non-pronominal) transitive object NP, it may be moved to the left over it (see section 2.1c):

> The agent showed around the buyer

(A)round may be used simply as an adverb:

> Today I just walked around
>
> The housekeeper is always moving things around
>
> The carousel went round and round

The walking and the moving were just 'here and there' (not with respect to anything in particular). And the carousel rotated about its central axis (which it must do).

Other examples of *(a)round* being used purely as an adverb include:

> Mother turned around to see who was calling her
>
> There's a fierce dog this way, you'd better go the other way round to the shop
>
> Don't play around with your food, just eat it!

As described in section 2.7, *(a)round* is one of only three prepositions (the others are *over* and *through*) which may follow its NP. One may say either of:

> Marco travelled around the world
>
> Marco travelled the world around

Postposing the preposition stresses the fact that the activity did extend over the whole of the space (or time) specified.

(A)round can be used to specify a measure, as in *a tree four foot around*. This can be viewed as a reduced form of a relative clause construction, as in:

> They are going to fell a tree (which is) four feet around (its trunk)

Allied to its 'here and there' sense, *(a)round* may mean 'somewhere near' when it is used with a verb of location, or 'approximately' when modifying a number word:

> Desmond lives round Dallas
>
> Around sixty people have been invited to the party
>
> Leslie only received around ten per cent of the vote

A statement such as *It happened around the turn of the century* combines the 'approximate' meaning of *(a)round* with the sense 'turn' (that is, from one century to the next).

12.2a (A)round *in phrasal verbs*

(A)round fills slot **a** in phrasal verbs of types V-a, V-NP-a, and V-a-p-NP. A number, of type V-a, simply have an unspecified meaning: 'doing any old thing, here and there, perhaps aimlessly'—*mess around, hang around, fool around*, and *knock around*.

- Some phrasal verbs show an extension of the spatial sense:

V-a	That rumour is <u>going around</u>	moving around in a circular-
V-a	That news is <u>getting around</u>	type path
V-a	Tony has been <u>sleeping around</u>	sleeping with people 'here and there, all over the place'

- Others have a more abstract meaning, dealing with 'turning from one physical state or opinion to another':

V-a	The patient <u>came round</u>	from unconsciousness into consciousness

V-NP-a   The doctor <u>brought/pulled</u> the patient <u>round</u>

V-a-p-N   We <u>came round to</u> John's   from disagreeing to agreeing
          opinion   with him

V-NP-a   We <u>talked</u> John <u>around</u>   from disagreeing to agreeing
                                                with us

- Another group of phrasal verbs go further, beyond the basic senses of *(a)round*:

V-NP-a   Let's just <u>kick</u> the idea <u>around</u>   discuss it informally

V-a-p-NP   He's never going to <u>get round to</u>   starting to do it
           repairing the roof

In the following phrasal verb, *(a)round* is in slot **p**:

V-p-NP   You need to <u>get round</u> Solomon   gain his confidence

Whether *round* or *around* is used in the examples quoted here reflects the form in the corpus example, or what came most naturally to me in constructing an example. In fact, either could be used in each sentence except that only *around* is used to modify a number word (*around fifteen books*), and the phrasal verb illustrated in *Tony has been <u>sleeping around</u>* does require *around*.

12.2b Contrasting over and (a)round

There are several kinds of contrast between *over* and *(a)round*. We can first look at:

> The maid walked over the garden, looking for the diamond ring she had dropped
>
> The visitor walked around the garden, marvelling at the display of flowers
>
> The agent looked over the house, making sure that it was all clean and shipshape
>
> The visitor looked around the house, admiring the panelling and candelabras

The first sentence of each pair, with *over*, implies a thorough examination (an extension from the 'moving from one side to the other' sense of *over*; see section 11.1a-2). In contrast, the *(a)round* alternatives indicate casual movement or attention, just 'here and there'.

There is less difference in effect between the two prepositions in:

Do come over/(a)round for dinner this evening!

We really ought to have the neighbours over/(a)round

In these sentences, *over* means 'moving across the gap between your/their place and ours', whereas *(a)round* is, essentially, 'moving along a trajectory', and it can be vague as to what kind of trajectory is involved (curved or straight). In actual fact, the *over* and *(a)round* alternatives are as close to being pragmatically identical as can be.

12.3 *About, concerning*

The Old English preposition/adverb *on-būtan* 'about' (literally 'on the outside') became *abūtan* and then modern day *about* /əˈbaut/. This is one of the ten most frequent prepositions in present-day English. It is unusual in that it frequently relates to a situation, or a happening, or a state of affairs, described through an NP with general meaning or a subordinate clause.

Many verbs and adjectives which can be followed by an NP or a subordinate clause introduced with *about* may also be followed by an NP introduced with a different preposition. The alternatives sometimes relate, in varying ways, to a single situation. Example sentences of similar meaning using *with* and *about* are:

Be careful with that emu egg

Be careful about how you handle that emu egg

Or the alternatives may have quite different meanings—compare *sorry for* and *sorry about*:

I'm sorry for that sick child

(my sympathies go out to the child)

I'm sorry about having eaten all the mangoes and left none for you

(I apologise for having done this)

The considerable set of such 'prepositional pairs' is presented in section 12.3c. Before this we need to outline the basic senses of *about*.

12.3a Basic senses

About does have a spatial sense, but this makes up a small portion of the total occurrences. It can replace *(a)round* in the meaning 'here and there':

> Today I just walked (a)round/about town
> There's a box of jewels buried (a)round/about here somewhere

About also functions as an adverb:

> Today I just walked about
> No one seems to be about

In its 'approximately' sense, *(a)round* can be replaced by *about*, with no difference in meaning:

> Leslie only received around/about ten per cent of the vote

However, *about* cannot replace *around* in: *It happened around the turn of the century*. This is because only *(a)round* includes within its meaning the nuance of 'turn' (as one century becomes another).

When the preposition *about* extends beyond spatial meaning, the NP or subordinate clause it introduces generally refers to a situation, or a happening, or a state of affairs. For example:

> John was sad about his books getting burnt in the fire
> I was uneasy about going out in the thunderstorm
> Are you serious about wanting to be an astronaut?
> I couldn't care less about the election result, all politicians are
>   crooks anyway

12.3b About *and* concerning

The verb *concern* was borrowed from French in the early sixteenth century. Its participle *concerning* /kən'sə:nɪŋ/ soon developed into a preposition.

Concerning 'in reference to' is, essentially, a specialised hyponym of *about*. Whereas *about* has wide usage across many registers of speech, preposition *concerning* is (a) found mostly in fairly formal speech, and (b) used when information is sought. The difference in formality is illustrated in:

Tubby asked Jacko about the lollypops

The inspectors asked the manager concerning discrepancies in the accounts

Concerning is found most often introducing an NP which modifies a noun; for example:

They were gathering [information [concerning techniques of fish-farming]]

I require [full details [concerning the proposed demolition of the town hall]]

For pretty well every occurrence of *concerning*, it could be replaced by *about*. The reverse is not the case; for instance, *concerning* would scarcely be acceptable in place of *about* for any of the example sentences given above.

12.3c About *and other prepositions*

As mentioned, many verbs and adjectives which may be followed by an NP (or subordinate clause) marked with *about* may alternatively take a peripheral NP introduced by another preposition The main possibilities here are: *of, for, by, with, at, towards, on, against, over* (we can refer to this as the 'other preposition').

There is a recurrent meaning contrast. The NP with the 'other preposition' typically has a fairly specific reference, relating to a person, a thing, a fact, or an incident. In contrast, the NP or subordinate clause with *about* will have more general reference—to a situation, or a happening, or a state of affairs. This can be illustrated in tabular form. (The number of the section dealing with the relevant sense of the 'other preposition' is given in parenthesis.)

		with the other preposition	*with* about
(a)	Aunt Meg complained	of ear-ache (5.2f-3)	about the hospital system
(b)	Mother is proud	of James (5.2f-3)	about James becoming a priest
(c)	Wilfred spoke	of his son (5.2g)	about his experiences in India

(d)	I am certain	of the date (5.2g)	about the cancellation of the party
(e)	Jed is sorry	for the cripple (5.3b-4)	about having let his parents down
(f)	The vicar enquired	for John (5.3c-3)	about how John is going
(g)	Sally doesn't care	for whiskey (5.3c-4)	about what other people do
(h)	Joe was worried	by the explosion (6.1c)	about the possible effects of the storm
(i)	Jacob is annoyed	with the boss (6.2d-2)	about the retail down-turn
(j)	I don't bother	with fools (6.2d-2)	about half-baked schemes
(k)	Joe is angry	at his wife (7.1d)	about not being allowed to take part
(l)	What are your feelings	towards your lover (7.3d)	about the political crisis
(m)	Marie was reticent	on that incident (9.1c-2)	about her achievements
(n)	Uncle cautioned Joey	against going (9.3a-1)	about the danger of the current situation
(o)	Tim and Jim argued	over the price (11.1a-1)	about the need to economise
(p)	Sue hesitated	over shaking hands (11.1a-1)	about whether to join the club

There are, of course, many other verbs and adjectives with these properties. They include *boast* for row (a); *be ashamed* for (b); *dream, hear, read,* and *tell* (someone) for (c); *be sure, be unsure, be doubtful,* and *be positive* for (d); *ask* for (f); *be pleased* for (i); *be mad* for (k); *be silent* for (m); and *warn* for (n).

As with many aspects of the use of prepositions, there is a great deal of individual variation. Occasionally, one might hear the prepositions reversed from what is presented in the table. For example: *Tim and Jim argued about the price* and *Tim and Jim argued over the need to economise.*

The scheme in the table is the canonical one. But the wonder of every language is the scope it provides for variation. (Some would call it sloppy, others innovative.)

There is a contrast between *over* and *about* which parallels that between *over* and *(a)round*, illustrated with *walk* and *look* in section 12.2b. As in the basic sense, *(a)round* and *about* are interchangeable here, with no difference in meaning.

An idiomatic use of *about* is in:

I'm sorry but I've got no money about me just now

This indicates that the person has no money on their person; it is typically used in the negative. There is extension from this to another idiom: *You'd better keep your wits about you.*

The adverbial phrase *out and about* is quite literal—come out of a place and wander about an area. Another adverbial phrase, *around and about* (the coordinands almost always being in this order) simply emphasises the vague 'here and there' spatial sense of both *(a)round* and *about*:

All day we just wandered around and about

About features in grammar within the semi-modal verb *be about to* 'be on the verge of doing something', as in *I'm about to sneeze.*

12.3d About *in prepositional verbs and phrasal verbs*

There are a couple of prepositional verbs which use *about*—*wonder about* (see section 4.1e-1) and *fret about*, plus a fair number of phrasal verbs.

In keeping with their similar basic meanings, some phrasal verbs of type V-a with *about* mirror those with *(a)round*. Alongside *mess around, hang around, fool around*, and *knock around*, there are *mess about, hang about, fool about*, and *knock about*, sharing an unspecified meaning: 'doing any old thing, here and there, perhaps aimlessly'.

There are further phrasal verbs of types V-a, and also V-NP-a, with *about* filling slot **a**. Their meanings constitute extensions from the meaning of *about* outlined above.

V-a	A reconciliation could <u>come about</u> through dialogue	eventuate
V-NP-a	The new manager plans to <u>bring</u> changes <u>about</u>	make eventuate

V-a	The rumour might <u>get about</u>	move here and there
V-NP-a	The editor <u>put</u> false news <u>about</u>	make move here and there
V-NP-a	The guards <u>knocked</u> the blind prisoner <u>about</u>	hit him/her here and there

There are also half-a-dozen phrasal verbs, of type V-p-NP which have *about* in slot **p**; for example:

V-p-NP	Dr Jones is <u>going about</u> his business	involved in
V-p-NP	Pablo <u>set about</u> the painting	getting involved in
V-p-NP	The guards <u>laid about</u> the blind prisoner	hit him/her here and there

* * *

The next short chapter discusses three adverbs which can expand to become prepositions. This is followed by a chapter dealing with the substantial issue of prepositions relating to time.

13

Separation

Apart(-from), aside(-from), away(-from)

Away /əˈweɪ/ continues Old English *on-weg* or *a-wag* (literally 'on one's way'). Noun *side* goes back to OE *sīde* with *a-* being added to create adverb *aside* /əˈsaɪd/ in the fourteenth century. And *apart* /əˈpaːt/ was taken over from French, also in the fourteenth century. The three adverbs each feature in some phrasal verbs. And they can each be extended to a phrasal preposition by adding *from*, giving *apart-from* /əˈpaːtfrəm=/, *aside-from* /əˈsaɪdfrəm=/, and *away-from* /əˈweɪfrəm=/. By virtue of the final *from*, each of the prepositions is a proclitic to a following NP.

English Prepositions: Their Meanings and Uses. R. M. W. Dixon. Oxford University Press (2021). © R. M. W. Dixon.
DOI: 10.1093/oso/9780198868682.003.0013

13.1 *Apart(-from)*

Adverb *apart* has a basic sense '(two or more items) spatially separated', as in:

> The illicit lovers moved apart when they saw their spouses
> approaching

Apart may be modified by a measure phrase:

> The duke and duchess live five miles apart
>
> You should plant the seedlings at least six inches apart

In its spatial sense, *apart* can be the opposite of *together* (see section 6.3):

> During the trial separation Marie and her husband lived apart but
> now they're living together again

Adverb *apart* requires an NP with plural reference. This can be in S (intransitive subject) function, as in *They live apart*, or in O (transitive object) function, as in *Keep the dogs apart!* The referents of the plural NP may be separated when the preposition *apart-from* is employed in place of the adverb. Thus:

> The duke and duchess live apart
>
> The duke lives apart-from the duchess
>
> The duchess lives apart-from the duke

The adverb may refer to a separation which is not strictly spatial but has a more abstract nature. (In the next example, *set NP apart* is a phrasal verb.)

> Each month Tommy <u>sets</u> some money <u>apart</u>, in case of an
> unexpected future need
>
>> (that is, he separated off this money, into a different account
>> from the everyday one)
>
> Opinions on the desirability of renovating the steeple are far apart

We also find adverb *apart* used to refer to something losing cohesion, or being separated into parts:

> My cousin's marriage fell apart
>
> Adrian took the machine apart, spread out all the bits, and then
> couldn't put it together again

Note that this provides another example of *together* as the opposite of *apart*.

Apart is in slot **a** for a phrasal verb of type V-NP-a, illustrated in:

Uncle Harry can't <u>tell</u> the twins <u>apart</u>

13.1a *Preposition* apart-from

There are more extensions from the spatial sense for preposition *apart-from* than for adverb a*part*.

Apart-from may refer to one thing separated from others by a wealth of achievement or excellence, as in:

Shakespeare is in a class apart-from all other dramatists

All other dramatists may be omitted (as understood). The preposition *apart-from* then has no following NP to cliticise to, and must be reduced to adverb *apart*:

Shakespeare is in a class apart

The preposition *apart-from* may be used to focus on one item, contrasting it with others, or just setting it off against a general background:

There was no one in the room that I recognised, apart-from Dr Scruggs
Apart-from New York I really don't care for big cities
Sheila is in good health, apart-from her lumbago

In these sentences, *apart-from* has a similar meaning to *except(-for)*; see section 6.4.

Another sense of the preposition indicates 'in addition to':

Apart-from their official talks, the leaders twice met privately
What are you studying this semester, apart-from Cosmic Theology?
The most important person present—apart-from Jules—was Jim
Apart-from the broken window, there was no real damage
Apart-from her smart appearance, what qualifications does Sue have for the position?

There is an alternative way of phrasing the last sentence, replacing preposition *apart-from* by adverb *apart* at the end of the NP *her smart appearance*:

Her smart appearance apart, what qualifications does Sue have for
the position?

There is a meaning difference here. The first sentence—with *apart from
her smart appearance*—implies that her appearance is a positive factor,
and enquires what other qualifications for the job Sue might have. The
second—with *her smart appearance apart*—implies that although her
appearance is pleasing, it does not count as a qualification for the
position.

A similar pair of sentences is:

Apart-from joking, what are we going to do about the crisis?
Joking apart, what are we going to do about the crisis?

13.2 Aside(-from)

In its basic spatial sense, adverb *aside* is equivalent to (and could be
replaced by) *to one side*. Examples are:

Matt took me aside and whispered the secret message
Fiona moved aside to let me go past
Maggie laid her work aside during the vacation
Michael pushed the beggar aside

As is usual, the adverb may be moved to the left before an object NP
(see section 2.1c):

Michael pushed aside the beggar

However, left movement is not possible over a pronoun as object. That
is, one may say *Michael pushed him aside*, but not **Michael pushed
aside him*.

Other common combinations include: *turn aside, throw aside*,
and *toss aside*. Also the very common phrasal verb *set NP aside*,
as in:

The government has <u>set aside</u> land for returned veterans
How much money have you <u>set aside</u> to cover our tax assessment?
The argument was strong but the judge <u>set</u> it <u>aside</u>

The phrasal verb *set NP apart* (mentioned in section 13.1) has essentially the same meaning as *set NP aside*, with the latter being far more frequent.

The spatial sense of *aside* may extend to abstract statements—*The judge set the argument aside* indicates that he did not consider it relevant in making his judgement. As another example, there can be a range of possibilities for what may be swept aside:

> Ronald swept aside the dirt on the floor/those who stood in his way/the current problems

Aside may (like *apart*) occur in slot **a** for a few phrasal verbs. There are *brush aside, sweep aside* (of type V-a), *set NP aside* (of type V-NP-a), and *stand aside* (also of type V-a), which can have a spatial or an abstract sense:

> We <u>stood aside</u> to let the procession through
>
> Because of a conflict of interest, I <u>stood aside</u> (when my wife's work plan was discussed)

13.2a Preposition aside-from

The main sense of *aside-from* is 'in addition to', similar to one of the senses of *apart-from* (see section 13.1a). However, there is a difference, as can be seen in:

> Apart-from the cabin staff, who will be attending the meeting?
>
> Aside-from the cabin staff, who will be attending the meeting?

The first sentence, with *apart-from*, implies that the cabin-staff will be important participants in the meeting. The second sentence, with *aside-from*, dismisses the cabin staff as being of little consequence and enquires who the main participants at the meeting will be.

There is as similar contrast between:

> What courses is Ben taking, apart-from Higher Mathematics
>
> What courses is Ben taking, aside-from Cake Decoration

The *apart-from* sentences acknowledges Higher Mathematics as a crucial course. In contrast, the speaker of the *aside-from* sentence plainly does not think much of Cake Decoration and wants to know if Ben is also taking courses with more significant content.

An alternative to *apart-from* is preposition *apart-of* /əˈpaːtəv=/, with similar meaning; this has a very low frequency today and may be considered colloquial.

Preposition *besides* also has an 'addition' sense; see section 9.4b. Interestingly, its meaning is closer to *apart-from* than to *aside-from*.

13.3 *Away(-from)*

Whereas *apart(-from)* and *aside(-from)* each describe a static separation, *away(-from)* implies movement. Moreover, it typically indicates increasing separation from something which is unpleasant and which is being avoided. For example:

> Max ran away-from an unhappy home
>
> Max jumped away-from the snake

Preposition *away-from* may omit the following NP, and then clitic component *from* /frəm=/ has to be dropped, reducing it to adverb *away*:

> Max ran away
>
> Max jumped away

The item which Max is separating himself from is now not stated, but it is understood to be something unwelcome.

Away(-from) has a fair range of meanings, relating to distance (preposition and adverb), disposal, diminution, commencement, and continuation (all of these almost exclusively just adverb).

13.3a Distance

Further examples of *away(-from)* describing beneficial separation are:

> Please move away-from the fire (so that you don't get burnt)!
>
> You'd better face away-from the blast (to avoid hurting your eyes)
>
> Molly will have a new life away-from her parents
>
> Let's have a holiday away-from home this year

Molly's life with her parents may have got constrained as she became older, and will be more free when she moves out. In the fourth sentence, a holiday should be a refreshing change from everyday routine, best achieved in a location different from home.

Matters are reversed when you hear someone say:

Stay away-from me!

Here it is the referent of the subject (understood to be *you*) which is deemed unwelcome, rather than the referent of the NP following *away-from*, as in the previous examples. This can be shortened to just: *Stay away!*

There need not necessarily be any unwelcome overtone. There is not, for instance, in the jocular advice *Away with you!*, nor in:

The boss is away(-from work) today

This week, our team is playing away (-from home)

Preposition *away-from* may be extended to more abstract meanings, as in:

Joseph turned away-from realistic painting to photography

Fashion is moving away-from traditional blacks and browns towards blues and reds

Separation may involve time (see section 14.6c) rather than space (again there is no unwelcome nuance):

The meeting is still two weeks away

He had been forty years away-from his homeland

13.3b Disposal

Adverb *away* may be used with a verb of action, describing the elimination of something which is unwanted:

You ought to throw/chuck away that food which is out-of-date

We'll have to clean away all the mould

In other circumstances, it is the act of elimination which is unwelcome:

Termites ate away at my house in the village, and eventually it collapsed

Or the 'disposal' may simply be a social convention:

Since her father had died, it had to be Uncle Ivan who gave Mary away at her wedding

A further sense simply describes removal or relocation, with no value judgement involved:

> Beryl put the winter clothes away in the closet

Adverb *away* may be modified to indicate the size of a separation:

> The CEO lives twenty miles away

13.3c Diminution

Whereas it requires some agent to effect disposal of an item (described by a transitive verb plus *away*), an item may all on its own gradually weaken (described by an intransitive verb plus *away*):

> The sound of the band faded away into the distance
> That iceberg will melt away within a couple of years
> His voice died away into a whisper

Also *waste away*, *wither away*, and *drain away*.

13.3d Commencement and continuation

Suppose that guns are primed and aimed. Then an officer orders:

> Fire away!

Here adverb *away* signals the start of the fusillade, which will be expected to persist. Further examples of continuation are:

> Peter worked away all day, without stopping
> The getaway car sped away and was soon out of sight

If someone enquires: *Can I ask you a few questions?*, you might respond: *Ask away!*

13.3e Away in a prepositional verb and in phrasal verbs

There is one prepositional verb involving away. This is *while away*, as in *The actor whiled away the time between engagements by playing the accordion in bars.*

Adverb *away* occurs in slot **a** for phrasal verbs of types V-a, V-NP-a, and V-a-p-NP. Most of them relate to senses just described:

TYPE	SENSE	
V-a	**Distance**	<u>Keep away</u>, I don't want you near me
V-a-p-NP		<u>Get away from</u> me, you miserable scoundrel!
V-a		He <u>stole away</u> in the dead of night and was never seen again
V-a-p-NP	**Disposal**	They are going to <u>do away with</u> capital punishment soon
V-a-p-NP	**Removal**	The robbers <u>got away with</u> $100,000 and three bars of gold
V-a	**Diminution**	Profits have <u>fallen away</u> this year, as rapidly as they rose last year
V-a		The centenarian <u>passed away</u> quietly in his sleep last night
V-a	**Continuation**	You'll get there in the end, just keep <u>pegging away</u>!

However, there are others which have a different meaning

V-a-p-NP	Susan did so well that she just <u>walked away with</u> the prize
V-NP-a	Jeff was scared of thunder but his wife tried to <u>laugh</u> it <u>away</u>

13.3f *Contrasting* off *and* away(-from)

There are a number of contexts in which either *off* (see section 9.2) or *away(-from)* may be used, with varying differences of meaning.

First we can compare the use of prepositions *off* and *away-from* in:

> Keep off the grass!
> Keep away-from the grass!

The first sentence, with *off*, orders the addressee to have no connection with the grass (that is, not to stand or walk on it). In contest, the sentence with *away-from* issues an instruction not to go near the grass; that is, to maintain a separation from it.

> Max was standing on the stage and then he ran off (it)
> Pete ran away-from the party

The sentence with *off* implies that Max had had a connection with the stage but then broke that connection. In the second sentence, Pete may or may not have been at the party; the point is that he moved so as to get a good distance from it.

There are other pairs where it is difficult to distinguish any difference in effect between the use of adverbs *off* and *away*. For instance: *The meeting is two weeks off/away* and *Profits have fallen off/away*. One could explain the *off* alternative as involving lack of connection and the *away* one as referring to separation; however, the alternatives have the same pragmatic result.

A fascinating contrast involves two phrasal verbs, of type V-NP-a, *laugh NP away* and *laugh NP off*:

> You can't just <u>laugh</u> a toothache <u>away</u>
> Dr Scruggs tried to <u>laugh off</u> his annoyance at the interruption

Laugh NP away means 'make little of it' whereas *laugh NP off* is used when someone pretends that what has happened is unimportant whereas in fact the opposite is the case.

* * *

The next chapter tackles the weighty matter of prepositions referring to time. There are six which are temporally dedicated, and a further thirty with secondary temporal senses.

14

Temporal

Since, because(-of); until/till,
up-until/up-till; during; after, afterward(s),
before, beforehand; past; and more

English Prepositions: Their Meanings and Uses. R. M. W. Dixon. Oxford University Press (2021). © R. M. W. Dixon.
DOI: 10.1093/oso/9780198868682.003.0014

There are three prepositions with an exclusively temporal meaning—*since*, *until/till*, and *during* (*since* also functions as a conjunction with the meaning 'consequence'). For three more, the primary meaning is temporal—*after* (and *afterward(s)*), *before* (and *beforehand*), and *past*. And a further two dozen of the prepositions discussed in previous chapters have a secondary sense relating to time.

A preposition with temporal meaning is more closely linked to the following NP than one with a spatial or relational sense. This is demonstrated by the possibilities for placement in questions. (The same results apply for other grammatical techniques of fronting such as relative clause formation; see section 2.2.)

Consider a statement which includes a non-temporal peripheral NP:

The highlanders surrendered to the lowlanders

If one wasn't sure who the surrender was directed towards, it would be possible just to substitute *who* for *the lowlanders*, creating an 'echo question': *The highlanders surrendered to who?* However, it is more usual to move the interrogative word (here *who*) to the beginning of the sentence. There are two ways of doing this (each equally acceptable for a sentence with *surrender*):

(a)   Fronting *who* and leaving the preposition in its original position:

Who did the highlanders surrender to?

(b)   Fronting preposition plus *who(m)*:

To whom did the highlanders surrender?

The (a) alternative is more common, and is acceptable for most non-temporal peripheral NPs. The (b) alternative is more restricted and is often only marginally acceptable, or else unacceptable. This is shown in:

The surgeon will operate on Trevor's hernia
(a)   What will the surgeon operate on?
(b)   ?On what will the surgeon operate?

The (a) alternative here is fine; the (b) sentence sounds awkward.

It should be noted that in many cases there is no clear 'acceptable'/'unacceptable' partition, but rather a continuum; the (b) sentence just quoted falls towards the 'unacceptable' end of the continuum.

In summary, for prepositions with a non-temporal meaning, (a) is generally alright and (b) often fairly dubious. Matters are entirely different for prepositions with a temporal sense. Here the (a) alternative would be unlikely to be used, while (b) is acceptable. This can be illustrated with *until* and *after*:

Jane worked here until Christmas

(a) *When did Jane work here until?

(b) Until when did Jane work here?

They signed a peace treaty after forty years of fighting

(a) *How many years of fighting did they sign a peace treaty after?

(b) After how many years of fighting did they sign a peace treaty?

It is interesting to compare non-temporal and temporal senses of other prepositions. For example, *for*. When used with a non-temporal sense, both questioning alternatives (a) and (b) are fine:

Mildred knitted socks for soldiers

(a) Who did Mildred knit socks for?

(b) For whom did Mildred knit socks?

However, things are rather different when *for* is used with a temporal meaning, as in:

Mildred knitted for three hours

(a) ?How many hours did Mildred knit for?

(b) For how many hours did Mildred knit?

Here alternative (a) is unlikely to be employed with (b) being far more felicitous.

The principle appears to be as follows: a preposition with temporal meaning is closely tied to its following NP. When the NP is put into question form, both preposition and NP may be moved to the front of the sentence but not the NP alone (leaving the preposition 'stranded'). That is, technique (b) is preferred over (a). When the preposition has a non-temporal sense, the opposite applies; here (a) is preferred over (b)—the NP can be detached and fronted, leaving the preposition behind. (See the general discussion of this in section 2.2.)

Turning to another topic, four of the temporal prepositions—*since, till/until, after*, and *before*—have an unusual grammatical property; they can mark a peripheral constituent which is either an NP or a declarative clause. These prepositions introduce reference to Time or to a Happening, and the latter may be realised as an NP, referring to the Happening, or a clause stating the Happening. This can be illustrated for *since* and *before*:

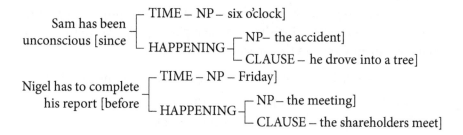

A 'traditional grammar' approach would doubtless consider *since* to be a conjunction in *Sam has been unconscious since he drove into a tree*. However *he drove into a tree* has the same syntactic and semantic status as *the accident* in *John has been unconscious since the accident*. The appropriate way of analysing this phenomenon is to recognise that *since*, as a preposition, can introduce a peripheral constituent which is either an NP or a clause.

Before behaves in the same way, as illustrated above, and so do *until/ till* and *after*. It appears that only these four temporal prepositions show this unusual property, of introducing a peripheral constituent which is a clause.

Sections 14.1–5 discuss temporal prepositions, one or two at a time. Then section 14.6 presents an analysis of types of temporal relationships, and how prepositions represent them.

14.1 *Since, because(-of)*

Although it goes back to *sīþ þan* 'after that' in Old English, *since* /sɪns/ only came into use as a preposition and conjunction after the fifteenth century.

We first deal with *since* as a preposition, when it has a temporal sense. Then as a conjunction, where the meaning is 'consequence', similar to—but far from identical with—the 'reason' sense of conjunction *because* and the associated preposition *because-of* (and also a minor use of *for*).

14.1a Temporal sense of preposition since

If a clause describing some activity or state includes a peripheral constituent *since X*—where X *is* an NP or a clause—this indicates that the activity/state commenced at the Time/Happening referred to by X and continues to and beyond the present. For example:

> Many people have been waiting since 4 a.m. to see the procession
> Agatha has been missing since last Thursday
> Alex has been depressed since he lost his job
> Ivan has had post-traumatic stress disorder since the war
> John has been a cripple since childhood

Two points should be particularly noted. First, no finishing time can be stated because the activity is continuing through the present time and into the indefinite future; that is, one cannot say **John has been a cripple since childhood until his operation*. Secondly, the main clause includes the auxiliary verb *have (. . . -en)* which describes an activity that commenced in the past and is still continuing now. One could not have past tense—for example, **John was a cripple since childhood*—because that would imply something which is finished. Note also that **John was a cripple since childhood until his operation* is ungrammatical; one would have to employ *from*, saying *John was a cripple from childhood until his operation*. See sections 14.2 and 14.6d.

Since, in its temporal function, may be modified by adverb *ever*. This is typically used when a longish time is involved, and it emphasises that the activity/state really has pertained over the whole period; for example, *John has been a cripple ever since childhood*.

A *since* temporal constituent typically comes at the end of a sentence. But if it is focused on, it may be placed at the beginning:

> (Ever) since childhood John has been a cripple

The NP or clause which would follow *since* may be anaphorically omitted if it was stated earlier in the sentence. For instance, a sentence-final *(ever) since the war* or *(ever) since he was injured in the war* may be reduced to just *ever since* in:

> Ivan was injured in the war and has had post-traumatic stress
>   disorder ever since

Ever is usually included before *since* when the preposition is divested of its following NP, as here. When it is referring to something already mentioned, as in the sentence just given, a full *since* constituent or the reduced form *ever since* is often placed clause initially:

> Ivan was injured in the war and ever since has had post-
>   traumatic stress disorder

There are two other constructions in which *since* may feature. In one of them a copula clause specifies a time span commencing with the event described by the NP following *since*. For example:

> It is five years since Richard set out on his pilgrimage
> It is more than a month since I saw you last

In the other construction, the main clause refers not to an extended activity/state, but to one or more separate events. For example:

> It was the most overwhelming electoral victory since 1933
> I've only seen Fiona three times since she got married

Note that *since* may not be modified by *ever* in the last four sentences. Nor can it be if negation is involved, in view of the fact that there is then no continuous state (just the lack of one). We can compare:

> He has been ill (ever) since Easter
> He hasn't been ill (*ever) since Easter

14.1b 'Consequence' sense of conjunction *since*

A quite different meaning attaches to *since* when it is used as a true conjunction, linking two clauses. First, some examples (note that the *since* clause generally comes first, although in some cases the order of clauses may be reversed).

> Since Mr Moggs owns the house, we had to ask his permission to
>   paint the kitchen
> Since Hannah is so clever, she should be able to solve the equation

Since one can be loyal to America and hate Trump, one can be
  fond of Russia while loathing Putin

Since Helen wouldn't say how much she paid, we had to make an
  educated guess

The semantic profile goes as follows. What is stated in the second clause is a consequence of what is stated in the first clause, which is introduced by *since*. Typically, the second clause includes a modality, as shown here by *have to*, *should*, and *can*.

It is possible to construct a sentence which is ambiguous, with *since* being assigned either a temporal or a consequence interpretation:

<blockquote>
Since she ate raw fish for breakfast, Mary has been feeling unwell
</blockquote>

TEMPORAL: from the time when she ate the raw fish, Mary has been feeling unwell

CONSEQUENCE: as a consequence of eating the raw fish, Mary became unwell

If *ever* were added before *since*, only the temporal meaning would be possible.

A constituent marked by *since* in its temporal sense typically comes at the end of the main clause. Such a temporal item is far more frequent than a clause introduced by *since* in its consequence sense, which is typically placed at the beginning of the sentence. If the order of clauses were reversed in the example just quoted—*Mary has been feeling unwell since she ate raw fish for breakfast*—this would likely to be accorded just the temporal meaning.

14.1c 'Reason' sense of conjunction because and preposition because-of

Noun *cause* was borrowed from Old French into Middle English during the thirteenth century; soon after, the phrase *by cause* developed into conjunction *because* /bɪˈkɔz/. Extending from section 5.2l, we can illustrate some examples of its use:

Adrian died young because he had lived a dissolute life

Joseph was executed because he had killed three people

I blew up the storehouse because the boss told me to

John was not allowed to vote because he was too young

Here the second clause, introduced with *because*, provides the reason for what was stated in the first clause. (The *because* clause may sometimes come first if it involves a general statement; for example: *Because he was too young, John was not allowed to vote*.)

The 'consequence' sense of *since* and the 'reason' sense of *because* are a little similar; they could be regarded as different aspects of 'cause'. We can construct a frame in which either may be used, but the cause-and-effect schemes are different:

> I cried because I was unhappy
>
>> (the reason that I cried was that I was unhappy)
>
> Since I was unhappy I cried
>
>> (I was unhappy and as a consequence of this I cried)

In fact, for only a small proportion of sentences with *since* in its 'consequence' sense could *because* be used instead. The same applies in the opposite direction.

Because is a conjunction and is followed by a clause describing an activity or a state. The activity/state could be expressed by an abstract noun, rather than a full clause, and then conjunction *because* adds *of* to become the phrasal preposition *because-of* /bɪˈkɔzəv=/. (This dates back to the fourteenth century.) We can compare (there is another example in section 5.2l):

> Justine hated her cousin because he lied
>
> Justine hated her cousin because-of his lies
>
> Cyril resigned because he couldn't stand the pressure
>
> Cyril resigned because-of the pressure
>
> John was not allowed to vote because he was too young
>
> John was not allowed to vote because-of his age

Both *because* and *because-of* may be modified by either *just* or *simply*, which emphasise that 'this really was the reason', as in:

> Mr Squiggs sacked Dick (just/simply) because he was always rude to everyone
>
> Mr Squiggs sacked Dick (just/simply) because-of his perpetual rudeness

It is instructive to compare the uses and meanings of *since* and *because*:

since + NP,   TEMPORAL
       clause

since + clause CONSE-   ← CAUSE → REASON *because*   + clause
                 QUENCE   REASON *because-of* + NP

It is relevant to add that the temporal sense of *since* is far more frequent than the consequence sense, and that conjunction *because* is much commoner than preposition *because-of*. (See also section 15.2e.)

Section 15.5 mentions a recent development of the preposition involving *because*.

Preposition *for* has carried forward a 'reason' sense from Old English, as in:

> I hid in the attic for I was mightily afraid of my cruel stepfather

This meaning of *for* has a low frequency today, being used more in the written than in the spoken mode, and sounding rather high-flown. It appears to convey a similar sense to *because*, indicating 'reason'. (There is another example in section 5.3j-2.)

14.2 *Until/till, up-until/up-till*

Preposition *til* entered Old English from Old Scandinavian, and has given rise to modern *till* /til/. In early Middle English this was combined with Old Norse *und* 'up to' to create *until* /ən'til/. In the present-day language, *till* and *until* carry the same meaning and are interchangeable. The only tendency is for the form *until* to be preferred as the first word in a sentence.

If a clause describing some activity or state includes a peripheral constituent *until/till X*—where X is an NP or a clause—this indicates that a continuing activity/state finished at X Time or at X Happening. For example:

> Every day, Lucy works till midnight
> Martha continued to write poems until her death/she died

Common phrases with *until/till* include: *until/till now, until/till recently, until/till late,* and *until/till later.*

Some *until/till* sentences may optionally include a *from* phrase which specifies the starting point of the state/activity, as in:

Every day, Lucy works from eleven a.m. till midnight

For others the implicit starting point is the present time, 'from now':

It will be two years until we see Johnny again
Be quiet till I tell you to speak

For the following sentence, it is assumed that the starting time was when Hannah commenced her run:

Hannah ran until she was out of breath

We saw that a sentence with *since* typically includes the auxiliary verb *have (... en)*; this describes an activity/state which commenced in the past and is still happening now. *Until/till* X states that the activity finished at the time described by X and is thus incompatible with the use of *have (...-en)*. The interesting consequence is that we cannot have a *since* constituent and an *until/till* constituent in the same sentence; see section 14.6d. *Until* specifies the finishing point, and there may be optional statement of a starting point, marked by *from*:

Martin worked at the farm (from March) till September

Since specifies a starting point but there can be no finishing point stated since the implication is that the state/activity extends to the present (and beyond):

Martin has worked at the farm since March

There is a fairly rare complex preposition *up-until/up-till* which is sometimes used in place of plain *until/till*:

The tribespeople continued to be enslaved up-until 1850
Martha continued to write poems up-until her death/she died

This adds the 'completion' sense of *up* (section 10.1d) to the meaning of *until/till*. *Up-until/up-till* X emphasise that the activity was both finished and completed by the time referred to by X. The complex preposition is used with past tense, and is unlikely to be found in a sentence referring to the future, such as *It will be two years until we see Johnny again* and *Be quiet until I tell you to speak*.

Until/till has a secondary sense, referring to place rather than to time:

He read the book until he reached the end

We drove on till we arrived at the mine

We didn't stop until we ran out of petrol

In fact, sentences such as these do indirectly refer to time: The last one is, more fully: *We didn't stop until the time at which we ran out of petrol*, and so on. (Note that *up-until/up-till* could not be used in such 'place' statements.)

An *until/till* constituent generally comes after the main clause. However, it may be placed in focus and then precedes the main clause—which is generally in past tense—and is in a different intonation group from it (shown in writing by a comma). For example:

(Up-)until her death/she died, Martha continued to write poems

(Up-)till the half-time whistle blew, our team were playing well

A rather different use of a constituent *until/till X* is when the main clause is in the negative. The meaning is that the positive realisation of the main clause only eventuates once the time reaches *X*. For example:

You can't drive until you've passed the test

Until his mother died, Alan didn't dare get married

We don't open till ten o'clock

Until more is known of the plan, I can't offer an opinion

We will never succeed until the system is changed

Until you learn to behave, you will get no money from me

For most of these sentences the *until/till* constituent may be placed finally or—with intonation break—initially. However, only final placement is possible if the main clause is a command:

Don't come until tomorrow/I tell you to

A few verbs—including *doubt* and *adjourn*—have an inherently negative meaning, and thus also accord with this scheme:

It is doubtful if a decision can be made until we have the full costings

The hearing is adjourned till the coroner recovers from flu

Note that here also the *until/till* constituent would usually come last.

14.3 *During*

During /'djuəriŋ/, the third preposition dedicated to time, came into English in the fourteenth century, from the present participle of the Old French verb *durer* 'last, endure' (the English verb *endure* is a cognate).

During is followed by an NP (never a clause) which refers either to a period of time or an event which lasts for a period of time. What is described by the main clause takes place within the specified time, either over the whole period or else at one or more points within it. See also section 14.6f.

First, some examples where the NP following *during* states a period of time:

> Sentries guarded the camp during the weekend
>
> There were several snowfalls during the winter
>
> Many people came to withdraw their savings during the hours that the bank was open
>
> Grandpa died during the night

Alternatively, the NP may refer to a Happening which extended over a period of time:

> Trevor kept up an incessant stream of chatter during lunch
>
> Aunt Jemima dozed off during the sermon
>
> During his visit, the Pope will bless the new hospital
>
> President Truman took over during the Second World War

An NP introduced by *during* generally follows the main clause. However, in many cases it could precede it, marked by comma intonation. (The *during* constituent coming first is less felicitous when the main clause describes a discrete Happening, such as *Grandpa died* or *President Truman took over*.)

There is one interesting difference between the three prepositions which have a dedicated temporal meaning. In framing a question, the NP (or clause) following *since* or *until/till* may be replaced by *when*. Thus:

STATEMENT	QUESTION
Jill has worked since noon	Since when has Jill worked?
Jill will work till noon	Till when will Jill work?

However, this does not apply *for during*. Instead, the whole of *during NP* is replaced by *when* in forming a question. For example:

STATEMENT	QUESTION
Prices rose during the 1940s	When did prices rise?
There was peace during the late king's reign	When was there peace?

That is, it is not permissible to say *during what* or *during when*, as one can say *since when* and *until/till when*. (One would have to say something like *during what time*.)

14.4 *After, afterward(s), before, beforehand*

Old English had prepositions *æfter* 'after, along, according to' and *beforan* 'before, in front of'. The latter was formed by prefixing *be-* (see section 6.1) to adverb *foran* 'in front, before'.

In the present-day language they constitute a pairing (see section 1.5), The major member *after* /'ɑːftə/ is significantly—although not vastly—more frequent than the minor member *before* /bi'fɔː/.and has a wider range of senses. Only *after* (of the six dedicated temporal prepositions) enters into phrasal verbs, and it also plays a role in a prepositional verb. And only *after* has a related prefix, deriving both nouns (*after-life*, *after-birth*) and adjectives (*after-school care*). However, unlike all the other pairings identified in section 1.5, when the two members of this pairing are conjoined, it is the minor member which generally comes first—that is, *before and after* (mirroring temporal sequence) is many times more common than *after and before*.

A peripheral phrase *after X* means 'later than the time shown by *X*' and *before X* means 'earlier than that time'. As illustrated at the beginning of this chapter, *X* may be an NP denoting a time (e.g. *midnight*), or an NP (*the examination*) or a clause (*I sat the examination*) describing a Happening.

The meanings of *after* and *before* primarily relate to time, but both also extend to space. Just *after* has more abstract uses, relating to 'wanting' and 'similarity'. As a preliminary to discussing these, it will be useful to examine the grammatical techniques for describing a sequence of Happenings, employing *after* and *before*.

Suppose that Tom went to church (C), and later he went to the pub (P). Using *after*, the clauses describing this sequence of activities could be in either order:

1   After John went to church he went to the pub
2   John went to the pub after he went to church

An alternative is to start by stating the initial activity, keeping *after* for later:

3   John went to church, and after (that/going to church) he went to the pub

In sentence 2 we get 'P after C' and in sentence 3 we get 'C, and after P' (with contrastive intonation). An alternative to 3, leaving no possibility for ambiguity, is to employ *afterwards* (the *and* can then be dispensed with):

4   John went to church, (and) afterwards he went to the pub

Note that the order of clauses in 3 and 4 corresponds to the temporal sequence of the activities.

In Old English, suffix *-weard* 'in the direction of' was added to *æfte*, producing *afterward* /'aːftəwəd/; a final optional *-s* /-z/ was added around 1300. This word has anaphoric function, referring back to something which had happened previously and was described earlier in the discourse:

> Henry was taken to hospital and died soon afterwards
> We saw Noel Coward at the Desert Inn and had dinner with
>   him afterwards

Alternatively, *(soon) afterwards* could be positioned at the beginning of the second clause, following *and*.

Things are slightly different with *before*. One could say:

5   John went to the pub and before that he went to the church

Note that the order of clauses here is opposite to the temporal sequence of the activities. *That* must be included in 5, whereas *that* is optional in 3. The important point is that there is no word *beforeward(s)* parallel to *afterward(s)*.

However, there is *beforehand* /biˈfɔːhand/, which appears to have been created in Middle English in imitation of *avant-main* 'in advance' in

Anglo-Norman (the dialect of Old French spoken by the Norman rulers of England following their invasion of 1066). Its meaning 'in advance' is illustrated in the following pair of sentences:

> He didn't tell us before the meeting what the meeting was about
> He didn't tell us beforehand what the meeting was about

14.4a Temporal sense

After 'later than' and *before* 'earlier than' have similar properties. As shown earlier in the chapter, they can be followed by an NP referring to a time, or an NP or a clause referring to a Happening. A further illustration of this is (see also section 14.6b):

The news came
[after/before
   TIME — NP — noon]
   HAPPENING —
     NP — the end of the party]
     CLAUSE — Sue delivered her speech]

The constituent following *after* or *before* may be anaphorically omitted:

> Mabel got divorced in April and shortly after/before (she got divorced) she re-wrote her will

Alongside *the day after tomorrow* there is *the day before yesterday. After* is typically used to indicate repetition—*day after day, time after time, one after another.*

14.4b Spatial sense

Here *before* has the sense 'in front of' with *after* indicating 'behind' (see section 11.2). For example:

> The president came after/before the prime minister in the procession

The spatial meaning here is allied to the temporal one—if the president were spatially 'before' ('in front of') the prime minister, he would be temporally visible 'before' ('earlier than') the president as the procession passed an observer.

   Before has a wider use in its spatial sense than does *after*. Examples include:

The pilgrim stood before the shrine, dazzled by its glory

Billy Graham spoke before ten thousand people

A large unexplored island lay before the explorer

After may carry the sense 'following', as in:

All the children flocked after the Pied Piper

The shaman went first and the tribesmen followed after, in single file

There is metaphorical extension in:

The task before us is a mighty one

After Nancy, Sebastian is the cleverest in the class

14.4c *Further senses of* after

An NP introduced by *after* may refer to something which is 'wanted'. For example:

Hugh is dead and the police are after the murderer

Sophie has lots of men after her (all wanting her to go out with them)

Mrs Munro was enquiring after (news concerning) Harold's state of health

The dog ran after the postman is likely to combine two senses—the dog is following the postman and at the same time it may be eager to bite him.

Another sense of *after* is 'in a similar (or identical) fashion to'. Instances of this include:

This painting is after Rubens (it is in the style of Rubens)

Our first child was named Victoria after her grandmother

After the continental manner, they kissed on both cheeks

14.4d After *in phrasal verbs*

A few phrasal verbs, all of type V-p-NP include *after* in slot **p**:

following   The dogs <u>made after</u> the rabbit at top speed

The police <u>kept after</u> the bandits until they finally trapped them

wanting   The porter <u>is after</u> a big tip

similarity   George <u>takes after</u> his father, in features and in attitudes

A further phrasal verb does not appear to relate to any of the senses of *after* just outlined. This is *look after*, as in: The *doctors and nurses <u>looked after</u> Aunt Helen very well indeed.*

14.4e Contrasting after *with other prepositions*

There are a few interesting contrasts between *after* and prepositions discussed in earlier chapters.

14.4e-1 *For, about,* and *after*

All three of these prepositions may be used following *ask* or *enquire*:

> We specifically asked for Dr Sells (rather than for any of the other GPs)
>
> We asked after Fred (wondering how he was progressing after the operation)
>
> We asked about Sandra (wondering, in general, how she was getting on)

In the first sentence *for* is used in its 'action directed towards a goal' sense (section 5.3c-3). In the second *after* has the 'wanting' sense. And the final one, using *about*, simply reflects general concern (see section 12.3c).

14.4e-2 *For* and *after*

Hanker requires a preposition; that is, it only occurs as part of a prepositional verb. The unusual feature is that either of two prepositions may be employed—*for* or *after*. There is a difference in meaning, albeit slight. *Hanker for* may relate to something which is achievable but unlikely (the 'mental aspiration' sense of *for*, section 5.3c-6) whereas *hanker after* (the 'wanting' sense of *after*) is more likely to relate to the unattainable. For example:

> Theodore hankered for a bigger house and a newer car
>
> Mavis hankered after all that is forbidden

The verbs *yearn*, *hunger*, and *lust* may also be followed by *for* or *after*, in similar fashion.

14.4e-3 *Behind* and *after*

Behind is essentially a spatial preposition but has a secondary sense relating to time. The reverse applies for *after*. Their primary senses take priority in:

> Please shut the door after you!
> Please shut the door behind you!

The *after* sentence connotes time—make shutting the door your next action once you go through it. In contrast, the *behind* sentence refers to space—place the door in the door frame once you have placed yourself beyond the door frame.

* * *

Temporal prepositions *until/till* and *after* may combine. *Joe stayed (on) after dinner* indicates that he was there later than the end of the meal. Then *Joe stayed until after dinner* states that the finishing point of the activity was later than the completion of the meal.

14.5 *Past*

Middle English borrowed the verb *pass* from Old French in the thirteenth century. Within a few years temporal preposition *past* /past/ developed out of the past participle of the verb.

The contrast of meaning with *after* can be illustrated by:

> Look at the clock, it's after your bedtime
> Look at the clock, it's past your bedtime

The first sentence, with *after*, simply identifies a point in time, one which is later than the addressee's regular bedtime. In contrast, preposition *past* (in accordance with its etymology) implies movement through time—the time shown on the clock has advanced to be later than the bedtime and is getting later and later still. (See also section 14.6b.)

Other sentences which indicate progression beyond a point of reference include:

> Jean is past her prime
> This cheese is past its use-by date

The time is half past seven

After would not be appropriate in any of these. Nor in:

Tom is past sixty (and moving towards seventy)

It is instructive to compare this with:

Tom is over sixty (and thus qualifies for free travel on public transport)

This is the 'on the far side of' sense of *over* (section 11.1a-3) and identifies Tom as being in the 'older than sixty' bracket. In contrast, using *past sixty* focuses on the fact that Tom's age is moving along.

There are just a few extensions from the basic temporal sense:

Mother is past caring (she has had to undergo so many indignities today, that she has moved beyond the point at which she would protest at any other indignity)

This car is past it (it has moved beyond the stage at which it could be repaired)

Preposition *past* extends into the spatial zone, but still with temporal underpinnings. Consider:

We ran past the church

The post office is just past the church

A spate of running takes time and the church was reached within this time span. Similarly, if one were walking, the time at which one reached the post office would be later than one's time at the church.

The following example provides a non-temporal spatial use:

He looked past the church at the hills

There is just a smidgen of extended meaning for the preposition *past*:

I wouldn't put it past Jules to try a trick like that on us

* * *

So far in this chapter we have surveyed the six prepositions with a specifically temporal orientation. Previous chapters dealt with relational and spatial prepositions, more than two dozen of which have a secondary temporal sense. It is now time to pull everything together and present the overall scheme of how time is described in English.

14.6 The mechanisms of time description

There is an intricate web of principles determining how prepositions are employed to describe temporal relations in English.

Time descriptions are in terms of the following items:

- **Time Label**: NP, e.g. *six o'clock, Monday afternoon, Christmas day, last month, 1945, the year the war ended, the anniversary of her husband's death, next year, yesterday, the moment you arrived.*
- **Unit of Time**: Noun, e.g. *second, minute, hour, day, month, year, century, weekend, lifetime, generation.*
- **Happening** (may only be used with *since, until/till, after,* and *before*): NP or clause, e.g. *he drove into a tree, the shareholders meet, Sue delivered her speech, Meg's father died.*
- **Event**: NP, e.g. *the accident, the meeting, the party, the debate, lunch.*

Note that Event is essentially a subtype of Happening (that is, every Event is a Happening).

According to the context, some words may have several functions, for example, *the debate*

- is treated as a Time Label (that is, as a unit, with no regard for its internal composition) in *Don was at the debate.*
- is treated as an Event (having a duration) in *Don slept through the debate.*

As another example, *night*

- is treated as a Time Label in *It's now eight o'clock at night in New York.*
- is treated as an Event in *There was a loud bang in the night.*

14.6a Time designation

This relates to a Time Label. Basically, *at* is used for an isolated point of time (*at noon, at the minute you arrived*; see section 7.1b), *in* for a point which is included within a time span (*in the afternoon, in the week just past*; section 8.1b), and **on** for anything which relates to 'day' (*on your birthday, on the sixteenth of June, on payday, on Monday afternoon*; section 9.1g). These varieties of time specification may be used in countless combinations, such as:

> Leo died at six o'clock in the morning on Thursday
>
> Theo died on Christmas Day in a windy winter at the end of the last century
>
> Cleo died in her sleep at dawn on the anniversary of her husband's death
>
> (an anniversary is always a day)

It is a fascinating point of English grammar that 'day' is accorded this special status. The reason is surely because 'day' is a natural unit of time, which every person is aware of. Whether 'day' is held to extend from midnight to midnight, or from dawn to dusk, or from dusk to dusk is a technicality. Each speaker of English is aware that 'today' is a different day from 'yesterday' and from 'tomorrow'. Hence, 'day' is accorded a special preposition, *on* (rather than *at* or *in*).

In contrast, 'second', 'minute', 'hour', and 'week' are artificial units. (We can add to these 'fortnight', an abbreviation from 'fourteen nights', which has wide currency in Britain and Australia but is unknown in the USA.) 'Month' could be a natural unit but isn't since convention recognises twelve 'calendar months' in the year, whereas there are in fact thirteen 'lunar months', which is the natural unit. 'Year' actually is the second natural unit, but it is of lesser immediacy than 'day'.

The use of the three prepositions *at*, *on*, and *in* is nicely contrasted in:

> The treaty will be signed at an hour on a day in a month to be specified

On is also used in several set phrases which relate to the 'connection' sense of the preposition, including *on time* and *on schedule*. Another use is in: *The clock strikes on the hour and on the half-hour*; this describes the minute hand coming into connection with numerals 12 and 6 on the face of the clock.

Further temporal senses of *in* are discussed in sections 14.6c and 14.6e.

Preposition **towards** (see section 7.3b) may be followed by an NP referring to a Time Label and has the meaning 'approaching', as in:

> The forecast is for rain towards the end of the week

14.6b Relative time

The relative chronology of two Happenings is shown by ***after*** or ***before*** (see section 14.4). As described earlier, these two prepositions may be followed by a clause or an NP.

In principle a sequence of Happenings could be described either as *X after Y* or as *Y before X*. This is only sometimes possible when X and Y appear to be unconnected. For example:

> Tom and Thea got married in Spain after the volcano erupted in Java
>
> The volcano erupted in Java before Tom and Thea got married in Spain

However a construction which employs *after* or *before* normally does involve a connection between the two Happenings. On hearing either of the last two examples, one might guess that Tom and Thea had been planning to spend their honeymoon on Java, or that there was some other link between the Happenings.

Typically, there is a relation of 'consequence' between the two Happenings such that *X before Y* could not be rephrased as *Y after X*, or vice versa. For example, this would scarcely be possible for:

> Meg inherited her father's business after he died
>
> The king resigned before the parliament could vote to dismiss him

An *after* or *before* constituent may often either follow or precede the main clause. *After Y, X* is particularly common since here the order of clauses reflects the order of the Happenings referred to. For example:

> After her father died, Meg inherited his business

Preposition ***with*** (see section 6.2b-8) has a minor use which combines the senses 'following' and 'consequence'. Unlike *after*, *with* may only be followed by an NP referring to an Event, not by a clause. For example, the last sentence can be slightly recast, while retaining essentially the same meaning:

> With her father's death, Meg inherited his business

With has an entirely temporal sense (with no 'consequence') in *Meg usually gets up with the sun*.

There are two prepositions which can contrast with *after* when it is used with a Time Label—**past** (section 14.5) and **beyond** (section 11.3a). For example:

391

Stephen worked after midnight

Stephen worked past midnight

Stephen worked beyond midnight

The sentence with *after* states that the time at which Stephen worked was later than midnight; he may or may not have worked earlier than midnight. Preposition *past* carries a sense of movement: midnight was a time through which Stephen passed as he worked (he may have only worked a short time longer). When one hears 'X is beyond Y' it is understood that X is a long way on the far side of Y; *Stephen worked beyond midnight* implies that he started before midnight and worked on far into the night.

The 'near to, not quite reaching' sense of **by** (section 6.1a) has an application to time, meaning 'earlier than', similar to *before*. However, there is a difference. We can compare:

You must be home before ten o'clock

You must be home by ten o'clock

The first sentence, with *before*, is in the nature of a general directive, such as might be placed on the wall of a dormitory. In contrast, the sentence with *by* is a specific instruction to someone who has often stayed out late in the past.

There are rather specialised expressions of relative time involving **behind** 'later than expected' and **ahead-of** 'earlier than expected' (section 11.2), illustrated in:

The building work is behind/ahead-of schedule

Damian's ideas are behind the times/ahead-of his time

As mentioned in section 11.2, adverbs **forward** and **back** can indicate temporal direction:

Ken looked forward to a lazy retirement

Jill looked back on an unhappy childhood

If someone makes a new resolution, the archaic-sounding adverb **forth** 'emanating from a source' (section 11.2d) can be used with a temporal meaning:

From that moment forth, Peter never took another drop of
    alcohol and lived a happy life

Complex preposition **up-to** (section 10.2a) can be used to indicate a temporal limit:

> Bjorn practises up-to six hours a day to keep in form

Different prepositions may be employed for telling the time. Whereas in British English one would say *ten to nine* and *twenty past nine,* Americans may say either *ten of nine* (with an archaic sense of *of*) or *ten till nine,* and *twenty after nine.* This is a bit of a mix. *After* and *past* mark relative time while *to* and *till* generally indicate the finishing point of a span of time.

14.6c Deferred time

Preposition **in** has different temporal meanings depending on the nature of the NP which follows it. Thus:

1   The election will be held in the middle of this month
2   The election will be held in six months (time)

In sentence 1 *in* is followed by an NP which is a Time Label (*in the middle of the month*), and *in* has its regular meaning of 'inclusion'. The NP in sentence 2 consists of a noun referring to a Unit of Time (*month*), modified by number *six,* and the meaning is totally different—the election will be held once six months have elapsed. (The word *time* may be included at the end of 2, or it could be omitted.)

The idea of deferred time can also be expressed, albeit in a slightly different way, through preposition **off,** at the end of its NP (section 9.2) or adverb **away** (section 13.3a):

> The election is six months off
>> (removed from the present)

> The election is six months away
>> (distance from the present)

In each case the head of the NP must be the name of a Unit of Time. We could have: *My retirement is in twenty-three years, The announcement of the winner is thirty-five minutes off,* and *The celebration is still five weeks away.*

Another technique for indicating deferred time is to use preposition **for** (see section 5.3f) with a negative main clause, as in:

They won't be voting for six months (yet)

Again, the head of the NP following *for* must be a Unit of Time. The final *yet* is optional.

14.6d A time span

Prepositions **to** (section 7.2) and **from** (section 7.4) mark starting point and finishing point respectively of a journey over land; for instance, *Julia walked from Kidlington to Oxford*. The same two prepositions do duty for indicating, in a straightforward manner, the starting point and finishing point for a span of time:

> Angela kept working from dawn to dusk
> Visiting hours are from two to three in the afternoon and from seven to eight in the evening

From and *to* may only be followed by an NP, here a Time Label. English also has more sophisticated means of describing a time span— with prepositions *since* and *until/till*, which may be followed by a clause describing a Happening. Briefly recapitulating from section 14.1, the NP or clause following **since** shows the starting point of a time span. The finishing point, which is not explicitly stated, is the moment of speaking:

> Since the theatre burnt down, John has been out of work
> I've been writing this same book since 1997

The activity (or lack thereof) which is referred to by the main clause may be continuous, as in the last two examples, or sporadic, as in:

> Margaret has been subject to fits of depression since her mother died

If one heard *Fred has been a member of the union since 1990*, this would imply that he has been a member continuously from 1990 to the present day. If, however, he had joined, resigned, joined again, resigned once more, and joined for a third time, then a qualification, such as, *off and on*, would need to be added in order for *since* to be used:

> Fred has been a member of the union, off and on, since 1990

The NP or clause following **until/till** describes the finishing point of a time span, so that this preposition is in a way complementary to *since*.

However, *since* and *unit/till* cannot be used in the same sentence; see the discussion in section 14.2. In most instances of use for *until/till* there is no statement of the starting point. It may be understood to be 'from now', as in:

> You won't be able to see the doctor till he returns from interstate
>
> Please keep working until five clock!

But in many instances the starting point is implicit—the time at which the activity described by the main clause commenced:

> Gently heat the soup until it simmers!
>
> The car kept breaking down till eventually it just gave up the ghost entirely

As shown in the last two sentences, the activity described by the main clause may be continuous or sporadic.

However, a starting point may be stated, marked by *from*:

> Xavier was talking from the moment he arrived until he departed

A finishing point may be marked by *to* or by *until/till*. It is worth noting that *until/till* can be used with or without an accompanying *from* phrase but that *to* requires one. We can say *He worked from eleven o'clock to noon*, or just *He worked from eleven o'clock* but not **He worked to noon*. It has to be *He worked till noon*.

Using just *from NP* and *to NP* is a matter-of-fact way of describing a span of time; this was illustrated in the first two examples of this section. In contrast, *until/till X* attaches special significance to the fact that the activity described by the main clause did extend to the time described by X.

Compare the following sentences:

> It rained from Monday to Saturday
>
> It rained from Monday until Saturday

It would be appropriate to say the first sentence during the wet seasons in the tropics, where six days of continuous rain is a regular occurrence. The second sentence, with *until*, might be said in a place which generally gets little rain; the fact that the downfall continued for so long is noteworthy, with *until* marking the surprising fact that the finishing point was not until Saturday.

14.6e Composition of a time span

The basic meaning of preposition *in* is 'enclosure' (see section 8.1) and this can apply equally to space (*in the kitchen*) or to time (*in the morning*).

If something happens at a point of time which is included in a time span, then *in* will be appropriate. Note that it must be followed by an NP (never a clause), referring to a Time Label or an Event. Examples include:

in the afternoon	in the past	in the next half-hour	in my lifetime
in the war	in the lecture	in the middle of lunch	in his sleep

Preposition **between** (section 12.1c) situates something in the space separating two objects; for example, *Ted stood between the oak tree and the elm tree.* And it identifies a time in the span separating two Time Labels. For example:

The fire started sometime between midnight and 2 a.m.

Between is also used to indicate the length of a time span within which either a time or an age lies:

The cottage will take between three and four months to build

Based on Sidney's medical history, his life expectation is
between 85 and 90 years

That is, to complete the cottage will require a time that is more than three and less than four months. And Sidney is expected to live to an age somewhere in the span from 85 to 90 years.

Prepositions **within** and **inside(-of)** indicate that some activity is completed in less than a given time span (section 8.3a):

The messenger should return within/inside(-of) thirty minutes

This means that the messenger is expected to return before thirty minutes is up. *Within* and *inside(-of)* have similar meanings. However it does seem that *within* is preferred for long time spans; for example, *We won't see world peace within my lifetime.*

(We can recall, from section 14.6c, that *The messenger should return in 30 minutes* has a quite different meaning—that the return will be after, not before, thirty minutes is up.)

14.6f A period of time

An Event is something which takes place over a period of time, and may not have a specifically stated starting point nor finishing point; for example: *the sermon, dinner, the war, the accident, the night*. When a main clause is followed by preposition ***during*** or ***throughout***, plus an NP referring to an Event, this states that what is described by the main clause takes place within the period of the Event. For example:

> Bill laughed during the performance
> Bill laughed throughout the performance

> It rained during the night
> It rained throughout the night

Throughout indicates that the activity was continuous: Bill's chuckles could be heard from beginning to end of the performance; and the rain did not let up once. *During* could convey the same meaning, or it could be used when the activity was only sporadic: Bill laughed several times, but not constantly; and there were several short sharp showers with periods of calm between them.

If there is a single incident within a period of time then only *during* can be used:

> Grandfather died during the night

During, which was discussed in section 14.3, is a dedicated temporal preposition. There is an account in sections 11.4c and 11.4d of ***through*** and *throughout* which have a primarily spatial meaning 'moving from one extremity to the other of a three-dimensional space'; both show a secondary sense referring to time. *Through* could have been employed in the sentences just quoted but *throughout* is more felicitous, emphasising 'in every part of'. (Another example of the contrast between temporal uses of *through* and *throughout* given in section 11.4d.)

There is an interesting contrast between *during* and the temporal use of *at* in:

> Jim Miller works as a lawyer during the week and as
>   a disc-jockey at the weekend

The longer period, *the week*, is here treated as an Event and takes *during*, whereas *the weekend* is regarded as a Time Label and is accorded preposition *at*.

Three other prepositions have limited use for referring to a period of time. They are illustrated in:

Over the years, Bill has made many generous donations

Across a lifetime of devotion, Jill has made many sacrifices

James was working round the clock to finish the project

Over (section 11.1a-1, and see section 11.4c-7b) is here employing its sense 'extends from one side to the other'. The basic sense of *across* (section 11.4b) is 'on a level path, from one extremity to the other'. *(A)round* describes moving in a circle (section 12.2) and may refer to time with a suitable NP; another example is: *We plant manioc all round the year.*

There are three prepositions which may follow—rather than precede—their NP (see section 2.7, and discussions of individual prepositions); these are *through*, *over*, and *(a)round*; this positioning emphasises that the activity takes place over the whole of the period specified. For example, *Hector slept the lecture through.*

Preposition *down* (section 10.3) refers to a 'lower position' which naturally extends to 'from one time period to later ones'. Thus:

Down untold generations, the Dukes of Bramcote have looked after their tenants well

This diamond necklace has been handed down from mother to daughter for generations

There is also one sense of preposition *for* which deals with a period of time (see section 5.3f), as in:

Felix works (for) four hours each day

The *for* may be omitted when the period of time is significantly lengthy (section 5.3f).

* * *

The final chapter looks at how prepositions have been—and are being—treated. They may be enjoined to behave in unnatural ways. They may be mistreated by foreign learners. In all aspects of language, there is dialectal variation but this only applies in minor ways for prepositions. And the matrix of a language is in a perpetual flux. How does, and might, this affect prepositions?

15

Do it your way

Language is a human attribute. It is in some ways like a human organism—it lives, fulfils its obligations, responds to new circumstances, is ready to deal with every sort of demand made upon it.

The nature and organisation of a language is determined by the language itself and by its community of users. Each person speaks their language in an entirely natural manner. They seldom think of what they're doing when they are speaking, just as most times they don't when they wash themselves or travel to work.

Language is basically a spoken medium. It is the defining feature of mankind, of *Homo sapiens*, as it evolved 100,000 years or so in the past. The artefact of writing was devised much more recently: perhaps 5,000 years ago in the Middle East and in China, and only within living memory in many communities. Writing is always an accessory. In every place, more time is devoted to speaking and listening than to reading and writing.

English Prepositions: Their Meanings and Uses. R. M. W. Dixon. Oxford University Press (2021). © R. M. W. Dixon.
DOI: 10.1093/oso/9780198868682.003.0015

Spoken language is hard to control. Not so writing. A nation may legislate to change the orthography, often to reflect a shifting political attitude. In 1928 Turkey was moving away from Islam and voted to replace the Arabic script with a Roman one. Kazakh had been written with an Arabic script for about a thousand years until, in 1929, the Soviet Union decreed that all its minority languages should use the Roman alphabet. Ten years later policies had changed and a Cyrillic alphabet was mandated. Now, with Kazakhstan having become an independent state, they are choosing to return to a Roman-type script.

Words may be targeted, with a push to remove loans which came from an unwelcome source and replace them with native forms. Together with its script reform, Turkish expunged loans from Arabic and Persian (but was content to retain those from French). In France there is an Academy which tries to control the vocabulary: thou shalt not use *weekend*, *email*, *software*, and many more. But most people pay little attention.

Some people do ruminate on how a language is structured. They may suggest changing bits of the grammar, to make it 'neater', 'more logical', perhaps 'more graceful'. There have been a few examples of such assaults upon English over the past few centuries.

Suppose that you had such a reform agenda. You might survey English to consider which parts of the grammar appeared to you to be rather unkempt, and could be tidied up to improve matters. You might single out three topics: word order, suffixal homonymy, and preposition placement.

(a) Word order. To a large extent, the words making up a sentence in English occur in a fixed order. For example:

[The new chef] [has cooked] [a chocolate cake]

The subject phrase, *the new chef* precedes the verb phrase, *has cooked*, and the object phrase, *a chocolate cake* follows it. Also, the words within each phrase occur in a fixed order.

However, the placement of some sentential adverbs is more fluid. Consider *now*, for instance. It can be placed in any of three positions:

- initially

  Now the new chef has cooked a chocolate cake

- finally

  The new chef has cooked a chocolate cake now

- after the first word of the verb phrase:

  The new chef has now cooked a chocolate cake

Isn't this untidy? Why don't we enforce a rule that a sentential adverb like *now* (or *obviously*, or *unexpectedly*, or quite a few more) must be placed after the first word of the verb phrase (or immediately before the verb phrase if it consists of a single word. For example, *The new chef now ate the chocolate cake*)?

This would move English further towards having a fixed word order. It would make the language simpler.

(b) Suffixal homonymy. Three important suffixes have exactly the same form in present-day English. The form written as *-s* (or *-es*) is used (i) for plural number on nouns (*doctor-s*); (ii) to mark a noun or NP as a possessor (*John-'s*, *[the tall doctor]-'s*); and (iii) on a verb in present tense when the subject is 3rd person singular (*[the doctor] know-s*).

The three suffixes have exactly the same pronunciation: /-iz/ after a sibilant (as in *horse-s* /hɔːs-iz/), /-s/ after a voiceless consonant (*cat-s* /kat-s/) and /-z/ elsewhere (*dog-s* /dɔg-z/, *cow-s* /kau-z/).

Having three suffixes with the same form but different meanings can be confusing. Suppose that you heard someone say:

1   /ðə=ˈmʌŋks kuk ˈfiʃiz/   (The monks cook fishes)

There are two instances of *-s*, each of which could have any of the three meanings. Both *cook* and *fish* do double duty as verb and as noun. Sentence 1 could be understood in any of three ways:

2   [The   monks]   [cook]   [fishes]
     ARTICLE   NOUN-PLURAL   VERB   NOUN-PLURAL

  (the monks are cooking fishes)

3   [The   monk's   cook]   [fishes]
     ARTICLE   NOUN-POSSESSOR   NOUN   VERB-3sg. PRESENT

  (the cook belonging to the monk is catching fishes)

4   [The   monks'   cook] [fishes]
     ARTICLE   NOUN-PLURAL-POSSESSOR NOUN   VERB-3sg. PRESENT
     (the cook belonging to the monks is catching fishes)

These meanings are distinguished, in writing, by placement of the apostrophe: *monks'* in 4, *monk's* in 3, and no apostrophe in 2. But the apostrophe isn't there in speaking. If you heard someone say /ðə=ˈmʌŋks kuk ˈfiʃiz/, out of context, you couldn't know which of the three meanings was intended.

There is at least a partial solution available. Possession can be marked by suffix *-s* or by preposition *of*. In many contexts one of the alternatives is preferred—*Sally's house* rather than *the house of Sally*, and *the front tyre of the bicycle* rather than *the bicycle's front tyre*. In other contexts either the *-'s* or the *of* construction is equally acceptable: *the table's leg* or *the leg of the table*. See section 5.2a-7.

What a reformer could do is recommend that possession should be exclusively marked by *of*, never by *-s*. Sentences 2–4 would now all be different:

2   The monks cook fishes
3'   The cook of the monk fishes
4'   The cook of the monks fishes

This reform would reduce ambiguity in the language.

(c) Preposition placement. A preposition marks the meaning and function of a peripheral NP which it precedes (hence the name pre-position). Consider:

1   [Michael brought an apple] [for the teacher]

Michael brought an apple provides the core of the sentence, with the peripheral NP, *for the teacher*, being an optional extra.

As described in section 2.2, there are a number of grammatical operations which can affect the placement of prepositions. Suppose that you wanted to know which person the apple was intended for. *The teacher* is replaced by *who*, which is moved to the beginning of the sentence. The interesting feature is that either (a) *who* leaves behind the preposition *for*, which now remains 'stranded' at the end of the sentence; or (b) *who* brings the preposition with it. Thus:

1 (a)   Who did Michael bring an apple for?
    (b)   For whom did Michael bring an apple?

The same two possibilities apply in relative clause formation. We can begin with two simple sentences:

I saw the white cottage

Jim lives in the white cottage

The second sentence can be embedded within the first as a relative clause. The common argument, *the white cottage*, is replaced by relative pronoun *which* at the beginning of the relative clause. We can have either (a) the preposition *in* is left behind at the end of the sentence, or (b) it moves with *which*:

2 (a) I saw the white cottage which Jim lives in

   (b) I saw the white cottage in which Jim lives

For almost all prepositions the (a) option is fine. The (b) alternative is sometimes alright—as in examples 1 and 2 just given—but is often of dubious acceptability. One of many examples of this is:

3 Sally composed a song about the eclipse

   (a) What did Sally compose a song about?

   (b) *About what did Sally compose a song?

In a prepositional verb, the simple verb plus preposition form a single unit which, in many cases may not be separated. That is, the (b) alternative is often not acceptable. For example:

4 Fred [disposed of] the rubbish

   (a) What did Fred [dispose of]?

   (b) *Of what did Fred dispose?

Phrasal verbs behave in a similar way, with preposition or adverb generally not being moveable away from the verb component:

5 The boss <u>laid off</u> the night shift workers

   (a) Who did the boss <u>lay off</u>?

   (b) *<u>Off</u> who(m) did the boss <u>lay</u>?

A preposition is prototypically followed by an NP. However, there are many circumstances—such as those just illustrated—where a sentence ends with a preposition.

The third option for a reformer is to suggest that 'stranded prepositions' not be allowed—that in every case alternative (b) should be employed in preference to (a).

* * *

Three opportunities have been offered for reform. The first, which could be done, would be to fix the placement of sentential adverbs and thus make the language simpler. The second, which could also be done, would be to mark possession exclusively by *of*, thus reducing ambiguity. The third would be to outlaw stranded prepositions; that is, to always choose the (b) alternative. It is hard to see what could be gained by this—neither simplicity nor any effect on ambiguity. And the vital point is that such a reform would be well nigh impossible, as can be seen from the examples quoted: (3b) is only marginally acceptable, (4b) is not at all acceptable, while (5b) is totally impossible.

But the 'no stranded preposition' proposal was pursued. This is now a story to tell.

15.1 Interfering busybodies

Up until the middle of the seventeenth century, the English people had spoken and written their language in a natural way. Its grammar served all needs. The vocabulary—recently expanded by manifold borrowings from French—was copious and yet eloquent. The plays of William Shakespeare achieved an eminence which has continued to surpass both contemporaries and successors. Ways of expression were spontaneous, untrammelled by stricture or edict.

There was, however, a spectre in the background. The Latin language, although unfamiliar to the populace at large, was revered by the scholarly elite, being held up as the acme of refinement. English and other modern languages were regarded as lesser tongues, lacking in incisiveness and lucidity. The grammar of Latin was to be admired and copied.

Latin does not permit any sentence to end with a preposition. This gave rise to the unfortunate proposal that in English the stranding of prepositions should be discouraged. Poet and essayist John Dryden promulgated this idea around 1670. Having sentences end with a preposition was observed in the works of such notables as Shakespeare and Ben Jonson and identified by Dryden as a 'mistake'. Indeed, Dryden noticed this 'fault' in his own earlier writings. In the first edition, in 1668, of Dryden's much-lauded essay *Of Dramatick Poesie*, there were as many stranded prepositions as in the work of any other writer of that time. They were eliminated from the second edition of his essay, in 1684.

Many were easily dealt with. For example:

1668   I cannot think so contemptibly of the age I live in

1684   I cannot think so contemptibly of the age in which I live

Others demanded a different technique. Consider:

1668   to a much higher degree of perfection than the French poets
can arrive at

The automatic rephrasing *than that at which the French can arrive* is clumsy, and Dryden preferred a rewrite:

1684   to a much higher degree of perfection than the French poets
can reasonably hope to reach

The proscription against isolated prepositions became a crusade. Dryden produced new versions of three of Shakespeare's plays, editing out end-placed prepositions. Many scholars and critics followed suit, so that an antipathy towards prepositions being separated from their NPs pervaded almost everything written about the language. Indeed, it reverberates until today.

The campaign gathered momentum through the eighteenth century. Grammarians warned against stranding, and the best writers strove to minimise it. In this way a criterion evolved—the best stylists used very few stand-alone prepositions; thus, work which followed this habit should be reckoned to be good style.

Robert Lowth, in his 1762 grammar, acknowledged sentence-final prepositions (as in *Horace is an author, whom I am much delighted with*) to be 'an Idiom which our language is strongly inclined to; it prevails in common conversation, and suits very well with the familiar style in writing; but the placing of the Preposition before the Relative is more graceful, as well as more perspicuous; and agrees much better with the solemn and elevated Style'. Dryden's wish to make English more like

Latin had indirectly led to the notion that a conscious avoidance of preposition stranding went hand-in-hand with grace and solemnity.

This view persisted. Goold Brown's 1844 grammar observed that a preposition is often separated from its NP, as in *Whom did he speak to?* 'But it is more dignified, and in general more graceful, to place the preposition before the pronoun' as, "*To whom did he speak?*" '. In *The Queen's English* (1864), Henry Alford acknowledged the prevalence of preposition stranding and advised that it 'is allowable in moderation, but must not be too often resorted to.'

The anguish concerning preposition stranding has gradually abated, but it has by no means disappeared. Sometimes there is no alternative (as with *What did Fred dispose of?*) but, when there is an alternative, pedantic schoolteachers may to this day enjoin their pupils to prefer it.

All of this has been absolutely unnecessary and unwelcome, a distraction from the serious business of using language in its many roles. In Shakespeare's day, prepositions found their place in a sentence quite naturally. Dryden and his clique simply interrupted the smooth operation of the language (a bit like throwing a log across a path, so that traffic has to detour around it), drawing attention to differences from and similarities to Latin, endowing the latter with a self-fulfilling aura of 'gracefulness'.

The current guide to style in the USA, by Strunk and White, suggests pragmatic reasons for where to put a preposition: 'Years ago, students were warned not to end a sentence with a preposition; time, of course, has softened that rigid decree. Not only is the preposition acceptable at the end, sometimes it is more effective in that spot than anywhere else. "A claw hammer, not an ax, was the tool he murdered her with". This is preferable to "A claw hammer, not an ax, was the tool with which he murdered her." Why? Because it sounds more violent, more like murder. A matter of ear.'

Another Latin-based proscription is that against what is oddly called a 'split infinitive'. In Latin grammar the term 'infinitive' was employed to refer to the form of a verb which—unlike the verb form in a main clause—was not marked for the person and number of a subject, and did show tense. This was a nominalisation, which functioned as an indeclinable neuter noun that could be head of an NP. For example *audī-re* 'hear-PRESENT.INFINITIVE'.

There is no corresponding form in English grammar for which the term 'infinitive' would be appropriate. What has happened is that preposition *to* plus the root form of a verb has been labelled 'infinitive', on the basis of translation equivalence from Latin. It is the custom to say that in the sentence *I want to hear that song* the sequence *to hear* is an 'infinitive'. And just as nothing may intrude between verb root and infinitive suffix in Latin (that is, not between verb root *audī-* and infinitive suffix *-re*), some people maintain that nothing should be allowed between *to* and *hear* in the English sentence—the 'infinitive' must not be 'split'. But it is absolutely natural to insert here an adverb such as *really* and to 'split the infinitive': *I want to really hear that song*. (The alternative **I want really to hear that song* is clumsy while **I want to hear really that song* is impossible.)

The avoidance of stranded prepositions is misguided. That concerning 'split infinitives' is simply foolish. Yet there are people who are fiercely insistent upon it.

15.2 Heads in the sand

Moving away from gratuitous pronouncements on how prepositions should be employed, we can now examine the extent to which dictionaries today provide comprehensive information on the meanings of prepositions.

The most common monosyllabic prepositions are on the whole dealt with adequately. However, many dictionaries display a somewhat cavalier attitude towards complex prepositions. These represent subtle semantic contrasts which are often not even acknowledged, let alone investigated.

This can be illustrated by quoting entries from six of the leading dictionaries, four American and two English:

- W3: *Webster's Third New International Dictionary of the English Language Unabridged*. ed. Philip B. Gove. 1961.
- Coll: *Merriam-Webster's Collegiate Dictionary*, 11th ed. ed. Frederick G. Mish. 2003.
- AH: *The American Heritage Dictionary of the English Language*, 3rd ed. ed. Anne H. Soukhanov. 1992.

- RH: *The Random House Dictionary of the English Language Unabridged*, 2nd ed. ed. Stuart B. Flexner. 1987.
- COD: *The Concise Oxford Dictionary of Current English*, 8th ed. ed. R. E. Allen. 1990.
- COB: *Collins Cobuild English Dictionary for Advanced Learners*. ed. John Sinclair. 2001.

15.2a Inside-of

In many contexts either of the prepositions *inside* and *inside-of* may be used. However—as stated in section 8.3—there is a definite tendency to prefer *inside* for motion and *inside-of* for location and time, as in:

Jack went inside the castle

Jack lives inside-of the castle

Jill will return inside-of a week

There is not a hint concerning this in the dictionaries. Three suggest that *inside-of* is colloquial or informal (an opinion with which I would not agree, since *inside-of* is encountered in formal styles) and one says that it is predominantly regional (which is also doubtful).

The entries for *inside of* are:

W3	within
Coll	inside
AH	within, inside
RH	inside, *informal*
COD	inside, *colloquial*
COB	inside, *more usual in American English*

Preposition *outside-of* is treated in similar fashion.

15.2b In-between

Prepositions *between* and *in-between* were discussed in section 12.1c-2.

In-between can be used instead of *between* in several of its spatial, locational, and temporal meanings, but not for the more abstract senses (for example, not in: *Jack and Jill have five cars between them*). We also showed that in some spatial contexts the two prepositions can have different meanings. Repeating an earlier example:

Peter ran between the goalposts

(he ran off or on the football field through the space between the goalposts)

Peter ran in-between the goalposts

(he ran back and forth in the space between the goalposts)

RH has a useful entry for *in between*, recognising two senses, the other five dictionaries simply don't bother. Here are their entries for *in between*:

W3   between

Coll   between

AH   between

COD   \<adverb = between\>

COB   \<no mention\>

15.2c Upon

As shown in section 9.1, *on*, *upon*, and *onto* constitute a triumvirate of prepositions, the meanings of each being shown by contrast with the meanings of the others. All six dictionaries do, of course, have full entries for *on*, and five do so for *onto*. The sixth, COD, says: 'The form *onto* is still not fully accepted in the way that *into* is, although it is in wide use. It is however useful in distinguishing sense as between *we drove on to the beach* (i.e. in that direction) and *we drove onto the beach* (i.e. in contact with it).' (It should be noted that *onto* came into use in the late sixteenth century.)

W3, RH, and COB have full entries for *upon* (which goes back to OE); however, the other three give short shrift to it. Their entries are:

Coll   on

AH   on

COD   on (*Upon* is sometimes more formal and is preferred in *once upon a time* and *upon my word*, and in uses such as *row upon row of seats* and *Christmas is almost upon us*.)

15.2d Off-of

Section 9.2b mentioned that, although *off-of* has been very occasionally used in British English since the mid-fifteenth century, its main use today is in American English. It is likely that its meaning there is not exactly the same as *off*, just as there are differences between *out* and *out-of* and between *inside* and *inside-of*.

I consulted the six dictionaries for help and insight. Their entries for *off of* are as follows:

W3	off
Coll	off. The *of* is often criticized as superfluous, a comment that is irrelevant, because *off of* is an idiom. It is much more common in speech than in edited writing and more common in American than in British.
AH	off. The compound preposition *off of* is generally regarded as informal and is best avoided in formal speech and writing: *He stepped off* (not *off of*) *the platform.*
RH	The phrasal preposition OFF OF is old in English, going back to the 16th century. Although usage guides reject it as redundant, recommending OFF without OF, the phrase is widespread in speech, including that of the educated: *Let's watch as the presidential candidates come off of the rostrum and down into the audience.* OFF OF is rare in edited writing, except to give the flavour of speech.
COD	slang, disputed use = off.
COB	<no mention>

All this tells us is that many people don't approve of *off-of*. However, it is much used in American English. Since I lack intuitions about this dialect, I have relied on looking at corpuses and quizzing American friends. A preliminary hypothesis is that *off-of* may be preferred for the temporal sense (as in *The late start sliced ten minutes off-of the time available for my presentation*). In the present state of knowledge I hesitate to venture further—to suggest, for instance, that *off-of* may be used more for spatial motion or more for location. A linguist whose first dialect is American is needed to investigate this matter. (See also the discussion of 'optional *of*' in section 5.2k.)

15.2e Since

Michael West, in his entry for *since* in *A general service list of English words* (1953: 458), mentions that 66 per cent of its occurrences are temporal. The remaining 34 per cent are described as '= *because*' with a note 'apt to confuse and easily avoided'. Presumably his advice is that *since* ought only to be used with its temporal meaning and for the rest *because* should be preferred.

It was shown in sections 14.1b–c that while conjunctions *since* and *because* have similar 'causal' meanings these are far from identical, that of *since* being described as 'consequence' and that of *because* as 'reason'. There are some contexts in which either *since* or *because* may be used, but many where only one is appropriate. For example:

> Since Fred is so tall, we'll ask him to clean the chandeliers
>
> I do it because I like it

Because could scarcely be used in the first sentence, and *since* would not be appropriate in the second.

The moral is that a learner is unlikely to benefit from the superficial observation that *since*, in its conjunction function, and *because* have similar meanings. There is no substitute for detailed analysis and comparison.

15.3 Variation

A language is not a monolith. There is a core, which is soft and malleable, wrapped around with coatings of distinctions—regional, generational, social, individual. There are no 'laws' for what to say or how to say it, just precedents and conventions.

In this book I have attempted to outline a set of basic principles which explain the meanings and uses of the main prepositions of English, integrating and contrasting them. They form a shifting matrix, responsive to the needs of language users, reflecting the world they serve.

It is important to acknowledge that there is no such thing as a uniquely 'correct' analysis of any linguistic phenomenon. Judgements are necessarily subjective. All one can do is put forward a set of interlocking statements which together provide a comprehensive description and explanation of the phenomenon. There may be alternatives, which are just as effective in a totally different way.

My aim in this book has been to characterise the system of prepositions in present-day English, focusing on the British/Australian variety which I speak and write natively. Most of the prepositions are rooted in spatial or temporal reference and these are taken as their basic senses. Extending out are more abstract meanings and I have grouped these, for each preposition, in terms of a series of senses.

The sense identified for a certain preposition in a particular sentence depends on the meanings of the lexical words involved. Consider two uses of *for*:

> Robin has a reputation for honesty
>
> Hilary has an aptitude for mathematics

These sentences have a similar structure but quite different import. The first falls under the sense of *for* 'reason for the subject having a certain quality' (section 5.3b-3), alongside *Michael is famous for his jokes*. In contrast, the second sentence belongs to the sense of *for* 'ability to achieve a purpose' (section 5.3c-1), together with *Edmund is getting fit for the climb ahead*. Both *reputation* and *aptitude* are abstract nouns but the former relates to an established quality and the latter to an established capability.

Speakers may vary in their choice of preposition. In section 1.1b the following sentences were contrasted:

> Kate thought of a solution to the problem
>
> Mark thought about a solution to the problem

The first sentence uses *of* in its 'knowledge' sense (section 5.2g)—Kate had been exercising her brain to come up with a solution. In the second sentence, Mark was doing something quite different, simply pondering on what a solution might be like, and perhaps how nice it would be to receive the prize offered for the correct solution; here preposition *about* is appropriate (section 12.3).

Language is not like a machine, a matter of pressing buttons. Each speaker makes their own choices and some may be more generous than others. Someone may use the second sentence above intending that the meaning should be that which we have associated with the first, or vice versa. A distinction is missed, sure, but this may be of little consequence for this speaker. The linguistic system provides a network of contrasting meanings; each user can employ as many of them as suits their purpose.

The verb *complain* may be followed by a peripheral NP introduced by either *of* or *about*:

> Aunt Meg complained of ear-ache
>
> Aunt Meg complained about the hospital system

Preposition *of*, in the first sentence, introduces an NP referring to a person's attitude towards a specific issue (see section 5.2f-3). This contrasts with *about*, in the second sentence, whose NP describes a general state of affairs (section 12.3c).

These sentences illustrate canonical meanings of the prepositions, which most speakers will adhere to. However, there is always fluidity— someone may say *Aunt Meg complained about her ear-ache* or *Aunt Meg complained of the hospital system* and still be understood (but perhaps considered a trifle uncouth).

The least common verbs may engender the most fluidity. As discussed in section 14.4e-2, *hanker* requires a following preposition; it may be *for*, relating to something which is achievable, or *after*, which is more likely to relate to the unattainable. For example:

> Sebastian hankered for status and recognition
>
> Elizabeth hankered after a fairer world

Some speakers may confuse these meanings, or just use *for* in all instances or just *after*. The contrast is subtle and not of the highest importance. (Similar comments apply for the verbs *yearn*, *hunger*, and *lust*.)

Nothing is ever static in a language. A preposition may develop new senses and discard old ones. Loss can be a gradual process; a certain sense may drop out of use from the standard dialect but continue on the periphery, in a regional variety.

In days gone by, *on* could be used where we would now employ *of* in its 'dissociation' sense (section 5.2h). An example is in a fifteenth-century version of the Middle English ballad of Sir Eglamour of Artois:

> Sir Eglamowre was...recovryd on hys wounde

This sense of *on* survives just in dialects from the north of England. My Lancashire grandfather (born in 1878) would say:

We'll soon be shut on him

(meaning: we'll soon be rid of him, he will soon be gone)

He was using *shut* in the meaning 'be free from something unwelcome', also now used only in non-standard dialects.

15.3a Across the Atlantic

There are interesting differences in the use of prepositions between Standard British English (BrE) and Standard American English (AmE). The same prepositions have tentacles of meaning spreading out in different directions in the two dialects.

We can begin with explanation of some notable divergences:

BrE   We're having a party at the weekend

AmE   We're having a party on the weekend

In BrE *the weekend* is regarded as a 'point of time' and accorded preposition *at*, whereas in AmE it is treated as a kind of 'day' (after all, a weekend does consist of two days) which requires *on* (see section 14.6a).

BrE   Ian is in the team for cricket

AmE   Jan is on the team for baseball

For BrE the 'part of a group' sense of *in* (section 8.1d) is used while AmE has the 'physical connection' sense of *on* (section 9.1a-1); perhaps abbreviated from: *Jan's name is on the team list for baseball.*

AmE often omits preposition *on* when referring to 'day' (section 14.6a):

BrE   The sale starts on Monday

AmE   The sale starts Monday

BrE   On Saturdays we go to see grandma

AmE   Saturdays we go to see grandma

For some temporal statements the two dialects employ different techniques:

BrE   Harriet works by day and studies by night

AmE   Harriet works days and studies nights

It is often the case that there are two forms, each occurring in both dialects, but with one form being more common in one dialect and the other in the other dialect. Quirk et al. (1985: 681) counted occurrences of *around* and *round* (section 12.2) in the LOB corpus (BrE) and the Brown corpus (AmE):

	BrE	AmE
around	245 = 42%	561 = 88%
round	336 = 58%	74 = 12 %

Among and *amongst* (section 12.1) are also found in both dialects; *among* is in each case the more common but *amongst* is better represented in BrE (Quirk et al. 1985: 680):

	BrE	AmE
among	313 = 87%	370 = 99%
amongst	45 = 13%	4 = 1%

In section 13.2a it was noted that phrasal prepositions *apart-from* and *aside-from* have similar—but not absolutely identical—meanings. *Aside-from* is far commoner than *apart-from* in AmE, with the reverse applying in BrE. There are other examples where both occur in each dialect but the preferences differ; they include:

preferred in BrE	preferred in AmE	
afterwards	afterward	see section 14.4
forwards	forward	see section 11.2e
towards	toward	see section 7.3

One difference between dialects involves description of a time span. An American would say:

The shop will be closed (from) Monday through Thursday

This is absolutely clear. The shop will be closed for four days, including Thursday. BrE does not use *through* with this temporal sense, and its equivalent is:

The shop will be closed from Monday to/until/till Thursday

This is unclear. Some people would take is as meaning that the closure was for three days, with Thursday being the day the shop opened again, while others would understand it to be saying that Thursday was the last day it was shut. It would be sensible for speakers of BrE to imitate their American cousins and adopt *through* as marker of a time span.

As has been mentioned several times (see section 14.6b), the BrE and AmE utilise different prepositions for telling the time:

sample time	BrE	AmE
8.40	twenty to nine	twenty of nine, twenty till nine
9.10	ten past nine	ten after nine

The brief survey has mentioned only a sample of differences between BrE and AmE which relate to prepositions, but it should be sufficient to signal the flavour of the whole.

Section 5.4 surveyed the prepositions used in ministerial titles—*for* in Australia, the UK, and Papua New Guinea, *of* in Canada, South Africa, India, and Nigeria, and a mixture of *for* and *of* in New Zealand. (Titles in the USA are framed in a somewhat different way.)

15.4 Not quite right

Many people across the world have English as a second language (L2) and use it on a regular basis. In fact they may well outnumber native speakers who have English as their first language (L1). These L2 users speak and write a form of the language which is intelligible but which differs from L1 English in a variety of ways. We can briefly survey some of these.

A typical divergence is due to interference from the L1. A Japanese take-away in Australia bears the sign:

   *Call us by 41038 2354

This uses preposition *by* rather than the standard *on*. In Japanese either the dative particle *ni* or the instrumental particle *de* is used with a phone number. *De* is often translated as *by*; for example, *basu de itta* 'I went by bus'. Hence the use of *by* in the take-away sign.

Other divergences by L2 speakers from the L1 norm involve taking two prepositions which are substitutable in some contexts and attempting to generalise on this. For example:

L2 *He died out of cancer

L1 He died from cancer

When *out-of* and *from* are used in their basic senses they can convey the same meaning; for example *He took the box from/out-of the cup-board* (see section 8.2e). But *from* is employed in a quite different sense 'source' (section 7.4b) in *He died from cancer*, and here *out-of* is not an alternative.

A study of the English of Spanish students revealed a symmetrical cross-over:

L2	L1 norm
*The woman saw at the man	The woman saw the man
*The woman looked the man	The woman looked at the man
*She heard to the man	She heard the man
*She listened him	She listened to him

See is here replaced by *see at*, and *look at* by *look*. On the same pattern, *hear* is replaced by *hear to* and *listen to* by *listen*.

There are many examples of a preposition being omitted, so that what was a peripheral NP appears to be reassigned to object function; for instance, **Craig confirmed me the time* when it should be *Craig confirmed the time to me*.

Which type(s) of complement clause a verb takes may be difficult for an L2 speaker to master, as shown by:

L2	L1
*I suggest him to go	I suggest that he should go
*I envisage to complete it soon	I envisage completing it soon
	I envisage that I will complete it soon

The L2 speaker expects *suggest* to take a TO complement clause, as *per-suade* does (*I persuaded him to go*); in fact it is restricted to the THAT variety. In the second example, *envisage* is also expected to take a TO clause, like *plan* (*I plan to complete it soon*); in fact it may only occur with an -ING or a THAT complement clause.

We frequently encounter a non-standard sentence from an L2 speaker which appears to be a blend of two related constructions:

L1	L2 blend
Tomorrow I go to Poland	
Tomorrow I leave for Poland	*Tomorrow I leave to Poland
A woman in her fifties	
A woman of fifty	*A woman of fifties
Don't blame the accident on Sue	
Don't blame Sue (for the accident)	*Don't blame on Sue

Since and *until/till* have rather intricate meanings (see sections 14.1–2). In keeping with this they pose a minefield of difficulty for L2 speakers. One non-standard use of *since* may be explained as a blend:

L1	L2 blend
I started to work on Kalaba in 1935	
I have worked on Kalaba since 1935	*I started to work on Kalaba since 1935

Until is typically used where *by* would be appropriate (see sections 14.6b and 6.1a):

> *I will draft the proposal until around 25th February
>
> *Please send the pdf to us until 7 April

This may in part be due to 'translating' from forms like German *bis* and French *jusqu'à ce que*.

There are many more ways in which L2 speakers rework English grammar—some amusing, a few cute, and all shedding light on how the human brain may grapple with an unfamiliar (or only partly familiar) system.

15.5 Moving forward

In Middle English times, many new prepositions were added to the language. Then things settled down; there has been relatively little change over the past few centuries. However, the world of communication is now evolving in unanticipated ways, with email, social media, and the like. Language is becoming more succinct. What sort of effect might this have on prepositions?

Some prepositions may expand their scope and others proportionately contract theirs. Eventually, a number of the least used prepositions may retreat into the state characterised by lexicographers as 'obsolete' (*forth*, *amid(st)*, and *concerning* might well be among the first to recede). *Apart-from* and *aside-from* have similar meanings and just one of them could be retained (which one would depend on whether AmE or BrE exercised the strongest influence). But the more likely changes are for some of the longer phrasal prepositions and complex prepositions to simply trim themselves down.

A few prepositions have two forms with pretty much the same sense. They relate to the addition, in Middle English times, of *-st* or *-s* to a noun or adjective to form an adverb or preposition (see section 1.10). Nowadays, both long and short forms can function as preposition with little or no difference in meaning; there may just be dialectal preferences.

It was mentioned in section 15.3 that *among* is far more common than *amongst*. In AmE *amongst* accounts for just one per cent of the combined occurrences of the two forms, and in BrE no more than thirteen per cent. The style sheet of Allen & Unwin, the leading Australian publisher, forbids any of the *-st* alternatives: no *amongst*, or *amidst*, or *whilst* (or *unbeknownst*). This may be an example which the whole world will follow.

Similar remarks can apply for *beside/besides*, *toward/towards*, *forward/forwards*, *backward/backwards*, and other forms ending in *-ward(s)*. Having alternative forms is a relic; why not just use the shorter one?

A number of prepositions may optionally include a final *of*, sometimes carrying just a little bit of a meaning difference. As mentioned in sections 8.3 and 15.2a, *inside-of* may be preferred when referring to time (*I'll be back inside-of thirty minutes*) and location (*He sheltered inside-of the church*) while just *inside* would be appropriate for motion (*He ran inside the church*). However, these are only preferences; in daily use both *inside* and *inside-of* may be substituted in virtually every context. Having two forms here is a luxury which could be dispensed with—just use *inside* and forget the *of*. (Similarly for *outside*.)

Preposition *out-of* is sometimes reduced to *out*; it could always be so, with minimal loss. *Off-of* is used, mostly in AmE, as an alternative to *off*; the *of* could just be discarded. Some phrasal prepositions in their current form require a final *of* or *to*, omitting this would shorten them without leading to any confusion: *ahead-of, in-front-of, instead-of, near-to* would become just *ahead, in-front, instead, near.* Adverbs *apart, aside,* and *away* add *from* to form a preposition. The *from* could be dispensed with, so that one form does duty as both preposition and adverb (this already happens with *in, out, on, off, over, behind,* and more).

Such shortenings would suit those social media channels which have a limit on the number of characters in each message. And this may at least partially explain the peculiar development of *because.*

Conjunction *because* and preposition *because-of* (see sections 5.2l and 14.1c) entered English in the fourteenth century. Quite recently both construction types have undergone reduction. First, when a copula clause follows conjunction *because* its copula subject and copula verb may be dropped, leaving just the copula complement. For example:

I need to lie down because   →   I need to lie down because tired
[I am tired]

No work tomorrow because   →   No work tomorrow because
[it is Sunday]   Sunday

Secondly, the preposition *because-of* may omit the *of* and also any modifiers within the following NP, as in:

I can't come [because-of my   →   I can't come because homework
homework]

The ground is wet [because   →   The ground is wet because rain
of the rain]

These reductions from two types of established construction have converged on a single new construction with a main clause followed by *because X*, where *X* is typically a single word (it can be of any word class).

Once established, the new *because* construction was extended; for example:

Of course evolution is true because science

Here *science* summarises something like 'because science tells us so'.

The *because* constriction is colloquial, being used for informal messaging. It can be highly elliptical as in:

Hot cocoa because need

This is shorthand for something like 'I'm drinking hot cocoa because I feel I need it.'

In this novel use *because* could hardly be called a preposition since it is not followed by a full NP: *my homework* becomes *homework*, and *the rain* reduces to just *rain*. It is something quite new, which the language has evolved to help it meet emerging needs.

The most frequent prepositions, *of* and *to*, tend to expand their ranges of use. An unexpected change, just in the colloquial register, is the replacement of verbal auxiliary *have* (in its reduced form *'ve*) by *of*. Thus:

standard orthographic form	I would've done it
phonological form	/'ai 'wʊd=əv 'dʌn=it/
innovated orthographic form	I would of done it

The phonological form is the same for the standard and innovated sentences. Preposition *of*, generally a proclitic /əv=/ to the following word, is here an enclitic /=əv/ to the preceding word, being phonologically identical to *'ve*, /=əv/. (See section 5.2l.)

If there are two ways of indicating some grammatical relation, then reducing these to a single method would be to simplify the language, At the beginning of this chapter it was noted that possession may be realised by preposition *of* or by suffix *-'s*. But the suffix is three-ways homonymous; it can also mark plural on a noun and 3rd person singular subject on a verb in present tense. Ambiguity would be reduced by always using *of* for possession. This could happen naturally; it might make things easier for some varieties of social media. Or a dictatorial ruler might decree it.

It was mentioned in section 15.4 that—across the world—English is being used on a regular basis by many people for whom it is only an L2. The great majority of international conferences are conducted in English, although there may be rather few L1 speakers among the participants (sometimes there are none). English is one of the three working languages of the European Union, yet of the 27 member nations only Ireland and Malta have English as an L1. A leading publisher, in Germany, puts out the majority of its books in English but there is no L1 speaker on the editorial staff; indeed, every message I have seen from this publisher includes a goodly sprinkling of 'errors'.

Over time, the non-standard habits of these hundreds of millions of L2 speakers and writers may have an effect on the language as a whole.

The linguistic practices of the L2 brigade may override what had been considered acceptable by L1 speakers. I have heard so many L2 friends use *suggest* with a TO complement clause (for example, *I suggest you to invite Irene*) that this verb may be added to the roster of verbs taking a TO clause; and there may be many more things like this. *Since* and *till* (the longer *until* may have been lost) are so difficult to master that they may either drop out of use, or else have their meanings simplified.

The possible changes outlined in this section are all rather minor. Surely, as the language adjusts itself to deal with such challenges as the future might bring, it may make significant adjustments. Partly for fun, we can muse on one.

Most prepositions have specific meanings, such that useful contrasts would be lost if they were combined. For instance, *above* and *below* could not without cost be replaced by *over* and *under* (see section 11.1). However, prepositions with the most general meanings are a different matter.

Of the three central spatial prepositions, *to* and *from* refer to motion and in their basic senses are used with a verb of motion, while *at* refers to location and in its basic sense occurs with a verb of rest:

> Boris went from the beach to the hotel
> Brenda stayed at the hotel

There are some languages which have a single preposition that would translate both *at* and *to*. Let us suppose that English should move down the same path, and innovate a combined preposition (replacing both *at* and *to*), which might have the form *ato*. Wouldn't this cause confusion? Very little, as can be seen by examining examples across a range of senses. First, six where the *ato* phrase follows a verb:

He sat ato the table	He walked ato the door
She looked ato him	She listened ato him
Sally swore ato Tom	Sally sang ato Tom

Now some where the *ato* phrase follows an adjective:

He was angry ato me	He was mean ato me
She is experienced ato the work	She is accustomed ato the work

Two pairs with mixed constructions:

He had a try ato driving the ute   He tried ato drive the ute

She is good ato cooking   She is able ato cook well

A pair with *ato* having temporal sense:

The meeting is ato two   The shop is open from nine ato five

For each row, *ato* in the left hand sentence replaces *at*, and *ato* in the right-hand one replaces *to*. In no case does using *ato* in place of *at* or *to* obscure the meaning.

There are just a handful of exceptions where *at* and *to* do contrast:

Jim threw the ball to Tom (for Tom to catch it)

Jim threw the ball at Tom (intending for it to hit Tom)

And *shout at/to, point at/to, get at/to, stick at/to,* all illustrated in section 7.2k-5. These could be dealt with in some other way. And they are a small inconvenience compared to the advantage of having one preposition in place of two. (This would perhaps be welcomed in a future world which valued concision ahead of redundancy.)

* * *

This final chapter has been intended to frame the story. A language is what its everyday body of users makes it. It does not need know-alls criticising where prepositions choose to dally, nor stopping an adverb from slipping in between *to* and a verb. We saw how the compilers of dictionaries tend to be selfishly selective, dealing with familiar prepositions but shying away from the real challenges.

The chapters in this volume have attempted to delineate the canonical meanings and uses for each preposition. However, these are only a guide. Each individual speaker will navigate their way around, coaxing the language to satisfy their whims. This is fine so long as intelligibility is not compromised. There is variation between regions which give character to a dialect. Foreign learners don't quite follow established conventions and the ways in which they deviate can be insightful. Finally, a pinch of speculation was offered, concerning what might conceivably happen next.

Be it as L2 or L1, this is *your* language. Value it. Cherish it. Let its gallery of prepositions tell a story, a story of your choice. Do it your way.

Sources and notes

Sources

As a basis for this study, I assembled a collection of several hundred sentences for each preposition and worked inductively from these. They came from a variety of sources. The compilations by Heaton (1965), Cowie and Mackin (1975), and West (1953) were invaluable. Example sentences in the COBUILD dictionary (Sinclair 2001) and the on-line Oxford English Dictionary were helpful. I also made use of the standard dictionaries, including Random House (Flexner 1987), American Heritage (Soukhanov 1992), Merriam-Webster's Collegiate (Mish 2003), and the finest dictionary of all, that by Samuel Johnson (1755). Various corpus collection were referred to, including the International Computer Archive of Modern English, *ICAME collection of English language corpora* (Bergen: Norwegian Computing Centre for the Humanities), plus the Australian corpus of English (ACE), the Lancaster-Oslo-Bergen (LOB) corpus, and the Brown corpus of American texts; also the Corpus of Contemporary American English (COCA). I did of course utilise my native speaker intuition, and what I heard in the course of participant observation.

Etymological information came from Mitchell (1985), Barnhart (1988), and the various dictionaries listed in the last paragraph.

There has been no previous volume which attempted to pursue a full and integrated examination of the semantics and syntax of the major prepositions in English, as this one does. Lindstromberg (2010) is a popular book with many drawings of things inside/outside/above/below other things; it has some handy comparative discussion, but little on grammar. A number of works cast in terms of a formal theory include a limited discussion of prepositions. For instance, Tyler and Evans (2003) has 53 pages on *over* and 121 pages providing nuggets of information on 17 other prepositions, replete with diagrams of a rather simplistic nature (but there is nothing on *from, by, with, since, until*, and 30 more). There are a number of articles each dealing with one (or sometimes two) prepositions, considered as isolates rather than as elements within the integrated system of the language as a whole. For example, Ferrando (1999) discusses some of the senses of *on* in terms of 'metaphor theory' and does not mention *upon* or *onto*, nor does he contrast *on* with *off, at, in, of, for, by*, and *to*. The two major grammars of English each includes useful—but far from comprehensive—discussions of prepositions: Pullum and Huddleston's long chapter on 'Prepositions and preposition phrases' in the Huddleston and Pullum grammar

425

(2002: 597–661) and the chapter on 'Prepositions and prepositional phrases' in the grammar by Quirk, Greenbaum, Leech, and Svartvik (1985: 655–716).

Notes

Chapter 1

1.6 Dixon (2007) is a comprehensive account of clitics in English.
1.9 The prefixes which are related to prepositions are discussed in Dixon (2014: 129–36, 144–52, 164–5).

Chapter 2

2.1 A peripheral NP, marked by a preposition—for example, *in the dense jungle*—is sometimes called a 'prepositional phrase', a misleading label since it is in fact a just a type of noun phrase. Recently, the implication of this nomenclature has been realised with the odd suggestion that the preposition should be regarded as the 'head' of a 'prepositional phrase' (see, among others, Huddleston and Pullum 2002: 598–9). But the head of the peripheral NP *in the dense jungle* is the same as the head of the plain NP *the dense jungle*; that is, it is the noun *jungle*. The head of any syntactic constituent must be a lexical element, not a grammatical marker.
2.5c A full account of complement clauses in English will be found in Dixon (1991: 32–50, 207–66; 2005: 36–53, 230–85).

Chapter 3

There have been a number of accounts of phrasal verbs in English; Kennedy (1920) and Bolinger (1971) are particularly recommended. Dixon (1982) provides a consolidated overview and a bibliography to 1979. For the history of the term 'phrasal verb' and alternative designations, see Bolinger (1971: 1) and Dixon (1982: 2–3). Kennedy (1920: 11–18) and Meyer (1975: 5–6) discuss the historical development of phrasal verbs in English.

Several criteria have been suggested for identifying a phrasal verb. Unfortunately, none stands up to scrutiny. Live (1965: 428) suggested substitutability by a one-word 'synonym', e. g. *postpone* for *put off*, *suppress* for *fight down*, and *inherit* for *come into*. This fails because (a) many phrasal verbs do not have a one-word synonym; and (b) quite a few verb-plus-preposition sequences which are not phrasal verbs (i.e. the constituents keep their basic meanings) have single-word synonyms, e.g. *enter* for *go in*, *extract* for *take out*. Other suggestions have involved: position of preposition, gapping, fronting, passive, and adverb insertion; the difficulties associated with each are discussed in

Dixon (1982: 5–9) and Bolinger (1971: 6–22). The only workable criteria are (i) a verb plus preposition combination qualifies as a phrasal verb if a speaker could not infer its meaning from the basic meanings of the components, and it thus requires a dictionary entry all of its own; and (ii) the preposition/adverb cannot be fronted but must remain with the simple verb component.

In recent years two volumes have been published on phrasal verbs; unfortunately, neither demonstrates any understanding of their syntactic structures and grammatical characteristics. Thim (2012) shows how German has phrasal verbs similar to those in English, while O'Dowd (1998) attempts a discourse-pragmatic explanation of their properties.

3.5 A number of further triggers have been suggested for left movement of a form in slot **a** over a preceding NP. These include: a preposition is more likely to move over an NP with inanimate referencee than over one with human reference; disyllabic prepositions are less open to left movement than monosyllabic ones (van Dongen 1919: 324–5 has counts to support this); and left movement is most likely over NPs with a general meaning, such as *things*, *matter*, and *idea*.

Chapter 4

Thim (2012: 30) employs the rather cute label 'cranberry verbs' for what I call 'prepositional verbs'. He only quotes a single example: *eke out*.

4.2c Fairly detailed discussion of *decide on*, *choose*, and related verbs will be found in Dixon (1991: 138–40, 254–5; 2005: 143–6, 274–5).

Chapter 5

Van Dam (1957: 4–23) discusses the 'cause', 'reason', and 'purpose' meanings of *for* in Old English.

5.1 There is a detailed account of nominalisations in English in Dixon (2014: 296–364).

5.4 I am most grateful to Michael Webster, Secretary of the Cabinet, New Zealand, for his thoughtful assistance with this section, and for granting permission to quote from his letter. An extract is from paragraph 2.32 of the *Cabinet Manual* <https:/www.dpmc.govt.nz/our-business-units/cabinet-office>. Reference is to the New Zealand Ministerial List as of 26 October 2017; this is subject to change, with the current list available at <https://dpmc.govt.nz/our-business-units/cabinet-office/ministers-and-their-portfolios/ministerial-list>. Ministerial titles for other nations were accessed from the web during February 2018.

5.5 When one is using language L as the meta-languages to describe the structure of the same language L, difficulties are always likely to arise. They are especially pervasive when dealing with the most central grammatical elements, such as *of* and *for*. I was several times wanting to write things like: 'The senses described for *for*…', and to avoid the 'for *for*' had to expand it to: 'The senses described for the preposition *for*…' And so on.

Chapter 7

7.3 Adverbs ending in *-ward(s)* bear stress on the initial components, with the *-ward(s)* element being unstressed /-wəd(z)/; for example *inward(s)* /ˈinwəd(z)/. However, preposition *toward(s)* has the *-ward(s)* component stressed, /təˈwɔːd(z)/. This may be because the first component, *to*, is generally a clitic /tə=/ and— unlike the initial elements of the adverbs—unstressed. There is more on suffix *-ward(s)* in Dixon (2014: 263–4, 376–7).

Chapter 8

For the history of *in*, see Sweet (1892: 206).
8.3b I am grateful to American colleagues for sharing their ideas concerning *off-of*: Rob Bradshaw and Hannah Sarvasy.

Chapter 11

11.1b The 'minimal pair' *Jim hung his jacket above the back of the chair* and *Jim hung his jacket over the back of the chair* is based on Tyler and Evans (2003: 111).

Chapter 14

14.2 The preposition *till* was followed by an NP from Old English times. The possibility of its being followed by a clause was added in the twelfth century. Aikhenvald (2011: 23 and note 19) integrates this into a general hypothesis concerning direction of change.
14.6a Wierzbicka (1993) discusses criteria for using *in*, *on*, and *at* in temporal expressions, but does not examine the full range of meanings for each preposition; her study fails to penetrate to the heart of the matter.

Chapter 15

Information on the history of orthographies for Kazakh was kindly provided by Irina Nevskaya and Saule Tazhibaeva. There is a comprehensive account of adverbs in English in Dixon (2005: 375–431).
15.1 Yañéz-Bouza's (2015) excellent study is the basis for a good deal of the information in this section, including quotations from Dryden (1668: 33, 72;

1684: 40, 89), Brown (1844: 173), and Alford (1864: 147–8). Quotation from Strunk (1979: 77–8). See also Davies (1951: 114–8), Warburg (1962), and Burchfield (2004: 617–8).

15.3a Much of the information in the section comes from Trudgill and Hannah (1982: 65–8) and Quirk et al. (1985: 677–94).

15.4 Information on Japanese was kindly provided by Nerida Jarkey. The work of Spanish students is quoted from Catalán (1996).

15.5 There is a book by McCulloch (2019) entitled *Because Internet: Understanding how language is changing*. I am grateful to Kate Burridge for information on the new *because X* construction.

There are instances of prepositions *to, for,* and *of*—which are generally proclitic to the following word—becoming merged with the preceding word. This applies for *to*, introducing a complement clause, for example *going to > gonna, have to > hafta, want to > wanna* (see Quirk et al. 1985: 1616). In cricket, a bowler may take six wickets while conceding sixty runs and is then said to have *six for sixty*. The fact that he has taken six wickets in an innings can be summed up by saying that *he has a sixfa* (< *six=for*). In England and Australia, *cuppa* (*cup=of*) is a short form for *cup of tea*.

A single preposition combines the meanings 'at' and 'to' in Boumaa Fijian; see Dixon (1988: 151–5).

Acknowledgements

As always, Alexandra Aikhenvald acted as a sounding board for all my notions, whilst also providing many ideas and nifty examples. I also owe thanks to Kate Burridge, Rob Bradshaw, Nerida Jarkey, Hannah Sarvasy and Michael Webster, Secretary of the Cabinet, New Zealand.

References

Aikhenvald, Alexandra Y. 2011. 'Versatile cases', pp. 1–43 of *Language at Large: Essays on Syntax and Semantics* by Alexandra Y. Aikhenvald and R. M. W. Dixon. Leiden: Brill.

Alford, Henry. 1864. *The Queen's English: Stray Notes on Speaking and Spelling*. London: Deighton and Bell.

Allen, R. E. 1990. Editor of *The Concise Oxford Dictionary of Current English*, 8th ed. Oxford: Clarendon Press.

Barnhart, Robert K. 1988. Editor of *Chambers Dictionary of Etymology*. Edinburgh: Chambers.

Bolinger, Dwight. 1971. *The Phrasal Verb in English*. Cambridge, MA: Harvard University Press.

Brown, Goold. 1844. *The Institutes of English Grammar, Methodically Arranged*. New York: S.S. and W. Woods.

Burchfield, R. W. 2004. *Fowler's Modern English Usage*, Revised Third Edition. Oxford: Oxford University Press.

Catalán, Rosa Maria Jiménez. 1996. 'Frequency and variability in errors in the use of English prepositions'. *Miscelánia: A Journal of English and American Studies* 17: 171–87.

Cowie, A. P. and Mackin, R. 1975. *Oxford Dictionary of Current Idiomatic English*. Vol 1, *Verbs with Prepositions and Particles*. Oxford: Oxford University Press.

Davies, Hugh Sykes. 1951. *Grammar without Tears*. London: The Bodley Head.

Dixon, R. M. W. 1982. 'The grammar of English phrasal verbs', *Australian Journal of Linguistics* 2: 1–42.

Dixon, R. M. W. 1988. *A Grammar of Boumaa Fijian*. Chicago: University of Chicago Press.

Dixon, R. M. W. 1991. *A New Approach to English Grammar, on Semantic Principles*. Oxford: Clarendon Press.

Dixon, R. M. W. 2005. *A Semantic Approach to English Grammar*. Oxford: Oxford University Press.

Dixon, R. M. W. 2007. 'Clitics in English', *English Studies* 88: 574–600.

Dixon, R. M. W. 2014. *Making New Words: Morphological Derivation in English*. Oxford: Oxford University Press.

Dryden, John. 1668. *Of Dramatick Poesie: An Essay*. London: J. Tonson.

Dryden, John. 1684. *An Essay of Dramatick Poesie*. The second edition. London: Henry Herringman.

Ferrando, Ignasi Navarro I. 1999. 'The metaphorical use of *on*', *Journal of English Studies* 1: 145–64.

Flexner, Stuart B. 1987. Editor in chief of *The Random House Dictionary of the English Language Unabridged*, 2nd ed. New York: Random House.

Gove, Philip B. 1961. Editor in chief of *Webster's Third New International Dictionary of the English Language Unabridged*. Springfield, MA: Merriam-Webster.

Heaton, J. B. 1965. *Prepositions and Adverbial Particles*. London: Longmans.

Huddleston, Rodney and Pullum, Geoffrey K. 2002. Chief authors of *The Cambridge Grammar of the English Language*. Cambridge: Cambridge University Press.

Johnson, Samuel. 1755. *A Dictionary of the English Language* . London: J. and P. Knapton, T. and T. Longman, C. Hitch and L. Hawes, A. Millar, and R. and J. Dodsley.

Kennedy, Arthur Garfield. 1920. *The Modern English Verb Adverb Construction*. Stanford University Publications in Language and Literature Vol. 1, No. 1. [Reissued by AMS Press, New York, 1967.]

Lindstromberg, Seth. 2010. *English Prepositions Explained*. Revised edition. Amsterdam: John Benjamins.

Live, Anna H. 1965. 'The discontinuous verb in English', *Word* 21: 428–51.

Lowth, Robert. 1762. *A short Introduction to English Grammar: With Critical Notes*. London: A. Miller and R. and J. Dodsley.

McCulloch, Gretchen. 2019. *Because Internet: Understanding How Language is Changing*. London: Harvill Secker.

Meyer, George A. 1975. *The Two-Word Verb: A Dictionary of the Verb-Preposition Phrases in American English*. The Hague: Mouton.

Mitchell, Bruce. 1985. *Old English Syntax*, 2 vols. Oxford: Clarendon Press.

Mish, Frederick G. 2003. Editor in chief of *Merriam-Webster's Collegiate Dictionary*, Eleventh Edition. Springfield, MA: Merriam-Webster.

O'Dowd, Elizabeth M. 1998. *Prepositions and Particles in English: A Discourse-Functional Approach*. New York: Oxford University Press.

Pullum, Geoffrey K. and Huddleston, Rodney. 2002. 'Prepositions and prepositional phrases', pp. 507–661 of *The Cambridge Grammar of the English Language*, Chief authors Rodney Huddleston and Geoffrey K. Pullum. Cambridge: Cambridge University Press.

Quirk, Randolph, Greenbaum, Sidney, Leech, Geoffrey, and Svartvik, Jan. 1985. *A Comprehensive Grammar of the English Language*. Harlow: Longman.

Sinclair, John. 2001. Founder editor in chief of *Collins Cobuild English Dictionary for Advanced Learners*. Glasgow: HarperCollins.

Soukhanov, Anne H. 1992. Executive editor of *The American Heritage Dictionary of the English Language*, 3rd ed. Boston: Houghton Mifflin.

Strunk, William, Jr. 1979. *The Elements of Style*, with Revisions, an Introduction, and a Chapter on Writing by E. B. White. Boston: Allen and Bacon.

Sweet, Henry. 1892. *A Short Historical English Grammar*. London: Oxford University Press.

Thim, Stefan. 2012. *Phrasal Verbs: The English Verb-Particle Construction and its History*. Berlin: De Gruyter Mouton.

Trudgill, Peter and Hannah, Jean. 1982. *International English: A Guide to Varieties of Standard English*. London: Edward Arnold.

Tyler, Andrea and Evans, Vyvyan. 2003. *The Semantics of English Prepositions: Spatial Scenes, Embodied Meaning and Cognition*. Cambridge: Cambridge University Press.

Van Dam, Johannes. 1957. *The Causal Clause and Causal Prepositions in Early Old English Prose*. Groningen: J. B. Wolters.

Van Dongen, W. A., Sr. 1919. '"He put on his hat" and "He put his hat *on*"', *Neophilologus: A Modern Language Quarterly* (Groningen) 4: 322–53.

Warburg, Jeremy. 1962. 'Notions of correctness', pp. 313–28 of Randolph Quirk, *The Use of English*. London: Longmans.

West, Michael. 1953. *A General Service List of English Words*. London: Longmans.

Wierzbicka, Anna. 1993. 'Why do we say *in* April, *on* Thursday, *at* 10 o'clock: In search of an explanation', *Studies in Language* 17: 437–54.

Yañéz-Bouza, Nuria. 2015. *Grammar, Rhetoric and Usage in English: Preposition Placement 1500–1900*. Cambridge: Cambridge University Press.

Index

Books by R. M. W. Dixon

BOOKS ON LINGUISTICS
Linguistic Science and Logic
What *is* Language? A New Approach to Linguistic Description
The Dyirbal Language of North Queensland
A Grammar of Yidiñ
The Languages of Australia
Where Have All the Adjectives Gone? And Other Essays in Semantics
and Syntax
Searching for Aboriginal Languages: Memoirs of a Field Worker
A Grammar of Boumaa Fijian
A New Approach to English Grammar, on Semantic Principles
Words of Our Country: Stories, Place Names and Vocabulary in Yidiny
Ergativity
The Rise and Fall of Languages
Australian Languages: Their Nature and Development
The Jarawara Language of Southern Amazonia
A Semantic Approach to English Grammar
Basic Linguistic Theory, Vol. 1, Methodology
Basic Linguistic Theory, Vol. 2, Grammatical Topics
Basic Linguistic Theory, Vol. 3, Further Grammatical Topics
I am a Linguist
Making New Words: Morphological Derivation in English
Edible Gender, Mother-in-law Style and Other Grammatical Wonders:
Studies in Dyirbal, Yidiñ and Warrgamay
Are Some Languages Better than Others?
"We Used to Eat People": Revelations of a Fiji Islands Traditional Village
The Unmasking of English Dictionaries
Australia's Original Languages: An Introduction
The Essence of Linguistic Analysis: An Integrated Approach

with Alexandra Y. Aikhenvald
Language at Large: Essays on Syntax and Semantics

with Grace Koch
Dyirbal Song Poetry: The Oral Literature of an Australian Rainforest
People

with Bruce Moore, W. S. Ramson and Mandy Thomas
Australian Aboriginal Words in English: Their Origin and Meaning

BOOKS ON MUSIC
with John Godrich
Recording the Blues

with John Godrich and Howard Rye
Blues and Gospel Records, 1890 - 1943

NOVELS *(under the name Hosanna Brown)*
I Spy, You Die
Death upon a Spear

EDITOR OF BOOKS ON LINGUISTICS
Grammatical Categories in Australian Languages
Studies in Ergativity

with Barry J. Blake
Handbook of Australian Languages, Vols 1–5

with Martin Duwell
The Honey Ant Men's Love Song, and Other Aboriginal Song Poems
Little Eva at Moonlight Creek: Further Aboriginal Song Poems